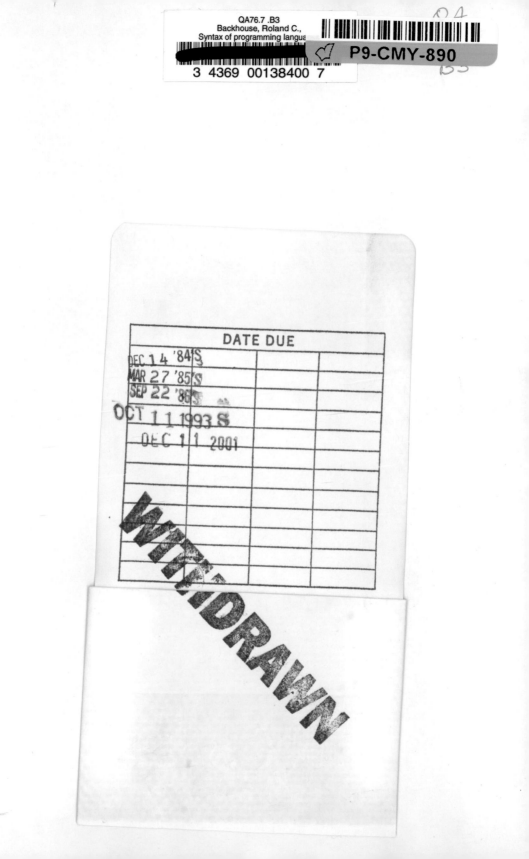

DATE DUE		
DEC 14 '84 S		
MAR 27 '85 S		
SEP 22 '86 S		
OCT 11 1993 S		
DEC 11 2001		

SYNTAX OF PROGRAMMING LANGUAGES
Theory and Practice

Prentice-Hall International
Series in Computer Science

C. A. R. Hoare, Series Editor

Published

BACKHOUSE, R. C., *Syntax of Programming Languages: Theory and Practice*
DUNCAN, F., *Microprocessor Programming and Software Development*
WELSH, J., and ELDER, J., *Introduction to PASCAL*

Future Titles

BAUER, F. and WOESSNER, H., *Algorithmic Language and Program Development*
HENDERSON, P., *Functional Programming*
JACKSON, M. A., *System Design*
JONES, C., *Software Development*
WELSH, J. and MCKEAG, M., *Structured System Programming*

SYNTAX OF PROGRAMMING LANGUAGES
LANGUAGES
Theory and Practice

ROLAND C. BACKHOUSE

Heriot-Watt University
Edinburgh, Scotland

Prentice/Hall International

ENGLEWOOD CLIFFS, NEW JERSEY   LONDON   NEW DELHI
SINGAPORE   SYDNEY   TOKYO   TORONTO   WELLINGTON

Library of Congress Cataloging in Publication Data

BACKHOUSE, ROLAND C   1948-
    Syntax of programming languages   ·

    Includes bibliographical references and index
    1. Programming languages (Electronic computers)—Syntax
    I. Title
    QA76.7.B3   001.6′424   78-22098
ISBN 0-13-879999-7

British Library Cataloguing in Publication Data

BACKHOUSE, ROLAND CARL
    Syntax of programming languages
    1. Programming language (Electronic computers)—Semantics
    I. Title
    001.6′424   QA76.7
ISBN 0-13-879999-7

ISBN 0-13-879999-7

PRENTICE-HALL INTERNATIONAL, INC., *London*
PRENTICE-HALL OF AUSTRALIA PTY., LTD., *Sydney*
PRENTICE-HALL OF CANADA, LTD., *Toronto*
PRENTICE-HALL OF INDIA PRIVATE LIMITED, *New Delhi*
PRENTICE-HALL OF JAPAN, INC., *Tokyo*
PRENTICE-HALL OF SOUTHEAST ASIA PTE., LTD., *Singapore*
PRENTICE-HALL, INC., *Englewood Cliffs*, *New Jersey*
WHITEHALL BOOKS LIMITED, *Wellington, New Zealand*

Printed in the United States of America

10   9   8   7   6   5   4   3   2

CONTENTS

PREFACE

The analysis of the syntax of programming languages is a topic which, deservedly, occupies a prominent position in computer-science curricula because of its relevance both to the practice of compiler construction and to the theory of computing. It is this bridge between theory and practice which I have chosen to stress.

The book is primarily directed towards computer-science students in the third or final year of an undergraduate degree course. It is assumed that the reader is familiar with the standard mathematical notation for sets and with the mathematical concept of proof, in particular proof by induction. The reader should have attended a course on the design of algorithms and data structures, preferably one in which the use of loop invariants to provide correctness proofs is an integral part. It is also preferable if the reader is familiar with PASCAL. However, I have always made a clear distinction between algorithms and programs so that the former can be understood without reference to any specific programming language.

Chapter 1 (Fundamentals) begins by introducing the principal concepts and terminology associated with context-free grammars, illustrating them with examples taken from the "Revised Report on ALGOL 60" as well as abstract examples. This is followed by a discussion of graph searching and its application to eliminating useless productions from a given context-free grammar. The material on graph searching is included in the "Fundamentals" because it is used extensively throughout the remainder of the book.

Chapter 2 discusses the variety of ways in which regular languages may be defined. The motivation for this chapter is the relationship between extended BNF and regular expressions (discussed in Chapter 3) and the use of a deterministic finite-state machine as the "heart" of an LR parser (Chapter 4). The material is standard but some of the presentation is novel—in particular, when designing an algorithm to convert a non-deterministic machine to a deterministic machine, I have taken care to stress the relationship to graph searching.

The emphasis in Chapter 3 is on the correspondence between parsing by recursive descent and the theory of LL parsing. The chapter begins by presenting a basic scheme for constructing a recursive-descent parser for a strong LL(k) grammar. This is followed by an algorithm for testing the strong LL(k) property, which is then specialized to the case $k = 1$. The chapter is concluded by a discussion of the relationship between the LL(k) and strong LL(k) properties, and of practical problems arising from the use of recursive descent.

The treatment of LR parsing in Chapter 4 is entirely non-standard and is notably shorter than Chapter 3. This is because, in my view, a study of recursive-descent parsers is much more fruitful for the non-specialist. I have, therefore, stressed the principles underlying an LR parser rather than the practical details of its construction.

Chapters 5 and 6 are an in-depth study of the theory of error repair and its application to the design of the error recovery in a recursive-descent syntax analyzer. Error recovery is, of course, an extremely important part of syntax analysis and a theory which stops short of this topic does not deserve to be called practical. The theory developed in Chapter 5 is based on the work of M. J. Fischer and R. A. Wagner (Sec. 5.1, string-to-string repair), R. A. Wagner (Sec. 5.2, regular language repair) and A. V. Aho and T. G. Peterson (Sec. 5.3, repair of context-free languages); my own contribution has been to unify the treatment of the three topics. I have preferred the term "repair" to the more prevalent "correction" because the former is less emotive and, in my view, more accurate. In Chapter 6 error recovery is seen as a compromise between efficiency constraints and the ideal of "least-cost" repair. Apart from a discussion of Wirth's recovery technique, which is included to motivate the ensuing development, the material in this chapter is entirely original.

Chapter 7 concludes the book by exposing the limitations of context-free grammars and encouraging the reader to a further study of the semantics of programming languages.

A feature of the text is the inclusion of an almost complete LL(1) test, implemented in PASCAL. This program, which is begun in Chapter 1 and extended in Chapter 3, has been included for two reasons. Firstly, I suspect that many students remain sceptical of the practicality of algorithms if they do not see them implemented. Secondly, and more importantly, I wanted to provide a basis for intellectually demanding but realistic projects which could be used to reinforce the material in the text. Project work is, quite rightly, a significant element in the training of a computer scientist, but too often its educational value is nullified by the sheer quantity of coding required, most of which is rather trivial in nature. The LL(1) test is, therefore, intentionally incomplete and the exercises request the reader to supply the missing procedures— between 50 and 100 additional lines of coding being required. As an aid to institutions recommending this text to their students I am willing to supply a copy of all programs and associated test data which were written during its preparation. Anyone interested should write to me at:

Department of Computer Science, Heriot-Watt University,
79 Grassmarket, Edinburgh, EH1 2HJ, Scotland.

A number of people have helped me to write this book, but first and foremost my thanks go to my wife, Hilary. The reviewers, Professor A. V. Aho, Dr. D. J. Cooke and Mrs. J. Hughes, have done an admirable job helping me to avoid many errors and offering a number of incisive comments. Thanks also go to Stuart Anderson, Simon Kestner, Nick Kotarski and Janet Meynell for their help in debugging the text. The PASCAL compiler used to debug the programs was written by Dag Langhmyr; without his efforts this book could not have been written. The assistance of Dave Cooper, John Fisher and Mike Staker has also been invaluable in ensuring that the PASCAL system was truly reliable. Dr. J. Welsh and Professor A. H. J. Sale have given advice on the technicalities of PASCAL for which I am very grateful, and a number of students have helped me by undertaking projects related to the material. I should like to mention particularly Jim Farquhar, Bryan MacGregor and Callum Mills. I would also like to thank Isabel Warrack for the excellent job she did of typing the manuscript, and my home department for the facilities it has made available to me. Finally, thanks go to Henry Hirschberg and Ron Decent of Prentice-Hall International and to Tony Hoare for providing encouragement at the opportune time.

Roland C. Backhouse

February, 1979

GLOSSARY OF SYMBOLS

$\in$	belongs to, is an element of
$\notin$	does not belong to
$\varnothing$	empty set
$\cup$	set union
$\cap$	set intersection
$\supseteq$	contains, is a superset of
$\subseteq$	is a subset of
$\sim$	not
$\wedge$	and
$\vee$	or
$\supset$	implies
iff	if and only if
$\forall$	for all
$\exists$	there exists
$\square$	end of a proof
$\rightarrow$	replacement symbol (productions)
$::=$	replacement symbol in ALGOL 60 Report
$\Rightarrow$	replacement symbol (derivation sequences)
$\nRightarrow$	does not generate
$\Rightarrow_l$	generates leftmost
$\Rightarrow_r$	generates rightmost
$\rightarrow$	replacement symbol (repairs)
$\longrightarrow$	replacement symbol (function definitions)
Λ	empty word
$\mid$	alternate sign in productions
$*$	reflexive and transitive closure, iteration zero or more times
$+$	transitive closure, iteration one or more times
O	order

SYNTAX OF PROGRAMMING LANGUAGES
Theory and Practice

1 FUNDAMENTALS

ALGOL 60 has lost a great deal of its popularity as a programming tool. It never succeeded in superseding FORTRAN, and has itself been superseded by programming languages like PASCAL and ALGOL 68. Nevertheless, I would venture to say that the contribution of ALGOL 60 to computing science will far outlive the contributions of PASCAL, ALGOL 68, FORTRAN or any other programming language in existence today. The main contribution of ALGOL 60 to computing is the standard it set for the *definition* of programming languages. The ALGOL 60 report introduced a method of defining the syntax of programming languages which has, subsequently, been used to define almost all programming languages of any merit. The method goes under a number of different names: *Backus Normal Form*, after its inventor J. Backus; *Backus–Naur Form* (BNF), after Backus and the editor of the report, P. Naur; and *context-free grammars*, the name suggested by N. Chomsky who independently (and prior to Backus) applied the method to defining the syntax of natural languages.

The definition of a programming language is normally split into two parts—the *syntax* and the *semantics* of the language. The syntax of the language specifies those combinations of symbols which are in the language. For example

begin real x; $x := 0$ **end**

is an ALGOL 60 program, but

begin end x **real**; $x := 0$

is not. The semantics of a language specifies the "meaning" of syntactically correct constructs in the language. In programming-language terms the semantics specifies, for each program in the language, an *input–output relation*; that is, the output of the program given a particular input. The ALGOL 60 report introduced a *formal* method of defining the syntax, but defined the semantics *informally* in English. Subsequently the theory of the syntax of programming languages, or *language theory* as it is commonly called, developed rapidly and has now, more or less, stabilized. In contrast, the theory of the semantics of programming languages has been slow to develop and has not yet stablized. The practical significance of this disparity is that the construction of the syntax-analysis phase of a compiler is now a highly reliable process tackled with ease by compiler writers; on the other hand the incorporation of code generation is much more difficult and often subject to debate.

This book introduces the reader to context-free grammars and presents a sample of the many theoretical results which relate to their use in defining programming languages. The main objectives of the book are to examine critically the value of context-free grammars as a definitional tool and, as a by-product, to convince the reader of the need for formal definitions and a sound *theory* of programming-language definition. We shall use the "Revised Report on the Algorithmic Language—ALGOL 60" [1.12] as the primary source of illustrative examples. This report, whilst now quite old in comparison to most computing-science literature (it was published in 1963), is one of the few classics and should be obligatory reading for all computing-science students. We would advise the reader to have a copy on hand when reading this text. (A list of the journals in which it has been published appears in the bibliography at the end of this chapter.) In subsequent sections we shall refer to the "Revised Report on ALGOL 60" or, simply, the "Revised Report" rather than give it its full title.

How are we to evaluate the definition of a programming language? We can obtain a number of criteria by looking at various methods of definition in common use and examining their inadequacies.

The method by which we all learnt our first programming language will undoubtedly have been by example. This is an excellent method but, unfortunately, suffers from the drawback that it can never be complete, since we can only ever see a finite number of examples. Everyone must, at some time, have asked the question "am I allowed to . . . ?". One should not blame oneself for not knowing the answer, nor should one blame one's teacher for not having already given the information—the method of definition is at fault. Thus our first criterion is:

C1. *The definition should provide a complete description of all aspects of the language.*

Examples are normally supplemented by verbal descriptions in order to rectify the last criticism. However English, like all natural languages, is full of ambiguities. In programming it is extremely important that we be quite unambiguous in everything we do. It is very important, therefore, that any language we use is also unambiguous or, if it is ambiguous, that such ambiguities be easily avoided.

There are two issues involved here and so we shall introduce some terminology to clarify them. When we define ALGOL 60 in English, there are two languages involved—ALGOL 60, the language being defined, which is called the *object language*, and English, the language used to make the definition, which is called the *metalanguage*. Now, it is a requirement of the word "definition" that the metalanguage be completely unambiguous, and this is the paramount motivation for a formalized or mathematical definition. However, in computing, we also impose the following requirement.

C2. *Any ambiguities in the object language should be intentional and immediately clear from the definition.*

In the event of a misunderstanding of a programming-language feature the compiler of the language is often referred to. A compiler does in fact define a language precisely and unambiguously, but it is perhaps the worst method of definition for a number of reasons. Firstly, there is no compiler to which the very first implementor of a language can refer. Secondly, there is no guarantee that two compilers of the same language agree. Finally, the compiler introduces a very large amount of machine-dependent detail which is irrelevant and confusing to the user. In summary, therefore:

C3. *The metalanguage should be easily understood and machine-independent.*

There are two parties interested in the definition of a programming language —the user and the compiler writer. Sometimes the requirements of these two parties are conflicting and there is growing evidence that, with regard to the semantics of a language, more than one mode of definition should be used. However there is one respect in which the compiler writer and user have a very strong mutual interest—the reliability of the compiler. Our final criterion is thus:

C4. *The method of definition should facilitate the systematic construction of a compiler.*

This book is based around a critical examination of the "Revised Report on ALGOL 60" with respect to these four criteria. The most important criterion is C4 and the success of the BNF definition of ALGOL 60 is very much due to the ease with which reliable syntax analyzers can now be written. For this reason discussion of techniques to facilitate the systematic construction of syntax analyzers occupies the major part of the text. Chapters 2–6 are all primarily concerned with this topic. Chapters 3 and 4 describe the two most important techniques used in syntax analyzers. The reader should not be put off by their names ("LL parsing" and "LR parsing") which are singularly meaningless and uninspiring. LL parsing is sometimes called parsing by "recursive descent" and is a very natural and easy technique to use. LR parsing is less natural but more powerful and is the technique normally used in so-called "translator writing systems" or "compiler-compilers" i.e. computer programs which input the definition of a language and output a compiler for that language. Chapter 2 includes preparatory material which is necessary to understand parts of all the remaining chapters. Error analysis is an extremely important part of syntax analysis and Chaps. 5 and 6 attempt to give it the thorough treatment it deserves. Chapter 5 develops a mathematical model of error repair which is then applied in Chap. 6 to the design of an error-recovery scheme.

Chapter 7 examines the "Revised Report on ALGOL 60" with respect to criterion C1. Surprisingly the context-free definition of ALGOL 60 does *not* completely define the syntax of ALGOL 60. We have learned to live with the limitations of the Report, but it is important to know exactly what they are! Chapter 7 is concluded by a discussion of some of the problems which have been caused by the lack of a formal method for completely defining the syntax and semantics of programming languages. It is hoped that the reader will then be motivated to go beyond this text and consult some of the references quoted in the bibliography of Chap. 7.

This first chapter includes in Sec. 1.1 the basic definitions and notation which are used throughout the text. Criterion C2 is then examined in Sec. 1.2. The word "ambiguous" is, of course, itself ambiguous. However in Sec. 1.2 we show how we can precisely characterize "ambiguous" context-free grammars. A test for ambiguity is delayed (for reasons which will become evident) until Chap. 3. The semantic ambiguities in the "Revised Report on ALGOL 60" are discussed in the final chapter.

A major emphasis in this book is on the design of efficient algorithms. The author agrees with the view of D. E. Knuth ("Computer Science and its Relation to Mathematics", *Computers and People*, September 1974, 8–11) that "computer science . . . is the study of algorithms". To set the tone of the remainder of the book a discussion of graph searching and its application to finding useless productions form the final two sections of this chapter. Although the connection of graph searching to language theory is not immediately apparent, it will repay the reader to study Sec. 1.3 thoroughly. It is referred to again and again in subsequent chapters and hence is one of the most important in the book.

1.1   BASIC DEFINITIONS

In this section we list a number of definitions and give examples illustrating them. The definitions will be used throughout the text and so it is desirable to memorize as many as possible. Those which are particularly important have been indicated by an asterisk (*).

Standard mathematical notation is used for sets (e.g. $\emptyset$ for the empty set, $\cup$ for set union). ALGOL 60 notation has been used for logical operations (e.g. $\supset$ for implication). If in doubt about the meaning of any symbol please refer to the glossary of symbols on p. xv.

1.1.1   Languages

Definition   An alphabet T is a finite set of symbols.

Example 1   The alphabet of ALGOL 60 includes the following symbols:

$$+ \quad - \quad \times \quad / \quad \div$$

$$a \quad b \quad c \quad \ldots \quad z$$

$$A \quad B \quad C \quad \ldots \quad Z$$

begin   real   end

$$; \quad : \quad ,$$

Definition   A sequence $s = t_1 t_2 \ldots t_n$ of symbols from some alphabet T is called a *string* or *word* over the alphabet T. The *length* of a string is the number of symbols in the word (in this case n). The operation of writing one string $v = b_1 b_2 \ldots b_m$ after a string $u = a_1 a_2 \ldots a_n$ to form the string $uv = a_1 a_2 \ldots a_n b_1 \ldots b_m$ is called the *concatenation* of u with v.

*Definition   It is useful to hypothesize the existence of a string of length 0 called *the empty word* and denoted by Λ. The empty word has the property that any word u concatenated with Λ is equal to u, and Λ concatenated with any word u is also equal to u. Symbolically this is

$$u\Lambda = u = \Lambda u \ .$$

More generally

$$u \Lambda v = uv$$

for all words u and v.

The empty word is denoted by $\langle empty \rangle$ in the "Revised Report on ALGOL 60". It is used there as a convenient way of allowing a label immediately before **end**. The example given in Sec. 4.4.2 of the "Revised Report" is

begin . . . ;   *John*:**end**

The interpretation is that between the colon and **end** there is a dummy statement which executes no operation.

*Definition T^* is the set of all strings of symbols over the alphabet T, including the empty word.

Definition   A *language L* (*over the alphabet T*) is a subset of T^*.

Example 2   Let $T = \{a, b\}$.
(a) $L_1 = T^* = \{A, a, b, aa, ab, ba, bb, aaa, \ldots\}$ is a language.
(b) $L_2 = \{a, ba, aab, bbbb\}$ is a language.
(c) $L_3 = \{a^p \mid p \text{ is prime}\}$ is a language.
(d) $L_4 = \{a^n b^n \mid n \geq 1\}$ is a language.
Note: a^n, where n is a positive integer, is defined to be the string $aaa . . . a$ consisting of n a's. a^0 is the empty word.

Example 3   Let T be the alphabet of ALGOL 60. Then the set of syntactically correct ALGOL 60 programs is a language.

It is important to recognize that our definition of "language" involves no concept of meaning. A language is simply a set of strings, and so language theory is the theory of the properties of sets of strings.

Definition   The *product $L \cdot L'$* of two languages L and L' is the set of words formed by concatenating a word from L with a word from L'.

Example 4 $L_2 \cdot \{a, bb\} = \{aa, baa, aaba, bbbba, abb, babb, aabbb, bbbbbb\}$.

Example 5 $L_3 \cdot L_4 = \{a^{n+p} b^n \mid p \text{ is prime and } n \geq 1\}$.

Very often we shall omit the dot and denote the product $L \cdot L'$ by simple juxtaposition, i.e. LL'.

Note: The product of two languages is not commutative. That is, in general, $L \cdot L' \neq L' \cdot L$.

Definition   The *powers* of a language L are defined inductively by:

$$L^0 = \{\Lambda\}$$
$$L^n = L \cdot L^{n-1} \text{ for } n \geq 1.$$

Using the properties of Λ it is easily shown that $L^1 = L$. For $n \geq 1, L^n$ is the set of all strings formed by concatenating together n strings from L.

Example 6 $L_2^1 = \{a, ba, aab, bbbb\}$.
$L_2^2 = \{aa, aba, aaab, abbbb, baa, baba, baaab, babbbb, aaba, aabba, aabaab,$
    $aabbbbb, bbbba, bbbbba, bbbbaab, bbbbbbbb\}$.

Definition   The *star* L^* of a language L is defined by:

$$L^* = L^0 \cup L^1 \cup L^2 \cup \cdots \cup L^n \cup \cdots.$$

L^* is often called the *Kleene closure* of L.

Definition   The *transitive closure* L^+ of a language L is defined by:

$$L^+ = L^1 \cup L^2 \cup L^3 \cup \cdots \cup L^n \cup \cdots.$$

1.1.2   Grammars

A language consisting of a finite number of strings can be defined simply by listing all those strings. However the languages with which we shall be concerned will normally be infinite. In this case we can use a *grammar* to define the language.

*Definition   A *grammar* consists of four items:
1.   A finite set N of *non-terminal symbols*.
2.   A finite set T of *terminal symbols*, where $N \cap T = \varnothing$.
3.   A distinguished symbol $S \in N$ called the *start* or *sentence* symbol.
4.   A set P of *productions* each of which has the form $u \to v$ where $u \in (N \cup T)^+$ and $v \in (N \cup T)^*$. We call u the *left-hand side* (lhs) and v the *right-hand side* (rhs) of the production.

Example 7   Definition of the syntax of ALGOL 60.

In the "Revised Report on ALGOL 60" the non-terminal symbols are all strings enclosed by ⟨ ⟩ (for example, ⟨*basic statement*⟩, ⟨*expression*⟩, ⟨*program*⟩). The terminal symbols have already been given in Example 1 and the start symbol is ⟨*program*⟩. The productions consist of all the rules defined in the syntax parts of the Report. A slightly different notation is used to that used here. Instead of "→" the notation "::=" is used and the symbol " | " is used to indicate alternate productions. For example the following definition appears in Sec. 2.4.1 of the "Revised Report".

⟨*identifier*⟩ ::= ⟨*letter*⟩ | ⟨*identifier*⟩ ⟨*letter*⟩ | ⟨*identifier*⟩ ⟨*digit*⟩

In our notation this definition would be written as three productions.

⟨*identifier*⟩→ ⟨*letter*⟩
⟨*identifier*⟩ → ⟨*identifier*⟩ ⟨*letter*⟩
⟨*identifier*⟩ → ⟨*identifier*⟩ ⟨*digit*⟩

Other examples of productions in the "Revised Report" are

⟨*program*⟩ → ⟨*block*⟩
⟨*assignment statement*⟩ → ⟨*left part list*⟩ ⟨*arithmetic expression*⟩

Example 8

1.   Let $N = \{A\}$.
2.   Let $T = \{a, b, c\}$.
3.   Let the start symbol be A.
4.   Let the productions be

$$A \rightarrow aAb \qquad A \rightarrow c$$

We shall normally abbreviate the definition of a grammar by writing "$G = (N, T, P, S)$, where P consists of . . . " as exemplified below.

Example 9

$G_1 = (\{A, B, C\}, \{a, b, c\}, P, A)$, where P consists of

$$
\begin{array}{ll}
A \rightarrow abc & A \rightarrow aBbc \\
Bb \rightarrow bB & Bc \rightarrow Cbcc \\
bC \rightarrow Cb & aC \rightarrow aaB \\
aC \rightarrow aa &
\end{array}
$$

In the above definition the non-terminal set is $\{A, B, C\}$, the terminal set is $\{a, b, c\}$ and A is the start symbol.

Example 10

$G_2 = (\{O, E\}, \{a\}, P, O)$, where P consists of

$$O \rightarrow a \qquad O \rightarrow aE$$
$$E \rightarrow aO$$

To understand how a grammar defines a language one should regard the symbol "$\rightarrow$" as an abbreviation for "may be replaced by". Starting with the start symbol of the grammar the productions may then be applied to strings of terminal and non-terminal symbols to produce a new string. This process is repeated until eventually the string produced is a terminal string (i.e. consists entirely of terminal symbols or is the empty word Λ). This final string is then a string of the language defined by the grammar.

To illustrate the process, consider Example 10. We begin with the string consisting of the start symbol O. There are two productions with lhs O, namely $O \rightarrow a$ and $O \rightarrow aE$. Thus we may replace O either by a or by aE. Taking the former choice we obtain the string consisting of the single terminal symbol a. Thus a is a string in the language defined by the grammar of Example 10. Alternatively, starting with O and using the production $O \rightarrow aE$ we obtain aE. This is not a terminal string because E is a non-terminal symbol. There is only one production with lhs E and so we have no choice but to replace E by aO, obtaining the string aaO. The process now repeats itself—we now have the choice of replacing O by aE or by a. Taking the former choice we obtain $aaaE$; taking the latter choice we obtain the terminal string aaa. Thus aaa is also a string in the language. Similarly, repeating the replacement process on $aaaE$ we can see that $aaaaa, aaaaaaa$ and indeed any string consisting of an odd number of a's is in the language. We can abbreviate the above description by simply writing:

$O \Rightarrow a$. Thus $a \in L(G_2)$.
$O \Rightarrow aE \Rightarrow aaO \Rightarrow aaa$. Thus $aaa \in L(G_2)$.
$O \Rightarrow aE \Rightarrow aaO \Rightarrow aaaE \Rightarrow aaaaO \Rightarrow aaaaa$. Thus $aaaaa \in L(G_2)$.
$\vdots$

Here $L(G_2)$ denotes the language *generated* by the grammar G_2. Clearly we have

$$L(G_2) = \{a^{2n+1} \mid n \geq 0\}.$$

A sequence of the form

$$u_1 \Rightarrow u_2 \Rightarrow u_3 \Rightarrow \cdots \Rightarrow u_m$$

will be called a *derivation sequence*.

At this stage the reader should be able to write down a few derivation sequences defined by the grammar of Example 8. By doing so one may deduce that the language generated by the grammar is $\{a^n c b^n \mid n \geq 0\}$, i.e. the set of all strings consisting of some arbitrary number n of a's followed by one c followed by a string of b's, where the number of b's equals the number of a's.

Example 9 is the most complex example. To discover the language generated we write down a few example derivation sequences, starting with the start symbol A.

$$A \Rightarrow abc$$

Thus $abc \in L(G_1)$.

$$
\begin{aligned}
A &\Rightarrow aBbc &\quad (1) \\
&\Rightarrow abBc &\quad (2) \\
&\Rightarrow abCbcc &\quad (3) \\
&\Rightarrow aCbbcc &\quad (4) \\
&\Rightarrow aabbcc &\quad (5)
\end{aligned}
$$

Thus $aabbcc \in L(G_1)$.

$$
\begin{aligned}
A &\Rightarrow aBbc &\quad (6) \\
&\Rightarrow abBc &\quad (7) \\
&\Rightarrow abCbcc &\quad (8) \\
&\Rightarrow aCbbcc &\quad (9) \\
&\Rightarrow aaBbbcc &\quad (10) \\
&\Rightarrow aabBbcc &\quad (11) \\
&\Rightarrow aabbBcc &\quad (12) \\
&\Rightarrow aabbCbccc &\quad (13) \\
&\Rightarrow aabCbbccc &\quad (14) \\
&\Rightarrow aaCbbbccc &\quad (15) \\
&\Rightarrow aaabbbccc &\quad (16)
\end{aligned}
$$

Thus $aaabbbccc \in L(G_1)$.

Note carefully how each line is generated from the preceding line by using a production to replace a substring by another string. Thus line (2) is generated from line (1) by replacing Bb by bB. Line (3) is generated from line (2) by replacing Bc by $Cbcc$. Table 1.1 shows how each line was generated from the preceding line.

We shall prove shortly that $L(G_1) = \{a^n b^n c^n \mid n \geq 1\}$, but let us first give a formal definition of the terms used in the last few paragraphs.

Definition Let $G = (N, T, P, S)$ be a grammar. A string w' is *immediately generated* by a string w if and only if $w = sut$, $w' = svt$ and $u \to v$ is a production of G, where s and t are arbitrary strings.

Line nos.	Strings		Production used
(1)→(2) , (6)→(7)	$aBbc$	$\Rightarrow abBc$	$Bb \rightarrow bB$
(2)→(3) , (7)→(8)	$abBc$	$\Rightarrow abCbcc$	$Bc \rightarrow Cbcc$
(3)→(4) , (8)→(9)	$abCbcc$	$\Rightarrow aCbbcc$	$bC \rightarrow Cb$
(4)→(5)	$aCbbcc$	$\Rightarrow aabbcc$	$aC \rightarrow aa$
(9)→(10)	$aCbbcc$	$\Rightarrow aaBbbcc$	$aC \rightarrow aaB$
(10)→(11)	$aaBbbcc$	$\Rightarrow aabBbcc$	$Bb \rightarrow bB$
(11)→(12)	$aabBbcc$	$\Rightarrow aabbBcc$	$Bb \rightarrow bB$
(12)→(13)	$aabbBcc$	$\Rightarrow aabbCbccc$	$Bc \rightarrow Cbcc$
(13)→(14)	$aabbCbccc$	$\Rightarrow aabCbbccc$	$bC \rightarrow Cb$
(14)→(15)	$aabCbbccc$	$\Rightarrow aaCbbbccc$	$bC \rightarrow Cb$
(15)→(16)	$aaCbbbccc$	$\Rightarrow aaabbbccc$	$aC \rightarrow aa$

Table 1.1

Definition   A string w' is *generated* by w if either $w' = w$ or there is a sequence of strings $w_0, w_1, \ldots, w_n$ such that $w = w_0$, $w' = w_n$ and w_i immediately generates w_{i+1} for each i, $0 \leq i < n$. The sequence

$$w_0 \Rightarrow w_1 \Rightarrow w_2 \Rightarrow \cdots \Rightarrow w_n$$

is called a *derivation sequence of length n*. We also say that w is a *derivation sequence of length* 0.

*Notation   We write $w \Rightarrow_G^* w'$ if w' is generated by w.

*Notation   We write $w \Rightarrow_G^+ w'$ if w' is generated by w using a derivation sequence of length *greater than* 0.

Normally, where no confusion is likely to arise, we shall omit the subscript G and write $w \Rightarrow^* w'$ or $w \Rightarrow^+ w'$.

*Definition   The *language generated* by G, denoted $L(G)$, is the set of all strings $w \in T^*$ such that $S \Rightarrow^* w$.

Definition   A word $w \in (N \cup T)^*$ is a *sentential form* of G if and only if $S \Rightarrow^* w$, and is a *sentence* of G if and only if $S \Rightarrow^* w$ and $w \in T^*$.

As an exercise in the use of the above notation let us return to Example 9 and prove that $L(G_1) = \{a^n b^n c^n \mid n \geq 1\}$. The proof is split into two parts: we first prove that

$$\{a^n b^n c^n \mid n \geq 1\} \subseteq L(G_1)$$

and, secondly, we prove that

$$\{a^n b^n c^n \mid n \geq 1\} \supseteq L(G_1).$$

We begin by making the following simple observations:

(a) $a^n B b^n c^n \quad\Rightarrow^* a^n b^n B c^n$
(b) $a^n b^n B c^n \quad\Rightarrow\; a^n b^n C b c^{n+1}$
(c) $a^n b^n C b c^{n+1} \Rightarrow^* a^n C b^{n+1} c^{n+1}$ $\Bigg\}$ for all $n \geq 1$.
(d) $a^n C b^{n+1} c^{n+1} \Rightarrow\; a^{n+1} b^{n+1} c^{n+1}$
(e) $a^n C b^{n+1} c^{n+1} \Rightarrow\; a^{n+1} B b^{n+1} c^{n+1}$

Of these (b), (d) and (e) are obvious since each simply involves applying a production in G_1. (a) and (c) are almost as obvious: $a^n B b^n c^n$ can be generated from $a^n B b^n c^n$ by n applications of the production $Bb \to bB$ and, similarly, $a^n C b^{n+1} c^{n+1}$ can be generated from $a^n b^n C b c^{n+1}$ by n applications of $bC \to Cb$.

Using (a)–(e) we can establish inductively that

$$\{a^n b^n c^n \mid n \geq 1\} \subseteq L(G_1).$$

The inductive hypothesis is that $a^n B b^n c^n$ and $a^n b^n c^n$ are both sentential forms of G_1 where $n \geq 1$. The basis, $n=1$, is trivial since there are productions $A \to abc$ and $A \to aBbc$ in G_1. Now, assuming the hypothesis is true of n, we have

$$A \Rightarrow^* a^n B b^n c^n \qquad \text{(the induction hypothesis)}$$
$$\Rightarrow^* a^n C b^{n+1} c^{n+1} \qquad \text{(using (a)–(c) above)}.$$

Therefore, using (d),

$$A \Rightarrow^* a^{n+1} b^{n+1} c^{n+1}$$

and, using (e),

$$A \Rightarrow^* a^{n+1} B b^{n+1} c^{n+1}$$

Thus the inductive hypothesis is true of $n+1$. We conclude that $A \Rightarrow^* a^n b^n c^n$ for all $n \geq 1$. That is,

$$L(G_1) \supseteq \{a^n b^n c^n \mid n \geq 1\}.$$

Now, for the second part of the proof we claim that all sentential forms of G_1 have one of the forms

$$A, \quad a^n b^n c^n, \quad a^n b^m B b^r c^n, \quad a^n b^m C b^{r+1} c^{n+1},$$

where $n \geq 1$, $m, r \geq 0$ and $m + r = n$. More formally, suppose $A \Rightarrow^* w$. Let us write $A \Rightarrow^k w$ if w can be generated from A using a derivation sequence of length k. We assert that, for all $k \geq 0$,

if $A \Rightarrow^k w$

then $w \in \{A\} \cup \{a^n b^n c^n \mid n \geq 1\}$
$\cup \{a^n b^m B b^r c^n \mid n \geq 1, \, m, r \geq 0 \text{ and } m + r = n\}$
$\cup \{a^n b^m C b^{r+1} c^{n+1} \mid n \geq 1, \, m, r \geq 0 \text{ and } m + r = n\}.$

The proof is by induction on k. The basis, $k=0$, is trivial since then $w=A$. Now, suppose the hypothesis is true for all derivation sequences of length k. Suppose $A \Rightarrow^{k+1} w$. Let v be such that $A \Rightarrow^k v \Rightarrow w$. Then v must have one of the forms A, $a^n b^n c^n$, $a^n b^m B b^r c^n$, $a^n b^m C b^{r+1} c^{n+1}$, where $n \geq 1$, $m, r \geq 0$ and $m + r = n$. Also, $v \Rightarrow w$. To re-establish the induction hypothesis we must therefore perform a case analysis on the possible forms of v and the productions that may be applied to each form. In this way one can show that w must also have one of the four forms. (The details are easily checked by the reader.) Thus the assertion holds whatever the value of k.

A special case of the assertion is when $w \in T^*$. Thus

$$\text{if} \quad A \Rightarrow^* w \text{ and } w \in T^* \quad \text{then} \quad w \in \{a^n b^n c^n \mid n \geq 1\}.$$

That is,

$$L(G_1) \subseteq \{a^n b^n c^n \mid n \geq 1\}.$$

This completes the proof.

1.1.3 Classification of Grammars

The notion of a grammar, as defined above, was originally introduced by Chomsky. He classified grammars into four types by imposing restrictions on the form of the productions. These four types are:

Type 0 No restriction on the productions.
Type 1 or *context-sensitive* All productions have the form $u \rightarrow v$ where $length(u) \leq length(v)$ and $u, v \in (N \cup T)^+$.
*Type 2 or *context-free* All productions have the form $A \rightarrow v$ where A is a non-terminal symbol and $v \in (N \cup T)^*$.
*Type 3 or *regular* A regular grammar can take one of two forms:
Either: All productions have the form $A \rightarrow tB$ or $A \rightarrow t$ where t is a terminal string (i.e. $t \in T^*$) and A and B are non-terminal symbols. This form is called a *right-linear* grammar.
Or: All productions have the form $A \rightarrow Bt$ or $A \rightarrow t$ where t is a terminal string and A and B are non-terminal symbols. This form is called a *left-linear* grammar.

*Definition A language is said to be a *regular language* if it can be generated by a regular grammar.

*Definition A language is said to be a *context-free language* if it can be generated by a context-free grammar.

Definition   A language is said to be a *context-sensitive language* if it can be generated by a context-sensitive grammar.

Examples

(a)   Example 8 is a context-free gammar, so $\{a^n c b^n \mid n \geq 0\}$ is a context-free language.

(b)   Example 9 is a context-sensitive grammar, so $\{a^n b^n c^n \mid n \geq 1\}$ is a context-sensitive language.

(c)   Example 10 is a regular grammar, so $\{a^{2n+1} \mid n \geq 0\}$ is a regular language.

(d)   The definition of the syntax of ALGOL 60 in the "Revised Report" uses a context-free grammar. However we shall see subsequently that this definition omits a number of aspects of the syntax of ALGOL 60 which cannot be defined using a context-free grammar. Thus the language defined by the Report is context-free but is not ALGOL 60!

Note: A regular grammar satisfies the properties of a context-free grammar but, in general, the converse is not true. Thus a regular language is also a context-free language.

According to the above definitions Λ is not allowed on the right-hand side of a production in a context-sensitive grammar but is allowed in a context-free grammar. This difference is not essential and it can be shown that if G is any context-free grammar then there is a context-free grammar G' which has no Λ-productions and is such that $L(G')=L(G)-\{\Lambda\}$. Clearly the grammar G' is also context-sensitive. Thus any context-free language is also context-sensitive provided we disregard the empty word should it be in the language.

1.2   AMBIGUITY IN CONTEXT-FREE GRAMMARS

An important requirement of a programming language is that it is unambiguous, or, at least, that any ambiguities in the language be immediately evident and easily avoided. We would like, therefore, to be able to examine the definition of a language and decide whether or not it is ambiguous. Before we can do this we must define precisely the meaning of "ambiguous". That is the objective of this section.

1.2.1   Bracketed Forms

We can get an idea of how ambiguity should be defined by examining simple arithmetic expressions. These are defined in Sec. 3.3 of the ALGOL report.

We shall abbreviate the definition contained therein to the following grammar:

Grammar A1 (Simple arithmetic expressions) Let $G_1 = (\{E, T, F, U\}$, $\{+, \times, (,), 0, 1, \ldots, 9\}, P_1, E)$, where P_1 consists of

$$E \to T \qquad\qquad E \to E + T$$
$$T \to F \qquad\qquad T \to T \times F$$
$$F \to U \qquad\qquad F \to (E)$$
$$U \to 0 \mid 1 \mid 2 \mid 3 \mid \ldots \mid 9$$

Grammar A1 has been obtained from Sec. 3.3.1 of the "Revised Report on ALGOL 60" by abbreviating ⟨*simple arithmetic expression*⟩ to E, ⟨*term*⟩ to T, ⟨*factor*⟩ to F and ⟨*unsigned number*⟩ to U. We have also omitted the exponentiation operator ↑, ⟨*variable*⟩s and **if . . . then . . . else** from arithmetic expressions. Note that we have also used " | " as in the "Revised Report" to abbreviate the ten productions with lhs U.

Grammar A1 appears, at first sight, to be unnecessarily complicated. An alternative grammar defining the same language is Grammar A2.

Grammar A2 Let $G_2 = (\{E, U\}, \{+, \times, (,), 0, 1, \ldots, 9\}, P_2, E)$, where P_2 consists of

$$E \to E + E \qquad\qquad E \to E \times E$$
$$E \to (E) \qquad\qquad E \to U$$
$$U \to 0 \mid 1 \mid 2 \mid \ldots \mid 9$$

Grammar A2 contains fewer non-terminals and fewer productions than A1. So why the extra complication? The reason, as we shall see, is that A1 is "unambiguous", whereas A2 is "ambiguous".

Given the expression $2 + 3 \times 5$ we would certainly be justified in declaring a grammar to be ambiguous if the expression can be interpreted as $(2 + (3 \times 5))$ or $((2 + 3) \times 5)$. Now bracketing an expression embodies a notion of structure, so how does a grammar give structure to strings? Let us look at how to derive $2 + 3 \times 5$ using our two grammars.

Using Grammar A2 we can generate $2 + 3 \times 5$ by the following derivation sequence:

$$E \Rightarrow_{A2} E + E \qquad \Rightarrow_{A2} E + E \times E$$
$$\Rightarrow_{A2} U + E \times E \Rightarrow_{A2} 2 + E \times E$$
$$\Rightarrow_{A2} 2 + U \times E \Rightarrow_{A2} 2 + 3 \times E$$
$$\Rightarrow_{A2} 2 + 3 \times U \Rightarrow_{A2} 2 + 3 \times 5$$

Now suppose that we rewrite the derivation sequence, but whenever we use a production $A \to w$ we replace A by $\langle w \rangle_A$ instead of w. In this way we obtain

$$E \Rightarrow \langle E + E \rangle_E$$
$$\Rightarrow \langle E + \langle E \times E \rangle_E \rangle_E$$
$$\Rightarrow \langle \langle U \rangle_E + \langle E \times E \rangle_E \rangle_E$$
$$\Rightarrow \langle \langle \langle 2 \rangle_U \rangle_E + \langle E \times E \rangle_E \rangle_E$$
$$\Rightarrow \langle \langle \langle 2 \rangle_U \rangle_E + \langle \langle U \rangle_E \times E \rangle_E \rangle_E$$
$$\Rightarrow \langle \langle \langle 2 \rangle_U \rangle_E + \langle \langle \langle 3 \rangle_U \rangle_E \times E \rangle_E \rangle_E$$
$$\Rightarrow \langle \langle \langle 2 \rangle_U \rangle_E + \langle \langle \langle 3 \rangle_U \rangle_E \times \langle U \rangle_E \rangle_E \rangle_E$$
$$\Rightarrow \langle \langle \langle 2 \rangle_U \rangle_E + \langle \langle \langle 3 \rangle_U \rangle_E \times \langle \langle 5 \rangle_U \rangle_E \rangle_E \rangle_E$$

The final expression is a little clumsy because there are a number of redundant brackets, but removing the two innermost brackets around each digit we obtain the string

$$\langle 2 + \langle 3 \times 5 \rangle_E \rangle_E \qquad (1.1)$$

Another way of generating $2 + 3 \times 5$ using grammar A2 is as follows:

$$E \Rightarrow_{A2} E \times E \qquad \Rightarrow_{A2} E + E \times E$$
$$\Rightarrow_{A2} U + E \times E \Rightarrow_{A2} 2 + E \times E$$
$$\Rightarrow_{A2} 2 + U \times E \Rightarrow_{A2} 2 + 3 \times E$$
$$\Rightarrow_{A2} 2 + 3 \times U \Rightarrow_{A2} 2 + 3 \times 5$$

If we now apply the same bracketing process to this derivation sequence the reader may readily verify that we obtain the bracketed form

$$\langle \langle \langle \langle 2 \rangle_U \rangle_E + \langle \langle 3 \rangle_U \rangle_E \rangle_E \times \langle \langle 5 \rangle_U \rangle_E \rangle_E$$

Again removing the two innermost brackets around each digit we obtain

$$\langle \langle 2 + 3 \rangle_E \times 5 \rangle_E \qquad (1.2)$$

By comparing (1.1) with (1.2) one can see why we declare Grammar A2 to be ambiguous.

On the other hand, using an *ad hoc* argument we can establish that grammar A1 brackets $2 + 3 \times 5$ in a unique way. Using Grammar A1 we can generate $2 + 3 \times 5$ as follows:

$$E \Rightarrow_{A1} E + T \qquad \Rightarrow_{A1} E + T \times F$$
$$\Rightarrow_{A1} T + T \times F \Rightarrow_{A1} F + T \times F \Rightarrow_{A1} U + T \times F \Rightarrow_{A1} 2 + T \times F$$
$$\Rightarrow_{A1} 2 + F \times F \Rightarrow_{A1} 2 + U \times F \Rightarrow_{A1} 2 + 3 \times F$$
$$\Rightarrow_{A1} 2 + 3 \times U \Rightarrow_{A1} 2 + 3 \times 5$$

Applying the bracketing process to this derivation sequence we would eventually produce the (rather horrifying) expression

$$\langle\langle\langle\langle\langle 2\rangle_U\rangle_F\rangle_T\rangle_E + \langle\langle\langle\langle 3\rangle_U\rangle_F\rangle_T \times \langle\langle 5\rangle_U\rangle_F\rangle_T\rangle_E$$

However removing surplus brackets the expression reduces to

$$\langle 2 + \langle 3 \times 5\rangle_T\rangle_E$$

Note that there are several different *derivation sequences* which generate $2+3\times 5$, but for each we obtain the same bracketed form. For instance, an alternative derivation sequence is

$$
\begin{aligned}
E &\Rightarrow_{A1} E+T \\
&\Rightarrow_{A1} T+T \quad\;\; \Rightarrow_{A1} F+T \quad\;\; \Rightarrow_{A1} U+T \quad\;\; \Rightarrow_{A1} 2+T \\
&\Rightarrow_{A1} 2+T\times F \Rightarrow_{A1} 2+F\times F \Rightarrow_{A1} 2+U\times F \Rightarrow_{A1} 2+3\times F \\
&\Rightarrow_{A1} 2+3\times U \Rightarrow_{A1} 2+3\times 5
\end{aligned}
$$

However, bracketing this derivation sequence would *not* result in a different bracketed form. The argument that the bracketed form is unique is straightforward. The first production used in any derivation sequence must be $E\to E+T$ because (a) this production must be used exactly once in order to introduce the "$+$" symbol and (b) if the first production were $E\to T$ the only way we can reintroduce "E" is to use $F\to(E)$, but this introduces "$($" and "$)$" which are not in our string. Having obtained the string $E+T$ we must have $E\Rightarrow^* 2$ and $T\Rightarrow^* 3\times 5$. The former can only be achieved using $E\Rightarrow T\Rightarrow F\Rightarrow U\Rightarrow 2$ and the latter only by $T\Rightarrow T\times F$ and then $T\Rightarrow^* 3$ and $F\Rightarrow^* 5$.

Unfortunately the above *ad hoc* argument is not of much use to us since it only considers a very special case. One might now ask "Is the bracketed form of $1+3\times 5\times 2+9$ unique?" Since there are infinitely many arithmetic expressions we need a more general argument to establish that the grammar is unambiguous.

1.2.2   Derivation trees and Ambiguity

The bracketed form of a string soon becomes messy and unreadable. A better, pictorial representation of the structure of a derivation is a *derivation tree*. Figures 1.1 (a) and (b) show the two derivation trees of $2+3\times 5$ in the Grammar A2; Fig. 1.2 shows the unique derivation tree of $2+3\times 5$ in the Grammar A1. Hopefully it is immediately obvious that Fig. 1.1 (a) corresponds to the bracketed form $\langle 2+\langle 3\times 5\rangle_E\rangle_E$ and Fig. 1.1 (b) to the form $\langle\langle 2+3\rangle_E\times 5\rangle_E$. The reader will no doubt agree that a derivation tree is clearer than the bracketed expression and so we shall define "derivation tree" formally but leave "bracketed form" informally defined.

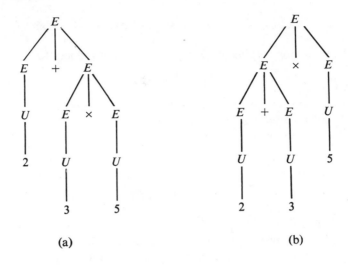

Fig. 1.1 (a) Derivation tree of $2+3\times5$ in Grammar A2; (b) alternative derivation tree of $2+3\times5$ in Grammar A2.

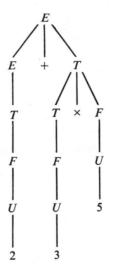

Fig. 1.2   Derivation tree of $2+3\times5$ in Grammar A1.

Definition   Let V be an arbitrary alphabet. A *labeled ordered tree D* consists of

(1)   a node n which is labeled by some $X \in V$ or by Λ;

(2)   an ordered set of k labeled ordered trees $D_1, \ldots, D_k$ where k is an arbitrary integer greater than or equal to zero.

The node n is called the *root* of the tree and $D_1, \ldots, D_k$ (if they exist, i.e. if $k>0$) are called the *subtrees* of the tree. If the tree D has no subtrees it is called a *leaf*. n is said to be the *father* of the roots $n_1, \ldots, n_k$ of $D_1, \ldots, D_k$.

Definition   A labeled ordered tree D is a *derivation tree* for a context-free grammar $G_S=(N,T,P,S)$ if

(a)   the root of the tree is labeled S, and

(b)   if $k>0$, $D_1, \ldots, D_k$ are the subtrees of D and the root of D_i is labeled A_i, then $S \rightarrow A_1 A_2 \ldots A_k$ is a production of P and D_i is a derivation tree for the grammar $G_{A_i}=(N,T,P,A_i)$.

The leaves of a derivation tree always spell out a sentential form if they are listed from left to right as they appear in the tree. Formally this is defined as follows.

Definition   The *frontier* of a derivation tree D is the string defined by the following recursive algorithm.

frontier$(D)=$**if** D *is a leaf* **then** *the label of* D
          else *frontier*$(D_1) \cdot$ *frontier*$(D_2) \cdots \cdot$ *frontier*(D_k)
          where $D_1, \ldots, D_k$ *are the subtrees of*
          D *and* $\cdot$ *denotes concatenation.*

The following theorem is immediate from the definitions.

Theorem 1.1 w is a sentential form of G if and only if w is the frontier of a derivation tree for G.

We now come to the main definition of this section.

Definition   A context-free grammar G is *ambiguous* if and only if there is a string $w \in L(G)$ such that w is the frontier of more than one derivation tree for G.

1.2.3   Examples of Ambiguous Grammars

In this subsection we discuss a number of features of ALGOL 60 and use these features to illustrate the concept of ambiguity.

Example 11   The "Revised Report on ALGOL 60" contains only one significant syntactic ambiguity. This appears in Sec. 2.6.1 where we find the
productions

$$\langle string \rangle \quad\quad\quad\to \text{`} \langle open\ string \rangle \text{'}$$
$$\langle open\ string \rangle \quad \to \langle proper\ string \rangle$$
$$\langle open\ string \rangle \quad \to \text{`} \langle open\ string \rangle \text{'}$$
$$\langle open\ string \rangle \quad \to \langle open\ string \rangle \ \langle open\ string \rangle$$
$$\langle proper\ string \rangle \to \langle empty \rangle \mid \langle any\ string\ of\ basic\ symbols$$
$$not\ containing\ \text{`}\ or\ \text{'} \rangle$$

The string '' '' '' is an example of an ⟨*open string*⟩ which is the frontier of
two distinct derivation trees (Figs. 1.3 (a) and (b)). The ambiguity is caused
by the use of the production

$$\langle open\ string \rangle \to \langle open\ string \rangle \ \langle open\ string \rangle$$

In this particular case the ambiguity can be resolved simply by replacing the
three productions with left-hand side ⟨*open string*⟩ by the two productions

$$\langle open\ string \rangle \to \langle proper\ string \rangle$$
$$\langle open\ string \rangle \to \langle open\ string \rangle \ \langle string \rangle \ \langle proper\ string \rangle$$

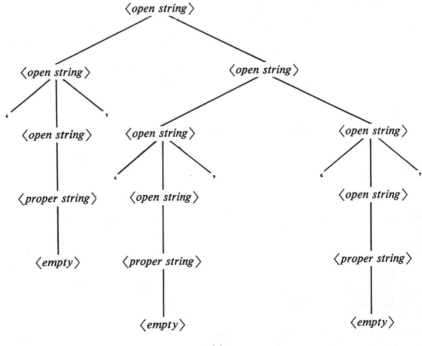

(a)

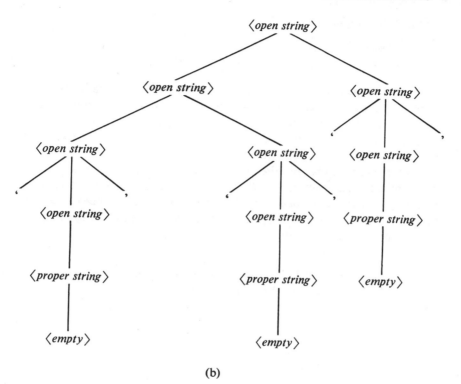

(b)

Fig. 1.3 An ambiguity in ALGOL 60.

In a more general form the ambiguity appears when there is a production of the form

$$A \rightarrow A \alpha A$$

(cf. $E \rightarrow E + E$) and, indeed, this is the most common cause of ambiguity introduced by novices to context-free definitions. To remove the ambiguity suppose that all the productions with left-hand side A are

$$A \rightarrow A \alpha A \qquad A \rightarrow \beta \qquad A \rightarrow \gamma \quad \ldots \quad A \rightarrow \omega$$

Let us regard α as an "operator" and $\beta, \gamma, \ldots, \omega$ as "operands". The language generated by A is any sequence of operands, where each pair of operands is separated by a single operator. A grammar generating the same language will be unambiguous if it rigidly specifies the order in which operators are to be applied. Here we shall choose to apply operators from right to left. This is achieved by replacing all the productions with left-hand side A

by the following productions:

$$A \to B \qquad A \to B\alpha A$$
$$B \to \beta \qquad B \to \gamma \quad \dots \quad B \to \omega$$

where B is a new non-terminal. The reader should compare the above productions with those in Grammar A1, noting that Grammar A1 defines a left-to-right order on application of operators. This process may not remove all ambiguities—$\alpha, \beta, \dots, \omega$ may be any strings of symbols and may include A—but it does remove one source of ambiguity.

There are a number of other minor ambiguities in the "Revised Report" concerning the recognition of $\langle identifier \rangle$ as either a $\langle primary \rangle$ or $\langle Boolean\ primary \rangle$ or $\langle procedure\ identifier \rangle$. However, as a consequence of the $uvwxy$ theorem to be discussed in Chap. 7, it is not easy to remove these ambiguities without impairing the clarity of the description.

Example 12   The most famous example of ambiguity is the dangling **else**. Consider the grammar with the productions

$$C \to \textbf{if}\ b\ \textbf{then}\ C\ \textbf{else}\ C$$
$$C \to \textbf{if}\ b\ \textbf{then}\ C$$
$$C \to s$$

The grammar is ambiguous since the string

> **if** b **then if** b **then** s **else** s

can be interpreted either as

> **if** b **then** (**if** b **then** s **else** s)

or as

> **if** b **then** (**if** b **then** s) **else** s

(see Figs. 1.4 (a) and (b)).

Referring to Sec. 4.5.1 of the "Revised Report" we can see that **if** . . . **then if** . . . is outlawed in ALGOL 60. For, in the definition of a $\langle conditional\ statement \rangle$, we find

> $\langle conditional\ statement \rangle ::= \langle if\ statement \rangle |$
> $\qquad\qquad\qquad\qquad\quad \langle if\ statement \rangle$ **else** $\langle statement \rangle$

where

> $\langle if\ statement \rangle ::= \langle if\ clause \rangle \langle unconditional\ statement \rangle$

Thus it is possible to write **if** . . . **then** . . . **else if** but not **if** . . . **then if** . . . . Nevertheless **if** . . . **then if** . . . is often allowed by ALGOL compilers—in such cases the interpretation defined by Fig. 1.4 (a) is invariably chosen.

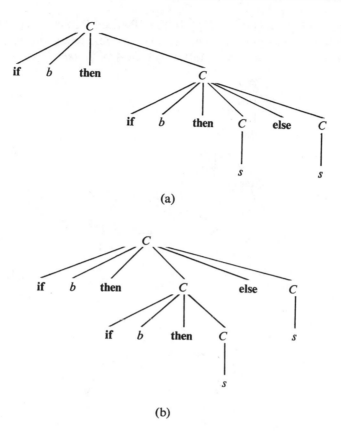

(a)

(b)

Fig. 1.4 Ambiguity in conditional statements.

Example 13 Our final example of ambiguity is in **for** statements. Consider the grammar with productions

$$S \rightarrow \textbf{if } b \textbf{ then } U$$
$$S \rightarrow \textbf{if } b \textbf{ then } U \textbf{ else } S$$
$$S \rightarrow a$$
$$U \rightarrow \textbf{for } c \textbf{ do } S$$
$$U \rightarrow a$$

Here we have avoided the ambiguity of **if** . . . **then if** as in the "Revised Report". But now the string

$$\textbf{if } b \textbf{ then for } c \textbf{ do if } b \textbf{ then } a \textbf{ else } a$$

is ambiguous (Figs. 1.5 (a) and (b)). In the "Revised Report on ALGOL 60" (Sec. 4.5.1) the ambiguity is again avoided by restricting the form of an ⟨*unconditional statement*⟩ so as not to include ⟨*for statement*⟩s.

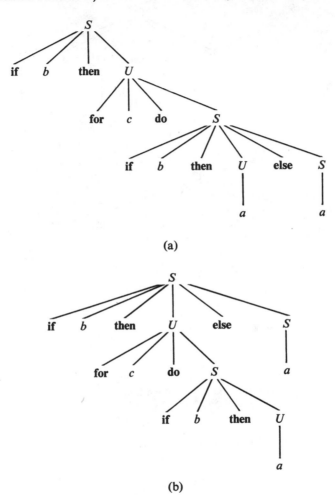

(a)

(b)

Fig. 1.5 Ambiguity in **for** statements.

1.2.4 A Negative Result

We conclude this section with a negative result. We shall not prove the result here since to do so we would need to include a considerable amount of background material.

Theorem 1.2 The problem of deciding whether a given context-free grammar is ambiguous is unsolvable.

This theorem is a bad way to have to start a book on Computer Science, particularly one which aims to stress the importance of algorithms! Nevertheless, the reader should not be put off by the result since it is a statement about a general problem. In particular cases we have seen that we can recognize ambiguities. Moreover we shall see in the chapters on LL and LR parsing that there are algorithms which reply either

"Yes, G is unambiguous"

or

"G may or may not be ambiguous"

to the question of whether G is ambiguous. Finally the property of ambiguity is (usually) a property of the grammar rather than the language and so, in practice, it is always possible to rewrite the definition of a "maybe ambiguous" grammar to ensure unambiguity. (There are nevertheless some languages which are "inherently ambiguous", i.e. there is no unambiguous context-free grammar defining the language. Fortunately problems of inherent ambiguity do not arise in programming languages.)

EXERCISES

In the following exercises only the productions in the grammar are specified. The non-terminals are the symbols which appear on the left-hand side of a production, and the terminals are the remaining symbols. Unless otherwise mentioned S is the start symbol.

1.1 Describe (in English) the language generated by the following grammar.

$$
\begin{array}{ll}
S \to S,E & S \to E \\
E \to E+T & E \to T \\
T \to T*F & T \to F \\
F \to a & F \to (E) \qquad F \to a[S]
\end{array}
$$

1.2 Use Sec. 3.4.1 of the "Revised Report on ALGOL 60" together with any other relevant sections to construct derivation trees for the following ⟨*Boolean expression*⟩s.

    (a) $a < b \equiv c \lor d$
    (b) **if if** a **then** $b < c$ **else** d **then** e **else** f

(*Hint:* Don't be surprised if the derivation trees are rather large.)

1.3 Check the following ALGOL statements for syntactic errors by referring to the relevant sections of the "Revised Report on ALGOL 60". If a statement is in error then give your reasons, quoting the relevant sections of the Report, and suggest how it may be written correctly.

(a) $y := $ **if** $a \lor b = c$ **then if** $b = d$ **then** 2
                        else if $b = e$ **then** 3 **else** 4 **else** 5
(b) let : $y := x + ($**if if** $p = q$ **then** t **else** r **then** 1 **else** 2)
(c) alpha $:= 21 \times$ **begin if** beta = gamma = delta
                        then alpha **else** 0 **end**
(d) **if** $a1 = a2$ **then for** $i := 1, 2$ **do** $a[i] := 0$
                        else $a[3] := 0$

For the identifiers a,b,c,d,e,p,q,t,r state what type(s) each may have in your corrected version of the statement.

Suggest reasons why each of the incorrect statements above is outlawed by the "Revised Report on ALGOL 60". Illustrate your answer by suitable examples.

1.4 The following is a grammar defining $\langle assignment\ statement \rangle$s in a hypothetical programming language.

$\langle assignment\ statement \rangle ::= \langle identifier \rangle := \langle expression \rangle$
$\langle expression \rangle \qquad\quad ::= \langle term \rangle + \langle expression \rangle \,|\, \langle term \rangle - \langle expression \rangle \,|$
$\qquad\qquad\qquad\qquad\quad \langle term \rangle \times \langle expression \rangle \,|\, -\langle term \rangle \,|\, \langle term \rangle$
$\langle term \rangle \qquad\qquad ::= \langle identifier \rangle \,|\, \langle digit \rangle \,|\, (\langle expression \rangle)$
$\langle digit \rangle \qquad\qquad ::= 0\,|\,1\,|\,2\,|\,3\,|\,4\,|\,5\,|\,6\,|\,7\,|\,8\,|\,9$
$\langle identifier \rangle \qquad\quad ::= a\,|\,b\,|\,c$

What is the value of a after each of the following assignments, assuming the above syntax?

$$a := 2 + 6 \times 3 \times 6$$
$$a := -(2 - 3 \times 2)$$
$$a := 2 + (3 - 2 \times 6)$$
$$a := 2 - 3 - 6$$

1.5 (a) Let G be defined by the following productions (where E is the start symbol):

$$E \rightarrow E + T \qquad E \rightarrow T$$
$$T \rightarrow T \times P \qquad T \rightarrow P$$
$$P \rightarrow u \qquad\quad P \rightarrow (E)$$

Show by example how this grammar imposes:
 (i) a left-to-right order on evaluation of arithmetic expressions, subject to:
 (ii) operator precedence of $\times$ over $+$.

How would you modify the grammar so that evaluation is right to left subject to rules of precedence?
(b) A subset of the programming language APL contains two binary operators ρ and ι and identifiers a, b and c. Evaluation is always from right to left and there is no operator precedence. Parentheses may be used to over-ride this order of evaluation.

Construct a grammar which defines the set of all expressions involving ρ, ι, a, b, c and parentheses (and) which imposes the above rules on their evaluation.

1.6 The following is the Backus Normal Form description of an expression $\langle EXP \rangle$ in some language. φ_1, φ_2 and φ_3 are operators.

$$\langle LIT \rangle \quad ::= A|B|C|D|E|F$$
$$\langle BASIC \rangle ::= \langle LIT \rangle | \langle BASIC \rangle \, \varphi_1 \, \langle LIT \rangle$$
$$\langle INTER \rangle ::= \langle BASIC \rangle | \langle INTER \rangle \, \varphi_3 \, \langle BASIC \rangle$$
$$\langle EXP \rangle \quad ::= \langle INTER \rangle | \varphi_2 \, \langle INTER \rangle | \langle EXP \rangle \, \varphi_2 \, \langle INTER \rangle$$

These formulas implicitly define the precedence of the operators φ_1, φ_2 and φ_3 in the evaluation of expressions. Deduce this precedence, giving your reasons, and hence parenthesize the following expression to show the order of evaluation.

$$\varphi_2 \, F \, \varphi_1 \, D \, \varphi_1 \, B \, \varphi_2 \, C \, \varphi_3 \, A$$

1.7 Describe the language defined by the following grammar and show that it is ambiguous.

$$
\begin{array}{ll}
S \rightarrow AB & S \rightarrow DC \\
A \rightarrow aA & A \rightarrow a \\
B \rightarrow bBc & B \rightarrow bc \\
C \rightarrow cC & C \rightarrow c \\
D \rightarrow aDb & D \rightarrow ab
\end{array}
$$

1.3 GRAPH SEARCHING

We shall now consider an abstract problem—that of finding a path through a graph. The problem may seem out of place in a text on language theory, but we shall have occasion to use the results presented here in a number of subsequent sections. In particular, in the next section we shall see an immediate application. The discussion of graph searching also provides an opportunity to demonstrate the style of algorithm development which is used throughout the text, as well as introducing concepts of program proving and the analysis of algorithms.

Definition A *directed graph H* is defined to be a pair consisting of a finite set of *nodes X* and a finite set of *arcs E*. Two mappings are defined from *E* into *X*, the first called the *from* component and the second called the *into* component. If *a* is an arc, these are denoted, respectively, by *a.from* and *a.into*. If *a.from* = *x* and *a.into* = *y*, the arc *a* is said to be *directed from x to y*.

Figure 1.6 is a diagrammatic representation of a directed graph. The set *X* of nodes in the graph may be identified with the set of integers $\{1, 2, 3, \ldots, 13\}$. The arcs are the lines connecting nodes, the arrow head pointing to the *into* component. For example, there are arcs from 1 to 2, from 2 to 3 and from 3 to 2.

It is important to note that our definition of a graph allows the possibility of more than one arc from a given node x to a given node y. For instance, in Fig. 1.6 there are two arcs from 2 to 11. Such duplication occurs frequently in the graphs we construct but always the important property is whether there is or is not an arc from x to y. It will be convenient, therefore, for us to refer to "an arc $\langle x, y \rangle$" rather than the long-winded but more precise description "an arc a with $a.from = x$ and $a.into = y$".

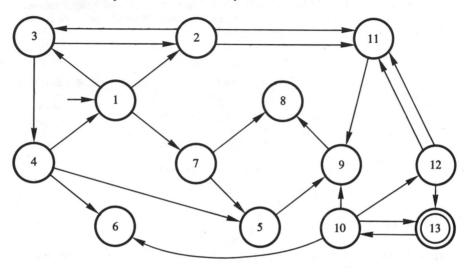

Fig. 1.6   A graph.

An *undirected graph* may be defined to be a graph H which has the property that, to each arc from x to y in the graph there is also a corresponding arc from y to x. In a diagrammatic representation of an undirected graph there are no arrow-heads on the arcs, a single line connecting nodes x and y being used to represent both an arc from x to y and the corresponding arc from y to x. In this text all the graphs we consider will be directed graphs. We shall, therefore, omit the adjective "directed" and simply talk about "graphs".

The problem we shall consider is this: Given two nodes s and f, is there a path from s to f in the graph? A *path from the node x to the node y* is defined to be a sequence of arcs $a_1, a_2, \ldots, a_t$, where $x = a_1.from$, $y = a_t.into$ and $a_i.into = a_{i+1}.from$ for each i $(1 \leq i \leq t-1)$. The path is said to be of *length t* (i.e. the number of arcs on the path). Additionally, it is useful to allow paths of length zero. Specifically, we say that there *is a path of length zero from each node to itself*. In this case the sequence of arcs is defined to be the empty sequence.

1.3.1 Developing an algorithm

Let us suppose that we wish to determine whether there is a path from node 1 to node 13 in the graph of Fig. 1.6. The *start node* (node 1) is indicated on the graph by an additional arrow, and a double circle has been used to indicate that node 13 is the *final node*.

A straightforward solution to this problem is based on the following ideas. We define a set, called *reached*, which consists of nodes which can be reached by paths from s. Initially *reached* is set to $\{s\}$. Now, if $x \in reached$ and there is an arc $\langle x, y \rangle$, y can also be reached from s. Conversely if $y \neq s$ and there is a path from s to y there must be an arc $\langle x, y \rangle$ from a node x which can also be reached from s. Thus to find whether f can be reached from s we repeat a process of adding to the set *reached* all nodes y to which there is an arc $\langle x, y \rangle$ from a node x already in *reached*. This is expressed by Algorithm 1.1.

Algorithm 1.1

```
var reached: set of node;
    s,f: node; {start and final nodes respectively}
begin reached := {s};
while (f ∉ reached) and (a change occurs in reached) do
    begin assertion 1: x ∈ reached ⊃ ∃ path from s to x;
    reached := reached ∪ directly-reachable(reached);
    end;
if f ∈ reached then write (' YES, THERE IS A PATH' )
               else write ( ' NO, THERE IS NOT A PATH' )
end.
```

Before developing the algorithm further, a number of general remarks are in order. In this book we shall develop a number of algorithms. Some of these algorithms will also be implemented as PASCAL programs. The notation used to describe algorithms will be based on the notation of PASCAL, on elementary mathematical notation for sets and on any additional notation defined in the text. Algorithms are distinct from programs in that they will generally involve data types and operations which are not primitive to PASCAL. Sometimes confusion can occur over what is intended by the algorithm. For example *reached* has been defined in Algorithm 1.1 to be of type *set of node*. This is intended to mean that *reached* is a set of nodes in the usual mathematical sense of the word set; it is *not* intended to mean that we have already chosen to implement *reached* as a PASCAL set. A PASCAL set is nothing more than a bit-vector and bears only a slight resemblance to the fundamental concept of a set! In order to avoid this confusion **set** in boldface type indicates the PASCAL meaning; more commonly, however, the appearance of set or *set* indicates the mathematical meaning. A second source of possible confusion is the use of functional notation, as in *directly-reachable* (*reached*). The use of this notation is not meant to imply that we shall construct a function *directly-reachable*. Instead, functional notation will be used whenever an operation appears which has not yet been expressed in terms primitive to PASCAL.

In Algorithm 1.1, *directly-reachable* (*reached*) is defined by: $y \in$ *directly-reachable* (*reached*) if, and only if, for some $x \in$ *reached* there is an arc $\langle x, y \rangle$ from x to y. Assuming this definition, we would claim that the algorithm is obviously correct. Nevertheless, we have added an assertion to the algorithm which will be used in Sec. 1.3.3 to verify its correctness.

The behavior of Algorithm 1.1 can be visualized as a wave spreading out from the start node s. Applied to our example, after the first iteration *reached* is {1,2,3,7} and after the second iteration *reached* is {1,2,3,7,4,5,8,11}. The algorithm terminates when either $f \in$ *reached* or no change occurs in *reached*.

Algorithm 1.1 contains a major source of inefficiency, namely, the re-computation of *directly-reachable* sets. For instance, in the example *directly-reachable*({1}) will be computed in every iteration, and *directly-reachable* ({2,3,7}) will be computed in every iteration except the first. This inefficiency can be removed by identifying a subset of the nodes which we will call the *frontier* set. *frontier* is defined to be the set of nodes newly added to *reached*. (The terminology has been chosen in order to suggest the analogy with a wave.)

Algorithm 1.2 shows how *frontier* and *reached* are calculated. A second assertion has been added to Algorithm 1.2. This assertion will be discussed more fully in Sec. 1.3.3, but, briefly, it expresses the property of *frontier* which enables us to claim that Algorithms 1.1 and 1.2 are equivalent. Note that *frontier* is the intersection of the sets *directly-reachable* (*frontier*) and ~ *reached*, where the latter denotes the set of all nodes which are not in *reached*.

Algorithm 1.2

```
var reached, frontier: set of node;
    s,f: node;
begin reached := frontier := {s};
while (f ∉ reached) and (a change occurs in reached) do
    begin
    assertion 1:  x ∈ reached ⊃ ∃ path from s to x;
    assertion 2:  reached ∪ directly-reachable(reached)
                     = reached ∪ directly-reachable(frontier);
    frontier := directly-reachable(frontier) ∩ (~reached);
    reached := reached ∪ frontier;
    end;
```

Algorithm 1.2 (Continued)

if $f \in$ *reached* then *write* (' *YES, THERE IS A PATH*')
                 else *write* (' *NO, THERE IS NOT A PATH*')
end.

The operations in Algorithm 1.2 are certainly not primitive to PASCAL. Algorithm 1.3 expands the statements in Algorithm 1.2 into statements which are much closer to a direct implementation. The control structures of Algorithms 1.2 and 1.3 are not identical, although the reader should have no difficulty in relating them to each other. Note also that the test for a change in *reached* has been replaced by the test (*frontier* $\neq \varnothing$).

Algorithm 1.3

Line No.		Symbolic frequency count
1	**var** *reached, frontier*: *set of node*;	
2	x, y, s, f: *node*;	
3	**begin** *reached* := *frontier* := $\{s\}$;	1
4	**while** ($f \notin$ *reached*) **and** (*frontier* $\neq \varnothing$) **do**	$\leq n$
5	**begin assertion** 1 ... ; **assertion** 2 ... ;	
6	*choose and remove x from frontier*;	$\leq n-1$
7	**for** *each arc a from x* **do**	$\leq \alpha$
8	**begin** *let y be a.into*;	$\leq \alpha$
9	**if** $y \notin$ *reached*	$\leq \alpha$
10	**then** *add y to reached and frontier*;	$\leq n-1$
11	**end**;	
12	**end**;	
13	**if** $f \in$ *reached*	1
14	**then** *write* (' *YES, THERE IS A PATH*')	≤ 1
15	**else** *write* (' *NO, THERE IS NOT A PATH*');	≤ 1
16	**end**.	

At this point it is worthwhile performing a detailed analysis of the frequency of execution of the statements in Algorithm 1.3.† Let n be the

---

†The analysis discussed here is commonly called a *worst-case analysis* because the maximum (or "worst") number of times each statement is executed is singled out for consideration. An *average-case analysis* attempts to predict the expected number of times each statement is executed. To perform such an analysis some information must be provided about the "average input". It is difficult to say what an "average graph" or, in later sections, what an "average grammar" is and so we shall not perform any average-case analyses. Throughout this book the worst-case execution time will be the sole criterion for comparing algorithms.

number of nodes and α be the number of arcs in the graph. Using this notation we have annotated Algorithm 1.3 with a *symbolic frequency count*. This count states how many times each statement will be executed, assuming arbitrary data. For instance, the initial statements are executed exactly once, and the two write statements are each either never executed or executed once only (i.e. $\leq$ 1 times). These counts are trivial—the analysis of the counts for the remaining statements is much more difficult.

The key property of the algorithm is expressed by the count attached to line 10. Here we are asserting that *each node y is added to reached at most once*. This assertion is obviously true, since no nodes are ever removed from *reached*, and, before adding *y* to *reached*, a check is made to ensure that it is not already in the set. All the remaining nontrivial counts are direct consequences of this property. For instance, consider line 6. Since the addition of nodes to *frontier* occurs simultaneously with the addition of nodes to *reached*, each node is added to *frontier* at most once and hence each node is removed from *frontier* at most once. Now *f* is never removed from *frontier*. Thus line 6 is executed at most $n-1$ times. Similarly we can argue that lines 7, 8 and 9 are executed at most α times, because each arc from each node will be accessed at most once.

The above analysis is encouraging. In any algorithm which performs a graph search of this kind, we would expect that for some inputs every arc of the graph must be accessed. In this sense Algorithm 1.3 is optimal. So, now is the time to think about choosing data structures.

1.3.2 Choice of Data Structures and Implementation

The data structure used to implement a particular data item should always be chosen by examination of the operations performed on that data item. This is well illustrated by the two items *frontier* and *reached* in Algorithm 1.3. Both *frontier* and *reached* are sets, but the operations performed on them are quite different. We shall see, therefore, that the data structures used to implement the two sets are also quite different.

Table 1.2 lists the data items used in Algorithm 1.3, together with the operations performed on them and the number of times each operation is executed. The data item *node* has not been included because its implementation is dependent upon the application; for simplicity, we assume here that nodes are represented by integers in the range 1 . . *n*. The value of *n* will be specified in the **const** section of the program.

Now, examining Table 1.2, it is clear that a suitable data structure for *reached* is a Boolean array *reached*, where $x \in reached$ if and only if *reached*[*x*] = true. The two frequently occurring operations of adding nodes to *reached* and testing for membership of *reached* can each be implemented using a single PASCAL instruction. The initialization of *reached* will require a **for** loop, but this is acceptable since the operation occurs once only. In contrast, *frontier* is best implemented using a stack. Adding nodes to *frontier* will then be represented by pushing items onto the stack, and removing a node will be represented by popping the top item. Note that the use of a stack is feasible because the analysis of Algorithm 1.3 does not depend on how x is chosen in line 6. Choosing the top stack item is as good as any other method. More detailed descriptions of these data structures are presented below.

const $n = $; {no. of nodes in the graph}
type $node = 1 .. n$;
     $frontierindex = 1 .. n$; $zeroorfrontierindex = 0 .. n$;
var   *reached*: **array** [*node*] **of** *Boolean*;
     top: *zeroorfrontierindex*;
     frontier: **array**[*frontierindex*] **of** *node*;

Table 1.2

Data item	Operations	Frequency	Data structure
reached	initialization	1	Boolean array
	add a node	$\leq n-1$	
	test for membership	$\leq \alpha + n$	
frontier	initialization	1	stack
	add a node	$\leq n-1$	
	choose and remove a node	$\leq n-1$	
	test for empty	$\leq n$	
graph	input	1	linear list of arcs
	given x: node, access each arc from x	at most once per arc	pointed to by x

As yet we are not in a position to choose data structures to represent the graph, since a major operation on the graph—its input—has still to be specified. We shall assume that the input file consists of the values of s and f followed by pairs of integers representing the arcs. The arcs are in a random order and are terminated by the end of the file.

Apart from its input, the only operation on the graph is, given a node x, to access each arc from x. The correctness and efficiency of the algorithm do not depend on the order in which arcs from x are accessed, so a suitable data structure is to store arcs from x in a linear list whose first element is pointed to by x. This data structure is also compatible with the specification of the input. Its description in PASCAL is presented below.

```
type arclink = ↑ arc;
     arc = record into: node; next: arclink;
            end;
var firstarcfrom: array[node] of arclink;
```

Note that, in this application, it is unnecessary to include a *from* component in the description of an arc.

We are now in a position to present a complete PASCAL program to perform graph searching.

Program 1.1

```
program graphsearch(input, output);
const n=  ; {n should be set equal to the no. of nodes}
type node = 1..n;
     arclink = ↑ arc;
     arc = record into: node; next: arclink;
            end;
     frontierindex = 1..n; zeroorfrontierindex = 0..n;
var   reached: array[node] of Boolean;
      top: zeroorfrontierindex;
      frontier: array[frontierindex] of node;
      s, f, x, y: node;
      parc: arclink;
      firstarcfrom: array[node] of arclink;

procedure inputgraph;
var from, into: node;
    parc: arclink;
    x: node;
begin  readln(s, f);
{initialize list of arcs from each node to nil}
for x := 1 to n do firstarcfrom[x] := nil;
{read each arc and add it to appropriate list}
read(from);
while not eof(input) do
     begin read(into); new(parc);
     parc↑.next := firstarcfrom[from]; firstarcfrom[from] := parc;
     parc↑.into := into;
     read(from);
     end;
end; {input graph}
```

Program 1.1   (Continued)

```
begin {main program}
inputgraph;
{initialize reached and frontier}
top := 1; frontier[top] := s;
for x := 1 to n do reached[x] := false; reached[s] := true;
while (top ≠ 0) and not reached[f] do
    begin x := frontier[top]; top := top − 1;
    {for each arc a from x add a.into to reached
    and frontier if not already reached}
    parc := firstarcfrom[x];
    while parc ≠ nil do
        begin y := parc↑.into; parc := parc↑. next;
        if not reached[y] then begin reached[y] := true;
                                  top := top + 1; frontier[top] := y;
                              end;
        end;
    end;
if reached[f] then writeln(' YES, THERE IS A PATH' )
              else writeln(' NO, THERE IS NOT A PATH' );
end.
```

1.3.3 Checking the Solution

The completion of a PASCAL program does not imply that the problem is solved! The final step in the solution of any problem is to check the accuracy of the solution. One way to check computer programs is to run them and inspect the output. This is an important part of the checking process and should always be done thoroughly. But it has its limitations, since it is rarely possible to guarantee the completeness of the check. Indeed *all* methods of checking have their limitations and no solution can ever be guaranteed to be *absolutely* correct. The aim of checking is to *increase* the level of confidence in the solution of a problem. *Program proving* is an important technique for doing this.

In order to prove a program two things need to be done. Firstly, one must establish that the program always terminates whatever the input. Secondly, one must show that the output meets the specification of the program. The proof is made a great deal easier if all steps in the development are also proven. Here we shall prove Algorithms 1.1 and 1.2 in detail and outline the proofs of Algorithm 1.3 and Program 1.1.

Lemma 1.3   Algorithms 1.1 and 1.2 always terminate.

Proof   Clearly it suffices to establish that the condition for terminating the **while** loop in both algorithms is always eventually satisfied. This is so, because at each iteration the number of nodes in *reached* either increases or remains constant. But it cannot increase indefinitely since the total number of nodes in a graph is finite.☐
(*Note:* ☐ indicates the end of a proof.)

The correctness of Algorithm 1.1 is expressed formally by Theorem 1.4.

Theorem 1.4   On termination of Algorithm 1.1, $f \in$ *reached* if and only if there is a path from s to f in the input graph.

The proof of Theorem 1.4 is split into two parts:

(a)   if $f \in$ *reached*, then there is a path from s to f, and
(b)   if there is a path from s to f, then $f \in$ *reached*.

Assertion 1 in Algorithm 1.1 enables us to complete part (a) of the proof. In general an *assertion* is used to express a property of the variables at some point in an algorithm whenever control of the execution of the algorithm is at that point. Assertion 1 expresses a property of s and *reached* whenever the body of the **while** loop is about to be executed. This property is true independently of the number of times the **while** loop is executed and is therefore called a *loop invariant*. Specifically assertion 1 states that for all $x \in$ *reached* there is a path from s to x. A special case of this assertion (when $x=f$) is part (a) of the proof of Theorem 1.4. The verification of loop invariants involves using simple mathematical induction on the number of times the body of the loop is executed. To illustrate this we shall formally verify assertion 1 in Algorithm 1.1.

Verification of assertion 1 (*Algorithm* 1.1)   The first time control reaches it, assertion 1 is true because *reached* $= \{s\}$ and, by definition, there is a path from s to s. Suppose that assertion 1 is true when the body of the loop has been executed k times $(k \geq 0)$. Suppose the body of the loop is executed $k+1$ times and let r and r' be the values of *reached* before and after the $(k+1)$th execution. By the induction hypothesis, if $x \in r$, then there is a path from s to x. Now $r' = r \cup$ *directly-reachable*(r). So to re-establish the induction hypothesis we only need to prove that if $y \in$ *directly-reachable*(r), then there is a path from s to y. Recall the definition of *directly-reachable*. $y \in$ *directly-reachable*(r) if and only if there is an arc a to y from some node $x \in r$. Now recall the definition of path. By the induction hypothesis, there is a path from

s to x, i.e. a sequence of arcs $a_1, a_2, \ldots, a_t$ where $a_1.from = s$ and $a_t.into = x$. (This sequence may be empty, in which case $s = x$.) But then $a_1, a_2, \ldots, a_t, a$ satisfies the definition of a path from s to y. Thus we have established the induction hypothesis for the $(k+1)$th execution of the **while** statement and we conclude that assertion 1 holds whatever the value of k. □

Let us now return to the proof of Theorem 1.4.

Proof of Theorem 1.4   By assertion 1 we have: if $f \in reached$ then there is a path from s to f in the graph. It remains to prove that, if there is a path from s to f then, on termination, $f \in reached$. In other words we must establish that Algorithm 1.1 does not terminate prematurely. The proof is by *reductio ad absurdum*; that is, we assume that the algorithm does not terminate correctly and establish a contradiction. Suppose that, on termination of Algorithm 1.1, $f \notin reached$ but there is a path from s to f. The condition for terminating the **while** loop is either $f \in reached$ or no change has occurred in *reached*. Since the former does not hold, the latter must. An alternative way of expressing this condition is

$$reached = reached \cup directly\text{-}reachable(reached).$$

Now $f = s$ contradicts our supposition, so suppose $f \neq s$. Let a path from s to f be $a_1, a_2, \ldots, a_t$, where $a_t.into = f$ and $a_1.from = s$. Let $x_0 = s$ and $x_j = a_j.into$ $(1 \leq j \leq t)$. Choose an index i such that $x_{i-1} \in reached$ and $x_t \notin reached$. Such an index exists since $s \in reached$ and $f \notin reached$. But then

$$x_t \in directly\text{-}reachable(\{x_{i-1}\})$$

and hence

$$reached \neq reached \cup directly\text{-}reachable(reached).$$

This is a contradiction and we deduce that either $f \in reached$ on termination, or there is no path from s to f. □

The reader will note that assertion 1 has been carried over into Algorithm 1.2. Assertion 2 is additional to Algorithm 1.2 and reflects the modification in the algorithm. It states that the new value of *reached* can be calculated by adding *directly-reachable(frontier)* rather than *directly-reachable(reached)* to *reached*. In other words, assertion 2 states that Algorithms 1.1 and 1.2 are equivalent with respect to the computation of *reached*. Provided that we can verify assertion 2, the proof of Algorithm 1.2 is identical to the proof of Algorithm 1.1. The verification of assertion 2 involves the use of mathematical induction and some simple properties of sets.

Verification of assertion 2 (*Algorithm* 1.2)   The first time control reaches it, assertion 2 is true because *reached*=*frontier*. Suppose that assertion 2 is true when the body of the loop has been executed k times ($k \geq 0$). Suppose the body of the loop is executed $k+1$ times. Let *fr* and *fr'* be the values of *frontier* and r and r' be the values of *reached* before and after the $(k+1)$th execution of the loop. Then, by inspection of Algorithm 1.2, we have

$$r' = r \cup fr' \tag{1.3}$$

Also, by the induction hypothesis,

$$r \cup \textit{directly-reachable}(r) = r \cup \textit{directly-reachable}(fr)$$
$$= r \cup (\textit{directly-reachable}\ (fr) \cap {\sim} r)$$
$$= r \cup fr'.$$

That is,

$$r' \supseteq \textit{directly-reachable}(r) \tag{1.4}$$

We must prove that

$$r' \cup \textit{directly-reachable}(r') = r' \cup \textit{directly-reachable}(fr').$$

The proof proceeds as follows.

$$r' \cup \textit{directly-reachable}(r') = r' \cup \textit{directly-reachable}(r \cup fr') \quad \text{(by (1.3))}$$
$$= r' \cup \textit{directly-reachable}(r)$$
$$\cup \textit{directly-reachable}(fr')$$
$$= r' \cup \textit{directly-reachable}(fr') \quad \text{(by (1.4))}.$$

We have thus established that assertion 2 is true on the $(k+1)$th execution of the **while** statement assuming that it is true on the kth execution. By induction we conclude that assertion 2 holds whatever the value of k.☐

It is worthwhile reviewing the verification of assertion 2 to see how it was constructed. The main steps in the proof are inequality (1.4) and the expansion of *directly-reachable*(r') into *directly-reachable*(r) $\cup$ *directly-reachable*(fr'). These two steps correspond directly with the informal argument given in Sec. 1.3.1 to justify the use of *frontier*, namely that any node *y* which is directly reachable from a node *x*, where *x* is in *reached* but not in *frontier* (cf. the expansion of *directly-reachable*(r')} will have already been added to *reached* (cf. inequality (1.4)). The two arguments complement each other very well. The informal argument adds clarity to the formal proof whilst the formal proof is concise, unambiguous and easily checked (by a machine if necessary).

Algorithm 1.3 is essentially a rewrite of Algorithm 1.2 with the calculation of *directly-reachable* expanded into more primitive operations. Thus no new assertions have been added to Algorithm 1.3 but assertions 1 and 2 have been carried over into it. We shall not perform a detailed proof of these assertions since no novel techniques are required. A major change in Algorithm 1.3 is the test for termination of the **while** loop. To check the validity of the new test we shall rewrite the proof of Theorem 1.4.

Theorem 1.5   On termination of Algorithm 1.3 $f \in$ *reached* if and only if there is a path from s to f in the input graph.

Proof   As in Theorem 1.4 the proof is split into two parts:
(a)   if $f \in$ *reached*, then there is a path from s to f, and
(b)   if there is a path from s to f, then $f \in$ *reached*.

Again the proof of part (a) follows easily from the proof of assertion 1 and so will be omitted. Part (b) involves examining the condition for termination. Suppose that, on termination of Algorithm 1.3, $f \notin$ *reached* but there is a path from s to f. Then we must also have *frontier* $= \varnothing$. Using assertion 2 (which we assume has already been proved)

$$reached \cup directly\text{-}reachable(reached)$$
$$= reached \cup directly\text{-}reachable(\varnothing) = reached.$$

Now the proof proceeds exactly as for Theorem 1.4 to which we refer the reader.☐

In order to prove Program 1.1 it is necessary to rephrase all arguments about *reached*, *frontier* and arcs of the graph in terms of their concrete representations. Thus "if $x \in$ *reached*" would be rewritten as "if *reached*[x]". "If $x \in$ *frontier*" would be rewritten as "if $\exists\ i$ such that *frontier*[i]$=x$". Unfortunately rewriting the definition of *directly-reachable* is much more complicated. Something like the following *preliminary* definition is required.

Let y *is in parc*, where y: *node* and *parc*: *arclink*, be defined recursively as

$$y \text{ is in parc} = false \qquad\qquad \textbf{if } parc = \textbf{nil}$$
$$= true \qquad\qquad\quad \textbf{if } y = parc\uparrow.into$$
$$= y \text{ is in } parc\uparrow.next \quad \textbf{otherwise}$$

If this process were carried to its logical completion it is doubtful whether it would increase one's confidence in the correctness of the program. Instead one would probably be left wondering whether the proof of correctness was correct! This is the point at which we will say "enough is enough". We shall never attempt to prove a PASCAL program and proofs of algorithms will be supplied with the sole objective of *increasing the level of confidence in the correctness of the algorithm*. Proofs will be discontinued where it is not clear that this objective will be achieved.

1.3.4   Summing Up

In Secs. 1.3.1, 1.3.2 and 1.3.3 we have developed and proved a relatively simple algorithm. The algorithms in the remainder of this book are often a great deal more complex, but none of them will be studied in as much detail. However, many of them embody a graph search, so a thorough understanding of Algorithm 1.3 and Program 1.1 will greatly assist the reader. Moreover the style of program development used in this text will always follow the pattern of the last three sections.

Let us summarize the steps in the development. We began by presenting a simple and compact algorithm to perform a graph search (Algorithm 1.1). The essential features of Algorithm 1.1 are

(a) it is simple,
(b) it is obviously correct, and
(c) it is expressed in terms natural to the problem.

At this stage in the development questions of efficiency and implementation are completely ignored. The next step is to repeat a process of analyzing the algorithm and modifying it in the light of the analysis. By "analyzing the algorithm" we mean looking for sources of inefficiency and identifying operations in the algorithm which are not primitive to the proposed implementation language. The final step is to choose data structures and rewrite the algorithm in terms of these data structures. Do not be tempted to choose data structures before the algorithm is fully developed. Doing so is a sure way of introducing unnecessary inefficiencies into the final implementation.

The way we have described it, the checking process would seem to be a *post mortem* act. This is not so. It has been presented in this way so as not to confuse the reader with too much detail at once. Normally every stage in the development should be checked as it is performed.

The reader may feel that we have wandered a long way from the topic of this book. To rectify that impression the next section shows how graph searching is used to eliminate so-called *useless* productions from a context-free grammar.

1.4 USELESS PRODUCTIONS

A "useless" production in a context-free grammar is one which cannot be used in the generation of a sentence in the language defined by the grammar. Useless productions are sometimes added to aid the English description of the language. For example the productions in Sec. 2.3 of the "Revised Report on ALGOL 60" which define ⟨*delimiter*⟩, ⟨*operator*⟩, ⟨*separator*⟩, etc. are all useless according to the definition given below. Detection of useless productions is a valuable exercise if only because it may highlight clerical errors in the grammar which otherwise go unnoticed. In addition, many of the algorithms presented in subsequent sections assume that the input grammar contains no useless productions. Here is the formal definition of "useless productions".

Definition   Let $G=(N,T,P,S)$ be a context-free grammar. The production $A \to \alpha$ is said to be *useful* if $S \Rightarrow^* uAw \Rightarrow u\alpha w \Rightarrow^* uvw$ for some $u,v,w \in T^*$. Otherwise the production $A \to \alpha$ is said to be *useless*.

Example 14   Let $G = (\{S,U,V,W\}, \{a\}, P, S)$, where P consists of

$$S \to aS \qquad S \to W \qquad S \to U$$
$$W \to aW \qquad U \to a$$
$$V \to aa$$

The useful productions in this grammar are

$$S \to aS \qquad S \to U \qquad U \to a$$

The production $V \to aa$ is useless because there is no way of introducing V into a sentential form (i.e. $S \not\Rightarrow^* uVw$ for any u,w). The productions $W \to aW$ and $S \to W$ are useless because W cannot be used to generate a terminal string (i.e. $W \not\Rightarrow^* w$ for any $w \in T^*$).

1.4.1 Rephrasing the Definition

The problem of determining which productions are useful splits up into two distinct problems. These are:

Problem 1   For each production $A \to \alpha$ determine whether $\alpha \Rightarrow^* v$ for some $v \in T^*$. (That is, determine whether α generates a terminal string.)

Problem 2   For each non-terminal A determine whether $S \Rightarrow^* uAw$ for some $u, w \in T^*$.

Problem 1 can be reduced further. Suppose $\alpha = X_1 X_2 \ldots X_m$, where $m \geq 0$ and $X_i \in N \cup T$ $(1 \leq i \leq m)$. Then $\alpha \Rightarrow^* v$ for some $v \in T^*$ if and only if, for all i $(1 \leq i \leq m)$, $X_i \Rightarrow^* v_i$ for some $v_i \in T^*$. Thus we replace Problem 1 by Problem 1':

Problem 1'   For each non-terminal A determine whether $A \Rightarrow^* v$ for some $v \in T^*$. That is, determine whether A is a *terminating* non-terminal.

Problem 2 can be simplified considerably if Problem 1' has already been solved. Suppose that in the grammar G every non-terminal A is terminating. Under this assumption Problem 2 becomes:

Problem 2′   For each non-terminal A determine whether $S \Rightarrow^* \beta A \gamma$ for some $\beta, \gamma \in (N \cup T)^*$. That is, determine whether A is an *accessible* non-terminal.

A program to remove useless productions will therefore involve computing the terminating non-terminals *followed by* the accessible non-terminals. However, Problem 2′ (computing the accessible non-terminals) is the easier to solve and so we shall consider it first.

1.4.2   Accessible Non-terminals

The solution of Problem 2′ is a direct application of graph searching. Given a grammar G, we construct a graph H in which the set of nodes is N, the set of non-terminals of G. There is an arc $\langle A, B \rangle$ in H if there is a production $A \rightarrow \mu B \eta$ in G, where $\mu, \eta \in (N \cup T)^*$. From the definitions of path and $\Rightarrow^*$, $S \Rightarrow^* \beta A \gamma$ for some $\beta, \gamma \in (N \cup T)^*$ if and only if there is a path from S to A in the graph H.

Example 15   Let $G = (\{S,A,B,C,D\}, \{a,b,c\}, P, S)$, where P consists of

$$
\begin{array}{lll}
S \rightarrow aB & S \rightarrow BC & \\
A \rightarrow aA & A \rightarrow c & A \rightarrow aDb \\
B \rightarrow DB & B \rightarrow C & \\
C \rightarrow b & D \rightarrow B &
\end{array}
$$

The graph H constructed from G is shown in Fig. 1.7. From H it can be seen that all productions involving A are useless and can be removed from G. Note the occurrence of two arcs from S to B corresponding to the two productions $S \rightarrow aB$ and $S \rightarrow BC$.

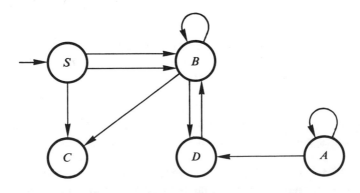

Fig. 1.7   Graph showing accessible non-terminals.

The task of implementing this solution to Problem 2′ and removing the requisite productions is left as an exercise for the reader.

1.4.3 Terminating Productions

The solution to Problem 1′ is very much like the solution to the graph-searching problem, although not identical. Let us define a set *terminating* which will contain both terminal and non-terminal symbols. Initially all terminal symbols are added to *terminating*. Subsequently the non-terminal A is added to *terminating* if there is a production $A \rightarrow X_1 X_2 \ldots X_m$, where either $m = 0$ (i.e. the right-hand side is Λ) or all of $X_1, X_2, \ldots, X_m$ are already in *terminating*. Clearly A will be added to *terminating* only if $A \Rightarrow^* v$ for some $v \in T^*$. This process is repeated until no change occurs in *terminating* (Algorithm 1.4).

Algorithm 1.4

type *symbol = non-terminal or terminal*;
var *terminating*: *set of symbol*;
　　　　terminating-productions: *set of production*;
begin *input grammar*; *terminating* := T; *terminating-productions* := $\varnothing$;
repeat assertion 1: $X \in terminating \supset X \Rightarrow^* v$ *for some* $v \in T^*$;
for *each production* $A \rightarrow X_1 X_2 \ldots X_m$ **do**
　　　begin
test rhs: **if** $\forall\, i\ (1 \leq i \leq m),\ X_i \in terminating$
　　　　　　then begin *add A to terminating*;
　　　　　　　　　　add $A \rightarrow X_1 X_2 \ldots X_m$ *to terminating-productions*;
　　　　　　　　　end;
　　　end;
until *no change occurs in terminating*;
end.

The proof of termination of Algorithm 1.4 is similar to the proof of termination of Algorithm 1.1. At each repeat the size of *terminating* either increases or remains constant. But it cannot increase indefinitely and the loop terminates when it remains constant. The proof of correctness is also very similar to that of Algorithm 1.1 and is left as an exercise for the reader. (Assertion 1 has been added to Algorithm 1.4 to assist the reader in this task.)

Two inefficiencies in Algorithm 1.4 can be identified. The first is the obvious one that whenever a production is added to the set of terminating productions it should never be considered again. The second inefficiency occurs in the statement labeled *test rhs*. As it stands, the test implies that each time a production is examined *every* element on the right-hand side is tested for membership of *terminating*. It would be preferable if, once the value of $X_i \in$ *terminating* has been found to be true, the test on X_i is never performed again. A simple way of conceptually achieving this is to remove each symbol X from the right-hand sides of productions when it is newly added to *terminating*. The left-hand side of the production is then declared to be terminating if there are no symbols remaining on the right-hand side. An example will help to clarify this procedure.

Example 16   Let $G = (\{A,B,C\}, \{a\}, P,A)$, where P consists of

$$A \rightarrow ABC \qquad A \rightarrow C$$
$$B \rightarrow Ca \qquad C \rightarrow a$$

Initially *terminating* = $\{a\}$, so we remove a from the right-hand side of $C \rightarrow a$ and $B \rightarrow Ca$ to obtain $C \rightarrow \Lambda$ and $B \rightarrow C$. Now C is added to *terminating*. Removing it from the right-hand sides in which it appears we obtain the productions

$$A \rightarrow AB \qquad A \rightarrow \Lambda$$
$$B \rightarrow \Lambda \qquad C \rightarrow \Lambda$$

Next A and B are added to *terminating* and removed from right-hand sides. All productions now have empty right-hand sides and *terminating* = $\{A,B,C,a\}$.

In practice it is possible to avoid *removing* symbols from the right-hand sides provided one ensures that each symbol is inspected once only. In this case it suffices to keep a count of the number of symbols remaining. When this count becomes zero the left-hand side is added to *terminating*. Algorithm 1.5 summarizes these deliberations. Note that, as in Algorithm 1.2, the set *frontier*, consisting of all symbols which have been newly added to *terminating*, has been identified. *lhs* and *rhs* are abbreviations of left-hand side and right-hand side, respectively. *length(p)* is the number of symbols remaining on the right-hand side of the production p. Note that if there are any empty productions in the grammar (productions having the form $A \rightarrow \Lambda$) their left-hand sides must also be added to *terminating*. (In Algorithm 1.4 such productions are detected by *test rhs*, since there is no i such that $1 \leq i \leq 0$.)

Algorithm 1.5

type *symbol = non-terminal or terminal*;
var *terminating, frontier*: *set of symbol*;
       terminating-productions: *set of production*;
       a: *terminal*; *A*: *non-terminal*; *X*: *symbol*;
       p: *production*;

Algorithm 1.5 (Continued)

begin *input grammar*; *terminating* := *frontier* := ∅ ;
      terminating-productions := ∅ ;
for *each a* ∈ *T* **do** *add a to frontier and terminating*;
for *each production p* **do**
      if (*length*(*p*)=0) **and** (*lhs*(*p*) ∉ *terminating*)
            then begin *add p to terminating-productions*;
                  add lhs(*p*) *to terminating and frontier*;
                  end;

while *frontier*≠∅ **do**
      begin *choose and remove X from frontier*;
            for *each occurrence of X on the rhs of each production p*
            do begin {*remove X from rhs*(*p*) }
                  length(*p*) := *length*(*p*)−1;
                  if *length*(*p*)=0
                        then begin *add p to terminating-productions*;
                              A := *lhs*(*p*);
                              if *A* ∉ *terminating*
                                    then *add A to terminating and frontier*;
                              end;
                  end;
            end;
end.

Before discussing the implementation of Algorithm 1.5 we need to specify the format of the input. We shall assume that the input file contains four items:

1. the string of characters which will be used to represent "→". (for example "::=");
2. a list of the non-terminal symbols;
3. a list of the terminal symbols;
4. a list of the productions.

It is convenient to agree on some fixed limit k of significant characters in each symbol and to introduce the type *alfa*=**packed array** [1..k] **of** *char*. Each symbol can then be any string of *non-blank* characters but only the first k are recorded. All symbols must be unique (including the representation of "→") and they are separated by blanks or the end of a line. Productions are separated by the end of a line. A string of k asterisks ('*') is reserved to separate the four items and to terminate the file.

One might argue that the lists of terminals and non-terminals are redundant and should be omitted because the non-terminals are those symbols which appear on the left-hand side of productions and the terminals are the remaining symbols appearing in productions. However, this argument is fallacious if there is a possibility of useless productions and, in any case, the two lists act as a further check against clerical errors in the preparation of the input file. They are not included in order to simplify the programming!

The data structures used to implement Algorithm 1.5 are much more complicated than those in Program 1.1, so let us try to design them by beginning with the simple operations and progressing to more complicated operations. When inputting the grammar, a major operation is checking uniqueness of the symbols and identifying symbols in productions. This immediately suggests the use of a hash table to store the character representations of each symbol. Since we also need to check that the left-hand sides of productions are, indeed, non-terminals, a field of each entry in the hash table will indicate the class of the symbol—either terminal or non-terminal. The character representation of the replacement operator is also stored in the hash table and its class is defined to be *neither*. *terminating* is analogous to *reached* in Algorithm 1.3 and is best implemented by associating a Boolean with each terminal or non-terminal symbol. How should symbols be represented? An obvious choice is to represent each symbol by its location in the hash table. Then *terminating* can be a field of the entry in the hash table and the test "**if** $X \in terminating$" can be implemented by "**if** $hashtable[h].terminating$", where h is the location of X in the hash table. As in Program 1.1, *frontier* can be implemented as a stack, each entry being of type *symbol*. The declarations in (1.5) summarize our progress so far.

> **type** *nonterminal* = *hashindex*; {*non-terminals and terminals are*}
>   *terminal*   = *hashindex*; {*represented by their location in*}
>   *symbol*   = *hashindex*; {*the hash table*   }
>   *symbolclass* = (*term, nonterm, neither*);
>   *hashtableentry* = **record** *sym*: *alfa*; {*character representation*}
>   **case** *class*: *symbolclass* **of**
>   *term, nonterm*: (*terminating*: *Boolean*);   (1.5)
>   *neither*: ( );
>   **end**;
>   *frontierindex* = 1 .. *n*; {*n* ≥ *total no. of symbols*}
>   *zeroorfrontierindex* = 0 .. *n*;
> **var** *frontier*: **array**[*frontierindex*] **of** *symbol*;
>   *top*: *zeroorfrontierindex*;
>   *hashtable*: **array**[*hashindex*] **of** *hashtableentry*;

Each production consists of a left-hand side (a non-terminal) and a right-hand side, the right-hand side being a list of symbols. We shall wish, of course, to output the useful productions, so we require pointers from the left-hand side to the first symbol on the right-hand side and from each right-hand side symbol to the next right-hand side symbol in the production. In addition, Algorithm 1.5 requires us to find each occurrence of a given symbol on the right-hand sides of productions. This suggests that we use pointers to chain together occurrences of the same symbol. We also need to add an additional field to each hash-table entry giving the first occurrence of the symbol on the right-hand side of a production. Finally, given an occurrence of a right-hand side symbol we must decrease the length of the production by 1. This means that firstly a field, called *length*, must be included in the description of a production, and secondly, a pointer to the production in which it appears must be associated with each right-hand side symbol. The appropriate PASCAL type declarations for productions and the modification to *hashtableentry* are given in (1.6).

```
type rhslink =↑ rhsitem;
     productionlink =↑ production;
     production = record lhs: nonterminal;
                    length: integer; firstrhsposn: rhslink;
                  end;
     rhssymbol = record h: symbol;   {location in hash table}
                    nextoccurrence: rhslink; {next occurrence of this symbol
                      on rhs of a production}
                  end;
     rhsitem = record x: rhssymbol;                              (1.6)
                    p: productionlink; {production in which symbol occurs}
                    next: rhslink; {next symbol on rhs of this production}
                  end;
     hashtableentry = record sym: alfa;
                        case class: symbolclass of
                        term, nonterm: (terminating: Boolean;
                                     firstoccurrence: rhslink);
                        neither: ( );
                      end;
```

Figure 1.8 illustrates this data structure when a grammar containing three productions has been read in but no further processing has occurred. The three productions are

$$S \to SAa \qquad A \to SB \qquad B \to ASAc$$

Note that the *h* field in *rhssymbol* is redundant. It has been included so that a run-time check on the pointers can be made. More redundancies of this nature ought to have been included in the program but have been omitted for brevity.

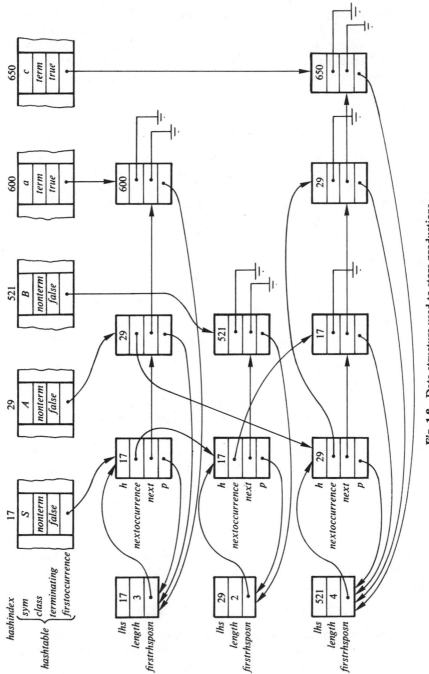

Fig. 1.8 Data structure used to store productions.

We are almost home. Only a few minor details concerning the hash table need to be considered. In Program 1.2 we have imposed an upper limit of 997 on the size of the hash table. Symbols are hashed to a location by assigning to each an integer value and taking that value modulo 997. Collisions are handled using the quadratic probing method. Although the input of the grammar forms the major part of Program 1.2, we shall not discuss it in depth. The reader may glean the details by examining Program 1.2. In outline, inputting the grammar involves reading the representation of the replacement symbol, then the non-terminals followed by the terminals and finally the productions. As each item is read, various checks are made and the item is printed out together with an error message, if necessary. Headings are inserted into the output to indicate which items are the non-terminals, which are the terminals etc. Additionally the initializations of *terminating* and *frontier* are performed during the input stage, as well as setting up the linked data structure.

The final consideration is the output of the terminating productions. Since they form only an intermediate stage in the check for useless productions (the next stage involves the solution of Problem 2') we have assumed no restrictions on the order of their output. Those productions whose right-hand side is the empty word are listed and output as soon as all input is complete. The remaining terminating productions are output as soon as they are discovered.

Program 1.2

```
program terminatingproductions(input, output);
label 1;
const primeno = 997; {size of hash table} primenomin1 = 996;
      allasterisks = ' ******* ';
      free = '        ';
      maxsymbollength = 7;
      n = primeno; {maximum no. of terminals and non-terminals}

type  hashindex = 0..primenomin1;  symbol = hashindex;
      nonterminal = hashindex;  terminal = hashindex;
      rhslink = ↑ rhsitem;
      productionlink = ↑ production;
      production = record lhs: nonterminal; length: integer;
                         firstrhsposn: rhslink;
                  end;
      rhssymbol = record h: symbol;
                         nextoccurrence: rhslink; {next occurrence of this}
                  end;                           {symbol on rhs of a prodn}
```

Program 1.2   (Continued)

rhsitem = **record** *x*: *rhssymbol*; *next*: *rhslink*;
          p: *productionlink*; {*production in which item occurs*}
        end;

symbolclass = (*term, nonterm, neither*);
{*alfa is predeclared as* **packed array** [1..7] **of** *char*}
hashtableentry = **record** *sym*: *alfa*;
                  case *class*: *symbolclass* **of**
                    term, nonterm: (*terminating*: *Boolean*;
                                      firstoccurrence: *rhslink*);
                    neither: ( );
            end;

frontierindex = 1..*n*; *zeroorfrontierindex* = 0..*n*;
emptyprodlink = ↑ *emptyprodlist*;
emptyprodlist = **record** *p*: *productionlink*; *next*: *emptyprodlink*;
               end;

var   *hashtable*: **array**[*hashindex*] **of** *hashtableentry*;
      frontier: **array**[*frontierindex*] **of** *symbol*;
      top: *zeroorfrontierindex*;
      p: *productionlink*; *rhsposn*: *rhslink*;
      found: *Boolean*; {*true iff cursymbol is in hash table*}
      h, curhashindex: *hashindex*; *o*: *integer*; {*no. of characters*}
      cursymbol: *alfa*;
      curchar: *char*; *replsymbol*: *alfa*;
      line: **array**[1..81] **of** *char*; *linelgth*: 0..81;
      chposn: *integer*; {*column no. of current character*}
      newline: *Boolean*;
      inputerror: *Boolean*;
      ep, firstemptyprod: *emptyprodlink*;

procedure *getsymbol*;
var *k*: 0..*maxsymbollength*;
   a: **array**[0..*maxsymbollength*] **of** *char*;
{*global variables* — *cursymbol, curhashindex, primeno*}
{*Sets cursymbol to the first maxsymbollength characters of the next symbol
in the input file and hashes these characters to obtain the location
curhashindex in the hash table*}

Program 1.2   (Continued)

procedure *getchar*;
var *ch*: *char*;
{*global variables — chposn, newline, line, linelgth*}
begin if *chposn* = *linelgth*;
      then begin if *eof(input)*
                    then begin *writeln*(' *** *INSUFFICIENT DATA*');
                          inputerror   := *true*; goto 1;
                        end;
             linelgth := 0; *write*(' ');
             while not *eoln(input)* do
                begin *read(ch)*; *write(ch)*;
                linelgth := *linelgth* + 1; *line*[*linelgth*] := *ch*;
                end;
             newline := *true*; *linelgth* := *linelgth* + 1;
             read(line[*linelgth*]);   {*end of line — blank read*}
             writeln; *curchar* := *line*[1]; *chposn* := 1;
             end
        else begin *chposn* := *chposn* + 1; *curchar* := *line*[*chposn*];
             end;
    end; {*getchar*}

begin {*getsymbol*}
newline := *false*;
repeat *getchar*;
until *curchar* ≠ ' ';
k := 0; *curhashindex* := 0;
repeat if *k* < *maxsymbollength* then
      begin *k* := *k* + 1; *a*[*k*] := *curchar*;
      curhashindex := ((*curhashindex*∗*o*) + *ord*(*a*[*k*])) mod *primeno*;
      end;
      getchar;
until *curchar* = ' ';
while *k* < *maxsymbollength* do
      begin {*pad a with blanks*}
      k := *k* + 1; *a*[*k*] := ' ';
      curhashindex := ((*curhashindex*∗*o*) + *ord*(*a*[*k*])) mod *primeno*;
      end;
pack(*a*, 1, *cursymbol*); {*unnecessary on other compilers*}
end; {*getsymbol*}

Program 1.2 (Continued)


```
procedure searchhashtableforcursymbol;
var nocollisions: 0..primeno;
    tableentry: alfa;
{global variables — cursymbol, found, curhashindex}
begin nocollisions := 0;  tableentry := hashtable[curhashindex].sym;
found := (tableentry = cursymbol);
while (tableentry ≠ free) and not found
        and (nocollisions < primeno div 2)
do begin nocollisions := nocollisions + 1;
    curhashindex := (curhashindex + nocollisions) mod primeno;
    tableentry := hashtable[curhashindex].sym;
    found := (tableentry = cursymbol);
    end;
if (tableentry ≠ free) and not found
then begin page(output);
    writeln(' *** TOO MANY SYMBOLS—HASH TABLE FULL');
    goto 1;
    end;
end; {search hash table}


procedure printproduction(p: productionlink);
const maxcharcount = 120; {max length of a line of output}
      indentlgth = 16; {2*(maxsymbollength + 1)}
      initialcharcount = 24; {3*(maxsymbollength + 1)}
var r: rhslink;  h: hashindex;  charcount: integer;
begin write(' ', hashtable[p↑.lhs].sym, ' ', replsymbol);
r := p↑.firstrhsposn;
while r ≠ nil do
    begin charcount := initialcharcount;
    while (r ≠ nil) and (charcount < maxcharcount)
    do begin h := r↑.x.h; write(' ', hashtable[h].sym);
        r := r↑.next;
        charcount := charcount + maxsymbollength + 1;
        end;
    if r ≠ nil then begin writeln; write(' ' : indentlgth);
                    end;
    end;
writeln;
end; {print production}
```

Program 1.2　(Continued)

procedure *readrepresentationofreplacementsymbol*;
begin *page*(*output*); *chposn* := 1; *linelgth* := 1;
writeln(' *REPRESENTATION OF REPLACEMENT SYMBOL*');
writeln(' ————————————————————————————');
getsymbol; *replsymbol* := *cursymbol*;
searchhashtableforcursymbol;
hashtable[*curhashindex*].*sym* := *cursymbol*;
hashtable[*curhashindex*].*class* := *neither*;
{*skip the row of asterisks*}
getsymbol;
if *cursymbol* ≠ *allasterisks*
then begin *writeln*(' *∗∗∗ ROW OF ASTERISKS EXPECTED*');
　　　inputerror := *true*;
　　end;
end; {*read representation*}

procedure *readin*(*kind*: *symbolclass*);
{*reads in terminal and non-terminal symbols*}
begin case *kind* **of** *nonterm*: **begin** *writeln*(' *NON-TERMINALS*');
　　　　　　　　　　　　　　writeln(' ————————————');
　　　　　　　　end;
　　　　　term: **begin** *writeln*(' *TERMINALS*');
　　　　　　　　　　writeln(' ——————————');
　　　　　　　end;
　　end;
chposn := 1; *linelgth* := 1; *getsymbol*;
while not (*cursymbol* = *allasterisks*) **do**
　　begin *searchhashtableforcursymbol*;
　　if *found* **then begin** *writeln*(' ' : *chposn* − 1,
　　　　　' × *SYMBOL ALREADY USED*');
　　　　　　　inputerror := *true*;
　　　　　　end;
　　with *hashtable*[*curhashindex*] **do**
　　　　begin *sym* := *cursymbol*; *firstoccurrence* := **nil**; *class* := *kind*;
　　　　case *kind* **of**
　　　　nonterm: *terminating* := *false*;
　　　　term: **begin** *terminating* := *true*;
　　　　　　　top := *top* + 1; *frontier*[*top*] := *curhashindex*;
　　　　　　end;
　　　　end;
　　　end;

Program 1.2   (Continued)

```
    getsymbol;
    end;
end; {read in terminals and non-terminals}


procedure readproductions;
var p: productionlink; r1,r2: rhslink;
{global variables— newline, chposn}
begin writeln(' PRODUCTIONS');
      writeln(' ——————————'); writeln;
getsymbol;
while cursymbol ≠ allasterisks do
    begin searchhashtableforcursymbol;
    if not found
    then begin writeln( ' ': chposn − 1,' × UNRECOGNIZABLE SYMBOL');
         inputerror := true;
         end
    else if hashtable[curhashindex].class ≠ nonterm
        then begin inputerror := true;
             writeln(' ': chposn − 1,
             ' × LHS MUST BE A NON-TERMINAL');
             end;
    {create new production link and set its lhs}
    new(p); with p↑ do begin lhs := curhashindex;
                        firstrhsposn := nil; length := 0;
                        end;
    getsymbol;
    {check that cursymbol is replacement symbol}
    if cursymbol ≠ replsymbol
    then begin writeln(' ': chposn − 1,
         ' × REPLACEMENT SYMBOL EXPECTED');
         inputerror := true;
         end;
    {read rhs of production}
    getsymbol;
    if newline
    then begin {empty production—add lhs to frontier}
         if not hashtable[p↑.lhs].terminating
         then begin top := top + 1; frontier[top] := p↑.lhs;
             hashtable[p↑.lhs].terminating := true;
             end
```

Program 1·2 (Continued)

```
        else begin inputerror := true;
            writeln(' ' :chposn−1, '×PRODUCTION REPEATED');
            end;
        {add p to list of empty productions}
        if firstemptyprod=nil
        then begin new(firstemptyprod); firstemptyprod↑.p := p;
            end
        else begin new(ep); ep↑.next := firstemptyprod;
            ep↑.p := p; firstemptyprod := ep;
            end;
        end
    else repeat searchhashtableforcursymbol;
        if not found or (hashtable[curhashindex].class=neither)
        then begin inputerror := true;
            writeln(' ' : chposn−1, '× UNRECOGNIZABLE SYMBOL');
            end
        else begin {create new rhsitem and set all links}
            p↑.length := p↑.length+1;
            new(r1); if p↑.firstrhsposn=nil then p↑.firstrhsposn := r1
                    else r2↑.next := r1;
            r2 := r1; r1↑.p := p;
            r1↑.x.h := curhashindex;
            if hashtable[curhashindex].firstoccurrence=nil
            then r1↑.x.nextoccurrence := nil
            else r1↑.x.nextoccurrence :=
                        hashtable[curhashindex].firstoccurrence;
            hashtable[curhashindex].firstoccurrence := r1;
            end;
        getsymbol;
        until newline;
    end;
end; {read productions}


begin {main program}
for h := 0 to primenomin1 do hashtable[h].sym := free;
top := 0; {frontier := ∅}
inputerror := false; firstemptyprod := nil;
o := ord('''')−ord('0'); {no. of characters—N.B. machine dependent}
readrepresentationofreplacementsymbol;
readin(nonterm); readin(term); readproductions;
```

Program 1·2 (Continued)

```
if inputerror then goto 1; page(output);
writeln(' TERMINATING PRODUCTIONS');
writeln('——————————————————————'); writeln;
{print out productions with empty word on rhs}
ep := firstemptyprod;
while ep ≠ nil do
    begin printproduction(ep↑.p); ep := ep↑.next;
    end;

while top ≠ 0 do
    begin {choose and remove X from frontier}
    h := frontier[top]; top := top − 1; {X is represented by its hash index}
    {remove X from rhs of all productions}
    rhsposn := hashtable[h].firstoccurrence;
    while rhsposn ≠ nil do
        begin p := rhsposn↑.p;
        if rhsposn↑.x.h ≠ h then writeln(' *** BUG IN PROGRAM');
        with p↑ do
            begin length := length − 1;
            if length = 0
            then begin printproduction(p);
                {add lhs to terminating and frontier}
                if not hashtable[lhs].terminating
                then begin hashtable[lhs].terminating := true;
                    top := top + 1; frontier[top]:= lhs;
                    end;
                end;
            end;
        rhsposn := rhsposn↑.x.nextoccurrence;
        end;
    end;
    1: page(output);
    if inputerror then writeln(' *** PROGRAM TERMINATED—',
                    'INPUT ERRORS')
            else writeln(' END OF OUTPUT');
end.
```

EXERCISES

1.8 Which are the useful productions in the following grammar?
$G = (\{A,B,C,D,E,F,H\}, \{a,b,c,d\}, P, A)$, where P consists of

$$
\begin{array}{ll}
A \to aDbF & A \to CH \\
B \to BaH & B \to b \\
C \to D & \\
D \to C & D \to \Lambda \\
E \to cEd & E \to b \\
F \to BF & \\
H \to CD & H \to a
\end{array}
$$

1.9 Prove that Problem 2 (Sec. 1.4.1) reduces to Problem 2′ when Problem 1′ has already been solved.

1.10 Establish the correctness of Algorithm 1.4.
(The assertion of correctness is:
$A \to X_1 X_2 \ldots X_m \in$ *terminating-productions* if and only if $\exists\, w \in T^*$ such that $A \Rightarrow X_1 X_2 \ldots X_m \Rightarrow^* w$).

1.11 Add a symbolic frequency count to each line of Algorithm 1.5, using the following notation. Let n be the number of non-terminal symbols and t be the number of terminal symbols. Let q be the number of productions and let l be the total length of the right-hand sides of productions in the input grammar. ($l = \Sigma_{p \in P}$ *length* (p) where *length* (p) is the *initial* length of the rhs of production p.) On the basis of the frequency count would you say that Algorithm 1.5 is efficient? Does Program 1.2 implement Algorithm 1.5 efficiently?

1.12 Incorporate into Program 1.2 the suggested solution to Problem 2′ (Sec. 1.4.1). Execute your program using the grammars in Example 14 and Exercise 1.8 as test data. (Note that the start symbol S must now be included in the input file.)

1.13 A non-terminal A is said to be *nullable* if $A \Rightarrow^* \Lambda$. The nullable non-terminals in the grammar of Exercise 1.8 are A, C, D and H. Develop and implement an algorithm which finds all the nullable non-terminals in a given grammar.
(*Hint:* The algorithm involves only a simple modification to Algorithm 1.5.)
    Please tackle this exercise. In future chapters we shall assume that its solution is known.

BIBLIOGRAPHIC NOTES

It is always interesting and often very illuminating to return to the source material on significant ideas. The definition of ALGOL 60 was first published in 1960 [1.11] but was revised in 1963 [1.12] after a number of ambiguities and contradictions in the original definition had been noticed. The examples of syntactic ambiguities presented in Sec. 1.2.3 are drawn from [1.11]. Chomsky was the first to propose the concept of a grammar used here, and the classification into the three types—regular, context-free and context-sensitive—appears in [1.3]. (Chomsky's definitions of the three types are actually a little different to those given here.) Considerable impetus was given to language theory when the correspondence between Chomsky's definitions and the definition of the syntax of ALGOL 60 was noticed. The two volumes by Aho and Ullman [1.2] provide an encyclopaedic account of results in language theory having application to compiling techniques. A very amusing justification of criterion C2 (ambiguities should be intentional and immediately evident) appears in [1.6]. Many texts on computability theory prove that the ambiguity problem is unsolvable. See, for example, Hopcroft and Ullman [1.7]. The design and analysis of algorithms is a topic which is central to computer science. In his series of books Knuth [1.9] analyzes the performance of many algorithms. [1.1] is an advanced text whilst [1.5] is a good introductory text. Manna [1.10] discusses the basic principles of program proving. The graph-searching technique used here is called "breadth-first search". An alternative technique, which is sometimes better when constraints on the paths are imposed, is called "depth-first search" [1.1]. Graph theory has many applications in computer science, many of which are discussed by Deo [1.4].

A concise summary of the programming language PASCAL can be found in [1.8]. Wirth [1.13] gives a more thorough and complete account of the language as well as presenting many example programs.

1.1 Aho, A. V., J. E. Hopcroft and J. D. Ullman, *The Design and Analysis of Algorithms*, Addison-Wesley, Reading, Mass. (1974).

1.2 Aho, A. V. and J. D. Ullman, *The Theory of Parsing, Translation and Compiling:* Vol. I, *Parsing* (1972); Vol. II, *Compiling* (1973), Prentice-Hall, Englewood Cliffs, N.J.

1.3 Chomsky, N., "On certain formal properties of grammars", *Info. and Control,* **2,** 137–67 (1959).

1.4 Deo, N., *Graph Theory with Applications to Engineering and Computer Science,* Prentice-Hall, Englewood Cliffs, N.J. (1974).

1.5 Goodman, S. E. and S. T. Hedetniemi, *Introduction to the Design and Analysis of Algorithms*, McGraw-Hill, New York (1977).

1.6 Hill, I. D., "Wouldn't it be nice if we could write computer programs in ordinary English—or would it?" *Comp. Bulletin*, 306–12 (June 1972).

1.7 Hopcroft, J. E. and J. D. Ullman, *Formal Languages and their Relation to Automata*, Addison-Wesley, Reading, Mass. (1969).

1.8 Jensen, K. and N. Wirth, *PASCAL User Manual and Report*, Corrected Reprint of the Second Edition, Springer Verlag, Berlin; Lecture Notes in Computer Science, **18** (1976).

1.9 Knuth, D. E., *The Art of Computer Programming:* Vol. 1, *Fundamental Algorithms* (1968); Vol. 2: *Seminumerical Algorithms* (1969); Vol. 3: *Sorting and Searching* (1973), Addison-Wesley, Reading, Mass.

1.10 Manna, Z., *Mathematical Theory of Computation*, McGraw-Hill, New York (1974).

1.11 Naur, P. (Ed.), "Report on the algorithmic language ALGOL 60", *Comm. ACM*, **3**, 299–314 (1960).

1.12 Naur, P. (Ed.), "Revised report on the algorithmic language—ALGOL 60", *Comm. ACM*, **6**, 1–20 (1963). Also in *The Computer Journal*, **5**, 349–67 (1963); *Numerische Mathematik*, **4**, 420–52 (1963).

1.13 Wirth, N., *Algorithms + Data Structures = Programs*, Prentice-Hall, Englewood Cliffs, N.J. (1976).

2 REGULAR LANGUAGES

A study of the theory of regular languages is often justified by the fact that they model the lexical analysis stage of a compiler. The lexical stage of a compiler *does* recognize a regular language (e.g. the set of identifiers) but it is also fair to say that a compiler writer *need not have* any knowledge of regular languages in order to program the lexical analyzer. Nevertheless a study of regular languages is fundamental to achieving a full understanding of the syntax of programming languages. The reasons for including the topic here are as follows.

1. Regular expressions (an alternative means of describing regular languages) are often used to supplement the context-free definition of a language. Such use adds both brevity and clarity to the definition. In later chapters the algorithms we describe assume a standard context-free definition of the language, but a thorough understanding of this chapter should enable the reader to extend the algorithms to handle regular expressions.
2. The material in this chapter on converting a non-deterministic machine to a deterministic machine (Sec. 2.3) is an essential preliminary to the discussion of LR-parsing in Chap. 4.
3. The class of regular languages is a simple but non-trivial subclass of the class of context-free languages. When faced with a difficult problem it is a good strategy to begin by tackling a special case of the problem. Some insight may then be obtained which enables one to proceed to the solution of the complete problem. In particular, the first step in the solution of a problem involving context-free languages could be to specialize the problem to regular languages. (This is the approach adopted in Chap. 5 on error repair. We begin by considering the repair

of spelling errors and then extrapolate from there to the repair of errors in regular languages and on to the repair of errors in context-free languages.)

4. The theory of regular languages has begun to have a significant impact on a number of practical problems outside the scope of this text. (See the Bibliographic Notes for references.) A study of the theory is important, therefore, even though its relevance to programming-language syntax may not be immediately apparent.

In outline the different sections in this chapter can be summarized as follows. Sections 2.1 and 2.2 cover two alternative methods of defining a regular language and their relationships to regular grammars. Transition diagrams, introduced in Sec. 2.1, are simply diagrammatic representations of regular grammars. They resemble flow diagrams whilst regular expressions, introduced in Sec. 2.2, correspond closely to **while . . . do** constructs. The parsing of regular languages can be achieved very efficiently using deterministic finite-state machines, but the description of a regular language leads naturally to a non-deterministic machine. Section 2.3 describes an algorithm for converting a non-deterministic machine to a deterministic machine. Finally, Sec. 2.4 applies the techniques of the preceding sections to the construction of a deterministic machine to recognize a ⟨*number*⟩ in ALGOL 60.

2.1 TRANSITION DIAGRAMS AND NON-DETERMINISTIC MACHINES

Very often a diagram can convey information much more clearly and succinctly than any number of words. Unfortunately diagrams are quite unintelligible to computers and one must use other means to communicate with them. The objective of this section is to show how regular grammars may be represented by "transition diagrams" and how one converts a regular grammar to a transition diagram or vice-versa. Let us first recall the definition of a regular grammar.

Definition A regular grammar is a grammar $G = (N, T, P, S)$ in which

Either: All productions have the form $A \rightarrow tB$ or $A \rightarrow t$ where t is a terminal string (i.e. $t \in T^*$) and A and B are non-terminal symbols (i.e. $A, B \in N$). This form is called a *right-linear* grammar.

Or: All productions have the form $A \rightarrow Bt$ or $A \rightarrow t$ where $t \in T^*$ and $A, B \in N$. This form is called a *left-linear* grammar.

(It is important to note that grammars in which left-linear productions are intermixed with right-linear productions are not regular. For example the grammar having productions

$$S \rightarrow aR \qquad S \rightarrow c \qquad R \rightarrow Sb$$

is not regular. Indeed, the language generated by this grammar is $\{a^n cb^n \mid n \geq 0\}$ and we shall show in Chap. 7 that it is impossible to define this language using a regular grammar.)

Consider the right-linear grammar $G=(\{S, R, U\}, \{a, b\}, P, S)$, where P consists of

$$\begin{array}{lll} S \rightarrow a & S \rightarrow bU & S \rightarrow bR \\ R \rightarrow abaU & R \rightarrow U & \\ U \rightarrow b & U \rightarrow aS & \end{array}$$

A diagrammatic representation of this grammar is shown in Fig. 2.1. The process used to construct Fig. 2.1 is a straightforward one. Here is a detailed description.

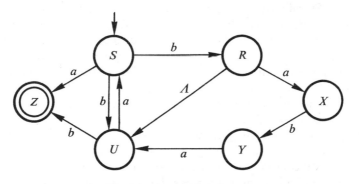

Fig. 2.1 A transition diagram.

1. There is a node for each non-terminal symbol in the grammar. There is also a single *final node* (the node labeled Z and indicated by two circles in Fig. 2.1). Additional nodes may also be added by steps 3, 4 and 5.
2. For each production of the form $A \rightarrow B$ there is an arc labeled Λ from the node A to the node B.
3. For each production of the form $A \rightarrow tB$ ($t \in T^+$) there is an arc labeled t from the node A to the node B (but see also step 5).
4. For each production of the form $A \rightarrow t$ there is an arc labeled t from the node A to the final node (but see also step 5).
5. Whenever steps 3 or 4 would have the effect of introducing an arc labeled by a string t where $length(t) > 1$, then a total of $length(t) - 1$ new nodes are added to the diagram and the arcs connecting these nodes are labeled with the individual letters of t.

Step 5 is imprecise but Fig. 2.1 is intended to clarify it. Corresponding to the production $R \rightarrow abaU$ two new nodes, arbitrarily labeled X and Y, have been added to the figure and arcs labeled respectively a, b and a have been drawn from R to X, from X to Y and from Y to U.

Fig. 2.1 is called a *transition diagram* and it depicts a *non-deterministic finite-state machine* (or *non-deterministic finite automaton*). In automata theory nodes in a graph are called *states* and the number of nodes is finite— hence "finite-state machine". The adjective "non-deterministic" is used to indicate that such a machine can be used to recognize words in a regular language but at certain points in the recognition process "non-deterministic" choices must be made. For instance, consider the string *babaaa*. This can be generated by our example grammar using the following derivation sequence:

$$S \Rightarrow bR \Rightarrow babaU \Rightarrow babaaS \Rightarrow babaaa$$

Equally the string *babaaa* can be recognized by Fig. 2.1 by traversing a path from S to Z. Specifically, we begin at the state S and then follow in turn the arc labeled b to R, the arcs labeled a, b and a to U, the arc labeled a to S and finally the arc labeled a to Z. Note that the sequence of arc labels spells out *babaaa* and the path corresponds closely to the derivation sequence. The recognition process is non-deterministic because a choice of which arc to follow must be made at the states S and R. A formal definition of a non-deterministic machine and the language recognized by such a machine has been postponed to Sec. 2.3.

The process of converting a left-linear grammar into a transition diagram is a little trickier, but its formulation has been left as an exercise for the reader. Instead, we shall consider the process the opposite way—converting a transition diagram into a left-linear grammar. Let us refer once again to Fig. 2.1. A left-linear grammar defining the same language is the grammar

$$G' = (\{S', R', X', Y', U', Z'\}, \{a, b\}, P', Z'),$$

where P' consists of

$$
\begin{array}{lll}
S' \rightarrow \Lambda & & \\
R' \rightarrow S'b & U' \rightarrow S'b & Z' \rightarrow S'a \\
U' \rightarrow R' & X' \rightarrow R'a & \\
Y' \rightarrow X'b & & \\
U' \rightarrow Y'a & & \\
Z' \rightarrow U'b & S' \rightarrow U'a &
\end{array}
$$

In this grammar "'" has been added to all the non-terminals in order to avoid any confusion with the non-terminals in the original grammar. All the productions except the first correspond to arcs in the graph—the production $A' \rightarrow B't$ has been introduced if there is an arc labeled t from B to A. The production $S' \to \Lambda$ is also added to the grammar, S being the start state of the machine. Note that the sentence symbol of the grammar is Z'. (Z is the final state of the machine.) The definition of a non-deterministic machine in Sec. 2.3 allows the possibility of having more than one final state. In such a case, if $Z_1, \ldots, Z_m$ are the final states a new non-terminal A, say is defined to be the start symbol and productions $A \to Z'_1$, $A \to Z'_2$, $\ldots$, $A \to Z'_m$ are added to the grammar.

The latter process is an unnatural one because, effectively, one has to think backwards! Consider again the input string *babaaa*. To generate this string using the grammar G' we use the derivation sequence

$$Z' \Rightarrow S'a \Rightarrow U'aa \Rightarrow Y'aaa \Rightarrow X'baaa$$

$$\Rightarrow R'abaaa \Rightarrow S'babaaa \Rightarrow babaaa$$

Note that the input symbols are introduced in reverse order. Thus the derivation sequence corresponds to starting at the final state and proceeding backwards to the start state. When the start state is reached the derivation sequence can be terminated using the production $S' \to \Lambda$.

2.2   REGULAR EXPRESSIONS

Transition diagrams look like flow diagrams. It is common to denounce flow diagrams and to prefer the use of **repeat** . . . **until** or **while** . . . **do** to express the structure of an algorithm. Analogously, instead of using a transition diagram or a grammar to define a regular language, one can use a regular expression. Regular expressions make abundant use of the * operator defined in Chap. 1. In fact, $T*$ is a regular expression. The * operator is used whenever something is repeated an indefinite number of times and is closely related to **while** . . . **do** in programming. In this section we discuss the conversion of a regular grammar to a regular expression and of a regular expression to a transition diagram. The development is informal because we shall never have occasion to program the techniques. However, the conversion of a regular grammar to a regular expression is important because it is the first of many examples of a problem being expressed as the solution of a system of simultaneous equations.

Definition A *regular expression* over the alphabet T and the *language denoted* by that expression are defined recursively as follows:

1. $\emptyset$ is a regular expression denoting the empty set.
2. Λ is a regular expression denoting $\{\Lambda\}$.
3. a where $a \in T$ is a regular expression denoting $\{a\}$.

4. If P and Q are regular expressons denoting the languages L_P and L_Q respectively, then

    (a) $(P+Q)$ is a regular expression denoting $L_P \cup L_Q$.

    (b) $(P \cdot Q)$ is a regular expression denoting $L_P \cdot L_Q$.

    (c) $(P*)$ is a regular expression denoting

$$\{A\} \cup L_P \cup L_P^2 \cup \cdots \cup L_P^n \cup \cdots$$

5. Nothing else is a regular expression.

Example 1   The following are regular expressions over the alphabet $T = \{0, 1\}$.

(a) $((0+1)*)$

(b) $(((0+1)*) \cdot 1)$

(c) $(((1*) \cdot 0) \cdot (1*))$

(d) $((((0+1)*) \cdot 1) + (((1*) \cdot 0) \cdot (1*)))$

The language denoted by Example 1(a) is the set of all strings consisting of an arbitrary number of 0s and 1s. This set has previously been denoted by $T*$. Example 1(b) denotes the set of all such strings in which the final symbol is 1. Example 1(c) denotes the set of all strings of 0s and 1s which include exactly one 0. Finally, Example 1(d) denotes the union of the sets denoted by 1(b) and 1(c).

    The proliferation of parentheses in these examples is confusing so we shall omit them wherever possible, assuming a left-to-right order of evaluation of operators and that their precedence is in the order *, $\cdot$, +. We shall also omit $\cdot$ and denote it by juxtaposition. Thus our examples may be abbreviated to

(a) $(0+1)*$

(b) $(0+1)*1$

(c) $1*01*$

(d) $(0+1)*1 + 1*01*$

Note that we have been very careful to say that a regular expression *denotes* a language. This is because, in general, there are lots of regular expressions which denote the same language. Sometimes these expressions differ in trivial ways—a and $a+\emptyset$ both denote $\{a\}$—but sometimes quite dissimilar expressions denote the same language—$(0+1)*$ and $(0*1)*0*$ both denote the set of all strings consisting of 0s and 1s. We shall say that two regular expressions are *equal* if and only if they denote the same set. Some examples of equalities between regular expressions are given below. All of these identities are easily checked and are rightly regarded as axiomatic.

A1 $(\alpha+\beta)+\gamma = \alpha+(\beta+\gamma)$ A2 $(\alpha \cdot \beta) \cdot \gamma = \alpha \cdot (\beta \cdot \gamma)$

A3 $\alpha+\beta \quad = \beta+\alpha$ A4 $\alpha+\alpha \quad = \alpha$

A5 $\alpha \cdot (\beta + \gamma) = (\alpha \cdot \beta) + (\alpha \cdot \gamma)$ A6 $(\beta + \gamma) \cdot \alpha = (\beta \cdot \alpha) + (\gamma \cdot \alpha)$

A7 $\alpha + \varnothing \quad = \alpha$ A8 $\alpha \cdot \varnothing \quad = \varnothing \quad = \varnothing \cdot \alpha$

A9 $\Lambda \cdot \alpha \quad = \alpha \quad = \alpha \cdot \Lambda$ A10 $\alpha^* \quad = \Lambda + \alpha \cdot \alpha^*$

A11 $\alpha^* \quad = (\Lambda + \alpha)^*$

Let us now consider the problem of finding a regular expression denoting $L(G)$ for a given regular grammar G. This problem may be solved by regarding the grammar G as defining a set of simultaneous equations. Consider, for example, a grammar having four productions:

$$S \to aS \qquad S \to bR \qquad S \to \Lambda$$
$$R \to aS$$

In place of these four productions we can write two simultaneous equations in $L(R)$ and $L(S)$. These are

$$L(S) = \{a\} \cdot L(S) \cup \{b\} \cdot L(R) \cup \{\Lambda\} \tag{2.1}$$
$$L(R) = \{a\} \cdot L(S)$$

(Note that $L(G) = L(S)$ by definition.) In the notation of regular expressions we dispense with { and }. We shall also abbreviate $L(S)$ and $L(R)$ to S and R, respectively. Thus equations (2.1) become

$$S = aS + bR + \Lambda \tag{2.2}$$
$$R = aS$$

A first step in the solution of (2.2) is to substitute the value of R into the equation for S. This gives

$$S = aS + baS + \Lambda \tag{2.3}$$

To solve (2.3) we need some rule allowing us to eliminate S from the right-hand side of the equation. The rule is stated below.

    R1   The equation $X = \alpha X + \beta$ has a solution $X = \alpha^* \beta$.

To justify R1, suppose X has two productions

$$X \to \alpha X \text{ and } X \to \beta$$

where $\alpha, \beta \in T^*$. Then $L(X) = \{\beta, \alpha\beta, \alpha\alpha\beta, \dots, \alpha^n\beta, \dots\}$ and a regular expression denoting this language is $\alpha^* \beta$.

Returning to (2.3), one may first use axiom A6 to obtain

$$S = (a + ba)S + \Lambda \tag{2.4}$$

and then apply R1:

$$S = (a+ba)^*\varLambda = (a+ba)^* \tag{2.5}$$

Alternatively, one can apply R1 to (2.3) twice, obtaining in turn

$$S = a^*(baS+\varLambda) = a^*baS+a^* \tag{2.6}$$

and

$$S = (a^*ba)^*a^* \tag{2.7}$$

Thus the language generated by the grammar can be denoted either by $(a+ba)^*$ or $(a^*ba)^*a^*$. Figure 2.2, which shows the transition diagram corresponding to the grammar, helps to check the correctness of these expressions. The * operators in the expressions correspond to cycles in the diagram and + operators indicate alternative paths. To perform a single cycle on node S the inputs a or ba are required. Thus $(a+ba)^*$ represents the set of all words which can be recognized by cycling on node S an arbitrary number of times.

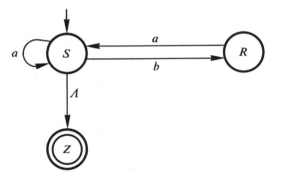

Fig. 2.2   Transition diagram recognizing $(a+ba)^*$.

In summary, to construct a regular expression denoting the language recognized by a regular grammar, the following two steps are executed:

1.   Construct a set of simultaneous equations in the form illustrated by (2.2).
2.   Solve these equations using the axioms A1–A11 and the rule R1.

Example 2
Let the grammar $G=(\{S, A, B\}, \{a, b\}, P, S)$, where P consists of

$$\begin{array}{lll} S \rightarrow aA & S \rightarrow bB & S \rightarrow b \\ A \rightarrow bA & A \rightarrow \varLambda & \\ B \rightarrow bS & & \end{array}$$

Firstly, let us rewrite the productions as a system of equations:

$$S = aA + bB + b$$
$$A = bA + \Lambda$$
$$B = bS$$

Using R1 and A9, we deduce that

$$A = b^*$$

Substituting A and B into the equation for S we obtain

$$S = ab^* + bbS + b$$
$$= bbS + ab^* + b$$
$$= (bb)^*(ab^* + b) \qquad \text{(by R1)}.$$

Thus $L(G) = (bb)^*(ab^* + b)$.

We shall not say any more about the method because it should already be very familiar to the reader! We presume that the reader is well acquainted with solving systems of equations when $+$ and $\cdot$ denote addition and multiplication of real numbers. It only remains for us to observe that the processes are almost identical. The axioms A1–A9 indicate that many algebraic properties of addition and multiplication are also true of $+$ and $\cdot$, and vice-versa. Two exceptions are the additional property A4 and the non-commutativity of concatenation (i.e. $\alpha \cdot \beta \neq \beta \cdot \alpha$). The rule R1 also has a close analog in real arithmetic. In real arithmetic the equation $X = aX + b$ has the solution

$$X = \frac{1}{(1-a)} \cdot b.$$

Morover, allowing a small amount of poetic licenee,

$$\frac{1}{1-a} = 1 + a + a^2 + \cdots.$$

Thus

$$X = b + ab + a^2b + \cdots.$$

In other words $1/(1-a)$ is directly analogous to a^*. The notation used in regular expressions is *deliberately* chosen to suggest the analogy with real arithmetic. It is an excellent illustration of Poincaré's dictum "Mathematics is the art of giving the same name to different things".

Before leaving this topic we must remark that the solution of a system of equations may not necessarily be unique. An example is the equation

$$X \doteq X + a. \qquad (2.8)$$

The solution given by R1 is

$$X = \Lambda^* a = a \qquad (2.9)$$

but other solutions are

$$X = a + b, \quad X = b^* a, \quad X = (a + b)^* \qquad (2.10)$$

Indeed, any value of X such that $X \supseteq \{a\}$ is a solution. The solution (2.9) is, however, the *appropriate* solution in the following sense. The equation (2.8) would arise if there were two productions with left-hand side X:

$$X \to X \quad \text{and} \quad X \to a$$

Thus $L(X) = \{a\}$. In subsequent chapters we shall construct and solve a number of different sets of simultaneous equations. In each case the solution may not be unique but we shall ensure that the appropriate solution is always calculated. The definition of "appropriate" differs in each case but, loosely speaking, it is the solution which corresponds to terminating derivation sequences in the grammar.

The final problem we have to describe is that of transforming a regular expression into a transition diagram. This is Algorithm 2.1. Algorithm 2.1 is recursive in line with the recursive definition of a regular expression.

Algorithm 2.1   Construction of a transition diagram from a given regular expression R such that the language recognized by the transition diagram equals the language denoted by R.

{The transition diagram for a given expression R has a single final node as well as a single start node. These will be denoted by f_R and s_R respectively.}

1.   If R is $\varnothing$, then the transition diagram for R is as shown in Fig. 2.3 (a).

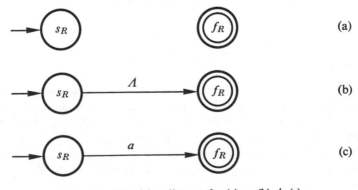

Fig. 2.3   Transition diagram for (a) $\varnothing$, (b) Λ, (c) a.

2. If R is Λ, then the transition diagram for R is as shown in Fig. 2.3(b).
3. If R is a, where $a \in T$, then the transition diagram for R is as shown in Fig. 2.3(c).

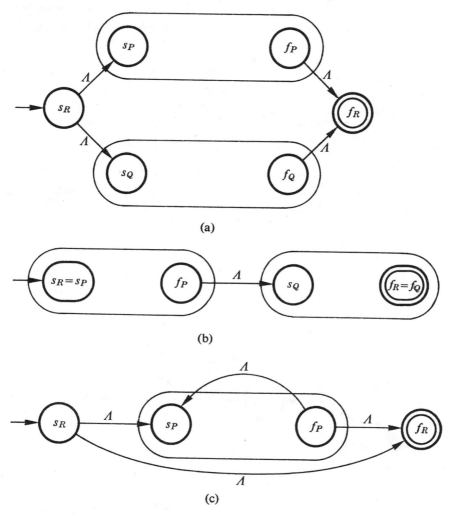

Fig. 2.4   Transition diagram for (a) $(P+Q)$, (b) $(P \cdot Q)$, (c) (P^*).

4. (a) If R has the form $(P+Q)$, then construct the transition diagrams for the expressions P and Q. Construct the transition diagram for R by creating two new nodes s_R and f_R and adding arcs labeled Λ from s_R to s_P and s_Q, and from f_P and f_Q to f_R. (See Fig. 2.4(a).)

(b) If R has the form $(P \cdot Q)$, then construct the transition diagrams for the expressions P and Q. Connect the node f_P to the node s_Q by an arc labeled Λ. Also let $s_R = s_P$ and $f_R = f_Q$. (See Fig. 2.4(b).)

(c) If R has the form (P^*), then construct the transition diagram for P. Create two new nodes s_R and f_R and add arcs labeled Λ from s_R to s_P, from f_P to s_P, from f_P to f_R and from s_R to f_R. (See Fig. 2.4(c).)

Example 3   Consider the regular expression $ab+c^*$. The steps involved in constructing the corresponding transition diagram are shown in Figs. 2.5(a), (b) and (c). (The transition diagrams for a, b and c are not shown as these are elementary.)

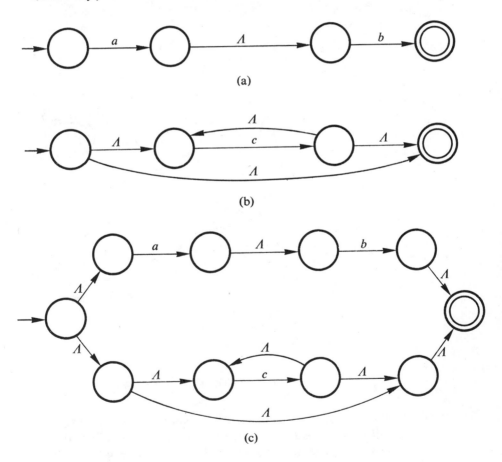

Fig. 2.5   Transition diagram for (a) ab, (b) c^*, (c) $ab+c^*$.

When performing hand calculations the number of Λ-arcs introduced by
Algorithm 2.1 is rather alarming. Indeed one can often spot shortcuts in the
construction process. Figure 2.6 shows a much smaller transition diagram for
$ab+c^*$. However, the number of arcs introduced by Algorithm 2.1 is not as
large as one might imagine. Let us measure the size of a regular expression
by the number of operators and operands in the expression. (Thus the size of
$ab+c^*$ is six, not forgetting the implicit $\cdot$ in ab.) Inspection of Algorithm 2.1
reveals that the number of nodes in the transition diagram is at most twice the
size of the expression (each operand introduces two nodes and each operator
introduces at most two nodes) and the number of arcs is at most four times
the size of the expression. Thus Algorithm 2.1 is quite efficient. It also has the
merit of being obviously correct. Moreover, in an actual implementation, the
incorporation of "shortcuts" into the algorithm may well prove to be quite
inefficient in comparison to generating the extra arcs.

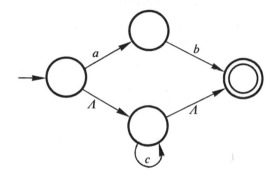

Fig. 2.6 Alternative transition diagram for $ab+c^*$.

2.3 CONVERTING A NON-DETERMINISTIC MACHINE INTO A DETERMINISTIC MACHINE

In Sec. 2.1 we introduced informally the concept of a non-deterministic
machine and the language recognized by such a machine. Here now is the
formal definition of a non-deterministic machine.

Definition A *non-deterministic* (*finite-state*) *machine* $\mathcal{N}$ is a 5-tuple
(Q, T, δ, S, F), where

1. Q is a finite non-empty set, elements of which are called *states*.
2. T is an alphabet.

3. δ is a mapping from $Q \times (T \cup \{\Lambda\})$ into the set of subsets of Q.
4. $S \in Q$ is the *start state*.
5. $F \subseteq Q$ is a non-empty set of *final states*.

State \\ Input	a	b	Λ
S	{Z}	{R,U}	∅
R	{X}	∅	{U}
X	∅	{Y}	∅
Y	{U}	∅	∅
U	{S}	{Z}	∅
Z	∅	∅	∅

Table 2.1 The transition function δ.

The function δ is called the *transition function*. Table 2.1 defines δ for the machine depicted by Fig. 2.1. (For ease of reference Fig. 2.1 has been reproduced in Fig. 2.7). Note that $\delta(A, t) = P$ if and only if for all $B \in P$ there is an arc labeled t from A to B in the figure. A special case of this is when $\delta(A, t) = \varnothing$ i.e. there are no arcs labeled t from the state A. The remaining elements of the 5-tuple are $Q = \{S, R, U, X, Y, Z\}$, $T = \{a, b\}$, $F = \{Z\}$ and the start state is S.

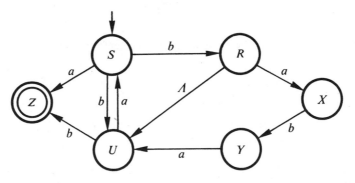

Fig. 2.7 A transition diagram.

Let us recall our informal description of the language recognized by a non-deterministic machine. The word w is in the language recognized by $\mathcal{N}$ if there is some path through $\mathcal{N}$ from the start state to a final state such that the arc labels on the path spell out w. Note that Λ-arcs (i.e. arcs labeled Λ) do not count in the spelling of w. For instance there is a path from S through

R and U to Z in Fig. 2.7 which spells out the word bb. Now, tracing such a path may involve a choice of arc to follow—when there is a Λ-arc from a given state (e.g. R in Fig. 2.7) or when there are two arcs labeled with the same symbol from a given state (e.g. the two arcs labeled b from S in Fig. 2.7). To automate this process one must, therefore, employ a graph-searching technique. If a machine is to be used often to recognize words in a language it is more efficient to factor out the graph search from the recognition process. This is achieved by replacing the non-deterministic machine by a deterministic machine—that is a machine in which no choices need to be made at any state for a given input symbol. Below we present the formal definition of a deterministic machine. The definition of the language recognized by a deterministic machine is simpler than the equivalent definition for a non-deterministic machine and so this is the order in which they are presented.

2.3.1 The Language Recognized by a Deterministic Machine

Definition A *deterministic (finite-state) machine* $\mathscr{D}$ is a 5-tuple (Q, T, δ, S, F), where
1. Q is a finite non-empty set, elements of which are called *states*.
2. T is an alphabet.
3. δ is a mapping from $Q \times T$ into Q.
4. $S \in Q$ is the *start state*.
5. $F \subseteq Q$ is a non-empty set of *final states*.

Note that the only difference between the definitions of a non-deterministic and a deterministic machine is in the definition of δ. We could have defined a deterministic machine to be a non-deterministic machine in which $\delta(q, \Lambda) = \varnothing$ and $\delta(q, t)$ is a singleton set (i.e. has exactly one element) for all $q \in Q$ and all $t \in T$.

Definition Let $\delta: Q \times T \longrightarrow Q$. The function $\delta^*: Q \times T^* \longrightarrow Q$ is defined by

$$\delta^*(q, \Lambda) = q \qquad \text{for all } q \in Q$$
$$\delta^*(q, tw) = \delta^*(\delta(q, t), w) \qquad \text{for all } q \in Q,\ t \in T \text{ and } w \in T^*.$$

The *language recognized* by the deterministic finite-state machine $\mathscr{D} = (Q, T, \delta, S, F)$ is the set of all words $w \in T^*$ such that $\delta^*(S, w) \in F$.

The latter definition requires some explanation. The $*$ in δ^* indicates that the function δ is to be applied an arbitrary number of times. If the input string is Λ, then δ is applied zero times and so the natural definition of $\delta^*(q, \Lambda)$ is q. If the input string has length greater than or equal to one, then δ is applied once to the first symbol of the input and then δ is applied repeatedly to the remainder of the input string, i.e. $\delta^*(q, tw) = \delta^*(\delta(q, t), w)$, where $t \in T$ and $w \in T^*$. The language recognized by the machine is then the set of all words which by repeated application of δ map the start state into a final state. Here is a concrete example.

Example 4   Consider the function δ defined by Table 2.2. Some examples of δ^* are

$$\delta^*(A, \Lambda) = A$$
$$\delta^*(B, \Lambda) = B$$
$$\delta^*(C, \Lambda) = C$$
$$\delta^*(A, a) = \delta^*(\delta(A, a), \Lambda) = \delta^*(C, \Lambda) = C$$
$$\delta^*(C, b) = \delta^*(\delta(C, b), \Lambda) = \delta^*(B, \Lambda) = B$$
$$\delta^*(A, ab) = \delta^*(\delta(A, a), b) = \delta^*(C, b) = B$$

State	Input	a	b
A		C	C
B		C	B
C		A	B

Table 2.2   Transition function.

An equally good description of δ^* is by an algorithm. (2.11) is an iterative algorithm corresponding to the recursive definition of δ^*. Note that * has been replaced by **while ... do**.

> {*Algorithm to determine whether a given input string ($\in T^*$) is in the language recognized by the deterministic machine $\mathscr{D} = (Q, T, \delta, S, F)$.*}
> *currentstate* $:= S$;
> *set nextsymbol to first symbol of input string*;
> **while** *input string not exhausted*   (2.11)
> **do begin** *currentstate* $:= \delta(currentstate, nextsymbol)$;
>   *get(nextsymbol)*;
>   **end**;
> **if** *currentstate* $\in F$ **then** *write ('INPUT RECOGNIZED')*
>   **else** *write ('INPUT NOT RECOGNIZED')*.

In (2.11) we assume the PASCAL convention with regard to recognizing the end of the input string. That is, the end of the input string is first recognized when an attempt is made to set *nextsymbol* when there are no symbols remaining. Thus if the input string is Λ, the initialization of *nextsymbol* sets the quantity *input string not exhausted* to *false* and the **while** statement is not executed. If the length of the input string is greater than zero, *get (nextsymbol)* sets *input string not exhausted* to *false* when an attempt is made to read beyond the last symbol in the input.

2.3.2 The Language Recognized by a Non-deterministic Machine

When the transition function δ of a non-deterministic machine is applied to a given state and given input symbol, one obtains a set of states. Accordingly δ^* (repeated application of δ) must be defined to map a set of states and an input symbol into a set of states. Here then is the definition of the language recognized by a non-deterministic machine.

Definition   Let 2^Q denote the set of all subsets of Q. Let $\delta: Q \times (T \cup \{\Lambda\}) \longrightarrow 2^Q$. Let the functionality of δ be extended to $2^Q \times (T \cup \{\Lambda\}) \longrightarrow 2^Q$ by

$$\delta(P, t) = \bigcup_{q \in P} \delta(q, t) \qquad \text{for all } P \subseteq Q.$$

The function $\delta^*: 2^Q \times T^* \longrightarrow 2^Q$ is defined by

$$\delta^*(\{q\}, \Lambda) = \{q\} \cup \delta^*(\delta(q, \Lambda), \Lambda)$$

$$\delta^*(\{q\}, t_1 t_2 \ldots t_n) = \delta^*(\delta(\ldots \delta(\delta^*(\delta(\delta^*(\{q\}, \Lambda), t_1), \Lambda), t_2), \ldots, t_n), \Lambda)$$

$$\delta^*(P, w) = \bigcup_{q \in P} \delta^*(\{q\}, w)$$

for all $q \in Q$, $P \subseteq Q$, $t_1, \ldots, t_n \in T$ $(n > 0)$ and $w \in T^*$.

The *language recognized* by the non-deterministic machine $\mathcal{N} = (Q, T, \delta, S, F)$ is the set of all words $w \in T^*$ such that $F \cap \delta^*(S, w) \neq \varnothing$.

The three clauses in the definition of δ^* may be justified as follows. When the input string is Λ the set of states which may be reached from q by repeated application of δ includes q itself (zero applications of δ) together with the set of all states which can be reached by a single application of δ followed by further repeated applications of δ. This is the first clause in the definition. The second clause states that a path starting at the state q which spells out $t_1 t_2 \ldots t_n$ consists of a sequence of Λ-arcs followed by an arc labeled t_1 followed by a sequence of Λ-arcs followed by an arc labeled t_2 etc. The path is terminated by an arc labeled t_n followed by a sequence of Λ-arcs. The third clause states that, if under some input string one may reach any of the states in the set P, and the remainder of the input is w, then the set of states which can be reached is the union of all the states which can be reached from the individual states in P. Note that, when $P = \varnothing$, we have $\delta^*(\varnothing, w) = \varnothing$.

Example 5   Consider the non-deterministic machine depicted by Fig. 2.8. The (extended) transition function δ is given by

$$
\begin{aligned}
\delta(\{A\}, \Lambda) &= \{C\} & \delta(\{A\}, a) &= \{B\} \\
\delta(\{B\}, \Lambda) &= \varnothing & \delta(\{B\}, a) &= \{D\} \\
\delta(\{C\}, \Lambda) &= \{E\} & \delta(\{C\}, a) &= \{D\} \\
\delta(\{D\}, \Lambda) &= \{E\} & \delta(\{D\}, a) &= \varnothing \\
\delta(\{E\}, \Lambda) &= \varnothing & \delta(\{E\}, a) &= \{B, D\}
\end{aligned}
$$

Some examples of δ^* are

$$
\begin{aligned}
\delta^*(\{A\}, \Lambda) &= \{A, C, E\} \\
\delta^*(\{A\}, a) &= \{B, D, E\} \\
\delta^*(\{C, D\}, a) &= \{B, D, E\} \\
\delta^*(\{C, D\}, aaa) &= \{B, D, E\}
\end{aligned}
$$

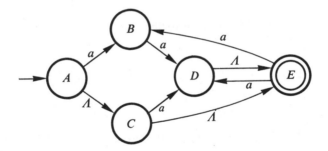

Fig. 2.8   A non-deterministic machine.

2.3.3   The Conversion Algorithm—An Example

The conversion of a non-deterministic machine to a deterministic machine is best explained by reference to an example. Consider the transition diagram in Fig. 2.7. The first step in the construction of a deterministic machine from this diagram is to create a state labeled $\{S\}$; S is the start state of the non-deterministic machine and $\{S\}$ is the start state of the deterministic machine. (See Fig. 2.9(a).) Now one constructs the arcs from this start state. Under input a the only state that can be reached from S in Fig. 2.7 is Z. A new state labeled $\{Z\}$ is, therefore, added to the deterministic machine and an arc labeled a is drawn connecting it to $\{S\}$ (Fig. 2.9(a)). Under input b the two states R and U can be reached from S. Thus we create a state $\{R, U\}$ and connect it to $\{S\}$ by an arc labeled b. Figure 2.9(a) summarizes all the steps so far.

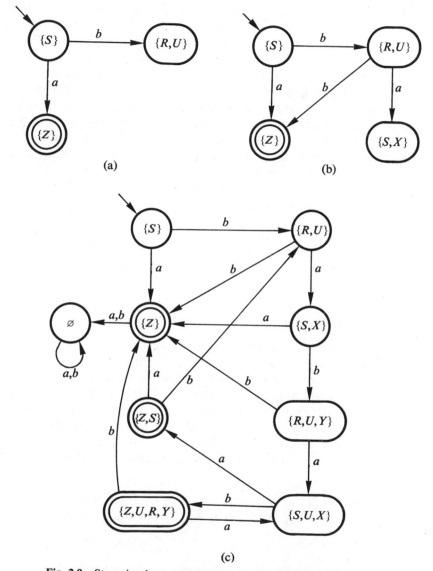

Fig. 2.9 Steps in the construction of a deterministic machine: (a) Step 1: arcs from $\{S\}$; (b) step 2: arcs from $\{R,U\}$; (c) the complete machine.

We must now add arcs from $\{R, U\}$ and from $\{Z\}$. From the state R in the non-deterministic machine one can reach either state S or state X under the input a. Also from U one can reach S under the input a. Thus from the state $\{R, U\}$ in the deterministic machine one can reach the state $\{S, X\}$. This new state has been added to Fig. 2.9(b) together with the connecting arc. Under input b the only state which can be reached from either R or U in the non-deterministic machine is the state Z. The state $\{Z\}$ has already been added to the deterministic machine and so only the new arc labeled b needs to be added from $\{R, U\}$ to $\{Z\}$. Figure 2.9(b) summarizes our steps at this point.

The essential principles involved in the construction are apparent from Figs. 2.9(a) and (b). Whenever a new state is introduced the arcs from that state must also be added. Such arcs may be to an existing node or may themselves cause a new state to be introduced. Figure 2.9(c) shows the end product—a deterministic machine which recognizes the same language as the non-deterministic machine of Fig. 2.7. (Figure 2.9(c) is deterministic because there are no Λ-arcs and there is exactly one arc labeled t, for each $t \in T$, from any given state.) Two extra details illustrated by Fig. 2.9(c) are (i) the final states are $\{Z\}$, $\{Z,S\}$ and $\{Z, U, R, Y\}$—these are the only states which include Z as an element, and (ii) the state $\varnothing$ has been added because there are no arcs from Z in the non-deterministic machine. $\varnothing$ is called the *error state* because any input string which causes it to be entered will not be recognized by the machine.

2.3.4   A Rigorous Development of the Conversion Algorithm

Now that the reader has a feel for it, we may begin to develop the conversion algorithm more rigorously. We remarked earlier that a graph search is required when using a non-deterministic machine to recognize words. This is immediately obvious from the definition of $\delta^*(\{q\}, \Lambda)$. Indeed the basic graph-searching algorithm described in Chap. 1 (Algorithm 1.1) is simply an iterative form of this recursive definition. *directly-reachable*($\{q\}$) identifies with $\delta(\{q\}, \Lambda)$ and *reached* is (an approximation to) $\delta^*(\{S\}, \Lambda)$. To improve the efficiency of the recognition process one makes use of the following theorem.

Theorem 2.1   Let $\mathcal{N} = (Q_{\mathcal{N}}, T, \delta_{\mathcal{N}}, S_{\mathcal{N}}, F_{\mathcal{N}})$ be a non-deterministic finite-state machine. Then, for all $n > 0$, $t_1, t_2, \ldots, t_n \in T$ and $P \subseteq Q_{\mathcal{N}}$,

$$\delta_{\mathcal{N}}^*(P, t_1 t_2 \ldots t_n) = \delta_{\mathcal{N}}^*(\ldots \delta_{\mathcal{N}}^*(\delta_{\mathcal{N}}^*(P, t_1), t_2), \ldots, t_n).$$

Theorem 2.1 is intuitively obvious although not immediately obvious from the definitions. So as not to interrupt the flow of our argument its proof appears as an appendix to this chapter.

The import of Theorem 2.1 is that one should preprocess the non-deterministic machine, calculating a function:

$$\delta_{\mathscr{D}}: 2^{Q_{\mathscr{N}}} \times T \longrightarrow 2^{Q_{\mathscr{N}}},$$

where

$$\delta_{\mathscr{D}}(P, t) = \delta_{\mathscr{N}}^{*}(P, t). \tag{2.12}$$

One can then test whether $w = t_1 t_2 \ldots t_n$ is recognized by $\mathscr{N}$ using (2.13).

$$\delta_{\mathscr{N}}^{*}(\{S_{\mathscr{N}}\}, t_1 t_2 \ldots t_n) = \delta_{\mathscr{D}}(\ldots \delta_{\mathscr{D}}(\delta_{\mathscr{D}}(\{S_{\mathscr{N}}\}, t_1), t_2), \ldots, t_n) \tag{2.13}$$

Equation (2.12) captures the major principles in the construction of a deterministic machine $\mathscr{D} = (Q_{\mathscr{D}}, T, \delta_{\mathscr{D}}, S_{\mathscr{D}}, F_{\mathscr{D}})$ from a non-deterministic machine $\mathscr{N}$. The state set $Q_{\mathscr{D}}$ is the set of all subsets of $Q_{\mathscr{N}}$ and the transition function $\delta_{\mathscr{D}}$ is as defined by (2.12). From (2.12) we also see that the start state of $\mathscr{D}$ is

$$S_{\mathscr{D}} = \{S_{\mathscr{N}}\} \tag{2.14}$$

Finally, the definition of the language recognized by $\mathscr{N}$ suggests the appropriate definition of the set of final states of $\mathscr{D}$, namely:
$P \in F_{\mathscr{D}}$ if and only if

either (i) $P = \{S_{\mathscr{N}}\}$ and $\delta_{\mathscr{N}}^{*}(\{S_{\mathscr{N}}\}, \Lambda) \cap F_{\mathscr{N}} \neq \varnothing$

or   (ii) $P = \delta_{\mathscr{N}}^{*}(\{S_{\mathscr{N}}\}, w)$ for some $w \in T^{+}$ and $P \cap F_{\mathscr{N}} \neq \varnothing$. $\left.\vphantom{\begin{array}{c}a\\a\end{array}}\right\}$ (2.15)

After further reflection, the preprocessing of $\mathscr{N}$ might not seem such a good idea. If the number of elements in $Q_{\mathscr{N}}$ is m, then the number of subsets of $Q_{\mathscr{N}}$ is 2^m. In other words $\delta_{\mathscr{D}}$ is going to be a mighty big function to tabulate! Fortunately, as evidenced by Fig. 2.9, it is rare in practice that one needs to tabulate the whole of $\delta_{\mathscr{D}}$. Only the values of $\delta_{\mathscr{D}}(P, t)$ for a relatively small number of subsets P of $Q_{\mathscr{N}}$ are required. The condition on P for calculating $\delta_{\mathscr{D}}(P, t)$ is that P should be "accessible" from $\{S_{\mathscr{N}}\}$. This is defined below.

Definition   Let $P \subseteq Q_{\mathscr{N}}$. Then P is said to be *accessible* if and only if $P = \{S_{\mathscr{N}}\}$ or there is some word $w \in T^{+}$ such that $\delta_{\mathscr{N}}^{*}(\{S_{\mathscr{N}}\}, w) = P$.

Figure 2.9(c) shows only the accessible subsets of $\{S, U, R, X, Y, Z\}$. Had we included all subsets the diagram would have had 64 states!

Let us summarize the discussion so far. To construct a deterministic machine $\mathscr{D}$ from a non-deterministic machine $\mathscr{N}$ we shall need to perform *two* graph searches. The first of these computes $\delta_{\mathscr{N}}^{*}(\{q\}, \Lambda)$, where $q \in Q_{\mathscr{N}}$. These values are used to compute $\delta_{\mathscr{N}}^{*}(\{q\}, t)$ which, from the definition of $\delta_{\mathscr{N}}^{*}$, is given by

$$\delta_{\mathscr{N}}^{*}(\{q\}, t) = \delta_{\mathscr{N}}^{*}(\delta_{\mathscr{N}}(\delta_{\mathscr{N}}^{*}(\{q\}, \Lambda), t), \Lambda). \tag{2.16}$$

The construction of Fig. 2.9(c) is a poor example of this; Fig. 2.5(c) gives a better idea of what is involved. The second graph search is necessary to find the accessible subsets of $Q_{\mathcal{N}}$. These subsets form the states of $\mathcal{D}$. The transition function of $\mathcal{D}$ is given by (2.12). Equation (2.17) is a more explicit statement of (2.12).

$$\delta_{\mathcal{D}}(P, t) = \bigcup_{q \in P} \delta_{\mathcal{N}}^*(\{q\}, t). \tag{2.17}$$

The start state of $\mathcal{D}$ is given by (2.14) and the final states of $\mathcal{D}$ are given by (2.15). We are now ready to express this algorithmically. Algorithm 2.2 consists mainly of two applications of Algorithm 1.3, but the terminology has been modified appropriately. (Some minor modifications have also been made to Algorithm 1.3 because we no longer wish to find whether a single node f is reachable from a given start node; instead we wish to find *all* nodes reachable from the start node.)

Algorithm 2.2   Conversion of a non-deterministic machine to a deterministic machine.

type *non-det state = non-deterministic state*;
    det state   = set of non-det state;
var *q, q', q'': non-det state*;
    d, d': det state;
    t: terminal;
    reached, non-det frontier: set of non-det state;
    det frontier: set of det state;
    estar: non-det state $\longrightarrow$ set of non-det state;
        {estar(q) = $\delta_{\mathcal{N}}^*(\{q\}, \Lambda)$}
    dnstar: non-det state $\times$ terminal $\longrightarrow$ set of non-det state;
        {dnstar(q, t) = $\delta_{\mathcal{N}}^*(\{q\}, t)$}

begin *{for each $q \in Q_{\mathcal{N}}$ perform graph search to calculate $\delta_{\mathcal{N}}^*(\{q\}, \Lambda)$}*
for *each $q \in Q_{\mathcal{N}}$* **do**
    begin *non-det frontier := reached := {q}*;
    repeat *choose and remove $q' \in$ non-det frontier*;
        for *each $q'' \in \delta_{\mathcal{N}}(q', \Lambda)$* **do**
            begin if *$q'' \notin$ reached*
                then *add q'' to reached and non-det frontier*;
        end;
    until *non-det frontier = $\varnothing$*;
    estar(q) := reached; *{ = $\delta_{\mathcal{N}}^*(\{q\}, \Lambda)$ }*
    end;

Algorithm 2.2　(Continued)

$\{Calculate\ \delta_{\mathcal{N}}^*(\{q\}, t)\}$
for *each* $q \in Q_{\mathcal{N}}$ **do**
　　for *each* $t \in T$ **do**
　　　　$dnstar(q, t) := estar(\delta_{\mathcal{N}}(estar(q), t))$;
$\{Perform\ graph\ search\ to\ find\ accessible\ states\ of\ \mathcal{D},\ simultaneously\ setting$
$\delta_{\mathcal{D}}\ and\ F_{\mathcal{D}}.\}$
$S_{\mathcal{D}} := \{S_{\mathcal{N}}\}$; **if** $estar(S_{\mathcal{N}}) \cap F_{\mathcal{N}} \neq \varnothing$ **then** $F_{\mathcal{D}} := \{S_{\mathcal{D}}\}$ **else** $F_{\mathcal{D}} := \varnothing$;
$Q_{\mathcal{D}} := det\ frontier := \{S_{\mathcal{D}}\}$;
repeat *choose and remove* $d \in det\ frontier$;
　　　$\{Construct\ arcs\ from\ d\text{—}each\ arc\ corresponds\ to\ a\ symbol\ t \in T.\}$
　　for *each* $t \in T$ **do**
　　　　begin $d' := \varnothing$;
　　　　$\{end\text{-}point\ of\ the\ arc,\ d',\ is\ the\ set\ of\ all\ non\text{-}deterministic\ states$
　　　　$q'\ reachable\ under\ input\ t\ from\ some\ q \in d.\}$
　　　　for *each* $q \in d$ **do** $d' := d' \cup dnstar(q, t)$;
　　　　if $d' \notin Q_{\mathcal{D}}$ **then begin** *add* d' *to* $Q_{\mathcal{D}}$ *and det frontier*;
　　　　　　　　　　　　$\{final\ state?\}$
　　　　　　　　　　　　if $F_{\mathcal{N}} \cap d' \neq \varnothing$
　　　　　　　　　　　　then $F_{\mathcal{D}} := F_{\mathcal{D}} \cup \{d'\}$;
　　　　　　　　　　　　end;
　　　　　　$\delta_{\mathcal{D}}(d, t) := d'$;
　　　　end;
until *det frontier* $= \varnothing$;
end.

The implementation of Algorithm 2.2 provides an interesting exercise in the choice of data structures. The data structures used in the implementation of Program 1.1 are certainly *not* applicable to the second graph search in Algorithm 2.2. The main stumbling block is the representation of deterministic states and the set $Q_{\mathcal{D}}$—the *potential* size of $Q_{\mathcal{D}}$ is just too big to contemplate and simple data structures—like a Boolean array—are out of the question. There are also a lot more non-primitive operations to be considered in Algorithm 2.2 than in Algorithm 1.3. So as not to spoil the reader's enjoyment no further hints will be provided and the reader is left to suggest suitable data structures. Note that there is no single "correct" answer to this problem.

2.4 NUMBERS IN ALGOL 60

As a concrete and sizable example of the techniques introduced in Secs. 2.1 to 2.3 we shall now construct a deterministic finite-state machine recognizing

⟨*unsigned integer*⟩   ::=   ⟨*digit*⟩ | ⟨*unsigned integer*⟩⟨*digit*⟩

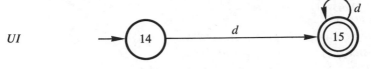

UI

⟨*integer*⟩   ::=   ⟨*unsigned integer*⟩ | + ⟨*unsigned integer*⟩ | − ⟨*unsigned integer*⟩

I

⟨*decimal fraction*⟩   ::=   •   ⟨*unsigned integer*⟩

DF

⟨*exponent part*⟩   ::=   10   ⟨*integer*⟩

EP

⟨*decimal number*⟩   ::=   ⟨*unsigned integer*⟩ | ⟨*decimal fraction*⟩ |

⟨*unsigned integer*⟩⟨*decimal fraction*⟩

DN

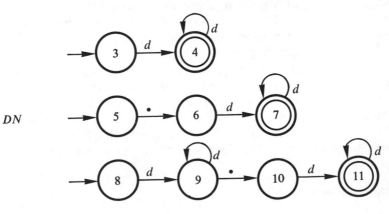

Fig. 2.10   ALGOL 60 ⟨*number*⟩

⟨*unsigned number*⟩   ::=   ⟨*decimal number*⟩|⟨*exponent part*⟩|

                          ⟨*decimal number*⟩⟨*exponent part*⟩

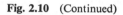

⟨*number*⟩   ::=   ⟨*unsigned number*⟩|+⟨*unsigned number*⟩||−⟨*unsigned number*⟩

Fig. 2.10   (Continued)

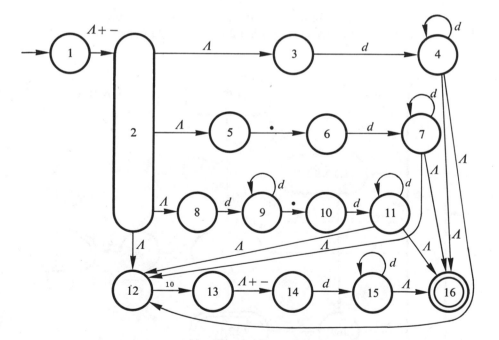

Fig. 2.11   Non-deterministic recognizer of an
ALGOL 60 ⟨*number*⟩.

real numbers in ALGOL 60. To do this we have taken the BNF description of
⟨*number*⟩ directly from Sec. 2.5.1 of the "Revised Report" and converted it
into a sequence of transition diagrams. These diagrams form Fig. 2.10, each
diagram being preceded by the productions from which it was derived. The
input alphabet is assumed to consist of the symbols +, −, ., 10 and *d*
(i.e. ⟨*digit*⟩). A square box represents a diagram which appears elsewhere.
Each diagram has been given a one- or two-letter name, the name being an
abbreviation of the non-terminal to which it corresponds. To complete a
diagram it is necessary to perform a macro-expansion of the square boxes
appearing in the diagram. This has been done in Fig. 2.11, which depicts a
non-deterministic machine which recognizes ALGOL 60 ⟨*number*⟩s. (Those
states in Fig. 2.10 which correspond to states in Fig. 2.11 have been numbered
accordingly.)

   The astute reader will have observed that, in some instances, Secs. 2.1 to
2.3 do not indicate how a diagram is to be constructed. In such cases (e.g. the
diagram for ⟨*unsigned number*⟩) common sense has been used to construct
the diagram.
   Having constructed a non-deterministic machine the next step is to construct
a deterministic machine using Algorithm 2.2. Figure 2.12 depicts the machine

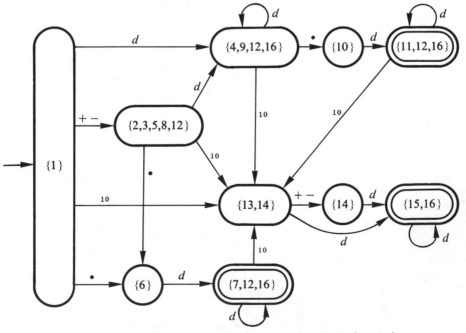

Fig. 2.12 Deterministic recognizer of an ALGOL 60 ⟨*number*⟩.

constructed in this way. (The numbering of the states in Fig. 2.11 also helps to relate the states of the deterministic machine to those of the non-deterministic machine.) For clarity the error state, $\varnothing$, has been omitted from Fig. 2.12.

Before concluding this chapter one final comment must be made about Algorithm 2.2. In Sec. 2.3 we took care to calculate only the accessible states of the deterministic machine with the objective of reducing the space required to store the transition function. Nevertheless the machine produced may well be larger than absolutely necessary. This is illustrated by Fig. 2.13 which also depicts a deterministic recognizer of ALGOL 60 ⟨*number*⟩s but has two fewer states than Fig. 2.12. This reduction has been effected by coalescing the state labeled {6} with the state labeled {10}, and the state labeled {7, 12, 16} with the state labeled {11, 12, 16}. This operation is valid because the coalesced states recognize the same languages. That is, if the start state of the machine depicted by Fig. 2.12 were redefined to be {7, 12, 16}, the language recognized by the new machine would be identical to the language recognized by the machine which has {11, 12, 16} as its start state. Similarly the language recognized by the machine with the start state {10} is identical to the language recognized by the machine with start state {6}. However, no other states of Fig. 2.12 may be coalesced without affecting the language recognized and so the machine depicted by Fig. 2.13 is minimal. In general it can be shown that, given any regular language L, there is a *unique minimal* machine which recognizes L and, more importantly, there is an efficient

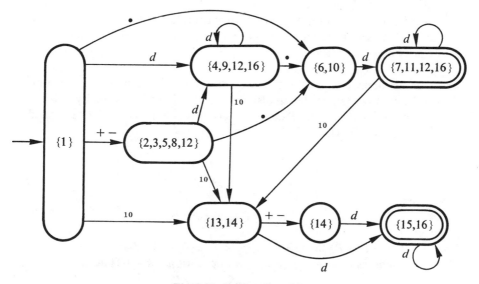

Fig. 2.13   Reduced machine.

algorithm to construct this *reduced* machine from a deterministic recognizer
of L. Regrettably we shall not discuss the algorithm here primarily because,
although it is easy to describe an inefficient algorithm, it is quite difficult to
design and implement a respectably efficient algorithm to perform this task.

Appendix—Proof of Theorem 2.1

The statement of Theorem 2.1 is reproduced below.

Theorem 2.1   Let $\mathcal{N} = (Q, T, \delta, S, F)$ be a non-deterministic finite-state
machine. Then, for all $n > 0$, $t_1, t_2, \ldots, t_n \in T$ and $P \subseteq Q$,

$$\delta^*(P, t_1 t_2 \ldots t_n) = \delta^*(\ldots \delta^*(\delta^*(P, t_1), t_2), \ldots, t_n). \qquad (2.18)$$

Verbally, a proof might proceed as follows.

Let $q \in P$. A path from q to q' which spells out $t_1 t_2 \ldots t_n$ consists of a
sequence of $\varLambda$-arcs followed by an arc labeled t_1 followed by a sequence of
$\varLambda$-arcs followed by an arc labeled t_2, etc. On the other hand, according to
(2.18) a path spelling out $t_1 t_2 \ldots t_n$ consists of (a sequence of $\varLambda$-arcs followed
by an arc labeled t_1 followed by a sequence of $\varLambda$-arcs) followed by (a sequence
of $\varLambda$-arcs followed by an arc labeled t_2 followed by a sequence of $\varLambda$-arcs), etc.
Thus a proof of Theorem 2.1 involves, essentially, a proof that a sequence of
$\varLambda$-arcs followed by a sequence of $\varLambda$-arcs is identical to a sequence of $\varLambda$-arcs.
(Hence, also, our statement that the theorem is "intuitively obvious".) In the
formal proof below we have introduced additional notation. Had we not
done so the proof would have seemed very complex, although it is not. The
moral is: think carefully about notation—it can obscure simple ideas, it can
also clarify complex ideas.

Proof of Theorem 2.1   Let $q \in Q$. Let $e: 2^Q \longrightarrow 2^Q$ denote the function
defined by $e(P) = \delta(P, \varLambda)$. Let us also denote function application by $\cdot$. Thus
$e \cdot P$ denotes $e(P)$ and $e \cdot e \cdot P$ denotes $e(e(P))$. Let $e^*: 2^Q \longrightarrow 2^Q$ be defined
by $e^* \cdot P = \delta^*(P, \varLambda)$. Then, clearly,

$$e^* \cdot P \supseteq P$$

and so

$$e^* \cdot e^* \cdot P \supseteq e^* \cdot P. \qquad (2.19)$$

Moreover

$$e^* \cdot P \supseteq e^* \cdot e^* \cdot P. \qquad (2.20)$$

For, if $q \in e^* \cdot e^* \cdot P$, then $\exists$ integers $n, m \geq 0$ such that $q \in e^n \cdot e^m \cdot P$.
(*Note*: e^m denotes $e \cdot e \cdot e \cdot \cdots \cdot e$, i.e. m applications of e.) That is,

$$q \in e^{n+m} \cdot P \subseteq e^* \cdot P.$$

From (2.19) and (2.20) we have

$$e^* \cdot e^* = e^*. \qquad (2.21)$$

(That is, a sequence of Λ-arcs followed by a sequence of Λ-arcs is identical to a sequence of Λ-arcs.) Now, returning to the use of parentheses to denote function application, we have by definition

$$\delta^*(P, t_1 \ldots t_n) = e^*(\delta(\cdots e^*(\delta(e^*(\delta(e^*(P), t_1)), t_2)), \ldots, t_n)).$$

Thus, applying (2.21)

$$\delta^*(P, t_1 \ldots t_n) = e^*(\delta(e^* \cdots (e^*(\delta(e^*(e^*(\delta(e^*(P), t_1))), t_2))), \ldots, t_n))$$
$$= \delta^*(\cdots \delta^*(\delta^*(P, t_1), t_2), \ldots, t_n). \qquad \square$$

EXERCISES

2.1 Construct transition diagrams corresponding to the following regular grammars.
 (a) $G_1 = (\{S,A,B,C,D\}, \{a,b,c,d\}, P, S)$, where P consists of

$$
\begin{array}{ll}
S \to aA & S \to B \\
A \to abS & A \to bB \\
B \to b & B \to cC \\
C \to D & \\
D \to bB & D \to d
\end{array}
$$

 (b) $G_2 = (\{S,A,B,C,D\}, \{a,b,c,d\}, P, S)$, where P consists of

$$
\begin{array}{ll}
S \to Aa & S \to B \\
A \to Cc & A \to Bb \\
B \to Bb & B \to a \\
C \to D & C \to Bab \\
D \to d &
\end{array}
$$

Use your transition diagrams to construct a *left-linear* grammar defining $L(G_1)$ and a *right-linear* grammar defining $L(G_2)$. Check your answers firstly by constructing derivation sequences for the following sentences.
(a) of G_1: *abb aababb b cd cbb*
(b) of G_2: *a aba aabca dca*
Secondly, construct a number of strings which are *not* sentences of G_1 or G_2 and check that the grammars you have constructed do not also generate these strings. Comment on the value of these checks.

2.2 Formalize (a) the process of converting a left-linear grammar into a transition diagram, and (b) the process of converting a transition diagram into a right-linear grammar.

2.3 Construct regular expressions denoting the following languages.
 (a) The set of statement lists. A statement list is a list of basic or dummy statements. Each statement in the list is separated from the next by one or

more semi-colons. In addition each statement may be labeled an arbitrary number of times. For example

$$b;l:b;l:l:;;b;;$$

is a statement list, where l denotes a label and b denotes a basic statement. Assume that l and b are terminal symbols.

(b)   COMMON statements in FORTRAN. An example of such a statement is the following

$$\text{COMMON } A,B(10),C/NAME1/X(5,5),Y/NAME2/Z$$

Assume that λ and μ are terminal symbols denoting an arbitrary identifier and constant, respectively. Assume also that arrays may have an arbitrary number of dimensions.

2.4   Construct regular expressions denoting the languages recognized by Figs. 2.14 (a) and (b).

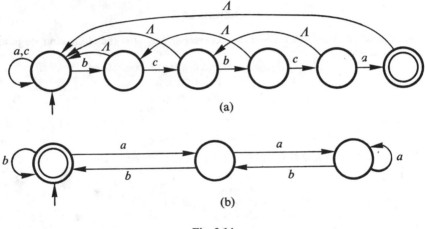

(a)

(b)

Fig. 2.14

2.5   Estimate how many states would be required to recognize all the ALGOL 60 reserved words. Comment on the suitability of using a finite-state machine to perform this task.

2.6   Construct deterministic machines equivalent to the non-deterministic machines shown in Figs. 2.15 (a) to (d).

2.7   Construct deterministic machines which recognize the following regular languages.
  (a) $((0^*+1)(1^*0))^*$
  (b) $(b+a(aa^*b)^*b)^*$
  (c) $(b+aa+ac+aaa+aac)^*$
  (d) $a(a+b)^*b(a+b)^*a(a+b)^*b(a+b)^*$

2.8   Construct a deterministic machine recognizing COMMON statements in FORTRAN (cf. Exercise 2.3(b)).

2.9 Assume that, in an implementation of ALGOL 60, all array bounds must be integer constants (signed or unsigned). Construct a deterministic machine recognizing declarations in ALGOL 60. Assume that λ and μ are terminal symbols representing ⟨*identifier*⟩ and ⟨*unsigned integer*⟩, respectively.

2.10 Construct non-deterministic machines recognizing the following sets. Assume that the alphabet $T = \{A,B,C,\ldots,Z\}$.

(a) The set of all strings composed of letters appearing in alphabetic order with no repetitions. (For example, *ACZ* is in the set, but *BA* is not.)

(b) The set of all strings in which at least one letter is repeated.

Suppose that the "size" of a deterministic machine is measured by the number of arcs in the machine which are directed from a non-error state to a non-error state. (For example, the machine in Fig. 2.9 (c) has size 14—the arcs from $\{Z\}$ to ∅ and from ∅ to ∅ are not counted.) Using this measure, estimate the size of deterministic machines equivalent to the non-deterministic machines you have constructed.

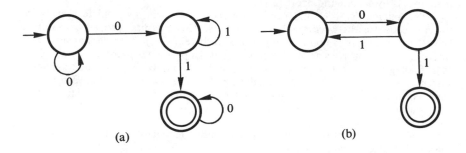

(a)   (b)

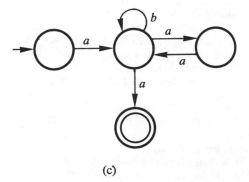

(c)

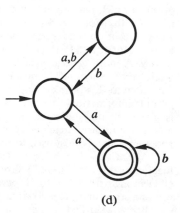

(d)

Fig. 2.15

2.11 Add an assertion to Algorithm 2.2 which expresses the property that the states of $\mathscr{D}$ are the accessible subsets of $Q_{\mathscr{N}}$. Prove inductively that your assertion is indeed a loop invariant.

2.12 Discuss the choice of data structures to implement Algorithm 2.2 efficiently. Assume that the number of states in the given non-deterministic machine is between 100 and 200 and that the deterministic machine is unlikely to have more than twice this number of states.

BIBLIOGRAPHIC NOTES

The material in this chapter forms part of a well-established area of automata theory and there are a large number of texts covering the topic in more detail. Hopcroft and Ullman [2.7] and Salomaa [2.13] discuss most of the important results, whilst Lewis *et al.* [2.9] argue in detail the relevance of the theory to the design of lexical analyzers. Minsky's book [2.10] is commendable for its readability and its discussion of the use of finite-state machines to model certain aspects of brain function. The classic paper on the relationship between non-deterministic and deterministic machines is by Rabin and Scott [2.11].

The axioms A1–A11 and rule of inference R1 form a complete system for proving equalities between regular expressions. This was first proved by Salomaa [2.12]. There are lots of practical applications where the objects under consideration obey the same properties as regular expressions. In particular path-finding problems (e.g. finding a shortest path between two points) can be expressed as solving a system of equations in a so-called regular algebra. The relationship between solving such equations and the techniques used commonly by numerical analysts (e.g. Gaussian elimination) has been studied by Backhouse and Carré [2.2]. We shall see such an application in Chap. 5.

A very practical application of non-deterministic machines is to "string matching" and "pattern matching". In its simplest form the problem is this. Given two strings u and v, is u a substring of v? There is an obvious algorithm to solve this problem which may involve comparing every symbol of u with almost every symbol of v. Knuth, Morris and Pratt [2.8] and Boyer and Moore [2.3] describe algorithms whose execution time is at worst proportional to the sum of the lengths of u and v. Knuth, Morris and Pratt [2.8] attribute the discovery of their algorithm to automata theory. A more general problem is, given a string u and a dictionary, is u in the dictionary? Aho and Corasick [2.1] have generalized the Knuth–Morris–Pratt algorithm to this problem and claim a ten-fold increase in the efficiency of a bibliographic information-retrieval system. The most general pattern-matching problem is, given a string u and a regular expression R, is u in R? Thompson [2.14] shows how a non-deterministic machine corresponding to R can be compiled into an IBM 7094 program which is then used to recognize u.

A relatively straightforward algorithm for minimizing the size of a deterministic machine is discussed in [2.9]. Gries [2.5] develops a PL/1 implementation of a more efficient algorithm due to Hopcroft [2.6]. Gries's paper is a good example of the use of a structured, top-down approach to the design of a complex algorithm.

Brzozowski [2.4] presents a direct method of converting a regular expression into a deterministic machine. His method is particularly interesting because it involves taking "derivatives" of the expression in a similar way to differentiating an arithmetic expression. This reinforces the argument for the suggestiveness of the notation used in regular expressions.

2.1 Aho, A. V. and M. J. Corasick, "Efficient string matching: An aid to bibliographic search" *Comm. ACM*, **18**, 333–40 (1975).

2.2 Backhouse, R. C. and B. A. Carré, "Regular algebra applied to path-finding problems", *J. Inst. Maths. Applics.*, **15**, 161–86 (1975).

2.3 Boyer, R. S. and J. Strother Moore, "A fast string searching algorithm", *Comm. ACM*, **20**, 762–72 (1977).

2.4 Brzozowski, J. A., "Derivatives of regular expressions", *J. ACM*, **11**, 481–94 (1964).

2.5 Gries, D., "Describing an algorithm by Hopcroft", *Acta Informatica*, **2**, 97–109 (1973).

2.6 Hopcroft, J. E., "An *n log n* algorithm for minimizing states in a finite automaton", in *Theory of Machines and Computations*, Academic Press, New York (1971), pp.189–96.

2.7 Hopcroft, J. E. and J. D. Ullman, *Formal Languages and their Relation to Automata*, Addison-Wesley, Reading, Mass. (1969).

2.8 Knuth, D. E., J. H. Morris and V. R. Pratt, "Fast pattern matching in strings", *SIAM J. Computing*, **6**, 323–50 (1977).

2.9 Lewis, P. M. II, D. J. Rosenkrantz and R. E. Stearns, *Compiler Design Theory*, Addison-Wesley, Reading, Mass. (1976).

2.10 Minsky, M., *Computation: Finite and Infinite Machines*, Prentice-Hall, London (1972).

2.11 Rabin, M. and D. Scott, "Finite automata and their decision problems", *IBM J. Res. Develop.*, **3**, 114–25 (1959).

2.12 Salomaa, A., "Two complete axiom systems for the algebra of regular events", *J. ACM*, **13**, 158–69 (1966).

2.13 Salomaa, A., *Theory of Automata*, Pergamon Press, Oxford (1969).

2.14 Thompson, K., "Regular expression search algorithm", *Comm. ACM*, **11**, 419–22 (1968).

3 LL PARSING

Syntax analysis is a very important phase of a compiler. The structure of the syntax analyzer can have a considerable bearing on the ease with which other parts of the compiler, such as the code generator, can be constructed. It is, therefore, a topic which deserves a thorough treatment.

It is an important requirement that syntax analyzers be simple and efficient; more specifically, they should operate in time proportional to the length of string being analyzed. In this chapter and the next we shall discuss two techniques which perform syntax analysis without backtracking, that is without revoking, at any stage, any earlier parsing decisions. The method described in this chapter is particularly attractive on account of its natural-ness. It is called parsing by *recursive descent* and is limited to grammars which satisfy the *LL(k) condition*. In Sec. 3.1 we describe the parsing method and introduce a stronger sufficiency condition for its applicability, called the *strong LL(k) condition*. Sections 3.2 and 3.3 are concerned with the problem of devising an efficient software tool which will test a given grammar for this property. Section 3.4 explores the theoretical limitations whilst, in contrast, Sec. 3.5 discusses ways of improving the practical feasibility and utility of the method.

3.1 SYNTAX ANALYSIS BY RECURSIVE DESCENT

In order to illustrate the ideas in this chapter we shall use the grammar in Table 3.1. For brevity lists of the non-terminals and terminals have been omitted. The non-terminals are the symbols enclosed by $\langle$ and $\rangle$ (e.g. $\langle program \rangle$, $\langle statement \rangle$) except for $\langle identifier \rangle$ and $\langle constant \rangle$, which are terminal symbols. The remaining symbols (e.g. ; $=>$ **begin**) are all terminal symbols and the sentence symbol is $\langle program \rangle$.

$\langle program \rangle$	::=	$\langle block \rangle$.
$\langle block \rangle$	::=	**begin** $\langle blocktail \rangle$
$\langle blocktail \rangle$	::=	$\langle declaration \rangle$ $\langle blocktail \rangle$ | $\langle statement\ list \rangle$ **end**
$\langle declaration \rangle$	::=	**label** $\langle idlist \rangle$ | **integer** $\langle idlist \rangle$
$\langle idlist \rangle$	::=	$\langle identifier \rangle$ $\langle rest\ of\ idlist \rangle$
$\langle rest\ of\ idlist \rangle$	::=	; | , $\langle idlist \rangle$
$\langle statement\ list \rangle$	::=	$\langle optional\ label\ part \rangle$ $\langle optional\ statement \rangle$ $\langle rest\ of\ list \rangle$
$\langle optional\ label\ part \rangle$	::=	$\langle empty \rangle$ | $\langle identifier \rangle$:
$\langle optional\ statement \rangle$	::=	$\langle empty \rangle$ | $\langle statement \rangle$
$\langle rest\ of\ list \rangle$	::=	$\langle empty \rangle$ | ; $\langle statement\ list \rangle$
$\langle statement \rangle$	::=	$\langle assignment \rangle$ | $\langle transfer \rangle$ | $\langle conditional \rangle$ | $\langle write \rangle$ | $\langle block \rangle$
$\langle assignment \rangle$	::=	$\langle expression \rangle$ => $\langle identifier \rangle$ $\langle rest\ of\ assignment\ list \rangle$
$\langle rest\ of\ assignment\ list \rangle$	::=	$\langle empty \rangle$ | => $\langle identifier \rangle$ $\langle rest\ of\ assignment\ list \rangle$
$\langle transfer \rangle$	::=	**goto** $\langle identifier \rangle$
$\langle conditional \rangle$	::=	**if** $\langle expression \rangle$ **then** $\langle statement\ list \rangle$ $\langle optional\ else \rangle$ **fi**
$\langle optional\ else \rangle$	::=	$\langle empty \rangle$ | **else** $\langle statement\ list \rangle$
$\langle write \rangle$	::=	**output** ($\langle output\ list \rangle$)
$\langle output\ list \rangle$	::=	$\langle expression \rangle$ $\langle more\ output \rangle$
$\langle more\ output \rangle$	::=	$\langle empty \rangle$ | , $\langle expression \rangle$ $\langle more\ output \rangle$
$\langle expression \rangle$	::=	$\langle exp1 \rangle$ $\langle rest\ of\ expression \rangle$
$\langle rest\ of\ expression \rangle$	::=	$\langle empty \rangle$ | $\langle relop \rangle$ $\langle exp1 \rangle$
$\langle exp1 \rangle$	::=	$\langle exp2 \rangle$ $\langle rest\ of\ exp1 \rangle$
$\langle rest\ of\ exp1 \rangle$	::=	$\langle empty \rangle$ | $\langle addop \rangle$ $\langle exp2 \rangle$ $\langle rest\ of\ exp1 \rangle$
$\langle exp2 \rangle$	::=	$\langle exp3 \rangle$ $\langle rest\ of\ exp2 \rangle$
$\langle rest\ of\ exp2 \rangle$	::=	$\langle empty \rangle$ | $\langle mulop \rangle$ $\langle exp3 \rangle$ $\langle rest\ of\ exp2 \rangle$
$\langle exp3 \rangle$	::=	$\langle positive\ exp3 \rangle$ | $-$ $\langle positive\ exp3 \rangle$
$\langle positive\ exp3 \rangle$	::=	**input** | $\langle identifier \rangle$ | $\langle constant \rangle$ | ($\langle expression \rangle$)
$\langle relop \rangle$	::=	< | > | =
$\langle addop \rangle$	::=	+ | $-$
$\langle mulop \rangle$	::=	× | /

Table 3.1   Definition of a Simple Programming Language

Here is an example of a program written in this language.

```
begin integer N, SUM, X;
      input => N;
      0 => SUM;
      begin label LOOP, FIN; integer ABS;
      LOOP: if N = 0 then goto FIN fi;
```

$$N - 1 => N; \textbf{input} => X;$$
$$\textbf{if } X < 0 \textbf{ then } - X => ABS \tag{3.1}$$
$$\textbf{else } X => ABS$$
$$\textbf{fi};$$
$$SUM + ABS => SUM;$$
$$\textbf{goto } LOOP;$$
$$FIN: \textbf{output}(SUM)$$
$$\textbf{end};$$

$$\textbf{end}.$$

Although the syntax is certainly non-trivial, the construction of a syntax analyzer for the language is surprisingly simple. The grammar has been designed specifically to allow an "LL" or "top-down" parsing technique to be used. Firstly for each symbol t in the terminal alphabet we write a procedure pt.[†] Examples of the procedures constructed for the symbols **label** and + are shown in (3.2) and (3.3).

> **procedure** *plabel*;
> **begin if** *nextsymbol* = *qlabel* **then** *advance input marker*   (3.2)
>   **else goto** 1
> **end**; {*plabel*}

> **procedure** *pplus*;
> **begin if** *nextsymbol* = *qplus* **then** *advance input marker*   (3.3)
>   **else goto** 1
> **end**; {*pplus*}

Each of these procedures assumes the existence of a globally declared value *nextsymbol* of type *terminal*. The type *terminal* is a scalar type, the elements of which are *qbegin*, *qend*, *qif*, . . . , *qplus*, etc,[†] i.e. all the terminal symbols of the grammar. The procedure *advance input marker* reads another symbol in the input stream and uses it to reset *nextsymbol*. The procedure pt will only be called when the next symbol should be t. If this is not the case a syntax error has been detected.

We shall consider the process of error repair in detail in Chaps. 5 and 6, but for the moment we shall assume that the analysis is aborted as soon as an error is detected. The label 1 referred to in (3.2) and (3.3) is thus a globally declared label. When control is transferred to it the message "*SYNTAX ERROR*" is printed and the analysis terminated.

[†]The prefix p on procedures and q on symbols ensures the absence of any clashes with reserved words.

The second step is to construct a procedure *pA* for each non-terminal, *A*, in the grammar. (3.4), (3.5) and (3.6) illustrate three of these procedures. Note carefully how the body of *pA* corresponds closely to the form of the right-hand sides of productions whose left-hand side is *A*. In the case of the procedure *pprogram* the correspondence is exact, since there is only one production with this left-hand side. In the other two procedures a choice must be made between right-hand sides of productions. In the procedure *pdeclaration* the choice is an easy one—if the next symbol is **label** the production

$$\langle declaration \rangle \rightarrow \textbf{label} \ \langle idlist \rangle$$

should be used; if the next symbol is **integer** the production used should be

$$\langle declaration \rangle \rightarrow \textbf{integer} \ \langle idlist \rangle$$

Otherwise there is an error in the input.

> **procedure** *pprogram*;
> **begin** *pblock*; *pdot*;   (3.4)
> **end**; {*pprogram*}

> **procedure** *pdeclaration*;
> **begin if** *nextsymbol* = *qlabel* **then begin** *plabel*; *pidlist*;
>   **end**
>   **else**
>   **if** *nextsymbol* = *qinteger* **then begin** *pinteger*; *pidlist*;   (3.5)
>   **end**
>   **else goto** 1;
> **end**; {*pdeclaration*}

> **procedure** *pstatement*;
> **begin if not** *nextsymbol* **in** [*qminus*, *qidentifier*, *qleftparenthesis*, *qinput*,
>   *qconstant*, *qgoto*, *qif*, *qoutput*, *qbegin*]
>   **then goto** 1;
>   **case** *nextsymbol* **of**
>   *qminus*, *qidentifier*, *qleftparenthesis*, *qinput*, *qconstant*:
>   *passignment*;   (3.6)
>   *qgoto*: *ptransfer*;
>   *qif*: *pconditional*;
>   *qoutput*: *pwrite*;
>   *qbegin*: *pblock*;
>   **end**;
> **end**; {*pstatement*}

The choice of production is not so easy in the procedure *pstatement*. However we note that

1. an ⟨*assignment*⟩ always begins with an ⟨*expression*⟩, which always begins with either −, ⟨*identifier*⟩, (, **input** or ⟨*constant*⟩;
2. a ⟨*transfer*⟩ always begins with **goto**;
3. a ⟨*conditional*⟩ always begins with **if**;
4. a ⟨*write*⟩ always begins with **output**;
5. a ⟨*block*⟩ always begins with **begin**.

Thus, in each case *nextsymbol* provides sufficient information to enable one to deduce the only possible choice of production which can lead to a correct parse.

As mentioned earlier, a procedure should be written for each non-terminal and each terminal symbol in the grammar. The body of the syntax analyzer then consists of a call to *advance input marker*, to initialize *nextsymbol*, followed by a call to the procedure *pprogram*. Two conditions need to be satisfied for the input to be a syntactically correct program. The first is that *pprogram* should terminate normally i.e. the statement **goto** 1 should never be executed. The second is that, on termination, the last input symbol has been read.

The procedures *pdeclaration* and *pstatement* require 1-*lookahead* to decide which production to match against. Other procedures in the grammar will need 2-*lookahead* to make the decision. To illustrate this, consider the non-terminal ⟨*optional label part*⟩. It can be seen from the derivation trees in Figs. 3.1(a) and 3.1(b) that ⟨*identifier*⟩ may be the 1-*lookahead* of both the productions

$$⟨optional\ label\ part⟩ → \Lambda$$

and

$$⟨optional\ label\ part⟩ → ⟨identifier⟩:$$

The dilemma may be resolved by ascertaining whether the symbol following ⟨*identifier*⟩ is " : ". If so the second production should be chosen; otherwise the first is the appropriate choice.

In general we shall say that a grammar is a *strong LL(k) grammar*, where k is a fixed positive integer, if a *k-lookahead* is always sufficient to choose between productions with the same left-hand side when parsing strings in the language defined by the grammar. It can be shown (using techniques discussed later) that the grammar of Table 3.1 is strong LL(2).

Before treating LL grammars formally, let us note that some grammars are not strong LL(k) for any value of k. Suppose that, in order to define ⟨*identifier*⟩, we used the productions

$$⟨identifier⟩ → ⟨identifier⟩\ ⟨letter⟩$$
$$⟨identifier⟩ → ⟨identifier⟩\ ⟨digit⟩$$
$$⟨identifier⟩ → ⟨letter⟩$$

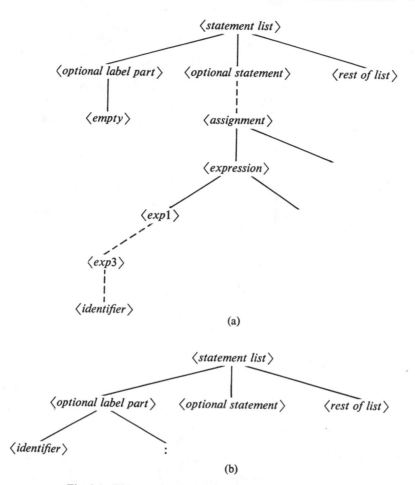

Fig. 3.1   The grammar in Table 3.1 is not strong LL(1).

Then, whatever value of k we pick, we can never hope to be able to parse ⟨*identifier*⟩s of length $\geq k$ using only *k-lookahead* to decide which production to apply. For example let us arbitrarily choose $k = 3$. Consider the trees shown in Figs. 3.2(a) and 3.2(b) and, in particular, consider the ringed productions. Both have the 3-*lookahead* "*AAA*" and so this is not sufficient information to tell us which production was used. The difficulty is caused by the fact that ⟨*identifier*⟩ is *left-recursive* i.e. there is a production ⟨*identifier*⟩ → ⟨*identifier*⟩... in which ⟨*identifier*⟩ is both the left-hand side and the left-most symbol on the right-hand side. (In general a non-terminal A is left-recursive if there is a string w such that $A \Rightarrow^+ Aw$.) Whenever left-recursion occurs the grammar will not be a strong LL(k) grammar for any value of k.

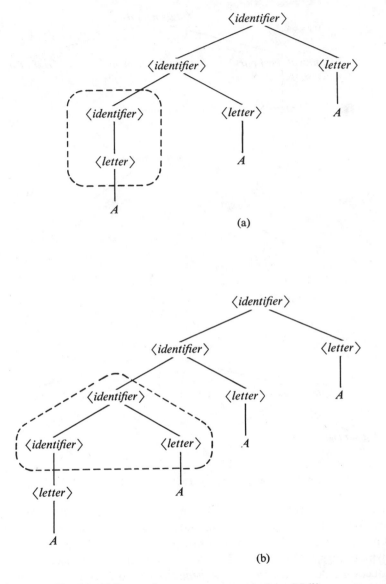

Fig. 3.2 Left-recursive grammars are not strong LL(k).

At this point the reader should ensure that he has a good intuitive grasp of the principles involved in the construction of a recursive-descent parser by constructing some more of the procedures required to parse the grammar in Table 3.1. Should the reader wish to implement the syntax analyzer, he will find the details of a lexical analyzer in the exercises. However, before doing so, it is advisable to refer to Sec. 3.5, which includes a number of general remarks about practical improvements to the method.

The only difficulty in the construction is the choice of production when a procedure is first entered. Particularly difficult are the productions with an empty right-hand side. It is tempting to treat empty productions as the default choice. For example the procedure corresponding to ⟨optional else⟩ might be written as in (3.7).

$$\textbf{procedure } \textit{poptionalelse};$$
$$\textbf{begin if } \textit{nextsymbol} = \textit{qelse}$$
$$\qquad \textbf{then begin } \textit{pelse}; \textit{pstatement} \qquad\qquad (3.7)$$
$$\qquad \textbf{end};$$
$$\textbf{end}; \ \{\textit{poptionalelse}\}$$

(3.7) illustrates how *not* to write the procedures. There are two reasons why. Firstly, we haven't established that **else** is not a possible 1-*lookahead* for the production ⟨optional else⟩ → Λ. Thus the syntax analyzer might flag errors which just aren't there! (Cf. the non-terminal ⟨optional label part⟩.) Secondly the omission of further tests on *nextsymbol* when *nextsymbol* ≠ *qelse* delays the detection of syntax errors. We shall have more to say about this in Chap. 6 but, briefly, it is a major cause of inappropriate error messages and poor error recovery in syntax analyzers. (3.8) shows how the procedure should be written.

$$\textbf{procedure } \textit{poptionalelse};$$
$$\textbf{begin if } \textit{nextsymbol} = \textit{qelse}$$
$$\qquad \textbf{then begin } \textit{pelse}; \textit{pstatement};$$
$$\qquad\qquad \textbf{end} \qquad\qquad\qquad\qquad (3.8)$$
$$\qquad \textbf{else if } \textit{nextsymbol} \neq \textit{qfi}$$
$$\qquad\qquad \textbf{then } \{\textit{error}\} \ \textbf{goto } 1;$$
$$\textbf{end}; \ \{\textit{poptionalelse}\}$$

Having gained some familiarity with the method and identified the main sources of difficulty it is our objective to formalize the method and to use our formalization to develop software tools to help us overcome the difficulties. We shall now present a number of definitions leading up to the definition of a strong LL(k) grammar. Also, to conclude this section, we have summarized the previous discussion by presenting a general schema for constructing a recursive-descent syntax analyzer which uses k-*lookahead* to effect parsing decisions.

Let $G = (N, T, P, S)$ be a context-free grammar. Henceforth we shall assume that all productions in G are useful (cf. Sec. 1.4).

Definition   The function $FIRST_k: T^* \longrightarrow T^*$ is defined by:

$$FIRST_k(x) = x \text{ if } length(x) \leq k$$
$$= u \text{ where } x = uv \text{ and } length(u) = k, \text{ otherwise.}$$

The function $FIRST_k$ is extended to languages in the natural way:

$$FIRST_k(L) = \{FIRST_k(x) \mid x \in L\}.$$

It is very important to note that $FIRST_k(L)$ may contain strings of length less than k. There are two reasons for this. The less important reason is that when the end of the input string has almost been reached, the *k-lookahead* will be a string with less than k symbols. More importantly, our definition makes the statement of Lemma 3.2, below, much more compact and, in consequence, simplifies the description of the algorithms used to calculate *k-lookahead*s. We shall use $T^{\leq k}$ to denote the subset of T^* consisting of strings of length less than or equal to k. Thus $FIRST_k(L) \subseteq T^{\leq k}$.

Definition   Let $A \rightarrow \alpha$ be a production of G. The *k-lookahead* of the production is a subset of T^* defined by:

$$k\text{-}lookahead(A \rightarrow \alpha) = FIRST_k(\{w \mid \exists\, \beta \in (N \cup T)^* \text{ and } u \in T^* \text{ such that}$$
$$S \Rightarrow^* uA\beta \Rightarrow u\alpha\beta \Rightarrow^* uw \in T^*\}).$$

Definition   The grammar G is said to be *strong LL(k)* if, for each distinct pair of productions $A \rightarrow \alpha$ and $A \rightarrow \beta$ in P with the same left-hand side,

$$k\text{-}lookahead(A \rightarrow \alpha) \cap k\text{-}lookahead(A \rightarrow \beta) = \varnothing.$$

Example 1   Referring to the grammar in Table 3.1, we have

$$1\text{-}lookahead(\langle declaration \rangle \rightarrow \textbf{label } \langle idlist \rangle) = \{\textbf{label}\}$$
and $\quad 1\text{-}lookahead(\langle declaration \rangle \rightarrow \textbf{integer } \langle idlist \rangle) = \{\textbf{integer}\}.$

Example 2   Let $G = (\{S, A\}, \{x, y\}, P, S)$, where P consists of

$$S \rightarrow yAx \qquad A \rightarrow yAy \qquad A \rightarrow x$$

Then $3\text{-}lookahead(A \rightarrow yAy) = \{yxy, yyx, yyy\}.$

If a grammar is strong LL(k) we can construct a parser for sentences of the grammar using the following scheme.

For each terminal symbol $a \in T$ we include a procedure *pa*:

procedure pa;
begin
if $nextsymbol = qa$ **then** *advance input marker*   (3.9)
                          else goto 1;
end; {pa}

For each non-terminal symbol $A \in N$ we include a procedure pA:

procedure pA;
var i: **integer**;
begin case *next k symbols* **in**
        k-lookahead $(A \to X_1 \dots X_m)$: **for** $i := 1$ **to** m **do** pX_i;   (3.10)
        k-lookahead $(A \to Y_1 \dots Y_n)$: **for** $i := 1$ **to** n **do** pY_i;
        $\vdots$
        k-lookahead $(A \to Z_1 \dots Z_r)$: **for** $i := 1$ **to** r **do** pZ_i;
        otherwise: goto 1;
        end;
end; {pA}

Note that in these procedures there is a case element for each production with left-hand side A. The **otherwise** element is executed when the *next k symbols* are not in the *k-lookahead* of any production with left-hand side A. The condition for G to be strong $LL(k)$ guarantees that only one of the cases will be executed and that this choice is the only choice which can lead to a successful parse.

Note also that if the production $A \to A$ is among those with left-hand side A, the corresponding case is

$$k\text{-}lookahead(A \to A):;$$

That is, a normal return is executed without advancing the input marker.

The final step is to assemble the procedures as indicated below.

begin label 1, 2;
var *next k symbols*: $T^{\leq k}$;
        k, *inputposn*: **integer**;
procedure *advance input marker*;
begin {*if called when inputposn is greater than the length of
the input string, an error has been detected and goto* 1
*should be executed. Otherwise, this procedure should
increment inputposn by* 1 *and set next k symbols to the
string of symbols from inputposn to inputposn+k−1.
If there are fewer than k symbols remaining, next k
symbols should be set to the remaining symbols. If*

there are no remaining symbols next k symbols should be set to Λ.}

. . .

end; {*advance input marker*}   (3.11)
⟨*procedure declarations*⟩
begin {*main program*}
inputposn := 0;
advance input marker; {*initialize next k symbols*}
{*call pS where S is the start symbol of the grammar*}
pS;
if *all input symbols have been read*
then begin *write* ('*NO SYNTAX ERRORS*'); **goto** 2
        end;
1: *write* ('*SYNTAX ERROR DETECTED-ANALYSIS ABORTED*');
2: **end**.

3.2 CHECKING THE STRONG LL(*k*) CONDITION

We have already emphasized that the main problem in constructing a recursive-descent syntax analyzer is the choice of productions when a procedure is first entered. To resolve this problem we need to be able to compute the *k-lookahead* of each production, for any given integer $k > 0$.

The definition of the *k-lookahead* sets is not too helpful as it stands. The reason is that *k-lookahead*($A \rightarrow \alpha$) is defined to be $FIRST_k(M)$ where M is a set which, generally, has an *infinite* number of elements. Now, we can define an infinite set using finite means (such as a grammar) but it is not possible for us to "calculate" such a set. The most we can do is to enumerate the elements *ad infinitum*. Our aim, therefore, is to redefine the *k-lookahead* sets in terms of other *finite* sets. This aim is realized by Corollary 3.3 below. The first step, however, is Theorem 3.1, which identifies two components in *k-lookahead*($A \rightarrow \alpha$)—namely, the set of strings which can be generated by α and the set of strings which may follow the non-terminal A in a sentence of the language. In all the definitions and theorems we assume we are given a grammar $G = (N, T, P, S)$ and an integer $k > 0$.

Definition   Let $\alpha = X_1 X_2 \ldots X_m \in (N \cup T)^+$. The *language generated by* α, denoted $L(\alpha)$, is defined to be

$$L(\alpha) = \{w \mid w \in T^* \text{ and } w = w_1 w_2 \ldots w_m, \text{ where } X_i \Rightarrow^* w_i \\ \text{for each } i, \ 1 \leq i \leq m\}.$$

In addition, *the language generated by A is*

$$L(A) = \{A\}.$$

Definition   Let $A \in N$. Then $FOLLOW_*(A)$ is defined by

$$FOLLOW_*(A) = \{w \mid w \in T^* \text{ and } S \Rightarrow^* uAw \text{ for some } u \in T^*\}$$

Also

$$FOLLOW_k(A) = FIRST_k(FOLLOW_*(A)).$$

The justification for these definitions is Theorem 3.1.

Theorem 3.1 $k\text{-}lookahead(A \to \alpha) = FIRST_k(L(\alpha) \cdot FOLLOW_*(A))$.

Proof Immediate from the definitions of $L(\alpha)$, $FOLLOW_*(A)$ and $k\text{-}lookahead(A \to \alpha)$. $\square$

A better characterization of *k-lookaheads* can be obtained by using Lemma 3.2.

Lemma 3.2   Let $L_1, L_2, \ldots, L_r \subseteq T^*$. Then

$$FIRST_k(L_1 \cdot L_2 \cdots \cdot L_r) = FIRST_k(FIRST_k(L_1) \cdot FIRST_k(L_2) \cdots \cdot FIRST_k(L_r)).$$

Proof We note that for two words u and $v \in T^*$

$$FIRST_k(u \cdot v) = FIRST_k(FIRST_k(u) \cdot FIRST_k(v))$$

since, if $length(u) \geq k$

$$FIRST_k(u \cdot v) = FIRST_k(u) = FIRST_k(FIRST_k(u) \cdot FIRST_k(v)).$$

and, if $length(u) = l < k$,

$$\begin{aligned}
FIRST_k(u \cdot v) &= u \cdot FIRST_{k-l}(v) \\
&= FIRST_k(u \cdot FIRST_{k-l}(v)) \\
&= FIRST_k(u \cdot FIRST_k(v)) \\
&= FIRST_k(FIRST_k(u) \cdot FIRST_k(v)).
\end{aligned}$$

Hence, for two languages L_1 and L_2.

$$\begin{aligned}
FIRST_k(L_1 \cdot L_2) &= \{FIRST_k(u \cdot v) \mid u \in L_1 \text{ and } v \in L_2\} \\
&= \{FIRST_k(FIRST_k(u) \cdot FIRST_k(v)) \mid u \in L_1 \text{ and } v \in L_2\} \\
&= FIRST_k(FIRST_k(L_1) \cdot FIRST_k(L_2)).
\end{aligned}$$

The general result for r languages follows easily by induction on r. $\square$

Corollary 3.3

$k\text{-}lookahead(A \to X_1 \ldots X_m)$
$= FIRST_k(FIRST_k(L(X_1)) \cdot \cdots \cdot FIRST_k(L(X_m)) \cdot FOLLOW_k(A))$ $(m > 0)$.

and $k\text{-}lookahead(A \to \Lambda) = FOLLOW_k(A)$.

Note that each of the sets $FIRST_k(L(X_i))$ and $FOLLOW_k(A)$ is a finite set (although $L(X_i)$ and $FOLLOW_*(A)$ are generally infinite). Thus, provided we can calculate these sets, we can also calculate the $k\text{-}lookahead$ of each production.

Algorithms for calculating the $FIRST_k$ and $FOLLOW_k$ sets are presented in Secs. 3.2.1 and 3.2.2. In each case the approach is the same—we characterize the sets by a system of simultaneous equations and then employ a simple iterative technique to solve the equations. Let us first consider the computation of the $FIRST_k$ sets.

3.2.1 Calculating $FIRST_k$ Sets

Suppose that we are given the grammar

$$G = (\{S, A\}, \{a, b\}, \{S \to aAS, S \to b, A \to ASb, A \to a\}, S)$$

and are asked to compute $FIRST_2(L(X))$ for each $X \in \{S, A, a, b\}$. This computation is easy for the terminal symbols—by definition, we have

$$FIRST_2(L(a)) = \{a\}$$

and   (3.12)

$$FIRST_2(L(b)) = \{b\}.$$

Now consider the non-terminals S and A. The first step in generating a string w from S must involve one of the two productions with left-hand side S. Thus

$$FIRST_2(L(S)) = FIRST_2(L(a) \cdot L(A) \cdot L(S)) \cup FIRST_2(L(b)). \quad (3.13)$$

Using Lemma 3.2 we may rewrite (3.13) in the form (3.14).

$$FIRST_2(L(S)) = FIRST_2(FIRST_2(L(a)) \cdot FIRST_2(L(A)) \cdot FIRST_2(L(S)))$$
$$\cup FIRST_2(L(b)). \quad (3.14)$$

Similarly (3.15) can be constructed from the productions with left-hand side A:

$$FIRST_2(L(A)) = FIRST_2(FIRST_2(L(A)) \cdot FIRST_2(L(S)) \cdot FIRST_2(L(b)))$$
$$\cup FIRST_2(L(a)). \quad (3.15)$$

The equations (3.12), (3.14) and (3.15) form a system of simultaneous equations in the unknowns $FIRST_2(L(a))$, $FIRST_2(L(b))$, $FIRST_2(L(S))$

and $FIRST_2(L(A))$. To ensure that this is well understood, let us rewrite the equations using the notation y_X for $FIRST_2(L(X))$:

$$
\begin{aligned}
y_a &= \{a\} \\
y_b &= \{b\} \\
y_S &= FIRST_2(y_a \cdot y_A \cdot y_S) \cup y_b \\
y_A &= FIRST_2(y_A \cdot y_S \cdot y_b) \cup y_a.
\end{aligned}
\tag{3.16}
$$

This is the second time that we have expressed a problem as finding a solution to a set of simultaneous equations. In Chap. 2 a regular expression denoting a regular language was calculated by solving a set of simultaneous equations. The technique used there was an *elimination technique*—the rule R1 enabled one to eliminate unknowns from the right-hand sides. Unfortunately, elimination techniques cannot be applied to (3.16) because the equations are *non-linear*, i.e., the underlying grammar is not left- or right-linear. For such equations a rule like R1 is difficult to formulate. However, one can use an *iterative technique* to solve the equations. An iterative technique involves firstly initializing the unknowns to some approximation to their actual values. Then the approximations are continually substituted into the right-hand sides to obtain new approximations. The substitution process is terminated when eventually the left-hand and right-hand sides are equal. Algorithm 3.1 applies this idea to the calculation of the $FIRST_k$ sets.

> {*Given a grammar $G=(N, T, P, S)$ and an integer $k>0$, this algorithm computes $FIRST_k(L(X))$ for each $X \in N \cup T$.*}
> **var** $F: N \cup T \longrightarrow T^{\leq k}$; {$F(X)$ *is an approximation to* $FIRST_k(L(X))$}
> **begin for** *each* $a \in T$ **do** $F(a) := \{a\}$;
>   **for** *each* $A \in N$ **do** $F(A) := \varnothing$;
>   **for** *each empty-word production* $A \rightarrow \Lambda$, *say* **do** $F(A) := \{\Lambda\}$;
>   **repeat assertion** 1: $(\forall\ X \in N \cup T)\ w \in F(X) \supset \exists\ x \in T^*$
>   *such that* $X \Rightarrow^* x$ *and* $w = FIRST_k(x)$;
>   **for** *each non-empty-word production in P* **do**
>   **begin** *let the production be* $A \rightarrow X_1 X_2 \ldots X_n$;
> $F(A) := F(A) \cup FIRST_k(F(X_1) \cdot F(X_2) \cdot \cdots \cdot F(X_n))$
>   **end**;
>   **until** *no change occurs in $F(A)$ for any $A \in N$*;
>   **assertion** *of correctness*: $(\forall\ X \in N \cup T)\ F(X) = FIRST_k(L(X))$;
> **end**.

Algorithm 3.1

The reader familiar with numerical analysis is likely to be sceptical of the correctness of Algorithm 3.1. Iterative techniques for solving equations

involving real arithmetic do not normally terminate in an absolute sense—
the values "converge" to the correct solution and the program is terminated
when the change in the values is within some specified tolerance. We must
therefore provide a proof that Algorithm 3.1 does indeed terminate. A second
cause for scepticism is that the solution of a system of equations, such as
(3.16), may not be unique. Indeed, it is easily verified that (3.17) and (3.18)
are both solutions of (3.16):

$$y_a = \{a\}, \quad y_b = \{b\}, \quad y_S = \{b, aa\}, \quad y_A = \{a, aa, ab\}, \tag{3.17}$$
$$y_a = \{a\}, \quad y_b = \{b\}, \quad y_S = \{b, aa, ab\}, \quad y_A = \{a, aa, ab, ba, bb\}. \tag{3.18}$$

The solution (3.17) is the *appropriate* solution because each string in y_X (where
$X = S$ or $X = A$) corresponds to a string which can be generated from X.
This is expressed precisely by assertion 1 in Algorithm 3.1. Assertion 1 has
two functions. Firstly it guarantees that Algorithm 3.1 calculates the appropriate solution and, secondly, it defines precisely what is meant by saying
that $F(A)$ is an "approximation" to $FIRST_k(L(A))$. An equivalent way of
expressing assertion 1 is $F(X) \subseteq FIRST_k(L(X))$. This is the form which has
been used in the proof of Theorem 3.4, which asserts that Algorithm 3.1 is
correct.

Theorem 3.4 Algorithm 3.1 correctly calculates $FIRST_k(L(A))$ for all
$A \in N$.

Proof We must prove that

(a) Algorithm 3.1 always terminates, and
(b) when it does, $F(A) = FIRST_k(L(A))$.

   (a) Algorithm 3.1 must terminate after at most $q(t+1)^k + 1$ repeats where
q is the number of non-terminal symbols and t is the number of terminal
symbols. This is because there are less than $(t+1)^k$ different words in $T^{\leq k}$ and
each repeat except the last must add at least one such word to one of the q sets
$F(A)$ for some $A \in N$.
   (b) We first prove that $F(A) \subseteq FIRST_k(L(A))$ for all $A \in N$ on termination of the algorithm. We do this by verifying assertion 1. That is, we show
that $F(A) \subseteq FIRST_k(L(A))$ at all times during the execution of the algorithm.
This is certainly true after initialization and before the first repeat. During
execution of a repeat, $F(A)$ can only be changed by the statement:

$$F(A) := F(A) \cup FIRST_k(F(X_1) \ldots F(X_n))$$

if there is a production $A \rightarrow X_1 X_2 \ldots X_n \in P$. Assume that before its execution $F(B) \subseteq FIRST_k(L(B))$ for all $B \in N$. Then w is added to $F(A)$ by the
statement if

$$w \in FIRST_k(F(X_1)\ldots F(X_n))$$
$$\subseteq FIRST_k(FIRST_k(L(X_1))\ldots FIRST_k(L(X_n)))$$
$$= FIRST_k(L(X_1)\ldots L(X_n)) \qquad \text{(Lemma 3.2)}$$
$$\subseteq FIRST_k(L(A)).$$

Hence $F(A) \subseteq FIRST_k(L(A))$ after execution of the statement. Thus $F(A) \subseteq FIRST_k(L(A))$ at all times during execution and so, in particular, on termination of the algorithm.

We now show that $F(A) \supseteq FIRST_k(L(A))$ on termination of the algorithm. Let the total number of repeats be r and let $F_m(A)$ be the value of $F(A)$ after m repeats if $m \leq r$, and let $F_m(A) = F_r(A)$ if $m > r$. We wish to show that $F_r(A) \supseteq FIRST_k(L(A))$.

Suppose $w \in FIRST_k(L(A))$. Then $\exists$ a word $x \in L(A)$ such that $w = FIRST_k(x)$. Suppose $A \Rightarrow^{p+1} x$. We shall prove, by induction on the length $p+1$ of the derivation sequence, that $w \in F_{p+1}(A)$. Certainly this is true for $p = 0$. For clearly, if $A \rightarrow x \in P$, then $FIRST_k(x)$ is added to $F_1(A)$. Now suppose for all $X \in N$ and for all $u \in L(X)$ with $X \Rightarrow^{\leq p} u$ that $FIRST_k(u) \in F_p(X)$. Suppose the derivation sequence for x is $A \Rightarrow X_1 X_2 \ldots X_n \Rightarrow^p u_1 u_2 \ldots u_n = x$. Clearly $X_i \Rightarrow^{\leq p} u_i$ for each i. Hence, by the induction hypothesis, $FIRST_k(u_i) \in F_p(X_i)$ for each i. Now for each i, let m_i be the smallest integer such that $FIRST_k(u_i) \in F_{m_i}(X_i)$, and let $m = max\{m_i\}$.

Since each $m_i \leq p$ (by induction), $m \leq p$. Moreover on the mth repeat $FIRST_k(u_j)$ is added to $F(X_j)$ for some j, and hence the algorithm does not terminate at this point (i.e. $m < r$). Now on the $(m+1)$th repeat

$$FIRST_k(F_m(X_1) \cdot F_m(X_2) \ldots F_m(X_n))$$

is added to $F(A)$. But

$$w = FIRST_k(u_1 u_2 \ldots u_n) = FIRST_k(FIRST_k(u_1) \ldots FIRST_k(u_n))$$
$$\in FIRST_k(F_m(X_1) \ldots F_m(X_n)).$$

That is, w is added to $F(A)$ at the $(m+1)$th repeat. Finally since $m \leq p$, $F_{m+1}(A) \subseteq F_{p+1}(A)$ and $w \in F_{p+1}(A)$. Thus the induction hypothesis is satisfied and so $F(A) \supseteq FIRST_k(L(A))$ on termination.

We have now proved that, on termination,

$$F(A) \subseteq FIRST_k(L(A)) \subseteq F(A).$$

Hence $F(A) = FIRST_k(L(A))$. $\square$

3.2.2 Calculating $FOLLOW_k$ Sets

The same approach can be used to design an algorithm to calculate the $FOLLOW_k$ sets. Let us consider once again the grammar

$$G = (\{S, A\}, \{a, b\}, \{S \to aAS, \ S \to b, \ A \to ASb, \ A \to a\}, \ S).$$

The construction of a set of equations for $FOLLOW_k(X)$, for each $X \in N$, is slightly tricky. Consider the non-terminal A and suppose we wish to calculate $FOLLOW_2(A)$. There are two instances of A on the right-hand side of a production, viz. within $S \to aAS$ and within $A \to ASb$. Figure 3.3(a) illustrates a general situation in which A is introduced by the first of these productions. By examination of Fig. 3.3(a) it is clear that

$$FOLLOW_*(A) \supseteq L(S) \cdot FOLLOW_*(S).$$

Similarly, by examination of Fig. 3.3(b),

$$FOLLOW_*(A) \supseteq L(S) \cdot \{b\} \cdot FOLLOW_*(A).$$

Since these two productions exhaust the possibilities for introducing A into a string we conclude that

$$FOLLOW_*(A) = L(S) \cdot FOLLOW_*(S) \cup L(S) \cdot \{b\} \cdot FOLLOW_*(A).$$

Hence, using Lemma 3.2,

$$FOLLOW_2(A) = FIRST_2(FIRST_2(L(S)) \cdot FOLLOW_2(S))$$
$$\cup FIRST_2(FIRST_2(L(S)) \cdot \{b\} \cdot FOLLOW_2(A)). \qquad (3.19)$$

Now consider the non-terminal S. There are *three* ways of introducing S into a sentential form. There are two occurrences of S on the rhs of productions—namely $S \to aAS$ and $A \to ASb$. But S is also itself a sentential form. In other words Λ may follow S. Thus the equation for $FOLLOW_2(S)$ is

$$FOLLOW_2(S) = \{\Lambda\} \cup FOLLOW_2(S) \cup FIRST_2(\{b\} \cdot FOLLOW_2(A)). \qquad (3.20)$$

(3.19) and (3.20) form a system of simultaneous equations in the unknowns $FOLLOW_2(A)$ and $FOLLOW_2(S)$. Again, the equations do not have a unique solution. The reader is left to verify that the appropriate solution is

$$FOLLOW_2(A) = \{b, aa, bb\}, \quad FOLLOW_2(S) = \{\Lambda, ba, bb\}.$$

In general terms, the equation for $FOLLOW_k(A)$ where $A \neq S$ and $A \in N$ is

$$FOLLOW_k(A) = \bigcup_{(\beta, B) \,\in\, R(A)} FIRST_k(FIRST_k(L(\beta)) \cdot FOLLOW_k(B)), \qquad (3.21)$$

where

$$R(A) = \{(\beta, B) \mid \exists \text{ occurrence of } A \text{ on the rhs of a production of the form } B \to \alpha A \beta\}.$$

The equation for $FOLLOW_k(S)$ is

$$FOLLOW_k(S) = \{\Lambda\} \cup \bigcup_{(\beta, B) \,\in\, R(S)} FIRST_k(FIRST_k(L(\beta)) \cdot FOLLOW_k(B)).$$
$$(3.22)$$

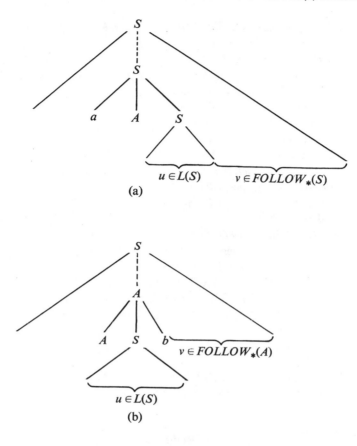

Fig. 3.3   Computing $FOLLOW_*(A)$.

Algorithm 3.2 uses an iterative technique to solve such a system of equations. The algorithm assumes that $FIRST_k(L(X))$ has been calculated and stored in $F(X)$ for each $X \in N \cup T$. The notation $FOL(A)$ means an approximation to $FOLLOW_k(A)$, where "approximation" is precisely defined by assertion 1. Also, as in Algorithm 3.1, assertion 1 guarantees that the appropriate solution to the equations (3.21) and (3.22) is found. One complication—the use of the variable L—has been introduced. Assertion 2, which is easily verified, explains its use. It should also be clear, after a moment's thought, why it is more efficient to access the rhs symbols from right to left rather than from left to right within the inner **for** loop. The proof of correctness of Algorithm 3.2 is one of the exercises.

{*Given a grammar* $G = (N, T, P, S)$, *an integer* $k > 0$ *and* $F(X)$ *for ea*
$X \in (N \cup T)$, *where* $F(X) = FIRST_k(L(X))$, *this algorithm calcula*
$FOLLOW_k(A)$ *for each* $A \in N$.}
var $FOL: N \longrightarrow T^{\leq k}$; {$FOL(A)$ *is an approximation to* $FOLLOW_k(A)$
    L: *set of strings each of length* $\leq k$;
    i: *integer*;
begin for *each* $A \in N$ **do** $FOL(A) := \varnothing$;
      $FOL(S) := \{\Lambda\}$;
repeat assertion 1: $(\forall A \in N)$ $u \in FOL(A) \supset \exists w \in T^*$
                such that $S \Rightarrow^* \alpha A w$ *and* $u = FIRST_k(w)$;
    for *each production in* P **do**
      begin *let production be* $A \rightarrow X_1 X_2 \ldots X_n$;
      if *rhs* $\notin T^*$
      then begin $L := FOL(A)$;
          if $X_n \in N$ **then** $FOL(X_n) := FOL(X_n) \cup L$;
          for $i := n - 1$ **downto** 1 **do**
            begin $L := FIRST_k(F(X_{i+1}) \cdot L)$;
            assertion $2 : L = FIRST_k(L(X_{i+1} \ldots X_n) \cdot FOL(A))$;
            if $X_i \in N$ **then** $FOL(X_i) := FOL(X_i) \cup L$;
            end;
          end;
      end;
until *no change occurs in* $FOL(A)$ *for any* $A \in N$;
assertion *of correctness*: $(\forall A \in N)$ $FOL(A) = FOLLOW_k(A)$;
end.

Algorithm 3.2

3.2.3 A Complete Example

This example gives a complete summary of the steps involved in testin
whether a given grammar is strong LL(k) for a given value of k and, if so
constructing an LL parser from the grammar.

The grammar we shall consider is $G = (\{S, R\}, \{a, b, c\}, P, S)$, wher
P consists of

$$S \rightarrow bRS \qquad S \rightarrow RcSa \qquad S \rightarrow \Lambda$$
$$R \rightarrow acR \qquad R \rightarrow b$$

G is not strong LL(1) because b is an element of the 1-*lookahead* of bot
$S \rightarrow bRS$ and $S \rightarrow RcSa$. We shall therefore test whether G is strong LL(2).

We first apply Algorithm 3.1 to find $FIRST_2(L(S))$ and $FIRST_2(L(R))$. The computation proceeds as follows:

$F(a) := \{a\}$; $F(b) := \{b\}$; $F(c) := \{c\}$;
$F(S) := F(R) := \varnothing$;
for $S \rightarrow \varLambda$ **do** $F(S) := \{\varLambda\}$;

First repeat
　for $R \rightarrow b$　　　**do** $F(R) := \varnothing \cup FIRST_2(\{b\}) = \{b\}$;
　for $R \rightarrow acR$　**do** $F(R) := \{b\} \cup FIRST_2(\{a\}\{c\}\{b\}) = \{b, ac\}$;
　for $S \rightarrow RcSa$ **do** $F(S) := \{\varLambda\} \cup FIRST_2(\{b, ac\}\{c\}\{\varLambda\}\{a\}) = \{\varLambda, bc, ac\}$;
　for $S \rightarrow bRS$ **do** $F(S) := \{\varLambda, bc, ac\} \cup FIRST_2(\{b\}\{b, ac\}\{\varLambda, bc, ac\})$
　　　　　　　　　　　$= \{\varLambda, bc, ac, bb, ba\}$;

Second repeat
　In the second repeat there is no change in $F(S)$ or $F(R)$ and so the algorithm terminates.

　We conclude that

$$FIRST_2(L(S)) = \{\varLambda, bc, ac, bb, ba\}$$

and

$$FIRST_2(L(R)) = \{b, ac\}.$$

Note that the number of repeats executed before termination depends very much on the order in which productions are chosen in the inner **for** statement. With foresight productions were chosen in the order which would ensure termination after one repeat. We now apply Algorithm 3.2 to find the $FOLLOW_2$ sets. Again, the ordering of the productions has been chosen to give the fewest number of repeats.

$FOL(S) := FOL(R) := \varnothing$;
$FOL(S) := \{\varLambda\}$;

First repeat
　for $S \rightarrow RcSa$ **do**
　　$L := \{\varLambda\}$;
　　for $i = 3$ **do** $L := FIRST_2(\{a\} \cdot \{\varLambda\}) = \{a\}$;
　　　　　　$FOL(S) := \{\varLambda\} \cup \{a\} = \{\varLambda, a\}$;
　　for $i = 2$ **do** $L := FIRST_2(\{\varLambda, bc, ac, bb, ba\} \cdot \{a\}) = \{a, bc, ac, bb, ba\}$;
　　for $i = 1$ **do** $L := FIRST_2(\{c\} \cdot \{a, bc, ac, bb, ba\}) = \{ca, cb\}$;
　　　　　　$FOL(R) := \varnothing \cup \{ca, cb\} = \{ca, cb\}$;
　for $S \rightarrow bRS$ **do**
　　$L := \{\varLambda, a\}$; $FOL(S) := \{\varLambda, a\}$;
　　for $i = 2$ **do** $L := FIRST_2(\{\varLambda, bc, ac, bb, ba\} \cdot \{\varLambda, a\})$

$$= \{\Lambda, a, bc, ac, bb, ba\};$$
$$FOL(R) := \{ca, cb\} \cup \{\Lambda, a, bc, ac, bb, ba\}$$
$$= \{\Lambda, a, bc, ac, bb, ba, ca, cb\};$$

for $S \rightarrow \Lambda$ **do** *nothing* ($rhs \in T^*$);
for $R \rightarrow acR$ **do** *no change occurs in FOL(R)*;
for $R \rightarrow b$ **do** *nothing.* ($rhs \in T^*$);

Second repeat
    for $S \rightarrow RcSa$ **do**
      $L := \{\Lambda, a\};$
      for $i = 3$ **do** $L := FIRST_2(\{a\} \cdot \{\Lambda, a\}) = \{a, aa\};$
                     $FOL(S) := \{\Lambda, a\} \cup \{a, aa\} = \{\Lambda, a, aa\};$
      for $i = 2$ **downto** 1 *no change occurs in FOL(R)*;
    for $S \rightarrow bRS$ **do**
      $L := \{\Lambda, a, aa\};$ *FOL(S) not changed*;
      for $i = 2$ **do** $L := \{\Lambda, a, aa, bc, ac, bb, ba\};$
                     $FOL(R) := \{\Lambda, a, aa, bc, ac, bb, ba, ca, cb\};$
      for $i = 1$ **do** *no change occurs in FOL*;
    for *remaining productions, no change occurs in FOL(S) or FOL(R)*.

Third repeat
    In the third repeat there is no change in $FOL(S)$ or $FOL(R)$ and so the algorithm terminates.

    We conclude that

$$FOLLOW_2(S) = \{\Lambda, a, aa\}$$

and

$$FOLLOW_2(R) = \{\Lambda, a, aa, bc, ac, bb, ba, ca, cb\}.$$

The penultimate step is to use Corollary 3.3 to calculate the lookaheads of each production. These are:

    2-lookahead($S \rightarrow RcSa$)
      $= FIRST_2(\{b, ac\} \{c\} \{\Lambda, bc, ac, bb, ba\} \{a\} \{\Lambda, a, aa\})$
      $= \{bc, ac\}$
    2-lookahead($S \rightarrow bRS$)
      $= FIRST_2(\{b\} \{b, ac\} \{\Lambda, bc, ac, bb, ba\} \{\Lambda, a, aa\})$
      $= \{bb, ba\}$
    2-lookahead($S \rightarrow \Lambda$)
      $= FIRST_2(\{\Lambda\} \{\Lambda, a, aa\})$
      $= \{\Lambda, a, aa\}$

2-*lookahead*($R \rightarrow acR$)
$$= FIRST_2(\{a\} \{c\} \{b, ac\} \{\Lambda, a, aa, bc, ac, bb, ba, ca, cb\})$$
$$= \{ac\}$$
2-*lookahead*($R \rightarrow b$)
$$= FIRST_2(\{b\} \{\Lambda, a, aa, bc, ac, bb, ba, ca, cb\})$$
$$= \{b, ba, bb, bc\}.$$

The final step is to compare productions with the same left-hand side. If two such productions have intersecting 2-*lookahead*s the grammar is not strong LL(2). However in our example it is soon checked that the productions with left-hand side S all have distinct lookahead sets, and so also do the productions with left-hand side R. We can therefore construct an LL parser from the productions and the lookaheads. This we have done in Program 3.1 which shows a PASCAL program to parse strings in the grammar. In order not to clutter the program with extraneous issues, it is assumed that the input consists only of as, bs and cs and is terminated by any character other than a, b or c.

Program 3.1

```
program simpleparser (input, output);
label 1, 2;
type leqtwosymbols = (empty, a, b, c, aa, ab, ac, ba, bb, bc, ca, cb, cc);
var  inputchar: char;
     nextsymbol, nextbutonesymbol: leqtwosymbols;
     nexttwosymbols: leqtwosymbols;
     symbol: array[char] of leqtwosymbols;
     concat: array[leqtwosymbols, leqtwosymbols] of leqtwosymbols;

function inputend: Boolean;
begin inputend := eof(input) or (not (inputchar in ['a', 'b', 'c']));
end; {inputend}

procedure advanceinputmarker;
begin nextsymbol := nextbutonesymbol;
      if not eof(input) then read(inputchar);
      if inputend then nextbutonesymbol := empty
              else begin write(inputchar);
                        nextbutonesymbol := symbol[inputchar];
                        end;
      nexttwosymbols := concat[nextsymbol, nextbutonesymbol];
end; {advance input marker}
```

```
procedure pa;
begin if nextsymbol = a then advanceinputmarker
                          else goto 1;
end;  {pa}

procedure pb;
begin if nextsymbol = b then advanceinputmarker
                          else goto 1;
end;  {pb}

procedure pc;
begin if nextsymbol = c then advanceinputmarker
                          else goto 1;
end;  {pc}

procedure pR;
begin {only one symbol is required to choose between the two productions
       with lhs R}
     case nextsymbol of
          a:  begin {chosen production is R→acR}
              pa; pc; pR;
              end;
          b:  {chosen production is R→b} pb;
          c, empty:  {error} goto 1;
     end;
end;  {pR}

procedure pS;
begin {two lookahead is required}
     case nexttwosymbols of
          ba, bb:  begin {chosen production is S→bRS}
                   pb; pR; pS;
                   end;
          bc, ac:  begin {chosen production is S→RcSa}
                   pR; pc; pS; pa;
                   end;
          empty, a, aa:  {chosen production is S→Λ};
          b, c, ab, ca, cb, cc:  {error} goto 1;
     end;
end;  {pS}

{main program}
begin {initialization}
symbol['a'] := a; symbol['b'] := b; symbol['c'] := c;
```

$concat[a, empty] := a$; $concat[b, empty] := b$; $concat[c, empty] := c$;
$concat[a, a] := aa$; $concat[a, b] := ab$; $concat[a, c] := ac$;
$concat[b, a] := ba$; $concat[b, b] := bb$; $concat[b, c] := bc$;
$concat[c, a] := ca$; $concat[c, b] := cb$; $concat[c, c] := cc$;
$concat[empty, empty] := empty$;
$read(inputchar)$; $write(' ')$;
if *inputend* **then begin** *nextsymbol* $:=$ *empty*; *nextbutonesymbol* $:=$ *empty*;
               end
         else **begin** *nextsymbol* $:=$ *symbol[inputchar]*;
              write(inputchar); *read(inputchar)*;
              if *inputend* **then** *nextbutonesymbol* $:=$ *empty*
              else begin *nextbutonesymbol* $:=$ *symbol[inputchar]*;
                write(inputchar);
              end;
           end;
nexttwosymbols $:=$ *concat[nextsymbol, nextbutonesymbol]*;
pS; *writeln*;
if *inputend* **then begin** *writeln(' NO SYNTAX ERRORS')*; **goto** 2;
             end;
1: *writeln*; *writeln(' SYNTAX ERROR DETECTED')*;
2: **end**.

3.2.4 A Test for Ambiguity

We remarked in Sec. 1.2 that, in general, it is impossible to test whether a grammar is unambiguous. On the other hand, Theorem 3.5 asserts that if a grammar is strong LL(k), for some integer k, then it is unambiguous. This is significant because it means that, if we take the trouble to write our context-free definition in a strong LL form, then not only can we construct a parser very easily but we have also ensured that the grammar is unambiguous. Conversely if we test whether a grammar is strong LL and find that it is not, then we have reason to suspect that it may be ambiguous.

The proof of the theorem is obvious. Indeed the theorem will always be true of classes of grammars which can be parsed "deterministically"—that is, for all classes of grammars for which a parsing algorithm exists which, when presented with a choice of next move (such as which production to use), can always make the choice irrevocably, or, synonymously, without "back-tracking".

Theorem 3.5 If the context-free grammar G is strong LL(k) for some integer k, then G is unambiguous.

Proof Suppose, contrary to the theorem, that G is strong LL(k) but also ambiguous. Let $w \in L(G)$ be a word which is the frontier of two distinct derivation trees T_1 and T_2. Suppose the nodes of the trees T_1 and T_2 are traversed simultaneously using a preorder traversal. That is, the nodes are visited in the order given by the following recursive procedure:

visit the root
traverse the subtrees in order from left to right.

Suppose the terminal or non-terminal symbols labeling the nodes of the two trees are compared as the trees are traversed. Let m_1 and m_2 be the first nodes of T_1 and T_2 which are encountered having distinct labels, B_1 and B_2 say. T_1 and T_2 both have roots labeled S (the start symbol of G) so m_1 and m_2 are interior nodes. Let n_1 and n_2 be the fathers of m_1 and m_2. By the choice of m_1 and m_2, n_1 and n_2 both have the same label, A, say. But T_1 and T_2 have the same frontier w. It follows, therefore, that there are two productions $A \rightarrow \alpha B_1 \gamma_1$ and $A \rightarrow \alpha B_2 \gamma_2$ (where $\alpha, \gamma_1, \gamma_2 \in (N \cup T)^*$) such that

$$k\text{-}lookahead(A \rightarrow \alpha B_1 \gamma_1) \cap k\text{-}lookahead(A \rightarrow \alpha B_2 \gamma_2) \neq \varnothing$$

in contradiction to the assumption that G is strong LL(k). Thus the theorem follows.   □

3.3 THE SPECIAL CASE $k=1$

It is very difficult to implement an efficient strong LL(k) test when k is an input parameter. The special case $k = 1$ is much simpler and is also the only case of practical importance for a number of reasons. Firstly, it is usual to try to design a language so that it is strong LL(1) except, perhaps, for a few productions which can be handled in an *ad hoc* manner. Secondly, if the syntax analyzer consistently requires more than one lookahead symbol, error recovery becomes difficult, complications arise in synchronizing error messages with the listing of the input and the efficiency of the syntax analyzer is seriously impaired. Accordingly, we shall not consider the general problem any further but, in this section, we shall develop a PASCAL program to test whether a given grammar G is strong LL(1). Let us begin by specializing the definitions in Sec. 3.1 to the case $k = 1$.

Definition Let $G = (N, T, P, S)$ be a context-free grammar with no useless productions. The functions *NULLABLE*, *FIRST* and *FOLLOW* are defined on $N \cup T$ as follows:

$$NULLABLE(X) = true \quad \text{if } X \Rightarrow^* \Lambda$$
$$= false \quad \text{otherwise}$$

$$FIRST(X) \quad = \{t \mid t \in T \text{ and } X \Rightarrow^* tw \text{ for some } w \in T^*\}$$

$$FOLLOW(X) = \{t \mid t \in T \cup \{\text{eof}\} \text{ and }$$
$$\textbf{S} \text{eof} \Rightarrow^* uXtw \text{ for some } u \in T^* \text{and } w \in (T \cup \{\text{eof}\})^*\}$$

The definition of *NULLABLE* is extended to strings $\alpha \in (N \cup T)^*$ as follows:

$$\begin{aligned} NULLABLE(\alpha) &= true \quad &\text{if } \alpha \Rightarrow^* \Lambda \\ &= false \quad &\text{otherwise} \end{aligned}$$

Definition The function *LOOKAHEAD* is defined on productions of G by

$$LOOKAHEAD(A \rightarrow X_1 \ldots X_m)$$
$$= \bigcup_{i \text{ s.t. } P_i} FIRST(X_i) \cup (\textbf{if } NULLABLE(X_1 \ldots X_m) \textbf{ then } FOLLOW(A) \textbf{ else } \varnothing)$$

where P_i denotes $1 \leq i \leq m$ and $NULLABLE(X_1 \ldots X_{i-1})$.

Definition The grammar G is said to be *strong LL(1)* if and only if for each pair of distinct productions $A \rightarrow \alpha$ and $A \rightarrow \beta$, say, having the same left-hand side, $LOOKAHEAD(A \rightarrow \alpha) \cap LOOKAHEAD(A \rightarrow \beta) = \varnothing$.

These definitions are not simply a rewrite of the definitions in Sec. 3.2 for the case $k = 1$. The major change is in the definition of *LOOKAHEAD*. This definition assumes that G contains no useless symbols. The reader is invited to indicate why. Two other differences introduced for convenience are (a) $FIRST(X)$ is not the same as $FIRST_1(L(X))$ since Λ may be an element of the latter but not the former. (b) To simplify the definition of *FOLLOW* we have assumed that all strings are terminated by a special symbol **eof** which is not an element of T. This means that every non-terminal is followed by at least one symbol and is equivalent to adding a new production $Z \rightarrow \textbf{S} \text{eof}$ to the grammar, where Z is a new sentence symbol. The grammar $G' = (N \cup \{Z\}, T \cup \{\text{eof}\}, P \cup \{Z \rightarrow \textbf{S} \text{eof}\}, Z)$ is called the *augmented form* of G. Henceforth we shall assume that G has already been augmented.

The reader may recall that the concept of a nullable non-terminal was introduced in Chap. 1. Exercise 1.13 asked the reader to modify Program 1.2 so as to compute the nullable non-terminals. This is the first step in the test for a strong LL(1) grammar and we shall assume that it has been completed. The next step is to design efficient algorithms to compute the *FIRST* and *FOLLOW* sets. Our starting point is Algorithms 3.1 and 3.2.

3.3.1 Graph Searching and the *FIRST* and *FOLLOW* Sets

Algorithms 3.1 and 3.2 are directly comparable to Algorithm 1.1, the basic graph-searching algorithm. In that algorithm a set of nodes was continually added to the set of reachable nodes, the main source of inefficiency being the repeated computation of the same set of nodes. Similarly, in Algorithms 3.1 and 3.2 the same strings are added again and again to $F(A)$ and $FOL(A)$. The parallel between the algorithms is closer still and, in fact, we can express the computation of the functions $FIRST$ and $FOLLOW$ as graph searches. The clue is to "invert" the algorithms—that is, rather than compute $FIRST(A)$ and $FOLLOW(A)$ for each $A \in N$, let us compute $FIRST^{-1}(t)$ and $FOLLOW^{-1}(t)$ for each $t \in T$. Here $FIRST^{-1}(t)$ is defined to be the set of symbols X such that $t \in FIRST(X)$ and $FOLLOW^{-1}(t)$ is defined likewise. (3.23) is essentially an "inversion" of the **repeat** statement in Algorithm 3.1.

> **for** *each* $t \in T$ **do**
>   **begin**
>   **repeat for** *each non-empty production in P* **do**
>   **begin** *let the production be* $A \rightarrow X_1 \ldots X_n$;
>   *add A to* $F^{-1}(t)$ *if* $\exists$ *i such that*   (3.23)
> $1 \leq i \leq n$, $NULLABLE(X_1 \ldots X_{i-1})$ *and* $X_i \in F^{-1}(t)$;
>   **end**;
>   **until** *no change occurs in* $F^{-1}(t)$;
>   **end**;

The reader may be able to spot the correspondence between Algorithm 1.1 and (3.23). If not, an example should make the correspondence unmistakable.

Example 3   Let $G = (\{R, S, U, V, Z\}, \{a, b, c, \mathbf{eof}\}, P, Z)$, where P consists of

$$Z \rightarrow S\mathbf{eof}$$
$$S \rightarrow abV$$
$$V \rightarrow UbU$$
$$U \rightarrow SR \qquad U \rightarrow VUU \qquad U \rightarrow \Lambda$$
$$R \rightarrow V \qquad R \rightarrow c$$

U is the only nullable non-terminal in this grammar. Armed with this information we can construct a graph which enables us to determine $FIRST(X)$ for each symbol X in the grammar. The graph is depicted in Fig. 3.4. There is a node in the graph for each symbol in $N \cup T$, with the exception of Z. The nodes corresponding to terminal symbols have been labeled with the symbol whilst, for each $A \in N$, the corresponding node has been labeled $FIRST(A)$. There is an arc from the node corresponding to X to the node corresponding to A if and only if there is a production $A \rightarrow \alpha X \beta$ in the grammar, where $\alpha = \Lambda$ or α is nullable. Thus the production $R \rightarrow V$ introduces an arc from $FIRST(V)$ to $FIRST(R)$. The production $V \rightarrow UbU$ introduces an arc from

FIRST(U) to *FIRST(V)* and an arc from *b* to *FIRST(V)*. (The latter arc is added because *U* is nullable.)

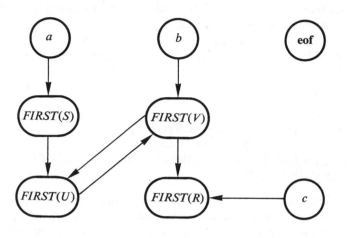

Fig 3.4   The *FIRST* graph.

It is clear from the method of constructing arcs that there is a path from the node labeled t ($t \in T$) to the node labeled *FIRST(A)* ($A \in N$) if and only if $A \Rightarrow^* t\alpha$ for some $\alpha \in (N \cup T)^*$ i.e. if and only if $t \in FIRST(A)$. From Fig. 3.4 we therefore deduce that

$$FIRST(S) = \{a\}$$
$$FIRST(U) = FIRST(V) = \{a, b\} \qquad (3.24)$$
$$FIRST(R) = \{a, b, c\}.$$

Further insight can be gained by comparing the graph in Fig. 3.4 with the system of equations defining the *FIRST* sets. The system of equations for the grammar of Example 3 is shown in (3.25).

$$
\begin{array}{ll}
FIRST(\text{eof}) = \{\text{eof}\} & FIRST(a) = \{a\} \\
FIRST(b) \ \ = \{b\} & FIRST(c) = \{c\} \\
FIRST(S) \ \ = FIRST(a) & \\
FIRST(V) \ \ = FIRST(U) \cup FIRST(b) & \qquad (3.25) \\
FIRST(U) \ \ = FIRST(S) \cup FIRST(V) & \\
FIRST(R) \ \ = FIRST(V) \cup FIRST(c) &
\end{array}
$$

The relationship between this set of equations and Fig. 3.4 is immediate— each arc in the graph corresponds to a term on the right-hand side of the equations.

Note that the cycle in the graph between the nodes *FIRST(U)* and *FIRST(V)* indicates that both *U* and *V* are left-recursive and so the grammar cannot be strong LL. Nevertheless, we shall continue to use this example to illustrate the construction of the *FOLLOW* sets.

Having identified the computation of *FIRST* with graph-searching it is natural to seek a similar result for *FOLLOW*. The clue is the system of equations defining the *FOLLOW* sets. (3.26) is the system of equations for our example grammar.

$$FOLLOW(S) = \{\textbf{eof}\} \cup FIRST(R)$$
$$FOLLOW(V) = FOLLOW(S) \cup FIRST(U) \cup FIRST(U)$$
$$\cup FOLLOW(U) \cup FOLLOW(R) \tag{3.26}$$
$$FOLLOW(U) = FIRST(b) \cup FOLLOW(V) \cup FIRST(U) \cup FOLLOW(U)$$
$$FOLLOW(R) = FOLLOW(U)$$

(3.26) has been used to construct Fig. 3.5. Again, arcs in the graph correspond to terms on the right-hand sides of the equations. Figure 3.6 is simply the combination of Figs. 3.4 and 3.5. In Fig. 3.6 there is a path from *t* to *FOLLOW(A)* if and only if $t \in FOLLOW(A)$. Thus we deduce that

$$FOLLOW(S) = FOLLOW(V) = FOLLOW(U) = FOLLOW(R)$$
$$= \{\textbf{eof}, a, b, c\} \tag{3.27}$$

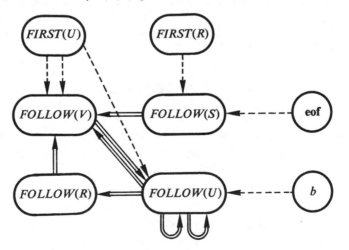

Fig. 3.5   The *FOLLOW* graph.

The construction of the system of equations (3.26) or, equivalently, Fig. 3.5 is slightly complicated. Two types of arc have been distinguished by the use of dotted and solid lines. To construct the arcs to *FOLLOW(A)* one

considers each occurrence of A on the right-hand side of a production. Let
such an occurrence be $B \rightarrow \alpha A \beta$. Now, if β has the form $\gamma X \delta$ and γ is nullable,
an arc is added from the node corresponding to $FIRST(X)$ to $FOLLOW(A)$.

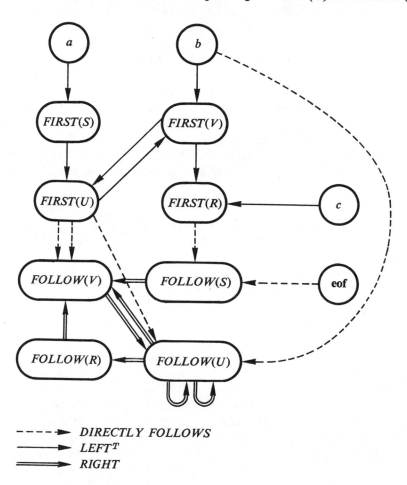

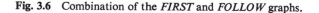

Fig. 3.6 Combination of the $FIRST$ and $FOLLOW$ graphs.

These are the dotted arcs in Fig. 3.5. For example, the arc from $FIRST(R)$
to $FOLLOW(S)$ is introduced by the occurrence of S in $U \rightarrow SR$. A second
example is the *two* dotted arcs from $FIRST(U)$ to $FOLLOW(V)$. One occurs
because U is adjacent to V in the production $U \rightarrow VUU$. The second occurs

because U is nullable and UU follows V in the production $U \rightarrow VUU$. The solid arcs in Fig. 3.5 connect $FOLLOW$ nodes to $FOLLOW$ nodes. In general, if A occurs in a production $B \rightarrow \alpha A \beta$ and β is nullable, then an arc is introduced from $FOLLOW(B)$ to $FOLLOW(A)$. This is because anything which can follow B can also follow A. Examples are the arcs from $FOLLOW(S)$ to $FOLLOW(V)$—this is caused by the occurrence of V in $S \rightarrow abV$—and from $FOLLOW(V)$ to $FOLLOW(U)$—arising from the occurrence of V in $U \rightarrow VUU$. Finally, one arc, which is easily forgotten but should not be, is that from **eof** to $FOLLOW(S)$. This arc corresponds to our convention that the input string is followed by an end-of-file marker and is introduced by the occurrence of S in the production $Z \rightarrow Seof$.

We can summarize the results of this section by defining three relations which we shall call $LEFT^T$, $RIGHT$ and $DIRECTLY FOLLOWS$. Theorem 3.6 expresses the computation of $FIRST$ and $FOLLOW$ in terms of these relations.

Definition Let $G = (N, T, P, Z)$ be a context-free grammar. The relation $LEFT^T$ is defined on $(N \cup T) \times N$ by $X LEFT^T A$ if and only if there is a production $A \rightarrow \alpha X \beta$ where α is nullable.

The relation $RIGHT$ is defined on $N \times N$ by $A RIGHT B$ if and only if there is a production $A \rightarrow \alpha B \beta$ where β is nullable.

The relation $DIRECTLY FOLLOWS$ is defined on $(N \cup T) \times N$ by $X DIRECTLY FOLLOWS A$ if and only if there is a production $B \rightarrow \alpha A \beta X \gamma$ where β is nullable.

Note that $X LEFT^T A$ if and only if there is an arc from the node corresponding to $FIRST(X)$ to the node $FIRST(A)$. Also $A RIGHT B$ if and only if there is a solid arc from $FOLLOW(A)$ to $FOLLOW(B)$. Finally, $X DIRECTLY FOLLOWS A$ if and only if there is a dotted arc from the node corresponding to $FIRST(X)$ to $FOLLOW(A)$. (The superscript T in $LEFT^T$ indicates that a matrix representation of $LEFT^T$ is the transpose of the matrix representation of $LEFT$. The relation $LEFT$ is defined by $A LEFT X$ if and only if there is a production $A \rightarrow \alpha X \beta$, where α is nullable.)

Definition The relations $(LEFT^T)^*$ and $RIGHT^*$ are defined as follows:

$X (LEFT^T)^* A$ if and only if $X = A$ or there is a sequence of symbols $X_0, X_1, \ldots, X_r$ where $r \geq 1$, $X = X_0$, $A = X_r$ and $X_{i-1} LEFT^T X_i$ for each i, $1 \leq i \leq r$.

$A RIGHT^* B$ if and only if $A = B$ or there is a sequence of symbols $A_0, A_1, \ldots, A_r$ where $r \geq 1$, $A = A_0$, $B = A_r$ and $A_{i-1} RIGHT A_i$ for each i, $1 \leq i \leq r$.

The relations $(LEFT^T)^*$ and $RIGHT^*$ correspond to paths through the relevant graphs. Observe once again the use of * to indicate an indefinite iteration.

Theorem 3.6 Let $G = (N, T, P, Z)$ be an augmented context-free grammar with no useless productions. Let $t \in T$ and $A \in N$. Then $A \in FIRST^{-1}(t)$ if and only if $t (LEFT^T)^* A$. Also $A \in FOLLOW^{-1}(t)$ if and only if for some $B \in N$ and $X \in N \cup T$, $X \in FIRST^{-1}(t)$, X DIRECTLY FOLLOWS B and B RIGHT*A.

Let $A \to \alpha \in P$. Then $t \in LOOKAHEAD(A \to \alpha)$ if and only if either α is nullable and $A \in FOLLOW^{-1}(t)$ or $\alpha = \beta X \gamma$ for some $\beta, \gamma \in (N \cup T)^*$, $X \in N \cup T$ where β is nullable and $X \in FIRST^{-1}(t)$.

3.3.2 An Efficient Algorithm

In principle a test for the strong LL(1) condition consists of first constructing the graph of the relations $LEFT^T$, DIRECTLY FOLLOWS and RIGHT and, secondly, performing a graph search to determine the FIRST and FOLLOW sets of each symbol. The LOOKAHEAD sets of each production can then be computed and compared in order to determine whether the grammar is strong LL(1). In practice all of these operations are intertwined and the resulting algorithm is quite difficult to follow. As a first step, Algorithm 3.3 describes the basic structure of the calculation of the FIRST and FOLLOW sets.

> {*augment G*} $P := P \cup \{Z \to \textbf{Seof}\}$; $T := T \cup \{\textbf{eof}\}$; $N := N \cup \{Z\}$;
> **for** *each* $t \in T$ **do**
>   **begin**
>   *perform a graph search to determine all X such that* $t (LEFT^T)^*$ X;
>   *add all such X to* $FIRST^{-1}(t)$;
>   **whenever** *some X is added to* $FIRST^{-1}(t)$ **do**
>   **begin**
>   *compute all B such that X* DIRECTLY FOLLOWS B;
>   **for** *each such B* **do**
>   **for** *each A such that B* RIGHT* A **do** *add A to* $FOLLOW^{-1}(t)$;
>   **end**;
>   **end**;

Algorithm 3.3

The next step is to incorporate the computation of LOOKAHEAD sets. This has been done in Algorithm 3.4. Additionally, the computation of DIRECTLY FOLLOWS has been refined in Algorithm 3.4.

augment G;
for *each t ∈ T* **do**
  begin
  perform a graph search to determine all X such that
    t (LEFT^T)* X; add all such X to FIRST$^{-1}(t)$;
  whenever *some X is added to FIRST$^{-1}(t)$* **do**
    begin
    for *each occurrence of X on the rhs of a production* **do**
      begin *let the occurrence be A→αXβ*;
      if α *is nullable*
      then *add t to LOOKAHEAD(A→αXβ), simultaneously*
        checking strong LL(1) condition;

addtopredecessors ⎰

      for *each non-terminal B preceding X on the rhs and*
        separated from X by nullable symbols **do**
      begin {*X DIRECTLY FOLLOWS B*}
      for *each A such that B RIGHT* A* **do**
        begin *add A to FOLLOW$^{-1}(t)$*;
        add t to lookahead of all nullable productions with
        lhs A, simultaneously checking strong LL(1)
        condition;
        end;
      end;

    end;
    end;
  end;

Algorithm 3.4

Algorithm 3.4 is already quite long and convoluted. Indeed, it is more complex than it looks, since our use of "*perform a graph search to*" and "**whenever**" disguise much of its complexity. In the final implementation, parts of Algorithm 3.4 have been delegated to procedures. One such part forms the procedure *addtopredecessors*, the body of which has been indicated in the algorithm. Additionally, a procedure *addtolookahead* has been written which adds a given terminal symbol to the lookahead of a given production, simultaneously checking the strong LL(1) condition.

Two important details are still outstanding. The first of these is the computation of *RIGHT**. This will, of course, involve a graph search. However, it is important to note that *RIGHT** is independent of the value of the terminal symbol *t* and so should be computed and tabulated before executing Algorithm 3.4. Secondly, efficiency dictates that the test "α *is nullable*"

involves a single operation rather than testing each symbol of α within the
loop. This is easily achieved by associating a Boolean quantity, *nullablepredecessors*, say, with each rhs position. The value of *nullablepredecessors*
for the ith position of $A \rightarrow X_1 \ldots X_n$ is *true* if and only if $i = 1$ or $i > 1$ and
all of $X_1 \ldots X_{i-1}$ are nullable. Algorithm 3.5 indicates these details as well as
explicitly including the computation of $(LEFT^T)^*$.

augment G;
compute nullable non-terminals; {Exercise 1.13}
{set nullablepredecessors}
for *each non-empty production* **do**
  begin *let the production be $A \rightarrow X_1 \ldots X_m$; null := true;*
  for $i := 1$ **to** m **do**
    begin *set nullablepredecessors of ith position to null;*
    null := null **and** *nullable$[X_i]$;*
    end;
  end;
construct RIGHT;
perform a graph search to calculate RIGHT*;
{ calculate LOOKAHEAD sets}
for *each $t \in T$* **do**
  begin *{perform a graph search to determine all X such that $t\ (LEFT^T)^*\ X$}*
  $(LEFT^T)^*(t) := \{t\}; frontier := \{t\};$
  repeat *choose and remove X from frontier;*
    $\{X \in FIRST^{-1}(t)\}$
    for *each occurrence of X on the rhs of a production* **do**
      begin *let the occurrence be $A \rightarrow \alpha X \beta$;*
      if α *is nullable*
      then begin *add t to LOOKAHEAD($A \rightarrow \alpha X \beta$), simultaneously*
              checking strong LL(1) condition;
        if $A \notin (LEFT^T)^*(t)$
        then *add A to frontier and $(LEFT^T)^*(t)$;*
        end;
      addtopredecessors(t, rhsposn); {see Algorithm 3.4}
      end;
  until *frontier $= \varnothing$;*
  end;

Algorithm 3.5

3.3.3 Implementing the Algorithm

The implementation of Algorithm 3.5 is long and arduous but straightforward. The most complicated data structure required is a linear list. Program 3.2 is the listing of a major part of a PASCAL implementation and

Table 3.2 is a sample output from the program. The input procedures are almost identical to those in Program 1.2 and have been omitted. Also omitted are the procedures *computeterminatingproductions*, *computesymbolsgenerated-byS* and *computenullablenonterminals*. The latter two procedures were set as exercises in Chap. 1.

LOOKAHEAD SETS

SL

PRODUCTION	SL	::=	ST	;	SL		
LOOKAHEAD	IF	ID					
PRODUCTION	SL	::=					
LOOKAHEAD	FI	ELSE	EOF				

ST

PRODUCTION	ST	::=	IF	U	THEN	SL	E	FI
LOOKAHEAD	IF							
PRODUCTION	ST	::=	U					
LOOKAHEAD	ID							

U

PRODUCTION	U	::=	ID
LOOKAHEAD	ID		

E

PRODUCTION	E	::=	ELSE	SL
LOOKAHEAD	ELSE			
PRODUCTION	E	::=		
LOOKAHEAD	FI			

END OF OUTPUT

Table 3.2   Output from Program 3.2.

The efficient computation of the relation *RIGHT* necessitates the introduction of the field *predecessor* in the definition of *rhsitem* and the field *lastrhsposn* in the definition of *production*. These two fields allow one to access the symbols on the right-hand side of a production beginning with the last symbol and proceeding from right to left to the first symbol. The setting of these fields (together with any operations required by *computesymbols-generatedbyS* and *computenullablenonterminals*) is the only modification necessary to the input procedures.

The function of the procedure *computesymbolsgeneratedbyS* is to find all symbols X such that $S \Rightarrow^* uXv$ for some $u,v \in T^*$. It should also create the following lists:

1. the useful terminals;
2. the useful non-terminals;
3. · the useful, non-empty productions (a production is non-empty if its right-hand side is not Λ);
4. the occurrences of each useful symbol on the right-hand side of useful productions.

The pointers *firstterminal*, *firstnonterminal* and *firstproduction* should be set to point to the first item in each of lists 1 to 3 respectively. The fields *firstoccurrence* of *hashtableentry* and *nextoccurrence* of *rhssymbol* should be used to form the fourth list.

The procedures *constructRIGHT* and *calculateRIGHTSTAR* construct the lists $RIGHT[A]$ and $RIGHTSTAR[A]$ for each non-terminal A, respectively. A graph search is used within *calculateRIGHTSTAR*, the variable *inrightstar* taking the place of *reached* in Program 1.1. The arcs are defined by the relation *RIGHT*. Similarly, *inlefttrstar* takes the place of *reached* in the graph search to compute the *FIRST* sets (procedure *constructFIRSTand-FOLLOWsets*). The value of the terminal symbol t is implicit in the variables *FOLLOW*, *inlookahead* and *inlefttrstar*. For example, $FOLLOW[A]$ is *true* if the current value of t has already been added to the *FOLLOW* set of A.

Normally items are added to the front of a list, this being the simplest method. However, terminal symbols are added to the rear of the list of lookahead symbols of a given production. This is for aesthetic reasons since it is better to output the terminal symbols in the order in which they were input to the program. Similarly *EOF* is added to the rear of the list of terminal symbols. Z is not added to the list of non-terminals because we do not wish to output the production with left-hand side Z. Note that augmenting the grammar takes place in two steps. Before any data have been read, Z and *EOF* are added to the hash table and their class is defined as *neither*. This prevents one from using these symbols within the grammar. When the grammar has been read the classes of Z and *EOF* are redefined and the production $Z \rightarrow S\ EOF$ is added.

The procedure *addtolookahead* is slightly complicated. If the terminal symbol t is already in the lookahead of production p when the procedure is called, then the grammar is certainly not strong LL(1). However, rather than output the single umbrella statement "not strong LL(1)" the program identifies the non-terminals which are not strong LL(1). For example, Table 3.3 illustrates the output for a very simple grammar. Note that A will be added twice to the lookahead of S, but it is the non-terminal R which prevents the grammar from being strong LL(1). The Boolean variable *nonLL1* has, therefore, been defined for each non-terminal symbol. On termination *nonLL1[A]* = *true* if and only if there are two distinct productions $A \to \alpha$ and $A \to \beta$ such that $LOOKAHEAD(A \to \alpha) \cap LOOKAHEAD(A \to \beta) \neq \varnothing$. The setting of *nonLL1* is the sole complication in *addtolookahead*.

LOOKAHEAD SETS

S

PRODUCTION	S	::=	R
LOOKAHEAD	A		

R		*** NOT STRONG LL(1) ***	
PRODUCTION	R	::=	A
LOOKAHEAD	A		
PRODUCTION	R	::=	A B
LOOKAHEAD	A		

END OF OUTPUT

Table 3.3 A non-LL(1) grammar.

The structures of *constructFIRSTandFOLLOWsets* and *addtopredecessors* follow closely their descriptions in Algorithms 3.4 and 3.5 and should require no further explanation.

Program 3.2

```
program LL1test(input,output);
label 1;
const primeno = 997;
      allasterisks = '*******';
      free = '       ';
      maxsymbollength = 7;
      n = primeno;

type hashindex = 0 .. primeno; symbol = hashindex;
     terminal = hashindex; nonterminal = hashindex;
     symbollink =↑ symbolitem;
     symbolitem = record X: symbol; next: symbollink;
                  end;
     rhslink =↑ rhsitem;
```

Program 3.2   (Continued)

productionlink $=\uparrow$ *production*;
production = **record** *lhs*: *nonterminal*; *length*: *integer*;
        firstrhsposn, lastrhsposn: *rhslink*;
        nextlhsoccurrence: *productionlink*;
        lookahead: **record** *first, last*: *symbollink*;
               end;
       next: *productionlink*;
     end;
rhssymbol = **record** *h*: *hashindex*;
        nextoccurrence: *rhslink*; {*next occurrence of this*
          symbol on rhs of a production}
     end;
rhsitem =   **record** *X*: *rhssymbol*;
        next, predecessor: *rhslink*;
        p: *productionlink*; {*production in which item occurs*}
        nullablepredecessors: *Boolean*;
     end;
symbolclass = (*term, nonterm, neither*);
hashtableentry = **record** *sym*: *alfa*;
        case *class*: *symbolclass* **of**
        term, nonterm: (*terminating*: *Boolean*;
          firstlhsoccurrence: *productionlink*;
          firstoccurrence: *rhslink*);
        neither: ( );
      end;
frontierindex = $1 .. n$; *zeroorfrontierindex* = $0 .. n$;

var   *hashtable*: **array**[*hashindex*] **of** *hashtableentry*;
   Z, S: *nonterminal*; *endoffile*: *terminal*;
   inputerror: *Boolean*;
   nullable: **array**[*symbol*] **of** *Boolean*;
     {*nullable*[*X*] = *true iff* $X \Rightarrow^* \Lambda$}
   firstproduction: *productionlink*; {*pointer to list of non-empty*
                  productions}
   RIGHT, RIGHTSTAR: **array**[*nonterminal*] **of** *symbollink*;
   firstterminal, firstnonterminal: *symbollink*;
     {*pointers to lists of useful terminals and non-terminals,*
      respectively}
   lastterminal, lastnonterminal: *symbollink*;
   nonLL1: **array**[*nonterminal*] **of** *Boolean*;

Program 3.2   (Continued)

nullableprodn: **array**[*nonterminal*] **of** *productionlink*;
{*nullableprodn*[*A*] *is* **nil** *if A is not nullable. Otherwise, it is the production with lhs A which has a nullable rhs. If more than one such production exists the grammar cannot be LL*(1) *and the execution is aborted.*}

{*The following variables are declared globally because of restrictions on the implementation used to debug the code. It is preferable to declare them locally to construct FIRSTandFOLLOWsets.*}
inlookahead, FOLLOW: **array**[*nonterminal*] **of** *Boolean*;
inlefttrstar: **array**[*symbol*] **of** *Boolean*;
{*Variables used in the input procedures have been omitted.*}

{*Refer to Program* 1.2 *for the text of the following procedures*}
procedure *getsymbol*;
. . .

procedure *searchhashtableforcursymbol*;
. . .

procedure *printproduction*(*p*: *productionlink*);
. . .

procedure *readrepresentationofreplacementsymbol*;
. . .

procedure *readin*(*kind*: *symbolclass*);
. . .

procedure *readproductions*;
{*Changes which need to be made are*:
1.   *Set lastrhsposn for each production.*
2.   *Set predecessor of each rhsposn.*
3.   *Changes necessitated by the computation of the nullable non-terminals and the symbols generated by S.*
4.   *Remove instructions adding productions to the list of empty productions.*}
. . .

procedure *readstartsymbol* (**var** *S*: *nonterminal*);
begin *writeln*; *writeln*(' *START SYMBOL*'); *writeln*(' —————');
writeln; *getsymbol*; *searchhashtableforcursymbol*;
if not *found* **then begin** *writeln*('   ': *chposn*−1, ' × *UNRECOGNIZABLE*',
                                ' *SYMBOL*');
                    inputerror := *true*;
                end

Program 3.2　(Continued)

else if *hashtable[curhashindex].class* $\neq$ *nonterm*
　　then begin *inputerror* := *true*;
　　　　　writeln (' '*: chposn* $- 1$, ' $\times$ *START SYMBOL MUST BE A'*,
　　　　　　　' *NON-TERMINAL'*);
　　　　end
　　else $S := curhashindex$;
{*skip the asterisks*}
getsymbol;
if *cursymbol* $\neq$ *allasterisks*
then begin *writeln*(' '*: chposn* $- 1$,' $\times$ *ROW OF ASTERISKS EXPECTED'*);
　　inputerror := *true*;
　　end;
end; {*read start symbol*}

procedure *computeterminatingproductions*; {*see Program 1.2*}
. . .

procedure *computesymbolsgeneratedbyS*;
{*Exercise: Involves using a graph search to find those symbols X such that*
$S \Rightarrow * \ldots X \ldots$.
The following lists should also be created.
　1.　*The useful terminals.*
　2.　*The useful non-terminals.*
　3.　*The useful, non-empty productions.*
　4.　*The occurrences of each useful symbol on the rhs of useful productions.*}
. . .

procedure *computenullablenonterminals*;
{*Exercise: Almost identical to the computation of the terminating*
productions. The following variables should be set on exit from the procedure.
　1.　*nullable*　　　*nullable[A] = true iff* $A \Rightarrow * \Lambda$.
　2.　*nullableprodn nullableprodn[A] is undefined if A is not nullable.*
　　　　　　Otherwise nullableprodn[A] = p where p↑.lhs = A and
　　　　　　the rhs of p is nullable. If more than one such
　　　　　　production occurs the execution should be terminated.}
. . .

procedure *addZandEOFtohashtable*;
var $i: 1 \ldots maxsymbollength$; a: **array**$[0 \ldots maxsymbollength]$ **of** *char*;
begin $a[1] := 'Z'$; *curhashindex* := $ord('Z')$ **mod** *primeno*;
for $i := 2$ **to** *maxsymbollength*

Program 3.2   (Continued)

do begin $a[i] := '$ $'; curhashindex := ((curhashindex * o) + ord('$ $'))$
                                   mod *primeno*
   end;

$pack(a, 1, cursymbol); searchhashtableforcursymbol; Z := curhashindex;$
$hashtable[Z].sym := cursymbol; hashtable[Z].class := neither;$
$a[1] := 'E'; curhashindex := ord('E') \textbf{ mod } primeno;$
$a[2] := 'O'; curhashindex := ((curhashindex * o) + ord('O')) \textbf{ mod } primeno;$
$a[3] := 'F'; curhashindex := ((curhashindex * o) + ord('F')) \textbf{ mod } primeno;$
for $i := 4$ **to** *maxsymbollength* **do**
      begin $a[i] := '$ $'; curhashindex := ((curhashindex*o) + ord('$ $'))$
                                   mod *primeno*
      end;
$pack(a, 1, cursymbol); searchhashtableforcursymbol;$
$endoffile := curhashindex;$
$hashtable[endoffile].sym := cursymbol; hashtable[endoffile].class := neither;$
end;   {*add Z and EOF to hashtable*}

procedure *addextraproduction*;
var p: *productionlink*; *rhsposn*: *rhslink*; *pt*: *symbollink*;
begin {*adds extra production* $Z \rightarrow$ Seof *to list*}
$hashtable[Z].class := nonterm; hashtable[endoffile].class := term;$
$new(p); p\uparrow.next := firstproduction; firstproduction := p;$
with $p\uparrow$ **do**
      begin $lhs := Z; nextlhsoccurrence := \textbf{nil};$
      $new(rhsposn); firstrhsposn := rhsposn; rhsposn\uparrow.p := p;$
      with $rhsposn\uparrow$ **do**
            begin $X.h := S; X.nextoccurrence := hashtable[S].firstoccurrence;$
            $hashtable[S].firstoccurrence := rhsposn; predecessor := \textbf{nil};$
            end;
      $new(rhsposn); lastrhsposn := rhsposn; rhsposn\uparrow.next := \textbf{nil};$
      $rhsposn\uparrow.predecessor := firstrhsposn; rhsposn\uparrow.p := p;$
      with $rhsposn\uparrow$ **do**
            begin $X.h := endoffile; X.nextoccurrence := \textbf{nil};$
            $hashtable[endoffile].firstoccurrence := rhsposn;$
            end;
      end;
$rhsposn := p\uparrow.firstrhsposn; rhsposn\uparrow.next := p\uparrow.lastrhsposn;$
$hashtable[Z].firstlhsoccurrence := p;$
$new(pt); pt\uparrow.X := endoffile; pt\uparrow.next := \textbf{nil};$

Program 3.2   (Continued)

```
if firstterminal = nil then firstterminal := pt
                        else lastterminal↑.next := pt;
lastterminal := pt;
end; {add extra production}

procedure setnullablepredecessors;
var p: productionlink; rhsposn: rhslink; null: Boolean;
begin p := firstproduction;
while p ≠ nil do
    begin rhsposn := p↑.firstrhsposn;
    repeat rhsposn↑.nullablepredecessors := true;
        if hashtable[rhsposn↑.X.h].class ≠ nonterm
        then null := false
        else null := nullable[rhsposn↑.X.h];
        rhsposn := rhsposn↑.next;
    until (rhsposn = nil) or not null;
    p := p↑.next;
    end;
end; {set nullablepredecessors}

procedure add(X: symbol; var pa: symbollink);
var pb: symbollink;
{adds the symbol X to the list of symbols pointed to by pa. No check is
made on whether X is already in the list}
begin new(pb); pb↑.X := X; pb↑.next := pa; pa := pb;
end; {add}

procedure constructRIGHT;
var p: productionlink; rhsposn: rhslink;
    X: symbol; lhs: nonterminal;
    pA: symbollink; null: Boolean;
begin {initialize RIGHT—RIGHT[A] is a pointer to a list of non-terminals
          B such that A RIGHT B}
pA := firstnonterminal;
while pA ≠ nil do
    begin RIGHT[pA↑.X] := nil; pA := pA↑.next;
    end;

p := firstproduction;
while p ≠ nil do
    begin rhsposn := p↑.lastrhsposn; lhs := p↑.lhs;
```

Program 3.2 (Continued)

```
    repeat  X := rhsposn↑.X.h;
        if hashtable[X].class = nonterm then begin  add(X, RIGHT[lhs]);
                                                     null := nullable[X];
                                              end
                                         else null := false;
            rhsposn := rhsposn↑.predecessor;
        until (rhsposn = nil) or not null;
        p := p↑.next;
        end;
end;  {construct RIGHT}


procedure calculateRIGHTSTAR;
var A, B, C: nonterminal; pA, pB, pC: symbollink;
    inrightstar: array[nonterminal] of Boolean;
    top: zeroorfrontierindex;
    frontier: array[frontierindex] of nonterminal;


begin {performs a graph search to compute the relation RIGHT*}
pA := firstnonterminal;
while pA ≠ nil do
    begin A := pA↑.X; pA := pA↑.next;
    {initialize RIGHTSTAR[A]—RIGHTSTAR[A] is a pointer to a list
     of non-terminals B such that A RIGHT* B}
    pB := firstnonterminal;
    while pB ≠ nil do
        begin B := pB↑.X; pB := pB↑.next; inrightstar[B] := false;
        end;
    RIGHTSTAR[A] := nil; add(A, RIGHTSTAR[A]);
    inrightstar[A] := true;
    top := 1; frontier[top] := A;
    repeat {remove top element}
        B := frontier[top]; top := top − 1; {A RIGHT* B}
        {Add all C such that B RIGHT C to RIGHTSTAR[A]}
        pC := RIGHT[B];
        while pC ≠ nil do
            begin C := pC↑.X; pC := pC↑.next;
            if not inrightstar[C]
            then begin inrightstar[C] := true; add(C, RIGHTSTAR[A]);
                top := top + 1; frontier[top] := C;
                end;
```

Program 3.2   (Continued)

```
            end;
       until top = 0;
       end;
end; {calculate RIGHT*}

procedure constructFIRSTandFOLLOWsets;
var t: terminal; A, lhs: nonterminal; X: symbol;
    p: productionlink; rhsposn: rhslink;
    pA, pt: symbollink;
    top: zeroorfrontierindex;
    frontier: array[frontierindex] of symbol;
    {Global variables: inlookahead, FOLLOW, inlefttrstar.
    inlookahead[A] = true iff t is in LOOKAHEAD(A→α) for some
                      production A→α.
    FOLLOW[A] = true iff t is in FOLLOW(A).
    inlefttrstar[A] = true iff t (LEFTᵀ)* A.}

    procedure addtolookahead(p: productionlink; t: terminal);
    label 1;
    var lhs: nonterminal; pt1, pt2: symbollink;
    begin lhs := p↑.lhs; pt1 := p↑.lookahead.last;
    {check if t is already in the lookahead of this production}
    if pt1 ≠ nil then if pt1↑.X = t then goto 1;
    {if t is in the lookahead of another production with this lhs
    then grammar is not LL(1)}
    if inlookahead[lhs] then nonLL1[lhs] := true
                        else inlookahead[lhs] := true;
    {add t to end of list of lookahead symbols for this production}
    new(pt2); pt2↑.X := t; pt2↑.next := nil;
    if pt1 = nil then p↑.lookahead.first := pt2
                 else pt1↑.next := pt2;
    p↑.lookahead.last := pt2;
1: end; {add to lookahead}

    procedure addtopredecessors(t: terminal; r: rhslink);
    {Adds t to the FOLLOW set of each non-terminal which precedes r in the
    production and is separated from r by nullable non-terminals}
    var r1: rhslink; X: symbol; B: nonterminal;
        null: Boolean; pB: symbollink; p: productionlink;
    begin r1 := r↑.predecessor; null := true;
    while (r1 ≠ nil) and null do
        begin X := r1↑.X.h; r1 := r1↑.predecessor;
```

Program 3.2   (Continued)

```
    if hashtable[X].class = term then null := false
    else begin null := nullable[X];
        if not FOLLOW[X]
        then begin {add t to FOLLOW(B) for all B such that X ⇒* ... B}
            pB := RIGHTSTAR[X];
            while pB ≠ nil do
                begin B := pB↑.X; FOLLOW[B] := true;
                pB := pB↑.next;
                if nullable[B]
                then begin p := nullableprodn[B];
                        {Note: it is assumed that there is at most one
                        nullable production with any given lhs. If not
                        the grammar is not LL and a suitable message
                        should be printed when nullable productions are
                        first detected}
                        addtolookahead(p, t);
                    end;
                end;
            end;
        end;
    end;
    end;   {add to predecessors}


{construct FIRST and FOLLOW sets}
begin pt := firstterminal;
while pt ≠ nil do
    begin t := pt↑.X; pt := pt↑.next;
    {initialize lefttrstar(t)}
    pA := firstnonterminal;
    while pA ≠ nil do
        begin A := pA↑.X; pA := pA↑.next; inlefttrstar[A] := false;
        inlookahead[A] := false; FOLLOW[A] := false;
        end;
    inlefttrstar[t] := true;
    {perform graph search to determine all X such that t (LEFT^T)* X}
    top := 1; frontier[top] := t;
    repeat {remove top element from frontier}
        X := frontier[top]; top := top−1; {X LEFT* t}
        {For each occurrence of X on rhs of a production do
```

Program 3.2   (Continued)

1. *Determine new elements to be added to* $(LEFT^T)^*(t)$.
2. *Add t to LOOKAHEAD set of productions involved in 1.*
3. *Add t to FOLLOW sets and to LOOKAHEAD of nullable*
   productions.}

```
            rhsposn := hashtable[X].firstoccurrence;
            while rhsposn ≠ nil do
                begin p := rhsposn↑.p; lhs := p↑.lhs;
                if rhsposn↑.nullablepredecessors
                then begin {X LEFT^T lhs and t (LEFT^T)* lhs}
                    addtolookahead(p, t);
                    if not inlefttrstar[lhs]
                    then begin inlefttrstar[lhs] := true;
                        top := top + 1; frontier[top] := lhs;
                        end;
                    end;
                addtopredecessors(t, rhsposn);
                rhsposn := rhsposn↑.X.nextoccurrence;
                end;
        until top = 0;
        end;
end; {construct FIRST and FOLLOW sets}


procedure printLOOKAHEADs;
const maxcharcount = 135;
var pA, pt: symbollink; A: nonterminal; t: terminal; top: zeroorfrontierindex;
    frontier: array[frontierindex] of nonterminal; p: productionlink;
    charcount: integer;
begin page(output); writeln(' LOOKAHEAD SETS');
writeln; writeln; writeln;
pA := firstnonterminal;
while pA ≠ nil do
    begin A := pA↑.X; pA := pA↑.next; write('   ', hashtable[A].sym);
    if nonLL1[A] then writeln('    ': 10, ' *** NOT STRONG LL(1) ***')
                else writeln;
    writeln; p := hashtable[A].firstlhsoccurrence;
    while p ≠ nil do
        begin write(' PRODUCTION', '   ': 8); printproduction(p); writeln;
        write(' LOOKAHEAD', '   ':10);
        pt := p↑.lookahead.first; charcount := 19 + maxsymbollength + 1;
```

Program 3.2   (Continued)

> **repeat**
>> **while** (*pt* ≠ **nil**) **and** (*charcount* < *maxcharcount*) **do**
>>> **begin** *write(hashtable[pt↑.X].sym, '   ')*; *pt* := *pt↑.next*;
>>> *charcount* := *charcount* + *maxsymbollength* + 1;
>>> **end**;
>> *writeln*; **if** *pt* ≠ **nil then** *write('   ':19)*;
>> **until** *pt* = **nil**;
>> *p* := *p↑.nextlhsoccurrence*;
>> *writeln*;
>> **end**;
> *writeln*; *writeln*; *writeln*;
> **end**;
end; {*print LOOKAHEADs*}

begin for *h* := 0 **to** *primeno* **do** *hashtable[h].sym* := *free*;
inputerror := *false*;
o := *ord('''')* − *ord('0')*;   {*no. of chars.—N.B. implementation dependent*}
addZandEOFtohashtable;
readrepresentationofreplacementsymbol;
readin(nonterm); *readin(term)*; *readproductions*;
readstartsymbol(S);
if *inputerror* **then goto** 1;
computeterminatingproductions;
computesymbolsgeneratedbyS;
computenullablenonterminals;
addextraproduction;
setnullablepredecessors;
constructRIGHT; *calculateRIGHTSTAR*;
constructFIRSTandFOLLOWsets;
printLOOKAHEADs;
1:   *page(output)*;
if *inputerror* **then** *writeln(' *** PROGRAM TERMINATED—INPUT'*,
         ' ERRORS')
>>> **else** *writeln(' END OF OUTPUT')*;

end.

3.4   LL(*k*) GRAMMARS

In this section we shall explore the theoretical question "What are the limitations of syntax analysis by recursive descent?" Some limitations have already come to light. The grammar must not be ambiguous and cannot contain any left-recursive non-terminals. In order to fix them exactly we need to ask the related question "What information is available to effect parsing decisions when using a recursive-descent syntax analyzer?" When a grammar is strong LL(k) two items of information are sufficient to make all parsing decisions. These are the non-terminal A currently being parsed and the k-lookahead at the point in the parse. Below we present an alternative definition of a strong LL(k) grammar which expresses this property in a novel way. First we need an auxiliary definition.

Definition   A derivation sequence $\alpha_0 \Rightarrow \alpha_1 \Rightarrow \alpha_2 \Rightarrow \cdots \Rightarrow \alpha_m$ is called a *leftmost derivation sequence* if and only if α_{i+1} is obtained from α_i by applying a production to the leftmost non-terminal in α_i for all i, $0 \leq i \leq m-1$.

Example 4   Let $G = (\{S, A\}, \{a, b\}, \{S \rightarrow AA, A \rightarrow a\}, S)$. Then

$$S \Rightarrow AA \Rightarrow aA \Rightarrow aa$$

is a leftmost derivation sequence, but

$$S \Rightarrow AA \Rightarrow Aa \Rightarrow aa$$

is not.

Notation   If $\alpha_0 \Rightarrow \alpha_1 \Rightarrow \alpha_2 \Rightarrow \cdots \Rightarrow \alpha_m$ is a leftmost derivation sequence we shall write

$$\alpha_0 \Rightarrow_l \alpha_1 \Rightarrow_l \alpha_2 \Rightarrow_l \cdots \Rightarrow_l \alpha_m$$

or

$$\alpha_0 \Rightarrow_l^* \alpha_m.$$

The motivation for the latter definition is that a recursive-descent syntax analyzer always constructs a leftmost derivation sequence. This is clearly true since the syntax analysis always proceeds from left to right through the right-hand side of each chosen production.

Definition   Let $G = (N, T, P, S)$ be a context-free grammar. G is said to be *strong LL(k)*, for some fixed integer $k > 0$, if whenever there are two leftmost derivations

1. $S \Rightarrow_l^* uA\gamma \Rightarrow_l u\alpha\gamma \Rightarrow_l^* ux \in T^*$, and
2. $S \Rightarrow_l^* vA\delta \Rightarrow_l v\beta\delta \Rightarrow_l^* vy \in T^*$

such that

3. $FIRST_k(x) = FIRST_k(y)$

it follows that

4. $\alpha = \beta$.

The above definition seems rather strange at first sight. The difficulty is caused by the contorted way of saying "there is a unique production such that . . .". Instead, the definition says "if there are two productions $A \to \alpha$ and $A \to \beta$ such that . . ., then they must be identical". To understand the definitions let us refer to Figs. 3.7(a) and (b). In Fig. 3.7(a) ux is the input string. Currently u has been successfully parsed and A is the non-terminal about to be parsed (i.e. the procedure pA has just been entered). After parsing A all the symbols of γ must be parsed. We shall refer to γ as the *open portion* of the parse and to u as the *closed portion* of the parse. $FIRST_k(x)$ is the *k-lookahead* at the current point in the parse. Figure 3.7(b) illustrates a second possibility for the current state of the parse. Now the definition of a strong LL(k) grammar states essentially this: Suppose we consider any state of the parse in which A is the non-terminal currently being parsed and the *k-lookahead* is w, say. Let us use this information to choose among productions with left-hand side A. *Any information provided by the open portion or the closed portion of the current state of the parse will be disregarded.* Then, if there is always a unique production which can give rise to such a state, the grammar is said to be strong LL(k). Contrast this with the definition of an LL(k) grammar which follows.

Definition Let $G = (N, T, P, S)$ be a context-free grammar. G is said to be LL(k), for some fixed integer $k > 0$, if whenever there are two leftmost derivations

1. $S \Rightarrow_l^* uA\gamma \Rightarrow_l u\alpha\gamma \Rightarrow_l^* ux \in T^*$, and
2. $S \Rightarrow_l^* uA\gamma \Rightarrow_l u\beta\gamma \Rightarrow_l^* uy \in T^*$

such that

3. $FIRST_k(x) = FIRST_k(y)$

it follows that

4. $\alpha = \beta$.

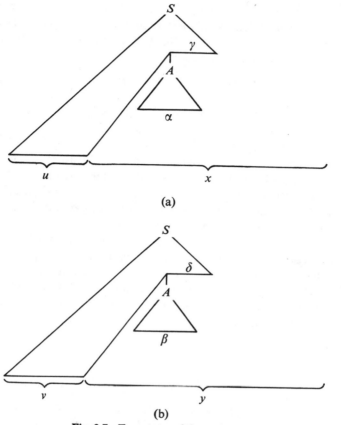

Fig. 3.7 Two states of the parse.

Once again the peculiar technique of saying "there is a unique production" has been used. Now, however, the definition captures *all* the information which can be used within a recursive-descent syntax analyzer. For, at any state in a recursive-descent parse the closed portion of the input string is certainly known. But the open portion is also known, because the sequence of productions used so far is known and the open portion consists of those portions of the right-hand sides which have not yet been parsed. A paraphrase of the definition is therefore as follows. Consider any state of a recursive-descent parse where a choice of production must be made. Suppose that one is allowed to look at the next k symbols in the input string. Then the grammar is LL(k) if there is a unique production which can give rise to this state.

Examples 5 and 6 illustrate the difference between strong LL grammars and LL grammars.

Example 5. Let $G = (\{S, A\}, \{a, b\}, \{S \to aAaa, S \to bAba, A \to b, A \to \Lambda\}, S)$. Clearly only one *lookahead* symbol is required to distinguish between the productions $S \to aAaa$ and $S \to bAba$. The grammar is not strong LL(2) (nor strong LL(1), of course) because

$$2\text{-}lookahead(A \to b) = \{ba, bb\}$$

and

$$2\text{-}lookahead(A \to \Lambda) = \{ba, aa\}.$$

However, the grammar is LL(2). We can prove this simply by exhibiting all states of the parse when A is about to be parsed—there are only two. (See Figs. 3.8(a) and (b).) Consider first Fig. 3.8(a). Here the closed portion is a and the open portion is aa. Now, if the 2-*lookahead* is aa (Fig. 3.9(a)), the correct choice of production is $A \to \Lambda$. On the other hand, if the 2-*lookahead* is ba, the production $A \to b$ is chosen (Fig. 3.9(b)). Now consider Fig. 3.8(b). Here the open portion is ba and the closed portion is b. If the 2-*lookahead* is ba the production $A \to \Lambda$ is chosen (Fig. 3.9(c)) and if the 2-*lookahead* is bb the production $A \to b$ is chosen (Fig. 3.9(d)). The additional information which allows the choices to be made is the manner in which A was introduced. To convert G into an equivalent *strong* LL(2) grammar it suffices to distinguish between occurrences of A. Thus, the grammar

$$G' = (\{S, A_1, A_2\}, \{a, b\}, P', S),$$

where P' consists of

$$
\begin{aligned}
S &\to aA_1aa & S &\to bA_2ba \\
A_1 &\to a & A_1 &\to \Lambda \\
A_2 &\to a & A_2 &\to \Lambda
\end{aligned}
$$

is equivalent to G and is also strong LL(2).

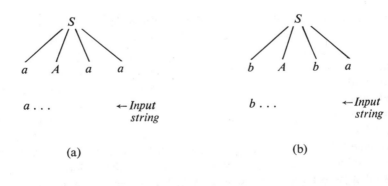

(a)   (b)

Fig. 3.8   States of the parse.

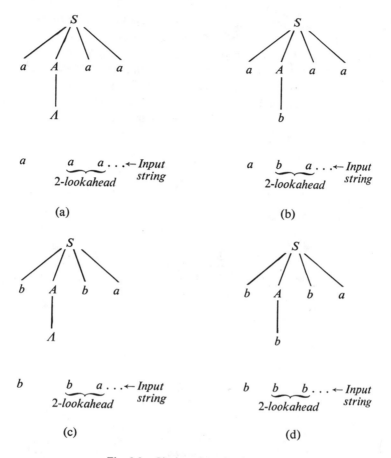

Fig. 3.9   Choice of productions.

Note that G is strong LL(3). The next example is a grammar which is LL(3) but not strong LL(k) for any value of k.

Example 6.   Let $G = (\{S, A, B\}, \{a, b, c\}, P, S)$, where P consists of

$$
\begin{array}{ll}
S \to aBA & S \to bBbA \\
B \to a & B \to ab \\
A \to abA & A \to c
\end{array}
$$

G is certainly not strong LL(3) for

$$3\text{-}lookahead(B \to a) = \{ac, aab, aba, abc\}$$

and

$$3\text{-}lookahead(B \to ab) = \{abc, aba, abb\}$$

(*aba* and *abc* are common elements). On the other hand, it is LL(3). Parsing
S or A presents no problems. The dilemma is when to choose $B \to a$ and
when to choose $B \to ab$, particularly when the 3-*lookahead* is *aba* or *abc*.
Consider, for example, *aba*. We need to examine two states of the parse
corresponding to the two ways of introducing B. These are depicted by Figs.
3.10(a) and (b). Clearly, in the first case (Fig. 3.10(a)) the appropriate choice
is $B \to ab$ whilst in the second case the choice is $B \to a$. Similarly the dilemma
can be resolved when the 3-*lookahead* is *abc*.

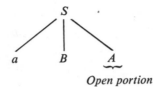

Open portion

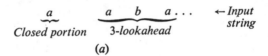

Closed portion   3-lookahead

(a)

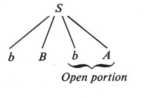

Open portion

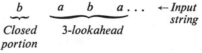

Closed
portion

(b)

Fig. 3.10   (a) Choice is $B \to ab$; (b) choice is $B \to a$.

To prove that the grammar is not strong LL(k) for any value of k let us
define

$$LOOKAHEAD_*(A \to \alpha) = \bigcup_{k > 0} k\text{-}lookahead\ (A \to \alpha).$$

Now

$$LOOKAHEAD_*(B \to a) = L_1 + L_2$$

where

$$L_1 = a + a(ab)^*(A + a + c)$$

and

$$L_2 = a + ab(ab)^*(\Lambda + a + c).$$

Also

$$LOOKAHEAD_*(B \to ab) = M_1 + M_2$$

where

$$M_1 = a + ab + ab(ab)^*(\Lambda + a + c)$$

and

$$M_2 = a + ab + abb\ (ab)^*(\Lambda + a + c).$$

(L_1 and M_1 are associated with the occurrence of B in $S \to aBA$. L_2 and M_2 are associated with the other occurrence of B.) Comparing M_1 and L_2 it is clear that $M_1 \cap L_2$ contains words of arbitrary length. Thus, for all $k > 0$, k-lookahead($B \to a$) $\cap$ k-lookahead($B \to ab$) $\neq \varnothing$ and the grammar is not strong LL(k) for any k. Note that $L_1 \cap M_1 = \{a\}$ and $L_2 \cap M_2 = \{a, ab\}$, so that by distinguishing the rhs occurrences of B one can easily construct an equivalent strong LL(3) grammar.

Examples 5 and 6 were contrived to highlight the difference between strong LL and LL grammars. The case of interest, however, is $k = 1$ and here we have the important result that an LL(1) grammar is also strong LL(1). Thus in Sec. 3.3 we could have abbreviated "strong LL(1)" to "LL(1)" throughout!

Theorem 3.7   The context-free grammar $G = (N, T, P, S)$ is strong LL(1) if and only if it is LL(1).

Proof   Clearly if G is strong LL(1) it is also LL(1). Suppose that G is not strong LL(1). Then, by definition, there are distinct productions $A \to \alpha$ and $A \to \beta$ such that, for some $u_1, u_2, v_1, v_2, w_1, w_2 \in T^*$ and $\gamma_1, \gamma_2 \in (N \cup T)^*$,

$$S \Rightarrow_l^* u_1 A \gamma_1 \Rightarrow_l u_1 \alpha \gamma_1 \Rightarrow_l^* u_1 v_1 \gamma_1 \Rightarrow_l^* u_1 v_1 w_1$$
$$S \Rightarrow_l^* u_2 A \gamma_2 \Rightarrow_l u_2 \beta \gamma_2 \Rightarrow_l^* u_2 v_2 \gamma_2 \Rightarrow_l^* u_2 v_2 w_2$$

and

$$FIRST_1(v_1 w_1) = FIRST_1(v_2 w_2).$$

We must prove that G is not LL(1). There are two cases to consider: (i) $v_1 = v_2 = \Lambda$, and (ii) one (or both) of v_1 and v_2 is not Λ.

In case (i) G is clearly not LL(1). (Indeed it is ambiguous.)

Consider case (ii). Without loss of generality we may assume that $v_1 \neq \Lambda$. Hence

$$FIRST_1(v_1 w_1) = FIRST_1(v_1) = FIRST_1(v_2 w_2).$$

But then the two derivation sequences

$$S \Rightarrow^*_l u_2 A \gamma_2 \Rightarrow_l u_2 \alpha \gamma_2 \Rightarrow^*_l u_2 v_1 \gamma_2 \Rightarrow^*_l u_2 v_1 w_2$$

and

$$S \Rightarrow^*_l u_2 A \gamma_2 \Rightarrow_l u_2 \beta \gamma_2 \Rightarrow^*_l u_2 v_2 \gamma_2 \Rightarrow^*_l u_2 v_2 w_2$$

satisfy the property

$$FIRST_1(v_1 w_2) = FIRST_1(v_1) = FIRST_1(v_2 w_2).$$

Thus, by definition, G is not LL(1).

We have proved that if G is strong LL(1), then it is also LL(1) and if G is not strong LL(1), then it is not LL(1). Thus G is strong LL(1) if and only if it is LL(1). □

The proof of Theorem 3.7 assumes that the definitions of a strong LL(k) grammar in this section and in Sec. 3.1 are equivalent. This is soon checked and has been left to the reader.

The foregoing results have all been highly theoretical. Let us conclude this section on a more practical note. Example 7 asserts that no programming language of any complexity can be LL. We ought, perhaps, to have mentioned this result at the very beginning of the chapter rather than towards the end!

Example 7   Consider a grammar having productions

⟨*expression*⟩	::= ⟨*Boolean expression*⟩ | ⟨*arithmetic expression*⟩
⟨*Boolean expression*⟩	::= ⟨*Boolean term*⟩ ⟨*rest of Boolean*⟩
⟨*rest of Boolean*⟩	::= ⟨*empty*⟩ | **or** ⟨*Boolean term*⟩
⟨*Boolean term*⟩	::= *true* | *false* | (⟨*Boolean expression*⟩)
⟨*arithmetic expression*⟩	::= ⟨*arithmetic term*⟩ ⟨*rest of arith.*⟩
⟨*rest of arith.*⟩	::= ⟨*empty*⟩ | + ⟨*arithmetic term*⟩
⟨*arithmetic term*⟩	::= 0 | 1 | (⟨*arithmetic expression*⟩)

Examples of expressions generated by this grammar are

true	*true* **or** *false*	(*true*)

and

0	0 + 1 + 1	((0 + 1) + 1)

The grammar is not ambiguous, nor is it left-recursive. Even so it is not LL(k) for any value of k. The reason is that, for all $k > 0$, we have the following two derivation sequences.

$$\langle expression \rangle \Rightarrow^*_l \langle expression \rangle \Rightarrow_l \langle Boolean\ expression \rangle$$
$$\Rightarrow^*_l (((\ldots(true)\ldots)))$$

and

$$\langle expression \rangle \Rightarrow_l^* \langle expression \rangle \Rightarrow_l \langle arithmetic\ expression \rangle$$
$$\Rightarrow_l^* (((\dots(0)\dots)))$$

where the number of opening parentheses is k in each case. Thus, the LL(k) condition is violated.

One might feel justified in dismissing recursive descent as a practical technique solely on the basis of this example. Nevertheless a number of commercially distributed compilers do perform syntax analysis in this way. For example all but one of the PASCAL compilers known to the author do so. A careful examination of the syntactic definition of PASCAL reveals an interesting phenomenon. According to the syntax diagrams the following expressions are all syntactically correct.

2 **or** 3   *true* * *false*   0 **or** *true* + 5

This fact is not publicized in the PASCAL Report because, of course, all PASCAL compilers should flag errors in each of them. The explanation is that such errors are easily detected during type checking but, if not, would thwart the use of recursive descent. Recursive descent has many advantages beyond syntax analysis and so it is preferable to relax the context-free definition of the language rather than use an alternative parsing technique.

3.5 PRACTICAL CONSIDERATIONS

To conclude this chapter we discuss three aspects of the practical use of recursive-descent syntax analysis. The first two are concerned with improving the efficiency and structure of the syntax analyzer. The third concerns the use of recursive descent even though the underlying grammar is not LL(1).

3.5.1 Eliminating Terminal Procedures

An obvious inefficiency, inherent in the scheme described in Sec. 3.1, occurs when tests on *nextsymbol* are duplicated within a terminal and a non-terminal procedure. The tests on *qlabel* within *plabel* ((3.2)) and *pdeclaration* ((3.5)) illustrate the phenomenon. In practice it is better *not* to write a procedure for each of the terminal symbols. Instead the action of advancing the input marker can always be initiated by the non-terminal procedures. In this way many redundant tests can be eliminated. (3.28) shows the procedure *pdeclaration* after eliminating *plabel* and *pinteger*.

procedure *pdeclaration*;
begin if *nextsymbol* = *qlabel* **then begin** *advance input marker*;
                                  pidlist;
                                  end

    else if *nextsymbol* = *qinteger* **then begin** *advance input marker*;   (3.28)
                                  pidlist;
                                  end

    else goto 1;
end;   {*pdeclaration*}

To reiterate, the procedures corresponding to the terminal symbols should be omitted and, instead, the appropriate action should be incorporated into the non-terminal procedures. This advice is offered from a practical viewpoint only. The merit of the scheme described in Sec. 3.1 is its uniform treatment of non-terminal and terminal symbols—conceptually it is a better scheme.

3.5.2   Extended BNF

Much more profound improvements in the technique of recursive descent can be achieved through an extension of BNF notation. The improvements are suggested both by programming considerations—the desire to remove unnecessary recursion—and by the need to improve the clarity of the definition of a language.

Two frequently occurring patterns are evident in Table 3.1. The first is the use of right recursion to define simple repetition. Examples are ⟨*statement list*⟩, ⟨*idlist*⟩ and ⟨*rest of exp*1⟩. The second is the use of ⟨*empty*⟩ to indicate an optional feature. Examples here are ⟨*optional else*⟩ and ⟨*optional label part*⟩. In Table 3.4 the grammar has been rewritten using an extended form of BNF. The principle extensions are the use of braces { } to indicate repetition and brackets [ ] to indicate optionality. Specifically, {⟨*item*⟩} denotes zero or more ⟨*item*⟩s and [⟨*item*⟩] denotes zero or one ⟨*item*⟩. {*a*} is, of course, *a** in disguise. In addition parentheses ( ) are used to group items together. Thus (*A* | *B*)*C* is equivalent to *AC* | *BC*. Effectively, the right-hand side of each production in Table 3.4 is a regular expression. (To be pedantic, [ ] is a new operator not considered in Sec. 2.2.)

When regular expressions were introduced in Sec. 2.2 the notation was deliberately chosen to suggest analogies with real arithmetic. Now our choice of notation is dictated by other consideration. The symbols "{" and "}" are called *meta-symbols* to indicate that they are not part of the object language but are being used to describe it. The symbol "→" is also a meta-symbol and, so far, we have tacitly assumed that it never appears on the right-hand side of a production. The introduction of additional notation necessitates that more care be taken to avoid confusing meta-symbols with the terminal or non-terminal symbols. Since almost all programming languages will include arithmetic expressions it is considered inadvisable to use *, + and • as meta-symbols. The use of {, }, [and] does not solve the problem—although braces are uncommon, brackets are terminal symbols in many programming languages. The solution adopted in Table 3.4 is to insist that all terminal symbols are enclosed by quotation marks. A period is also used to indicate the end of each production.

$\langle program \rangle$	::=	$\langle block \rangle$ "." .
$\langle block \rangle$	::=	"begin" {$\langle declaration \rangle$} $\langle statement\ list \rangle$ "end" .
$\langle declaration \rangle$	::=	("label" | "integer") " $\langle identifier \rangle$ "
		{"," " $\langle identifier \rangle$ " } ";" .
$\langle statement\ list \rangle$	::=	[" $\langle identifier \rangle$ " ":"] [$\langle statement \rangle$]
		{";" [" $\langle identifier \rangle$ " ":"] [$\langle statement \rangle$]} .
$\langle statement \rangle$	::=	$\langle assignment \rangle$ | $\langle transfer \rangle$ | $\langle conditional \rangle$ |
		$\langle write \rangle$ | $\langle block \rangle$.
$\langle assignment \rangle$	::=	$\langle expression \rangle$ " = > " " $\langle identifier \rangle$ "
		{" = > " " $\langle identifier \rangle$ "} .
$\langle transfer \rangle$	::=	"goto" " $\langle identifier \rangle$ " .
$\langle conditional \rangle$	::=	"if" $\langle expression \rangle$ "then" $\langle statement\ list \rangle$
		["else" $\langle statement\ list \rangle$] "fi" .
$\langle write \rangle$	::=	"output" "(" $\langle expression \rangle$ {"," $\langle expression \rangle$} ")" .
$\langle expression \rangle$	::=	$\langle exp1 \rangle$ [(" < " | " > " | " = ") $\langle exp1 \rangle$] .
$\langle exp1 \rangle$	::=	$\langle exp2 \rangle$ {(" + " | " - ") $\langle exp2 \rangle$} .
$\langle exp2 \rangle$	::=	$\langle exp3 \rangle$ {(" × " | "/") $\langle exp3 \rangle$} .
$\langle exp3 \rangle$	::=	[" - "] ("input" | " $\langle identifier \rangle$ " | " $\langle constant \rangle$ " |
		"(" $\langle expression \rangle$ ")") .

Table 3.4 Extended BNF Definition of a Simple Programming Language.

The main advantage imparted by the notation is to the structure of the recursive procedures. The constructs {$\langle item \rangle$} and [$\langle item \rangle$] transcribe to **while . . . do** *pitem* and **if . . . then** *pitem*, respectively. (The conditions under which *pitem* is called still need to be evaluated.) (3.29) and (3.30) show how the procedures corresponding to $\langle expression \rangle$ and $\langle exp1 \rangle$ might be constructed from Table 3.4.

> **procedure** *pexpression*;
> **begin** *pexp1*;
> **if** *nextsymbol* **in** [*qlessthan, qgreaterthan, qequal*] **then**   (3.29)
>   **begin** *advance input marker*; *pexp1*;
>   **end**;
> **end**; {*pexpression*}

```
procedure pexp1;
begin pexp2;
while (nextsymbol = qplus) or (nextsymbol = qminus) do        (3.30)
    begin advance input marker; pexp2;
    end;
end;  {pexp1}
```

Table 3.4 is eminently clearer than Table 3.1, but Table 3.1 is a better indicator of the number of parsing decisions that have to be resolved. Table 3.1 was constructed from Table 3.4 (not the other way round) using the principles developed in Chap. 2. Such a transformation could be automated and added to Program 3.2. This task is left as a worthwhile project for the interested reader.

Sometimes a compiler writer is presented with a standard context-free grammar which is not LL(1), and his first task is to transform it into an LL(1) form. No complete prescription can ever be provided for the transformation because, as observed in Sec. 3.4, there are languages which cannot be described by an LL grammar. Nevertheless, by making the fullest possible use of extended BNF one is often able to transform a grammar into a form which is suitable for parsing by recursive descent. The next example serves to illustrate this process.

Example 8   Consider the following list of productions taken from Sec. 4.1.1 of the "Revised Report on ALGOL 60".

$\langle compound\ tail\rangle$ ::= $\langle statement\rangle$ **end** | $\langle statement\rangle$; $\langle compound\ tail\rangle$
$\langle block\ head\rangle$ ::= **begin** $\langle declaration\rangle$ | $\langle block\ head\rangle$; $\langle declaration\rangle$
$\langle unlabelled\ compound\rangle$ ::= **begin** $\langle compound\ tail\rangle$
$\langle unlabelled\ block\rangle$ ::= $\langle block\ head\rangle$; $\langle compound\ tail\rangle$ (3.31)
$\langle compound\ statement\rangle$ ::= $\langle unlabelled\ compound\rangle$ | $\langle label\rangle$:
                                    $\langle compound\ statement\rangle$
$\langle block\rangle$ ::= $\langle unlabelled\ block\rangle$ | $\langle label\rangle$:$\langle block\rangle$
$\langle program\rangle$ ::= $\langle block\rangle$ | $\langle compound\ statement\rangle$

The transformation of these productions to an extended BNF form amenable to parsing by recursive descent provides an interesting application of the techniques for manipulating regular expressions discussed in Sec. 2.2. We shall assume that $\langle statement\rangle$ cannot begin with **end** or with any symbol which can begin a $\langle declaration\rangle$. $\langle label\rangle$ is regarded as a terminal symbol.

Recursion—both left and right—is used extensively in (3.31) to define simple iteration. To transform the grammar to LL(1) form one must certainly remove the left-recursion in the definition of $\langle block\ head\rangle$. It is also preferable to remove the right-recursion in the definitions of $\langle block\rangle$, $\langle compound$

statement⟩ and ⟨*compound tail*⟩. This is achieved using the rule R1 (Sec. 2.2)—in its left- and right-linear forms. The resulting extended BNF productions are given by (3.32).

$$
\begin{aligned}
&\langle compound\ tail\rangle &&::= \{\langle statement\rangle"";""\}\ \langle statement\rangle\ ""end"".\\
&\langle block\ head\rangle &&::= ""\mathbf{begin}""\ \langle declaration\rangle\ \{"";""\ \langle declaration\rangle\}. &&(3.32)\\
&\langle compound\ statement\rangle &&::= \{\langle label\rangle\ ""{:}""\}\ \langle unlabelled\ compound\rangle.\\
&\langle block\rangle &&::= \{\langle label\rangle\ ""{:}""\}\ \langle unlabelled\ block\rangle.
\end{aligned}
$$

In its present form ⟨*compound tail*⟩ is not LL(1) because one cannot decide when to terminate the **while** loop which checks for {⟨*statement*⟩ ";"} and when to check for ⟨*statement*⟩ "end". The problem is resolved using the easily proved identity of regular expressions $(ab)^*a = a(ba)^*$. ⟨*compound tail*⟩ has been redefined in (3.33) using this identity.

$$\langle compound\ tail\rangle ::= \langle statement\rangle\ \{"";""\ \langle statement\rangle\}\ ""\mathbf{end}"". \tag{3.33}$$

The remaining non-terminal which is non-LL(1) is ⟨*program*⟩—both ⟨*block*⟩ and ⟨*compound statement*⟩ can begin with ⟨*label*⟩ or **begin**. Here the strategy is to factor out the common features of the alternatives, but to do so we first need to perform a number of substitutions. (3.34) is the definition of ⟨*program*⟩ after eliminating all the other non-terminals.

$$
\begin{aligned}
\langle program\rangle ::= \ &\{\langle label\rangle\ ""{:}""\}\ ""\mathbf{begin}""\ \langle statement\rangle\ \{"";""\ \langle statement\rangle\}\ ""\mathbf{end}""\ |\\
&\{\langle label\rangle\ ""{:}""\}\ ""\mathbf{begin}""\ \langle declaration\rangle &&(3.34)\\
&\{"";""\ \langle declaration\rangle\}\ "";""\ \langle statement\rangle\\
&\{"";""\ \langle statement\rangle\}\ ""\mathbf{end}"".
\end{aligned}
$$

The final step, factoring out the common parts of the alternatives, results in an extended BNF definition of ⟨*program*⟩ which can be used in a recursive-descent syntax analyzer.

$$
\begin{aligned}
\langle program\rangle ::= \ &\{\langle label\rangle\ ""{:}""\}\ ""\mathbf{begin}"" &&(3.35)\\
&[\langle declaration\rangle\ \{"";""\langle declaration\rangle\}\ "";""]\\
&\langle statement\rangle\ \{"";""\ \langle statement\rangle\}\ ""\mathbf{end}"".
\end{aligned}
$$

3.5.3 Overcoming Non-LL(1) Features

Non-LL(1) features of a programming language can be overcome in a variety of ways. We saw in Sec. 3.4 that expressions, Boolean and arithmetic, cannot be recognized by an LL parser. The solution advocated there—the use of a type checker—also provides a solution to the non-LL(1) feature of the simple programming language defined in Table 3.1. We recall that the grammar is strong LL(2) but not LL(1) because ⟨*identifier*⟩ can begin both an ⟨*optional label part*⟩ or a ⟨*statement*⟩ which follows ⟨*optional label part*⟩. This is an instance of a commonly occurring non-LL(1) feature in programming languages. An ⟨*identifier*⟩ might also be the first symbol of a procedure call, an array variable, a record descriptor or just a simple variable. In each case *2-lookahead* would resolve the problem but *it is more usual to use the information provided by the symbol table.* Of course this does not help if the identifier has not been declared (a not infrequent occurrence) but it is the simpler strategy and it avoids problems of synchronizing error messages with the program listing.

It is a matter of opinion whether ambiguous features should be allowed in programming languages. It is a fact that they often are. For example, PASCAL allows all the ambiguities discussed in Sec. 1.2.3. The reason they are not outlawed is that, by chance, they cause no hiccoughs in a recursive-descent syntax analyzer. Consider the following extended BNF definition of S:

$$S ::= \text{"if"} \ B \ \text{"then"} \ S \ [\text{"else"} \ S] \mid U.$$

S is ambiguous but procedure pS ((3.36)) will, in fact, parse S correctly (i.e. detect a syntax error in the input string u if and only if $u \notin L(S)$). It is no longer obvious that pS is correct—the action taken when *nextsymbol* = *qelse* is in doubt, but it is very likely that a number of compiler writers have constructed such a procedure without realizing that any problem existed!

```
procedure pS;
begin
if nextsymbol = qif
then begin pif; pB; pthen; pS;
        if nextsymbol = qelse then begin pelse; pS;     (3.36)
                                    end;

    end
else pU;
end;   {pS}
```

EXERCISES

3.1 Which of the following are strong $LL(1)$, $LL(2)$ or $LL(3)$ grammars?

(a) $S \rightarrow aA$ $A \rightarrow S$ $A \rightarrow \Lambda$

(b) $S \rightarrow C$ $S \rightarrow D$
$C \rightarrow aC$ $C \rightarrow c$
$D \rightarrow aD$ $D \rightarrow d$

(c) $S \rightarrow AB$ $A \rightarrow a$
$B \rightarrow CD$ $B \rightarrow aE$
$C \rightarrow ab$ $D \rightarrow bb$
$E \rightarrow bba$

(d) $S \rightarrow aAS$ $S \rightarrow b$
     $A \rightarrow a$ $A \rightarrow bS$
(e) $S \rightarrow AB$ $A \rightarrow aAb$ $A \rightarrow c$
     $B \rightarrow bB$ $B \rightarrow c$
(f) $S \rightarrow AB$ $A \rightarrow Ba$ $A \rightarrow \Lambda$
     $B \rightarrow Cb$ $B \rightarrow C$
     $C \rightarrow c$ $C \rightarrow \Lambda$
(g) $S \rightarrow aSbS$ $S \rightarrow \Lambda$
(h) $S \rightarrow aaSbb$ $S \rightarrow a$ $S \rightarrow \Lambda$
(i) $S \rightarrow aAaB$ $S \rightarrow bAbB$
     $A \rightarrow a$ $A \rightarrow ab$
     $B \rightarrow aB$ $B \rightarrow a$
(j) $S \rightarrow AS$ $S \rightarrow \Lambda$
     $A \rightarrow aA$ $A \rightarrow b$
(k) $S \rightarrow BA$
     $A \rightarrow +BA$ $A \rightarrow \Lambda$
     $B \rightarrow DC$
     $C \rightarrow *DC$ $C \rightarrow \Lambda$
     $D \rightarrow (S)$ $D \rightarrow a$
(l) $S \rightarrow aSBA$ $S \rightarrow bASB$ $S \rightarrow c$
     $A \rightarrow a$
     $B \rightarrow a$ $B \rightarrow \Lambda$

3.2 Prove that if all symbols of G are useful and there is a left-recursive non-terminal in G, then G is not LL(k) for any value of k.

3.3 The following grammar defines regular expressions over the alphabet $\{a,b\}$. The numeral 1 has been used to denote the empty word instead of Λ to avoid confusion with an empty production. The start symbol is E. Transform the grammar to LL(1) form.

$$E \rightarrow E+T \qquad E \rightarrow T$$
$$T \rightarrow TF \qquad T \rightarrow F$$
$$F \rightarrow P* \qquad F \rightarrow P$$
$$P \rightarrow \varnothing \qquad P \rightarrow 1$$
$$P \rightarrow a \qquad P \rightarrow b$$

3.4 Implement a syntax analyzer for the language described by Table 3.4.

A significant part of this task is the construction of a lexical analyzer. The function of the lexical analyzer is

(a) to list the data as they are read in;
(b) to output to the syntax analyzer the value of the next symbol in the output;
(c) to remove comments and blanks.

The procedure *getsymbol* in Program 1.2 performs a similar, although simpler, task and can be used as a basis. Two tables need to be constructed. The first should contain the string of characters forming each reserved word together with its scalar value. The second, indexed by characters, should contain the scalar value corresponding to each character. The declaration and initialization of these two tables is illustrated below.

const *maxnoreswords* = 11;
type *terminal* = (*qbegin, qend, ..., qplus, ..., qnil*);
{*qnil is a spurious symbol*}
var   *resword*: **array**[1 .. *maxnoreswords*] **of record** *sym*: *terminal*;
                                                    string: *alfa*;
                                             end;
symb: **array**[*char*] **of** *terminal*;
...
resword[1].*sym* := *qbegin*; *resword*[1].*string* := ' *BEGIN* ';
...
symb['+'] := *qplus*;
...

The action of *getsymbol* depends on whether the first character of the next symbol is a letter, a digit, the symbol "=" (which can be *qequal* or can begin "=>") or otherwise. In the first case the remaining letters and/or digits of the next symbol should be packed into a word and the reserved word table searched. In the last case the table *symb* can be used directly to convert the character into a terminal symbol.

3.5 Compute the $FIRST_2$ and $FOLLOW_2$ sets for each non-terminal in the following grammars:

(a) $S \rightarrow aRTb$ $S \rightarrow bRR$
      $R \rightarrow cRd$ $R \rightarrow \Lambda$
      $T \rightarrow RS$ $T \rightarrow TaT$

(b) $S \rightarrow ABC$ $S \rightarrow BCA$
      $A \rightarrow abc$ $A \rightarrow BC$
      $B \rightarrow SAa$ $B \rightarrow C$
      $C \rightarrow cCB$ $C \rightarrow \Lambda$

3.6 Prove the correctness of Algorithm 3.2.

3.7 Construct graphs corresponding to the relations $LEFT^T$, *RIGHT* and *DIR-ECTLY FOLLOWS* from the following grammars. Use the graphs to compute the *lookahead* set of each production.

(a)   ⟨*statement*⟩ → ⟨*basic statement*⟩ | ⟨*case statement*⟩ |
                    ⟨*compound statement*⟩ | Λ
      ⟨*case statement*⟩ → **case** ⟨*identifier*⟩ **is begin** ⟨*case list*⟩ **end**
      ⟨*case list*⟩ → ⟨*case clause*⟩ | ⟨*case clause*⟩ ; ⟨*case list*⟩
      ⟨*case clause*⟩ → ⟨*identifier*⟩ **do** ⟨*statement*⟩
      ⟨*compound statement*⟩ → **begin** ⟨*statement list*⟩ **end**
      ⟨*statement list*⟩ → ⟨*statement*⟩ | ⟨*statement*⟩ ; ⟨*statement list*⟩

(b) $S \rightarrow aABC$ $S \rightarrow DEF$
      $A \rightarrow SG$ $A \rightarrow BaC$
      $B \rightarrow bBd$ $B \rightarrow \Lambda$ $B \rightarrow F$
      $C \rightarrow BS$ $C \rightarrow c$
      $D \rightarrow FG$
      $E \rightarrow a$
      $F \rightarrow \Lambda$ $F \rightarrow EBa$
      $G \rightarrow BF$

3.8 A new high-level assembly language, called XPOSTFIX, has been proposed. The principal features of this language are:

1. All expressions (Boolean or arithmetic) are written in postfix notation, commas being used to separate operators and operands.
2. The language allows conditional statements involving
$$\textbf{if} \ldots \textbf{then} \ldots \quad \text{or} \quad \textbf{if} \ldots \textbf{then} \ldots \textbf{else} \ldots \quad .$$
3. The language also includes statements of the form
$$\textbf{while} \ldots \textbf{do} \ldots \quad .$$

An example of a ⟨*statement*⟩ in XPOSTFIX might be

    while $a,b, \neq$ **do**
      begin
        $a, 1, a, +, := \ ;$
        if $a,n,>$ **then** $a,n, := \ ;$
        if d **then** $a,b, :=$ **else** $a, 1, :=$
      end

Construct an unambiguous context-free grammar which could be used to describe the syntax of ⟨*statement*⟩s in XPOSTFIX.

Prove that your grammar is indeed unambiguous.

You may assume the following:

(a) ⟨*identifier*⟩ and ⟨*number*⟩ are terminal symbols of your grammar.
(b) Expressions (Boolean or arithmetic) do not involve parentheses.
(c) Boolean expressions involve only the operators $\neq, =$ and $>$.
(d) Arithmetic expressions involve only the binary operators $+$ and $\times$.

3.9 Construct an extended BNF definition of extended BNF. That is, construct a grammar which defines the syntax of productions in extended BNF. Assume that ⟨*character*⟩ and ⟨*identifier*⟩ are terminal symbols of your grammar. Check that your grammar can be parsed by recursive descent by converting it to LL(1) form.

3.10 Complete Program 1.2. Analyze the performance of each procedure in the program and use your analysis to suggest where the program might be improved. If a monitoring facility is available to you which counts the actual number of times each statement is executed then use it to evaluate your theoretical predictions.

3.11 (Programming project.) Extend Program 1.2 so that it will accept grammars in extended BNF notation. Consider the two possibilities

1. converting the grammar to standard BNF form and then checking the LL(1) condition;
2. redesigning the LL(1) check to handle the additional notation directly.

BIBLIOGRAPHIC NOTES

The method of recursive descent has been popularized by its use in a PASCAL compiler [3.8] but its origins can be traced back to Conway [3.2]. The theory of LL parsing was developed first by Lewis and Stearns [3.5] and later by Rosenkrantz and Stearns [3.6]. Lewis and Rosenkrantz [3.4] describe the application of the theory in an ALGOL compiler. Wirth [3.9] presents a complete compiler, written in PASCAL, of a simple programming language. The extended BNF notation used in

Sec. 3.5 is that suggested by Wirth [3.10]. Aho *et al.* [3.1] discuss the extension of LL parsing (and LR parsing) to ambiguous grammars and present a sufficient condition for establishing the correctness of such a parser.

The basic principles used to design an efficient LL(1) test have a wide application. A much deeper study of the method, including the discussion of further examples, can be found in [3.3] and [3.7]. The topic is worth pursuing because it provides a further application of the use of regular expressions and their identities.

3.1 Aho, A. V., S. C. Johnson and J. D. Ullman, "Deterministic parsing of ambiguous grammars", *Comm. ACM*, **18**, 441–52 (1975).

3.2 Conway, M. E., "Design of a separable transition-diagram compiler", *Comm. ACM*, **6**, 396–408 (1963).

3.3 Hunt, H. B. III, T. G. Szymanski and J. D. Ullman, "Operations on sparse relations", *Comm. ACM*, **20**, 171–6 (1977).

3.4 Lewis, P. M. II and D. J. Rosenkrantz, "An ALGOL compiler designed using automata theory", *Proc. Symposium on Computers and Automata, Microwave Research Institute Symposia Series*, **21**, 75–88 (1971). Polytechnic Institute of Brooklyn, N.Y.

3.5 Lewis, P. M. II and R. E. Stearns, "Syntax-directed transduction", *J. ACM*, **15**, 464–88 (1968).

3.6 Rosenkrantz, D. J. and R. E. Stearns, "Properties of deterministic top-down grammars", *Inf. and Control*, **17**, 226–56 (1970).

3.7 Szymanski, T. G. and Ullman, J. D., "Evaluating relational expressions with dense and sparse arguments", *SIAM J. Comput.*, **6**, 109–22 (1977).

3.8 Wirth, N., "The design of a PASCAL compiler", *Software—Practice and Experience*, **1**, 309–33 (1971).

3.9 Wirth, N., *Algorithms + Data Structures = Programs*, Prentice-Hall, Englewood Cliffs, N.J. (1976).

3.10 Wirth, N., "What can we do about the unnecessary diversity of notation for syntactic definitions?" *Comm. ACM*, **20**, 822–3 (1977).

4 LR PARSING

In this chapter we shall present an account of the LR parsing technique. This technique is theoretically superior to the LL technique and a great deal of effort has been expended in making it practically viable. An excellent account of its practical application in compilers has been given by Aho and Ullman [4.3].

The LR technique is *fundamentally* important because it captures the essence of all left-to-right no-backtracking parsing algorithms. It is our intention, therefore, to emphasize the principles of LR parsing rather than the techniques necessary to make it practically viable. As a practical alternative to the LL technique (more precisely, recursive descent) LR parsing suffers because it is unnatural and does not offer the rich structure which so facilitates the incorporation of error recovery and code generation in an LL parser. On the other hand, LR parsing is the more powerful technique (we shall prove in Sec. 4.3 that any $LL(k)$ grammar is also $LR(k)$) and proven software tools are readily available to construct an LR parser from a given grammar.

In Sec. 4.1 we present the $LR(0)$ parsing algorithm which forms the basis for subsequent discussions of the $LR(k)$ and $SLR(k)$ algorithms. The LR technique is not easy to understand and the reader will need to exercise some patience when reading Sec. 4.1. Section 4.2 discusses $LR(k)$ and $SLR(k)$ grammars. Grammars are rarely $LR(0)$ and, although they are often $LR(1)$, the construction of an $LR(1)$ parser is generally accepted as impractical for typical programming languages. The "simple" LR (SLR for short) technique embodies a way of approximating the LR technique, thus enabling such parsers to be constructed. The final section, Sec. 4.3, provides a number of theoretical comparisons of LL, LR and SLR grammars.

4.1 LR(0) GRAMMARS

4.1.1 The Basic Parsing Algorithm

Section 3.4 introduced a concept of fundamental importance to parsing, namely, the *contextual information* used to effect parsing decisions. A strong LL parser uses less information than an LL parser and so a grammar may be LL(k) but not strong LL(k). In general one can assess the power of a parsing technique by examining how much of the information available is actually being used. The LR technique is of great theoretical and practical importance because it contrives to use *all* the information available in a left-to-right no-backtracking parse.

The LR technique works "bottom up" whilst the LL technique works "top down". Figures 4.1(a) and (b) contrast the order in which a derivation tree is constructed by both parsing methods. An LL parser sets itself the goal of parsing S (Fig. 4.1(a)). This goal is then replaced by the goal of matching the first input symbol with a and then parsing B. The goal of parsing B is then replaced by the goal of parsing A and then finding the symbol b. And so it goes on. An LR parser begins with the input string and attempts to "reduce" it to S (Fig. 4.1(b)). The first step is to reduce aab to aAb; this is then reduced to aB and finally aB is reduced to S. Contextual information is needed in the reduction process to recognize when a substring α, say, can be replaced by the non-terminal A, say—it is not sufficient to know that there is a production $A \rightarrow \alpha$ in the grammar. To fix this idea let us consider an example.

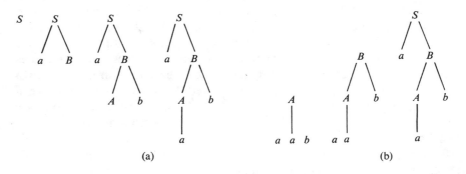

(a)   (b)

Fig. 4.1 Construction of a derivation tree: (a) LL parser; (b) LR parser.

Example 1   Let $G = (\{S, A, B\}, \{a, b\}, P, S)$, where P consists of

$$S \rightarrow aAb \qquad S \rightarrow aaBba$$
$$A \rightarrow Aa \qquad A \rightarrow b$$
$$B \rightarrow \Lambda$$

(Note that A is left-recursive. Left-recursion presents no particular problems to LR parsers.) The symbol b is the rhs of one production and also appears in the rhs of two other productions. Thus, knowing that b appears in an input string provides insufficient information to decide whether it can be replaced by A or is part of one of the productions $S \to aAb$ or $S \to aaBba$. However, the use of more contextual information allows one to resolve the dilemma. Figures 4.2(a), (b) and (c) show three situations in which b is the next symbol in the input string. The appropriate action is to reduce b to A only in the case of Fig. 4.2(a). In other words, we shall say that *in the LR(0) context ab the input string is reduced by the production $A \to b$.* Table 4.1 shows the context in which each of the productions would precipitate a reduce action. (Section 4.1.2 shows how Table 4.1 was constructed as well as defining precisely the terms introduced above.)

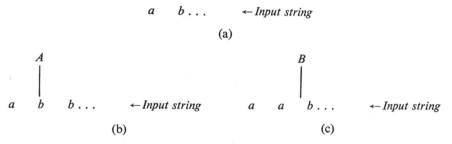

Fig. 4.2 Actions taken when b is the next symbol in the input string: (a) reduce b to A; (b) reduce aAb to S; (c) read the next symbol.

Production	LR(0) context
$S \to aAb$	$\{aAb\}$
$S \to aaBba$	$\{aaBba\}$
$A \to Aa$	$\{aAa\}$
$A \to b$	$\{ab\}$
$B \to \Lambda$	$\{aa\}$

Table 4.1   LR(0) contexts defined by Example 1.

Example 1 is particularly simple because there is exactly one string in the LR(0) context of each production. The general situation is that the LR(0) context consists of a possibly infinite set of strings. The LR(0) parsing technique is based on the idea of calculating the LR(0) context of each production and determining whether there are any "clashes" between productions. If not, the contexts are used to control the parsing process, which simply reduces the right-hand side of a production to its left-hand side whenever possible until the input string has been reduced to S. The grammar of Example 1 is LR(0).

Example 2   Let $G = (\{S\}, \{a\}, \{S \rightarrow Sa, S \rightarrow a\}, S)$.

The LR(0) contexts of the two productions in this grammar are $\{Sa\}$ and $\{a\}$, respectively. That is, if a is the first symbol in the input string, then it is reduced to S. Subsequently, if an initial portion of the input string has been reduced to S and a is the next symbol in the input string, then Sa is reduced to S.

Although there is no clash between the LR(0) contexts the grammar is, none the less, *not* a so-called LR(0) grammar. The reason is that, intuitively, we need 1-lookahead when a reduction to S has just been made in order to determine whether the input string has been completely parsed or further symbols remain. To reflect this we shall, henceforth, always augment the given grammar G with a new non-terminal Z and a new production $Z \rightarrow S$. The latter production needs to be included in the calculation of the LR(0) contexts. For the grammar of Example 2 we have

$$LR(0)CONTEXT(Z \rightarrow S) = \{S\}.$$

Moreover S is a prefix[†] of Sa, i.e. the LR(0) context of $Z \rightarrow S$ "clashes" with the LR(0) context of $S \rightarrow Sa$.

Algorithm 4.1 outlines the LR(0) parsing algorithm more formally. It makes use of a function *FIRST* which is identical to that defined in Chap. 3 except that its functionality has been extended in the obvious way. Strictly 4.1 is not an algorithm because it will loop indefinitely if the input string is not a sentence. The detection of errors will be incorporated into a subsequent refinement of the algorithm.

$\{G = (N, T, P, Z)$ *is a context-free grammar augmented by the production*
$Z \rightarrow S$ *where Z is a new non-terminal*$\}$
var u, x: T^*; α, β, γ: $(N \cup T)^*$; A: *non-terminal*;
       n: *integer*;
       $FIRST_n$: $(N \cup T)^* \longrightarrow (N \cup T)^{\leq n}$;
begin *let the input string be* u; $\gamma := u$;
repeat $n := 0$;
      while $FIRST_n(\gamma) \notin LR(0)CONTEXT(A \rightarrow \alpha)$ *for any production* $A \rightarrow \alpha$
      do $n := n + 1$;
      reduce: *suppose* $FIRST_n(\gamma) \in LR(0)CONTEXT(A \rightarrow \alpha)$;
                let $FIRST_n(\gamma) = \beta\alpha$ *and* $\gamma = \beta\alpha x$;
                $\{$*replace* α *by* $A\}$ $\gamma := \beta A x$;
until $A = Z$;
end.

Algorithm 4.1 Basic LR(0) parsing algorithm.

---

†The string α is said to be a *prefix* of the string β if there is a string γ such that $\beta = \alpha\gamma$. Thus α is always a prefix of α.

4.1.2 Calculating the LR(0) Contexts

We shall now consider the question of defining and calculating the LR(0) contexts. To be exact, the contexts are not actually "calculated" but are defined by a grammar. The startling feature of the defining grammar, which is of crucial importance, is that it is *regular*.

When defining the contexts it is important to note that the current state of the parse is all that is relevant to the next parsing decision; how that state was reached is insignificant. For example, in Figs. 4.3(a) and (b) the input string has been reduced to *aA*. If the remainder of the input string is the same, then the subsequent parsing actions will be identical; the fact that the initial portions of the input strings are different is irrelevant. Our first step, therefore, is to identify those sentential forms which can be generated in the intermediate stages of an LR parser.

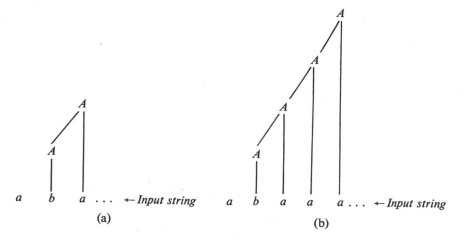

Fig. 4.3   Input string has been reduced to *aA*.

Consider three productions $A \to BC$, $B \to \beta$ and $C \to \gamma$ and suppose these productions are used to generate some sentence in $L(A)$. In reconstructing the parse using a left-to-right bottom-up parsing technique the use of the production $B \to \beta$ would be recognized first, followed later by $C \to \gamma$. In reverse this corresponds to generating the input string using

$$A \Rightarrow BC \Rightarrow B\gamma \Rightarrow^* Bv \Rightarrow \beta v \Rightarrow^* uv$$

where $u, v \in T^*$. In other words, productions are applied to the non-terminals on the rhs from right to left. The first step, therefore, is to define a *rightmost derivation sequence*.

Definition Let $G = (N, T, P, Z)$ be a context-free grammar. The sequence $\alpha_0 \Rightarrow \alpha_1 \Rightarrow \alpha_2 \Rightarrow \cdots \Rightarrow \alpha_n$ is a *rightmost derivation sequence* if and only if, for all i, $0 \leq i \leq n-1$, $\alpha_i = \beta_i A_i u_i$ and $\alpha_{i+1} = \beta_i \gamma_i u_i$ for some $u_i \in T^*$, $\beta_i \in (N \cup T)^*$ and $A_i \to \gamma_i \in P$.

Example 3 Let

$$G = (\{S, A, Z\}, \{a, b\}, \{S \to aASAb, A \to a, S \to c, Z \to S\}, Z).$$

The derivation sequence

$$Z \Rightarrow S \Rightarrow aASAb \Rightarrow aASab \Rightarrow aAcab \Rightarrow aacab$$

is a rightmost derivation sequence.
The derivation sequence

$$S \Rightarrow aASAb \Rightarrow aAcAb$$

is not a rightmost derivation sequence.

Notation We shall write $\alpha_0 \Rightarrow^*_r \alpha_n$ if $\alpha_0 = \alpha_n$ or there is a rightmost derivation sequence $\alpha_0 \Rightarrow \alpha_1 \Rightarrow \cdots \Rightarrow \alpha_n$.

Definition Let $G = (N, T, P, Z)$ be a context-free grammar. The $LR(0)$ *context* of the production $A \to \alpha$ is defined by

$$LR(0)CONTEXT(A \to \alpha) = \{\gamma \mid \gamma = \beta\alpha \text{ and } Z \Rightarrow^*_r \beta A w \Rightarrow_r \beta\alpha w \text{ for some } w \in T^*\}.$$

In words, the $LR(0)$ context of a production is the set of all strings which form the entire prefix, up to and including the rhs of the production, of a sentential form which uses that production in the final step of a rightmost derivation sequence. The reader is invited to check that Table 4.1 satisfies the definition.

All the strings in the $LR(0)$ context of $A \to \alpha$ have the form $\beta\alpha$ for some β. It seems natural, therefore, to redefine the $LR(0)$ context as the product of a set with $\{\alpha\}$. This we shall now do.

Definition Let $G = (N, T, P, Z)$ be a context-free grammar. The *left context* is defined for each $A \in N$ by

$$LEFTCONTEXT(A) = \{\beta \mid Z \Rightarrow^*_r \beta A w \text{ for some } w \in T^*\}.$$

Lemma 4.1

$$LR(0)CONTEXT(A \to \alpha) = LEFTCONTEXT(A) \cdot \{\alpha\}.$$

Proof Obvious. □

An analysis of the problem of determining $LEFTCONTEXT(A)$ follows the same pattern as used in the determination of $FIRST_k(A)$ and $FOLLOW_k(A)$ in Sec. 3.2. That is, we investigate all ways in which A can be introduced into a sentential form and include each as a term on the right-hand side of a system of simultaneous equations. Thus, because $Z \Rightarrow_r^* Z$ and Z is assumed not to appear on the rhs of any production, we have

$$LEFTCONTEXT(Z) = \{\Lambda\} \tag{4.1}$$

Moreover, if $B \to \gamma A\delta$ is a production of G, then

$$LEFTCONTEXT(A) \supseteq LEFTCONTEXT(B) \cdot \{\gamma\} \tag{4.2}$$

That is, $LEFTCONTEXT(B) \cdot \{\gamma\}$ is a term on the right-hand side of the equation for $LEFTCONTEXT(A)$. (We assume, as always, that G contains no useless productions.) Let us illustrate this with an example.

Example 4   Let $G = (\{S, A, B, Z\}, \{a, b\}, P, Z)$, where P consists of

$$Z \to S$$
$$S \to aSAB \qquad S \to BA$$
$$A \to aA \qquad A \to B$$
$$B \to b$$

The system of equations defining the left contexts is given by (4.3).

$$
\left.
\begin{aligned}
&LEFTCONTEXT(Z) = \{\Lambda\} \\
&LEFTCONTEXT(S) = LEFTCONTEXT(Z) \cup \\
&\qquad\qquad\qquad LEFTCONTEXT(S) \cdot \{a\} \\
&LEFTCONTEXT(A) = LEFTCONTEXT(S) \cdot \{aS\} \cup \\
&\qquad\qquad\qquad LEFTCONTEXT(S) \cdot \{B\} \cup \\
&\qquad\qquad\qquad LEFTCONTEXT(A) \cdot \{a\} \\
&LEFTCONTEXT(B) = LEFTCONTEXT(S) \cdot \{aSA\} \cup \\
&\qquad\qquad\qquad LEFTCONTEXT(S) \cup LEFTCONTEXT(A)
\end{aligned}
\right\} (4.3)
$$

Each term on the right-hand side of (4.3) corresponds to an inequality of the type (4.2), except $\{\Lambda\}$, which corresponds to (4.1).

The important feature of these equations is that they are *left-linear* and hence correspond to a *regular grammar*. In (4.4) we have written this grammar explicitly. Note that S, A and B are *terminal* symbols of the grammar. This is because strings γ in the left contexts are elements of $(N \cup T)^*$ and not just T^*. The non-terminal corresponding to $LEFTCONTEXT(R)$ has been abbreviated to $[R]$. No start symbol has been specified because we are interested in the language generated by each non-terminal.

$G_{LC} = (\{[S], [A], [B], [Z]\}, \{S, A, B, a, b\}, P_{LC},)$, where P_{LC} consists of

$$
\left.
\begin{array}{lll}
[Z] \rightarrow \Lambda & & \\
[S] \rightarrow [Z] & [S] \rightarrow [S]a & \\
[A] \rightarrow [S]aS & [A] \rightarrow [S]B & [A] \rightarrow [A]a \\
[B] \rightarrow [S]aSA & [B] \rightarrow [S] & [B] \rightarrow [A]
\end{array}
\right\} \quad (4.4)
$$

Since the equations are regular, we can solve them, obtaining regular expressions for the left contexts. Equations (4.5) show the solution of (4.3) and equations (4.6) combine (4.5) and Lemma 4.1 to give the LR(0) context of each production.

$$
\left.
\begin{array}{l}
LEFTCONTEXT(Z) = \Lambda \\
LEFTCONTEXT(S) = a^* \\
LEFTCONTEXT(A) = a^*(aS+B)a^* \\
LEFTCONTEXT(B) = a^*(aSA+\Lambda) + a^*(aS+B)a^*
\end{array}
\right\} \quad (4.5)
$$

$$
\left.
\begin{array}{ll}
LR(0)CONTEXT(Z \rightarrow S) & = S \\
LR(0)CONTEXT(S \rightarrow aSAB) & = a^*aSAB \\
LR(0)CONTEXT(S \rightarrow BA) & = a^*BA \\
LR(0)CONTEXT(A \rightarrow aA) & = a^*(aS+B)a^*aA \\
LR(0)CONTEXT(A \rightarrow B) & = a^*(aS+B)a^*B \\
LR(0)CONTEXT(B \rightarrow b) & = a^*(aSAb+b) + a^*(aS+B)a^*b
\end{array}
\right\} \quad (4.6)
$$

The use of regular expressions to describe the contexts is inessential to the process of constructing an LR parser. However, the example grammars we shall consider are all very small and it is clearer to display the contexts in this way. From now on, therefore, we shall use the notation of regular expressions without further comment.

4.1.3 Developing the Parsing Algorithm

One cannot over-emphasize the importance of the observation that the left contexts are regular. It is the key to the success of the LR parsing technique.

The first step in the construction of an LR parser for a context-free grammar G is to construct a deterministic machine to recognize the union of the LR(0) contexts. (A non-deterministic machine could be used but would slow down the parsing process). This machine is referred to as the *characteristic machine* of the grammar G. Each of the final states of the characteristic machine is labeled by the production to which it corresponds. (Figure 4.4 illustrates the characteristic machine of the grammar defined in Example 4, i.e. the machine recognizing the contexts in (4.6).) The transition function δ can then be used to effect the test in the **while** loop of Algorithm 4.1. Algorithm

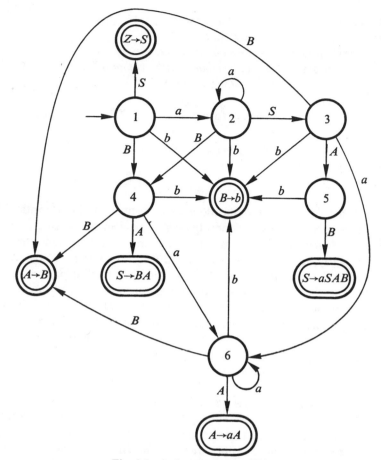

Fig. 4.4 A characteristic machine.

4.2 is the result of making this modification. (Note that, like Algorithm 4.1, Algorithm 4.2 is not strictly an algorithm since it expects *u* to be syntactically correct.)

Algorithm 4.2

$\{G = (N, T, P, Z)$ *is an augmented context-free grammar*$\}$

var u, x: T^*; α, β, γ: $(N \cup T)^*$; *state: state set*;

      A: *non-terminal*; *symbol: terminal or non-terminal*;

      n: *integer*;

      $FIRST_n$: $(N \cup T)^* \longrightarrow (N \cup T)^{\leq n}$;

      δ: *state set* $\times T \longrightarrow$ *state set*; $\{\delta$ *is the transition function of the*

                 characteristic machine of G — the machine recognizing

                 the LR(0) contexts$\}$

begin *let the input string be* u; $\gamma := u$;
repeat $n := 0$; *state* := *start state*;
    while *state is not labeled by a production* **do**
        begin $n := n+1$; *symbol* := *nth symbol of* γ;
                state := $\delta(state, symbol)$;
        end;
    reduce: *suppose label of state is* $A \to \alpha$, $FIRST_n(\gamma) = \beta\alpha$ *and*
        $\gamma = \beta\alpha x$;
        {*replace* α *by* A} $\gamma := \beta A x$;
until $A = Z$;
end.

A number of further modifications have been made in Algorithm 4.3. The main modification involves an obvious improvement to Algorithm 4.2. We note that before a reduction is made γ has the form $\beta\alpha x$, and afterwards $\gamma = \beta A x$. Clearly, it is unnecessary to reread β; one can continue by reading A provided one records the action of the parser when reading β. This one can do by stacking the current state before each transition, and unstacking the appropriate number of states during a reduction. In addition it is convenient to regard the input as a stack from which symbols are removed when required and onto which the appropriate lhs symbol is pushed whenever a reduction is performed. The string γ in Algorithm 4.2 is equal to μ concatenated with the input stack in Algorithm 4.3. The length of μ is always one less than the length of the state stack, the precise relationship between μ and the state stack being indicated by assertion 4. Assertions 1 and 2 form the crux of the correctness proof and will be discussed shortly. Both rely on the assumption that G is a so-called LR(0) grammar. Assertions 3 and 5 are tautologous with the properties required of the transition function δ. That is we cannot "prove" them but we insist that a state is labeled by a production if and only if assertion 5 is valid and $\delta^*(start\ state, \mu) \neq error\ state$ if and only if assertion 3 is valid. The detection of errors occurs as soon as an initial portion of the input string cannot be recognized as forming part of the LR(0) context of any production, i.e. when the current state is an error state or the input stack has been exhausted. In Algorithm 4.3 no recovery action is taken in such circumstances; instead, the syntax analysis is aborted. Example 5 illustrates the action of the algorithm and should help to resolve any outstanding ambiguities in its description.

{$G = (N, T, P, Z)$ *is an augmented context-free grammar*}
assumption: G *is LR(0)*;
var u: T^*; α, μ: $(N \cup T)^*$; A: *non-terminal*; *symbol*: $N \cup T$;
    state: *state set*;

input stack: $(N \cup \{\varLambda\}) \cdot T^*$;
state stack: $(state\ set)^*$;
δ: state set $\times T \longrightarrow$ state set;   {*transition function of the characteristic*
                                        machine of G}
begin *let the input string be u;*
input stack := *u;   state stack* := {*start state*}; μ := $\varLambda$;
state := *start state*;
repeat
    while *state is not labeled by a production* **do**
        begin assertion 1: $Z \Rightarrow^* u \supset Z \Rightarrow^*_r \mu \cdot (input\ stack)$;
        assertion 2: $\mu \cdot (input\ stack) \Rightarrow^*_r u$;
        assertion 3: $\exists\ w \in T^*$ *such that* $Z \Rightarrow^*_r \mu w$;
        assertion 4: *1st element of state stack = start state*
            and $\forall\ i\ (2 \leq i \leq length(state\ stack))$ *i th state on state stack*
            $= \delta^*(start\ state, FIRST_{i-1}(\mu))$;
        if *input stack* $= \varLambda$ **then** *abort analysis*
                    else *remove symbol from input stack*;
        μ := $\mu \cdot symbol$;   *state* := $\delta(state, symbol)$;
        if *state = error state* **then** *abort analysis*;
        push state onto state stack;
        end;
  reduce: *suppose label of state is* $A \rightarrow \alpha$;
        assertion 5: $\mu = \eta\alpha$ *for some* $\eta \in (N \cup T)^*$
            and $\exists\ x \in T^*$ *such that* $Z \Rightarrow^*_r \eta Ax \Rightarrow_r \eta\alpha x$;
        remove length(α) states from top of state stack;
        remove length(α) symbols from end of μ;
        add A to input stack;
until $A = Z$;
assertion *of correctness*: *input stack* = {Z} *if and only if* $Z \Rightarrow^* u$;
end.

Algorithm 4.3

Example 5   Table 4.2 indicates the action of Algorithm 4.3 when parsing the
input string *abbabb*. The grammar is that given in Example 4 and the transition
function δ is defined by Fig. 4.4. (Again, for clarity, the error state has been
omitted from Fig. 4.4). We recall that an LR parser constructs a *rightmost*
derivation sequence in reverse. This derivation sequence has been shown in
the final column of Table 4.2. Between reductions the string $\gamma = \mu \cdot (input$
stack) remains constant although symbols are removed from the top (i.e.
the left end) of the input stack and added to the right end of μ. Note that

immediately prior to performing a reduction the string μ is in the LR(0) context of the associated production. For example, all of ab, aBb, $aSab$ and $aSAb$ are in

$$LR(0)CONTEXT(B \to b) = a^*(aSAb+b)+a^*(aS+B)a^*b.$$

Table 4.2   Parsing *abbabb*

	State	State stack	μ	Input stack	Derivation sequence
	1	1	Λ	abbabb	abbabb
	2	1 2	a	bbabb	⇑
	$B \to b$	1 2 $B \to b$	ab	babb	
reduce	2	1 2	a	Bbabb	aBbabb
	4	1 2 4	aB	babb	⇑
	$B \to b$	1 2 4 $B \to b$	aBb	abb	
reduce	4	1 2 4	aB	Babb	aBBabb
	$A \to B$	1 2 4 $A \to B$	aBB	abb	⇑
reduce	4	1 2 4	aB	Aabb	aBAabb
	$S \to BA$	1 2 4 $S \to BA$	aBA	abb	⇑
reduce	2	1 2	a	Sabb	aSabb
	3	1 2 3	aS	abb	⇑
	6	1 2 3 6	aSa	bb	
	$B \to b$	1 2 3 6 $B \to b$	aSab	b	
reduce	6	1 2 3 6	aSa	Bb	aSaBb
	$A \to B$	1 2 3 6 $A \to B$	aSaB	b	⇑
reduce	6	1 2 3 6	aSa	Ab	aSaAb
	$A \to aA$	1 2 3 6 $A \to aA$	aSaA	b	⇑
reduce	3	1 2 3	aS	Ab	aSAb
	5	1 2 3 5	aSA	b	⇑
	$B \to b$	1 2 3 5 $B \to b$	aSAb	Λ	
reduce	5	1 2 3 5	aSA	B	aSAB
	$S \to aSAB$	1 2 3 5 $S \to aSAB$	aSAB	Λ	⇑
reduce	1	1	Λ	S	S
	$Z \to S$	1 $Z \to S$	S	Λ	⇑
reduce	1	1	Λ	Z	Z

4.1.4   The LR(0) Condition

Algorithm 4.3 is not guaranteed to work for all grammars. A fundamental assumption is that the decision to reduce the input string is correct. The validity of this assumption for any given grammar G depends on whether the LR(0) contexts provide sufficient information to uniquely define the parsing action. The *LR(0) condition*, defined below, is a sufficient condition for the correctness of Algorithm 4.3. Using it we shall verify assertion 1 and then proceed to providing the correctness proof.

Intuitively, there are two conditions which, when satisfied by the grammar G, guarantee the validity of assertion 1. Firstly, no state should be labeled with more than one production. This condition is implicitly assumed in the wording of Algorithm 4.3. Secondly, if a state is entered which is labeled by a production, then it should not be possible to choose the alternative action of continuing to read input symbols. A succinct statement of the two requirements is contained in the following definition.

Definition   Let $G = (N, T, P, Z)$ be an (augmented) context-free grammar. G is said to be LR(0) if and only if

$$\text{if } \theta \in LR(0)CONTEXT(A \to \alpha)$$

and

$$\theta w \in LR(0)CONTEXT(B \to \omega),$$

where $A \to \alpha \in P$, $B \to \omega \in P$, $\theta \in (N \cup T)^*$ and $w \in T^*$, then

$$w = \Lambda, \ A = B \text{ and } \alpha = \omega.$$

An equivalent way of defining the LR(0) condition is to stipulate that each reduce state in the deterministic recognizer of the LR(0) contexts should be labeled by a unique production and have no exit arcs labeled by terminal symbols. Thus, by inspection of Fig. 4.4, the grammar of Example 4 is LR(0).

Example 6   Let $G = (\{E, T, F, Z\}, \{a, +, \times, (,)\}, P, Z)$, where P consists of

$$
\begin{aligned}
&Z \to E \\
&E \to E + T \qquad E \to T \\
&T \to T \times F \qquad T \to F \\
&F \to a \qquad\quad\ F \to (E)
\end{aligned}
$$

This grammar is not LR(0) because

$$T \in LR(0)CONTEXT(E \to T) \qquad \text{and} \qquad T \times a \in LR(0)CONTEXT(F \to a).$$

Also

$$E \in LR(0)CONTEXT(Z \to E) \qquad \text{and} \qquad E + a \in LR(0)CONTEXT(F \to a).$$

In both cases we need 1-lookahead to recognize whether a reduction should be made or whether further input symbols should be read.

The following lemmas lead up to the proof of correctness of Algorithm 4.3 when G is $LR(0)$. They assume the validity of assertions 3 and 5 which, as we remarked earlier, embody the basic properties of the LR(0) contexts and the transition function δ used to recognize them.

Lemma 4.2 (Verification of assertion 1).
    If $G = (N, T, P, Z)$ is LR(0), then assertion 1 is a valid loop invariant of Algorithm 4.3.

Proof Let γ denote $\mu \cdot (input\ stack)$ (i.e. μ concatenated with the contents of the input stack). We need to establish that (4.7) is a loop invariant.

$$Z \Rightarrow^* u \supset Z \Rightarrow_r^* \gamma \tag{4.7}$$

If $Z \not\Rightarrow^* u$ we have nothing to prove, so let us assume that $Z \Rightarrow^* u$.

    Initially $u = \gamma$ and so (4.7) is valid. Suppose at some subsequent stage (4.7) is violated. Consider the first occasion that this occurs. It must follow a reduction because γ is invariant during execution of the **while** statement. Before the reduction we have, by assertion 5,

$$Z \Rightarrow_r^* \gamma = \eta\alpha x \quad \text{for some } \alpha, \eta \in (N \cup T)^* \text{ and } x \in T^*,$$

where $\eta\alpha \in LR(0)CONTEXT(A \to \alpha)$ for some $A \to \alpha \in P$. Now, after the reduction, the hypothesis is $Z \not\Rightarrow_r^* \eta Ax$. Let us suppose, therefore, that a rightmost derivation of $\eta\alpha x$ is actually:

$$Z \Rightarrow_r^* \beta By \Rightarrow_r \beta\omega y = \eta\alpha x,$$

where $\omega, \beta \in (N \cup T)^*$ and $y \in T^*$. Then

$$\beta\omega \in LR(0)CONTEXT(B \to \omega)$$

and

$$\beta\omega y = \eta\alpha x.$$

But this implies that either $\beta\omega = \eta\alpha w$, for some $w \in T^*$, or $\eta\alpha = \beta\omega v$, for some $v \in T^*$. That is, G is not LR(0). Thus we have proved that if assertion 1 is violated, G cannot be LR(0). Consequently, if G is LR(0), assertion 1 is a loop invariant. $\square$

    The LR(0) condition is also sufficient to prove assertion 2. This proof is left as an exercise. Note that, obviously, $\mu \cdot (input\ stack) \Rightarrow^* u$. The difficulty is to prove that the derivation is a rightmost one. The declaration of *input stack* provides a hint—one must establish that the input stack can never contain more than one non-terminal.
    In Theorem 4.4 we prove that the algorithm always terminates. A *fallacious* argument in support of this might proceed as follows. Firstly, the **while** statement in Algorithm 4.3 always terminates because each time its

body is executed the length of the input stack decreases. However, should the input stack become empty the analysis is aborted. So far the argument is correct. It remains to prove that the **repeat** statement terminates. Now, every time the **repeat** statement is executed γ is reduced. But at most $length(u)$ reductions can occur and so the **repeat** terminates. The fallacy here is that a "reduction" causes a decrease ("reduction") in the length of γ. In fact, if the production used in a reduce step is of the form $A \rightarrow \Lambda$, then the length of γ increases! Our proof of termination must, therefore, be rather different.

In outline the argument is as follows. First we claim (Lemma 4.3) that any sentence of G has a unique rightmost derivation sequence. Using this property we can conclude that if the input string is syntactically correct then the algorithm will terminate. Now if the input u is not syntactically correct we can identify a longest prefix v of u which contains no syntax errors. We then argue that the parsing of u proceeds normally until the point at which the symbol following v is removed from the input stack. At this point an error is detected and the analysis is aborted.

Lemma 4.3 Let $G = (N, T, P, Z)$ be an LR(0) grammar. Suppose $Z \Rightarrow_r^* u \in T^*$. Then there exists a unique rightmost derivation of u from Z.

Proof Suppose

$$Z = \alpha_n \Rightarrow_r \alpha_{n-1} \Rightarrow_r \cdots \Rightarrow_r \alpha_0 = u$$

and

$$Z = \beta_m \Rightarrow_r \beta_{m-1} \Rightarrow_r \cdots \Rightarrow_r \beta_0 = u$$

are two distinct rightmost derivations of u from Z. Let i be that index such that $\beta_j = \alpha_j$ for all $j < i$ but $\beta_i \neq \alpha_i$. Let $\alpha_i = \eta A x$ and $\alpha_{i-1} = \eta \psi x$, where $x \in T^*$. Let $\beta_i = \omega B y$ and $\beta_{i-1} = \omega \chi y$, where $y \in T^*$. Without loss of generality suppose $length(x) \geq length(y)$. Then, as $\beta_{i-1} = \alpha_{i-1}$ but $\beta_i \neq \alpha_i$, we have

$$\eta \psi \in LR(0)CONTEXT(A \rightarrow \psi)$$

is a prefix of

$$\omega \chi \in LR(0)CONTEXT(B \rightarrow \chi)$$

and G cannot be LR(0). Thus if G is LR(0), there cannot be two rightmost derivations of u. $\square$

Corollary If G is $LR(0)$, then G is unambiguous.

Proof Obvious, since u has a unique rightmost derivation if and only if there is a unique derivation tree for u. $\square$

Theorem 4.4 Suppose $G = (N, T, P, Z)$ is an LR(0) grammar. Then Algorithm 4.3 always terminates. Moreover, the algorithm terminates normally (i.e. is not aborted) with only the symbol Z on the input stack if and only if $Z \Rightarrow^* u$.

Proof We have already observed that the **while** loop in Algorithm 4.3 will always terminate. We need to establish that the **repeat** statement terminates or, equally, that the total number of reductions is finite.

   We shall consider two cases, namely, when the input string u is and is not a sentence of G.

   If u is a sentence of G then, by the corollary to Lemma 4.3, there is a unique rightmost derivation of u from Z. Moreover, assertions 1 and 2 guarantee that the algorithm constructs this derivation in reverse. Thus the total number of reductions is equal to the number of steps in the derivation and is finite. Finally, on termination, by assertion 1, we must have $\mu \cdot$ (*input stack*) $= Z$. That is, Z is the only symbol on the input stack.

   Now suppose u is not a sentence of G. Here we encounter three possibilities:

1. $u = vw$, where $w \in T^+$ and $Z \Rightarrow_r^* v$.
2. $Z \Rightarrow_r^* v = uw$, where $v, w \in T^+$.
3. Some prefix of u cannot be a prefix of a sentence of G. In this case let x be the longest prefix of u such that $Z \Rightarrow_r^* xw$ for some $w \in T^+$, and let $v = xw$ and $u = xaw'$, where $a \in T$.

   In each case we have defined a string $v \in L(G)$ and related to u. Let us compare the actions of the parser when parsing u and when parsing v. The actions are uniquely defined for v and, by the above argument, cause Algorithm 4.3 to terminate with Z on the input stack. Thus, when parsing u the computation will proceed identically up to the point where u differs from v. In case (1) the algorithm will terminate with Zw on the input stack. In case (2) an error will be recognized when an attempt is made to read from an empty input stack and in case (3) when the symbol a is read, δ^*(*start state*, $\mu \cdot a$) $= error\ state$ by the choice of x. Thus, in cases (2) and (3) the analysis is aborted, and in case (1) the algorithm terminates but Z is not the only symbol left on the input stack. $\square$

4.2   LR(k) AND SLR(k) GRAMMARS

4.2.1   LR(k) Grammars

It is rare for grammars to satisfy the LR(0) condition. Example 6 illustrated a simple grammar for arithmetic expressions which is not LR(0). Usually programming languages can be described by LR(1) grammars. That is they may be parsed using one lookahead symbol, in addition to the LR(0) contexts, to decide when reductions are to be performed.

In general, if a grammar is LR(k) for some integer k, the grammar may be parsed using a parsing algorithm essentially identical to the LR(0) algorithm except that reductions are delayed by k symbols. Algorithm 4.4 is the basic LR(k) parsing algorithm. It assumes that G has been augmented by a new production $Z \rightarrow Seof^k$ and that all input strings are terminated by k **eof** symbols (i.e. eof^k). This is for technical reasons similar to those used to justify the introduction of $Z \rightarrow S$ in the LR(0) parsing algorithm.

> $\{G = (N, T, P, Z)$ *is a context-free grammar augmented by the production* $Z \rightarrow Seof^k$. Z *is a new non-terminal and* **eof** *is a new terminal symbol.*$\}$
> **var** $u, v, x \colon T^*$; $\alpha, \beta, \gamma \colon (N \cup T)^*$;
> $\quad n \colon$ *integer*; $A \colon$ *non-terminal*;
> **begin** *let the input string be* u; $\gamma := ueof^k$;
> **repeat** $n := 0$;
> $\qquad$ **while** $FIRST_n(\gamma) \notin LR(k)CONTEXT(A \rightarrow \alpha)$ *for any production* $A \rightarrow \alpha$
> $\qquad \qquad$ **do** $n := n + 1$;
> $\qquad$ *reduce*: *suppose* $FIRST_n(\gamma) \in LR(k)CONTEXT(A \rightarrow \alpha)$;
> $\qquad \qquad$ *let* $FIRST_n(\gamma) = \beta\alpha v$ *where* $length(v) = k$;
> $\qquad \qquad$ *let* $\gamma = \beta\alpha vx$;
> $\qquad \qquad$ $\{$*replace* α *by* $A\}$ $\gamma := \beta A vx$;
> **until** $A = Z$;
> **end.**

Algorithm 4.4   Basic LR(k) parsing algorithm.

Algorithm 4.4 makes use of the LR(k) contexts. These are defined analogously to the LR(0) contexts as follows.

Definition   Let $G = (N, T, P, Z)$ be a context-free grammar which has been augmented by the production $Z \rightarrow Seof^k$ where $k \geq 0$. The *LR(k) context* of the production $A \rightarrow \alpha$ is defined by

$$LR(k)CONTEXT(A \rightarrow \alpha) = \{\gamma \mid \gamma = \beta\alpha u \in (N \cup T)^* T^k$$
$$\text{where } Z \underset{r}{\overset{*}{\Rightarrow}} \beta A u w \Rightarrow_r \beta\alpha u w$$
$$\text{for some } u \in T^k \text{ and } w \in T^*\}.$$

The calculation of the LR(k) contexts of each production is a little more complicated when $k > 0$ but follows the same pattern as when $k = 0$. All strings in the LR(k) context of $A \rightarrow \alpha$ have the form $\beta\alpha u$, where $u \in FOLLOW_k(A)$. We therefore propose the following definition.

Definition   Let $G = (N, T, P, Z)$ be a context-free grammar. Let $A \in N$ and $u \in FOLLOW_k(A)$. The *left context* of the pair (A, u) is defined to be

$$LEFTCONTEXT(A, u) = \{\beta \mid Z \Rightarrow_r^* \beta Auw \text{ for some } w \in T^*\}.$$

Lemma 4.6

$$LR(k)CONTEXT(A \to \alpha) = \bigcup_{u \in FOLLOW_k(A)} LEFTCONTEXT(A, u) \cdot \{\alpha u\}.$$

Note that the functionality of *LEFTCONTEXT* has been extended from its earlier definition.

An analysis of the problem of determining $LEFTCONTEXT(A, u)$ soon yields the following solution. (Cf. the calculation of $LEFTCONTEXT(A)$ in Sec. 4.1.2).

Suppose $B \to \gamma A \delta$ is a production of G, $v \in FOLLOW_k(B)$ and $u \in FIRST_k(L(\delta) \cdot v)$. Then, clearly,

$$u \in FOLLOW_k(A)$$

and

$$LEFTCONTEXT(A, u) \supseteq LEFTCONTEXT(B, v) \cdot \{\gamma\}. \qquad (4.8)$$

Thus, to calculate $LEFTCONTEXT(A, u)$, we construct a grammar whose non-terminal alphabet contains a symbol $[A, u]$ corresponding to each non-terminal A of G and each $u \in FOLLOW_k(A)$. The terminal alphabet is $N \cup T$ and there is a production

$$[A, u] \to [B, v]\gamma \qquad (4.9)$$

corresponding to every instance of an inclusion (4.8) which may be deduced from the productions of G. Finally, one more production is added to the grammar, namely

$$[Z, \Lambda] \to \Lambda \qquad (4.10)$$

The language generated by $[A, u]$ is then the left context of the pair (A, u). Note that, once again, the grammar is left-linear and so the left contexts and the LR(k) contexts are *regular*.

The final definition is the LR(k) condition. This is entirely analogous to our earlier definition of the LR(0) condition.

Definition   Let $G = (N, T, P, Z)$ be an (augmented) context-free grammar. Let $k \geq 0$. G is said to be LR(k) if and only if

$$\text{if } \theta \in LR(k)CONTEXT(A \to \alpha)$$

and

$$\theta w \in LR(k)CONTEXT(B \to \omega),$$

where $A \rightarrow \alpha \in P$, $B \rightarrow \omega \in P$, $\theta \in (N \cup T)^*$ and $w \in T^*$, then
$$w = \Lambda, \quad A = B \quad \text{and} \quad \alpha = \omega.$$

Let us illustrate the application of (4.9), (4.10) and Lemma 4.6 to check whether a simple grammar is LR(1).

Example 7   Let $G = (\{Z, S, A, B, C, D\}, \{a, b, \text{eof}\}, P, Z)$, where P consists of

$$
\begin{aligned}
&Z \rightarrow S\text{eof}\\
&S \rightarrow CbBA\\
&A \rightarrow ab \qquad\qquad A \rightarrow Aab\\
&B \rightarrow C \qquad\qquad\;\; B \rightarrow Db\\
&C \rightarrow a \qquad\qquad\;\; D \rightarrow a
\end{aligned}
$$

Using the techniques of Chap. 3 one soon verifies that

$$
\begin{aligned}
FOLLOW(S) &= \{\text{eof}\}\\
FOLLOW(A) &= \{\text{eof}, a\}\\
FOLLOW(B) &= \{a\}\\
FOLLOW(C) &= \{a, b\}\\
FOLLOW(D) &= \{b\}
\end{aligned}
$$

Thus the grammar G_{LC}, defining the left contexts, has non-terminal symbols:

$$\{[Z, \Lambda], [S, \text{eof}], [A, \text{eof}], [A, a], [B, a], [C, a], [C, b], [D, b]\}$$

and productions

$$
\begin{array}{ll}
[Z, \Lambda] \rightarrow \Lambda & \text{from (4.10)}\\
[S, \text{eof}] \rightarrow [Z, \Lambda] & \text{from } Z \rightarrow S\text{eof}\\
[C, b] \rightarrow [S, \text{eof}] & \\
[B, a] \rightarrow [S, \text{eof}]Cb & \left.\right\} \text{ from } S \rightarrow CbBA\\
[A, \text{eof}] \rightarrow [S, \text{eof}]CbB & \\
[A, a] \rightarrow [A, \text{eof}] & \left.\right\} \text{ from } A \rightarrow Aab\\
[A, a] \rightarrow [A, a] & \\
[C, a] \rightarrow [B, a] & \text{from } B \rightarrow C\\
[D, b] \rightarrow [B, a] & \text{from } B \rightarrow Db
\end{array}
$$

Normally one would test the LR(k) condition by constructing a deterministic recognizer of the LR(k) contexts of the productions and checking whether a state, is labeled by two distinct productions or is labeled by one production but has an exit labeled by a terminal symbol. This grammar has been chosen partly because all the left contexts are finite. The test is thus made simpler because we can enumerate the context of each production and compare them without constructing a deterministic machine. Specifically the left contexts are as follows:

$$LEFTCONTEXT(Z, \Lambda) = LEFTCONTEXT(S, \mathbf{eof})$$
$$= LEFTCONTEXT(C, b) = \Lambda$$
$$LEFTCONTEXT(B, a) = LEFTCONTEXT(C, a)$$
$$= LEFTCONTEXT(D, b) = Cb$$
$$LEFTCONTEXT(A, a) = LEFTCONTEXT(A, \mathbf{eof}) = CbB$$

Thus, applying Lemma 4.6 we obtain

$$
\left.
\begin{array}{ll}
LR(1)CONTEXT(Z \to S\mathbf{eof}) & = S\mathbf{eof} \\
LR(1)CONTEXT(S \to CbBA) & = CbBA\mathbf{eof} \\
LR(1)CONTEXT(A \to ab) & = CbBaba + CbBab\mathbf{eof} \\
LR(1)CONTEXT(A \to Aab) & = CbBAaba + CbBAab\mathbf{eof} \\
LR(1)CONTEXT(B \to C) & = CbCa \\
LR(1)CONTEXT(B \to Db) & = CbDba \\
LR(1)CONTEXT(C \to a) & = ab + Cbaa \\
LR(1)CONTEXT(D \to a) & = Cbab
\end{array}
\right\} \quad (4.11)
$$

By inspection this grammar is clearly LR(1).

4.2.2 Simple LR(k) Grammars

A major drawback to the LR parsing technique is the size of the grammar defining the left contexts. The simple grammar in Example 6 provides a good example. If one calculates the grammar G_{LC} when $k = 1$, one finds that there are twenty-seven productions. Yet the grammar itself has only seven productions and ten terminal and non-terminal symbols. In general terms if the grammar G has n non-terminals and t terminal symbols, there are potentially $(n-1) \cdot t^k + 1$ non-terminals in G_{LC}. This is to be compared with n—the number of non-terminals in G_{LC} when the LR(0) condition is to be tested. Now in a typical programming language there may be between 50 and 100 terminal symbols and so, in the worst case, testing the LR(1) condition may involve a grammar over 50 times the size needed to test the LR(0) condition. This also suggests that a deterministic recognizer of the LR(1) contexts is substantially larger than a deterministic recognizer of the LR(0) contexts. This is borne out by experience. Indeed it has been found impossible to construct a recognizer for the LR(1) contexts of any practical programming language. Instead various techniques have been suggested to compute "approximations" to the LR(k) contexts of the productions and to use these approximations as the basis of an LR parser. The technique we shall describe is applicable to the so-called "simple" LR(k) grammars. Again, in all the definitions we shall assume that the grammar G has been augmented by a production of the form $Z \to S\mathbf{eof}^k$.

Definition   The *simple LR(k) context* of the production $A \rightarrow \alpha$ in the grammar G is defined by

$$SLR(k)CONTEXT(A \rightarrow \alpha) = LR(0)CONTEXT(A \rightarrow \alpha) \cdot FOLLOW_k(A)$$

Definition   The grammar G is said to be a *simple LR(k) grammar* if and only if
$$\text{if } \theta \in SLR(k)CONTEXT(A \rightarrow \alpha)$$
and
$$\theta w \in SLR(k)CONTEXT(B \rightarrow \beta),$$
where $A \rightarrow \alpha \in P$, $B \rightarrow \beta \in P$, $\theta \in (N \cup T)^*$ and $w \in T^*$, then
$$w = \Lambda, A = B \text{ and } \alpha = \beta.$$

The motivation for the definition of the simple contexts is twofold. Firstly, the simple LR(k) context is an approximation to the LR(k) context of a production which can be computed "simply" from the LR(0) contexts. We have already shown how to calculate $FOLLOW_k(A)$ in Chap. 3. To calculate the simple contexts one only has to concatenate $FOLLOW_k(A)$ with the LR(0) contexts. The simple contexts are an approximation to the LR(k) contexts in the sense that

$$SLR(k)CONTEXT(A \rightarrow \alpha) \supseteq LR(k)CONTEXT(A \rightarrow \alpha) \qquad (4.12)$$

but they may not be equal. (4.12) is easily verified. To demonstrate that the inequality may be strict, consider a grammar having productions

$$S \rightarrow aAa \qquad S \rightarrow bAb$$
$$A \rightarrow a$$

The LR(1) context of $A \rightarrow a$ is $\{aaa, bab\}$, whereas its SLR(1) context is $\{aa, ba\} \cdot \{a, b\} = \{aaa, aab, baa, bab\}$.

The second motivation for the definition is to "patch" the LR(0) parsing algorithm to make it work for non-LR(0) grammars. Algorithm 4.5 is the algorithm used to parse SLR(1) grammars. The **while** statement in the algorithm is almost identical to that in Algorithm 4.3 and so its body has been omitted. The function of this statement is to read symbols until a string has been encountered which is in the LR(0) context of some production, i.e. just as in Algorithm 4.3. Now, however, when the **while** statement terminates there may not be a uniquely defined action. There is the possibility of a reduce action but perhaps by more than one production. There is also the possibility that the appropriate action is to continue reading input symbols. When the grammar is SLR(1), the dilemma may be resolved by "looking ahead" at the next symbol in the input string. This is the function of the sequence of statements labeled *possible reduction* in Algorithm 4.5. Specifically, the state q in the deterministic recognizer of the LR(0) contexts is a *final* state if, for some production $A \rightarrow \alpha$ and some $\theta \in (N \cup T)^*$

$$\delta^*(start\ state,\ \theta) = q \quad \text{and} \quad \theta \in LR(0)CONTEXT(A \rightarrow \alpha).$$

That is, in state q there is a possibility of a reduce action. Now with each final state q and each terminal symbol t, there is associated an action (see Algorithm 4.5). The action is to *reduce* if $t \in FOLLOW(A)$. The action is to make a state transition if, for some $w \in T^*$ and some production $B \rightarrow \beta$, $\theta tw \in LR(0)CONTEXT(B \rightarrow \beta)$. Finally, if neither of these actions is possible an error has been detected and the analysis is aborted.

Algorithm 4.5   Simple LR(1) parsing algorithm.

$\{G = (N, T, P, Z)$ *is a context-free grammar augmented by the production* $Z \rightarrow$ **S**eof *where Z is a new non-terminal and* **eof** *is a new terminal symbol*$\}$
assumption: *G is SLR*(1);
type *action* = **record case** *kind*: (*reduce, transition, error*) **of**
$\qquad\qquad\qquad\qquad$ *reduce*: (*p*: *production*);
$\qquad\qquad\qquad\qquad$ *transition, error*: ( );
$\qquad\qquad$ **end**;
var *u*: T^*; α, μ: $(N \cup T)^*$; *A*: *non-terminal*; *nextsymbol*: *terminal*;
$\qquad$ *input stack*: $(N \cup \{A\}) \cdot T^*$;
$\qquad$ *state stack*: (*state set*)*;
$\qquad$ δ: *state set* $\times T \longrightarrow$ *state set*;
$\qquad$ $\{An\ action\ is\ associated\ with\ each\ final\ state\ and\ each\ terminal\ symbol\}$
$\qquad$ *a*: *final state set* $\times T \longrightarrow$ *action*;
begin *let the input string be u*;
input stack := *u*; *state stack* := {*start state*}; μ := Λ;
state := *start state*;
repeat
$\qquad$ **while** *state is not a final state* **do**
$\qquad\qquad$ **begin** $\{See\ Algorithm\ 4.3\ for\ body\ of\ \textbf{while}\ statement\}$
$\qquad\qquad$ **end**;
$\qquad$ *possible reduction*:
$\qquad\qquad$ *let nextsymbol be symbol on top of input stack*;
$\qquad\qquad$ **case** *a*(*state, nextsymbol*).*kind* **of**
$\qquad\qquad\qquad$ *reduce*: **begin** *let a*(*state, nextsymbol*).*p be* $A \rightarrow \alpha$;
$\qquad\qquad\qquad\qquad$ *remove length*(α) *states from top of state stack*;
$\qquad\qquad\qquad\qquad$ *remove length*(α) *symbols from end of* μ;
$\qquad\qquad\qquad\qquad$ *add A to input stack*;
$\qquad\qquad\qquad$ **end**;

    transition: **begin** $\mu := \mu \cdot nextsymbol$;
            remove nextsymbol from input stack;
            $state := \delta\,(state, nextsymbol)$;
            push state onto state stack;
            end;
    error: *abort analysis*
  end;
until *reduction to Z has been performed*;
end.

Example 8   Let $G = (\{S, A, Z\},\ \{a, b, c\}\ P, Z)$, where P consists of

$$Z \to S$$
$$S \rightarrowtail Sb \qquad S \to bAa$$
$$A \to aSc \qquad A \to a \qquad A \to aSb$$

In order to test whether the grammar is SLR(1), one calculates the LR(0) contexts and the *FOLLOW* sets of each non-terminal. We leave the reader to check our calculations.

$$
\begin{aligned}
LR(0)CONTEXT(Z \to S) &= S \\
LR(0)CONTEXT(S \rightarrowtail Sb) &= (ba)^*Sb \\
LR(0)CONTEXT(S \to bAa) &= (ba)^*bAa \\
LR(0)CONTEXT(A \to aSc) &= (ba)^*baSc \\
LR(0)CONTEXT(A \to a) &= (ba)^*ba \\
LR(0)CONTEXT(A \to aSb) &= (ba)^*baSb \\
FOLLOW(A) &= a \\
FOLLOW(S) &= \Lambda + b + c
\end{aligned}
$$

Figure 4.5 shows a deterministic recognizer of the LR(0) contexts. The final states have been numbered from 1 to 6. In states 2, 4 and 5 the action is uniquely defined. However, in state 6 there is a dilemma between reducing by $S \rightarrowtail Sb$ or $A \to aSb$. In states 1 and 3 the dilemma is between continuing to read input symbols or reducing. In each case the appropriate action may be determined by looking at the next symbol in the input string. Table 4.3 indicates the action to be taken in each of the states 1, 3 and 6: e.g., in state 6 the action is to reduce using $A \to aSb$ if the next symbol is a. This is because $a \in FOLLOW(A)$, but $a \notin FOLLOW(S)$. Similarly the action is to reduce using $S \rightarrowtail Sb$ if the next symbol is b, c or **eof** because neither b, c nor **eof** is in $FOLLOW(A)$, but all are in $FOLLOW(S)$. (Strictly Λ and not **eof** is in $FOLLOW(S)$. We are assuming that the grammar has also been "patched" by changing $Z \to S$ to $Z \to S$**eof** as soon as it was discovered that it is not $LR(0)$.)

These actions correspond to recognizing the simple $LR(1)$ contexts which are exhibited below. Note that they satisfy the $SLR(1)$ condition.

$$SLR(1)CONTEXT(Z \to Seof) = Seof$$
$$SLR(1)CONTEXT(S \to Sb) = (ba)^*Sb(\text{eof}+b+c)$$
$$SLR(1)CONTEXT(S \to bAa) = (ba)^*bAa(\text{eof}+b+c)$$
$$SLR(1)CONTEXT(A \to aSc) = (ba)^*ba\,Sca$$
$$SLR(1)CONTEXT(A \to a) = (ba)^*baa$$
$$SLR(1)CONTEXT(A \to aSb) = (ba)^*baSba$$

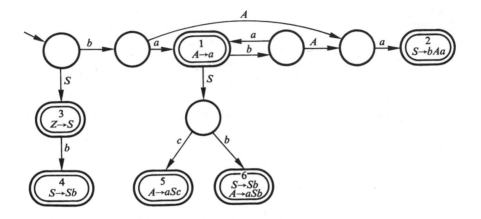

Fig. 4.5   Characteristic machine of Example 8.

State	Lookahead	action.kind	production
1	a	reduce	$A \to a$
	b	transition	
	c	error	
	eof	error	
3	a	error	
	b	transition	
	c	error	
	eof	reduce	$Z \to S$
6	a	reduce	$A \to aSb$
	b	reduce	$S \to Sb$
	c	reduce	$S \to Sb$
	eof	reduce	$S \to Sb$

Table 4.3   Simple LR(1) actions.

Does Algorithm 4.5 really work? To be sure of this we need to establish two properties of the algorithm. We must prove that no "error" will be detected when the input string is syntactically correct and, conversely, that an error is detected when the string is not syntactically correct.

The first property is reasonably obvious from the inequality (4.12). There are two points where an error can be flagged. The first is in the body of the **while** statement. Here the argument used to support Algorithm 4.3 can be applied, although now the proof of assertion 1 must be altered to make use of the SLR(1) condition rather than the LR(0) condition. The second point at which an error can be detected is when a reduction is possible. Here (4.12) can be applied directly. For, if an error is detected when the next symbol is t, say, then μt is not a prefix of the SLR(1) context of any production and so cannot prefix the LR(1) context of any production. Thus μt cannot prefix a sentential form.

The second property is not so obvious, again because of the inequality (4.12)—it can happen that, when a possible reduction is announced, the values of μ and the next symbol—t, say—are such that $Z \overset{*}{\Rightarrow} \mu tw$ for any $w \in T^*$ but no error is flagged. The saving grace of the algorithm is that the symbol t is read twice—once as the lookahead symbol when no error is detected but also once within the **while** statement when an error will be recognized.

The above discussion has been somewhat informal. Exercise 4.9 asks the reader to formalize the argument using the proof of correctness of Algorithm 4.3 as a guideline.

4.3 THEORETICAL COMPARISONS

The objective of this section is to compare the "power" of the various parsing methods discussed in this chapter and the last. The most outstanding result is that any LL(k) grammar is also LR(k). This, together with our use of left-recursion in Example 8, indicates that LR parsers have substantially fewer limitations than LL parsers and, therefore, allow a language designer much more freedom in his choice of syntax. Against this must be posed the pragmatic arguments in favour of LL parsing presented in the introduction to this chapter and the second notable result in this section—namely, an SLR(1) grammar may not be LL(1). We shall begin with the negative results.

Theorem 4.5　There are grammars which are LR(1) but not SLR(k) for any value of k.

Proof　Let us return to the grammar of Example 7. We recall that this grammar is LR(1). However we can prove that it is not SLR(k) for any value of k. For let us consider the productions $C \to a$ and $D \to a$. The LR(0) contexts of these productions are given by (4.13).

$$LR(0)CONTEXT(C \to a) = a + Cba$$
$$LR(0)CONTEXT(D \to a) = Cba \tag{4.13}$$

((4.13) may be deduced by discarding the last symbol of the LR(1) contexts given in (4.11).)

Now let us compute $FOLLOW_*(C)$ and $FOLLOW_*(D)$.

$$FOLLOW_*(C) = b \cdot L(B) \cdot L(A) + L(A)$$
$$= b(a+ab)ab(ab)^* + ab(ab)^*$$

and

$$FOLLOW_*(D) = b \cdot L(A)$$
$$= bab(ab)^*. \tag{4.14}$$

Combining (4.13) and (4.14) we have

$$SLR(*)CONTEXT(C \to a) = (a + Cba)[b(a+ab)ab(ab)^* + ab(ab)^*]$$

and

$$SLR(*)CONTEXT(D \to a) = Cbabab(ab)^*. \tag{4.15}$$

(The SLR(*) context is formed by concatenating the LR(0) context of $A \to \alpha$ with $FOLLOW_*(A)$.)

It remains for us to observe that

$$Cbabab(ab)^+ \subseteq SLR(*)CONTEXT(C \to a) \cap SLR(*)CONTEXT(D \to a)$$

That is

$$SLR(k)CONTEXT(C \to a) \cap SLR(k)CONTEXT(D \to a) \neq \varnothing$$

for all integers $k > 0$. □

Theorem 4.6   There are grammars which are LL(1) but not SLR(1).

Proof   The grammar having productions

$$Z \to Seof \quad S \to AaAb \quad S \to BbBa \quad A \to \Lambda \quad B \to \Lambda$$

is clearly LL(1). However

$$SLR(1)CONTEXT(B \to \Lambda) = (\Lambda + Bb) \cdot (a+b)$$
$$= a+b+Bb(a+b)$$

and

$$SLR(1)CONTEXT(A \to \Lambda) = (\Lambda + Aa) \cdot (a+b)$$
$$= a+b+Aa(a+b)$$

That is, the grammar is not SLR(1). □

Now we shall turn to the positive results.

Theorem 4.7   Every SLR(k) grammar is also LR(k).

Proof   Immediate from the inequality

$$SLR(k)CONTEXT(A \to \alpha) \supseteq LR(k)CONTEXT(A \to \alpha). \quad \square$$

The next theorem is of classical importance. Intuitively it appears obvious. In an LL parse the decision to use the production $A \to \alpha$, say, must be made at a point where a string in the language generated by A is first encountered; in an LR parse the decision is made *after* such a string has been read. Thus more information is available for use by an LR parser than by an LL parser. A concrete example is the grammar in Table 3.1 (p.93). We recall that this grammar is strong LL(2) but not LL(1) because of the difficulty in recognizing whether $\langle identifier \rangle$ begins an $\langle optional\ label\ part \rangle$ or is part of an $\langle expression \rangle$. The grammar is LR(1). No problem arises in deciding when to reduce $\langle identifier \rangle$ because the decision is delayed in an LR parse until the symbol following $\langle identifier \rangle$ has been read. Moreover, the remaining productions are all LL(1) and so we can infer from Theorem 4.8 that they also satisfy the LR(1) condition. It is, nevertheless, quite difficult to provide a wholly rigorous proof of Theorem 4.8 and we shall be content with a semiformal proof.

Theorem 4.8   Let k be a fixed positive integer. Let $G = (N, T, P, Z)$ be an augmented LL(k) grammar with no useless productions. Then G is also LR(k).

Proof   Suppose that $G = (N, T, P, Z)$ is an LL(k) grammar with no useless productions. Let $A \to \alpha$ and $B \to \beta$ be productions in G and suppose

$$\theta \in LR(k)CONTEXT(A \to \alpha)$$

and

$$\theta w \in LR(k)CONTEXT(B \to \beta), \qquad (4.16)$$

where

$$\theta \in (N \cup T)^* \text{ and } w \in T^*.$$

We shall show that $A = B$, $\alpha = \beta$ and $w = \Lambda$.

Consider first the case when A or B is Z. The only production with left-hand side Z is $Z \to S \text{eof}^k$, where S is the sentence symbol before augmentation of G. This production also has LR(k) context equal to $\{S \text{eof}^k\}$. Now, G is unambiguous since it is LL(k). So $S \Rightarrow^+ S$ is impossible and we can immediately infer that $A = B = Z$, $\theta = \alpha = \beta = S \text{eof}^k$ and $w = \Lambda$.

Let us turn to the case when both A and B are not equal to Z. Here we can assert that, for some $u_1, u_2 \in T^k$, $v_1\ v_2 \in T^*$ and $\omega_1, \omega_2 \in (N \cup T)^*$,

$$Z \underset{r}{\overset{*}{\Rightarrow}} \omega_1 A u_1 v_1 \underset{r}{\Rightarrow} \omega_1 \alpha u_1 v_1 \tag{4.17}$$

and

$$Z \underset{r}{\overset{*}{\Rightarrow}} \omega_2 B u_2 v_2 \underset{r}{\Rightarrow} \omega_2 \beta u_2 v_2 \tag{4.18}$$

where

$$\theta = \omega_1 \alpha u_1 \text{ and } \theta w = \omega_2 \beta u_2. \tag{4.19}$$

(The fact that $length(u_1) = length(u_2) = k$ is important and is the reason for our first dismissing the case $A = Z$ or $B = Z$.)

Consider derivation trees corresponding to the derivation sequences (4.17) and (4.18) and let us identify the nodes labeled A and B in these trees (see Figs. 4.6(a) and (b)). Suppose the ancestors of A are labeled by the non-terminals $Z = C_0, C_1, C_2, \ldots, C_{n-1}$ and the ancestors of B are labeled by the non-terminals $Z = D_0, D_1, \ldots, D_{m-1}$. Also let $C_n = A$ and $D_m = B$. Now let $x \in T^*$ be any string such that $\omega_1 \alpha \Rightarrow^* x$ and consider the derivation trees of $x u_1 v_1$ and $x u_1 w v_2$ (Figs. 4.7(a) and (b)).

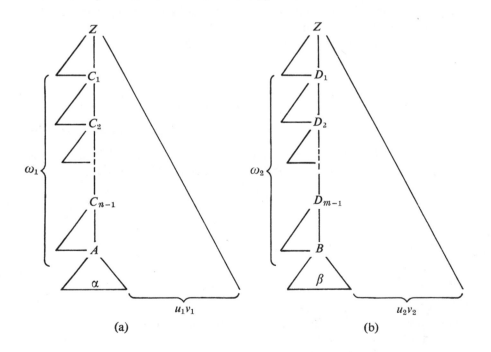

Fig. 4.6 Derivations of θ and θw: (a) $\theta = \omega_1 \alpha u_1$; (b) $\theta w = \omega_2 \beta u_2$.

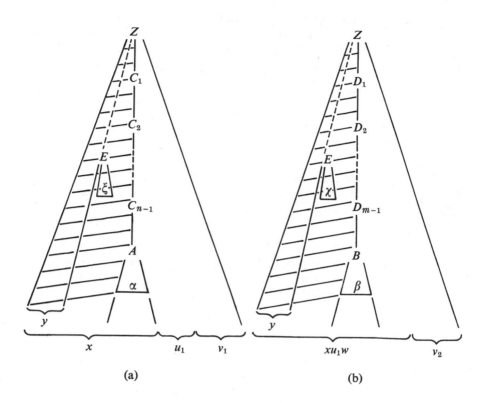

Fig. 4.7   Proof of Theorem 4.8: (a) $\theta = \omega_1 \alpha u_1 \Rightarrow^* x u_1$; (b) $\theta w = \omega_2 \beta u_2 \Rightarrow^* x u_1 w$.

In leftmost derivations of xu_1v_1 and xu_1wv_2 it is the shaded portions of the trees in Figs. 4.7(a) and (b) which are constructed. Now, it is not hard to see that, because G is $LL(k)$, the shaded portions are isomorphic. For, if not, let us "grow" each tree in parallel with constructing a leftmost derivation sequence and identify the first instant at which the trees differ. Then we must have, for some $y \in T^*$, $E \in N$ and $\gamma, \xi, \chi \in (N \cup T)^*$

$$Z \Rightarrow^*_l yE\gamma \Rightarrow_l y\xi\gamma \Rightarrow^*_l xu_1v_1$$

and

$$Z \Rightarrow^*_l yE\gamma \Rightarrow_l y\chi\gamma \Rightarrow^*_l xu_1wv_2.$$

Moreover y is a prefix of x and so

$$FIRST_{k+length(y)}(xu_1v_1) = FIRST_{k+length(y)}(xu_1wv_2).$$

This contradicts the hypothesis that G is $LL(k)$.

But this argument applies equally well to the paths $Z, C_1, C_2, \ldots, C_{n-1}, A$ and $Z, D_1, D_2, \ldots, D_{m-1}, B$ in the tree. We must, therefore, have $m = n$ and $C_i = D_i$ for all i, $0 \leq i \leq m$, in order that G be LL(k). Thus $A = B$. Furthermore $\alpha = \beta$ or, again, G cannot be LL(k). But then $\omega_1\alpha = \omega_2\beta$ and so

$$length(\theta) = length(\omega_1\alpha u_1) = length(\omega_1\alpha) + k$$
$$= length(\omega_2\beta) + k = length(\omega_2\beta u_2).$$
$$= length(\theta w).$$

Hence

$$w = \Lambda.$$

Summarizing, we have established that if (4.16) holds and G is LL(k), then $A = B$, $\alpha = \beta$ and $w = \Lambda$. We conclude, therefore, that G is also LR(k). □

EXERCISES

4.1 Express the left contexts of each non-terminal in the following grammars as a regular expression. (The non-terminals are denoted by capital letters, the terminals by small letters. S is always the sentence symbol.)

(a) $S \rightarrow A$ $S \rightarrow B$
     $A \rightarrow aAb$ $A \rightarrow c$
     $B \rightarrow aBb$ $B \rightarrow d$

(b) $S \rightarrow aASb$ $S \rightarrow b$
     $A \rightarrow bbAc$ $A \rightarrow aA$ $A \rightarrow c$

(c) $S \rightarrow SaSb$ $S \rightarrow R$ $S \rightarrow \Lambda$
     $R \rightarrow cRcR$ $R \rightarrow d$

(d) $S \rightarrow Sab$ $S \rightarrow bR$
     $R \rightarrow S$ $R \rightarrow a$

(e) $S \rightarrow cAc$
     $A \rightarrow CaBc$ $A \rightarrow BbCc$
     $B \rightarrow \Lambda$
     $C \rightarrow \Lambda$ $C \rightarrow bC$

(f) $S \rightarrow S+A$ $S \rightarrow A$
     $A \rightarrow (S)$ $A \rightarrow a(S)$ $A \rightarrow a$

4.2 Construct a table like Table 4.2 which shows the sequence of actions executed by Algorithm 4.3 when parsing the following strings. The grammar in question is that in Example 4 and its characteristic machine is shown in Fig. 4.4. (N.B. You may discover syntax errors in the strings.)

$$aababbbbb \quad abbba \quad aaaa$$

4.3 Verify assertion 2 in Algorithm 4.3.

4.4 Which of the grammars in Exercise 4.1 are LL(1)? Which are LR(0), SLR(1) or LR(1)? (Don't forget to augment the grammars before checking.)

4.5 Construct the characteristic machine for the grammar in Exercise 4.1(a).

4.6 What condition(s) must be satisfied by a regular language in order that it can be generated by an LR(0) grammar?

4.7 Prove or disprove the following:
    (a)   every regular language can be defined by an LL(1) grammar;
    (b)   every regular language can be defined by an LR(1) grammar;
    (c)   every regular language can be defined by a *left-linear* grammar which is also LR(1).

4.8 (Not intrinsically difficult but long. Care and precision are required.) Construct the characteristic machine of the grammar in Example 5. Show that the grammar is SLR(1).

4.9 Formalize the proof of correctness of Algorithm 4.5, using the correctness proof of Algorithm 4.3 as a guideline.

BIBLIOGRAPHIC NOTES

The LR(k) parsing technique was initially developed by Knuth [4.9] but it wasn't until *circa* 1970 that the method became a practical proposition [4.7, 4.10]. Since then considerable effort has been expended on improving the technique. [4.4–7, 4.10–13] are but a selection from the literature on this topic. The LALR technique is discussed in [4.5, 4.7, 4.11]. The survey by Aho and Johnson [4.1] forms a valuable guide to the literature up to 1974.

    The proof of Theorem 4.7 is due to Heilbrunner [4.8]. Heilbrunner also presents an LL(1) grammar which is not LALR(1), contradicting a claim made in [4.1]. The two books by Aho and Ullman [4.2, 4.3] cover almost every aspect of syntax analysis in greater or lesser detail. [4.3] is oriented to the practitioner; [4.2] develops the theory formally and rigorously. Knuth [4.9] offered two approaches to the construction of LR parsers, the first of which has been discussed in this text. It is the second approach which is presented in [4.2, 4.3].

4.1 Aho, A. V. and S. C. Johnson, "LR Parsing", *Computing Surveys*, **6**, 99–124 (1974).

4.2 Aho, A. V. and J. D. Ullman, *The Theory of Parsing, Translation and Compiling*: Vol. I: *Parsing* (1972); Vol. II: *Compiling* (1973), Prentice-Hall, Englewood Cliffs, N.J.

4.3 Aho, A. V. and J. D. Ullman, *Principles of Compiler Design*, Addison-Wesley, Reading, Mass (1977).

4.4 Aho, A. V. and J. D. Ullman, "A technique for speeding up LR(k) parsers", *SIAM J. Computing*, **2**, 106–27 (1973).

4.5 Anderson, T., J. Eve and J. J. Horning, "Efficient LR(1) parsers", *Acta Informatica*, **2**, 12–39 (1973).

4.6 Backhouse, R. C., "An alternative⁻approach to the improvement of LR parsers", *Acta Informatica*, **6**, 277–96 (1976).

4.7 DeRemer, F. L., "Simple LR(k) grammars", *Comm. ACM*, **14**, 453–60 (1971).

4.8 Heilbrunner, S., "Using item grammars to prove LR(k) theorems", *Bericht Nr.* 7701 (Dez. 1977), Hochschule der Bundeswehr München, Fachbereich Informatik.

4.9 Knuth, D. E., "On the translation of languages from left to right", *Info. and Control*, **8**, 607–39 (1965).

4.10 Korenjak, A. J., "A practical method for constructing LR(k) processors", *Comm. ACM*, **12**, 613–23 (1969).

4.11 Lalonde, W. R., E. S. Lee and J. J. Horning, "An LALR(k) parser generator", *Proc. IFIP Congress* 71, North Holland: Amsterdam pp. 153–7 (1971).

4.12 Pager, D., "On eliminating unit productions from LR(k) parsers", *Springer-Verlag Lecture Notes in Computer Science*, **14**, "Automata Languages and Programming" pp. 242–54.

4.13 Pager, D., "A practical general method for constructing LR(k) parsers", *Acta Informatica*, **7**, 249–68 (1977).

5   ERROR REPAIR

In many environments the majority of programs submitted to a compiler contain syntax errors and so it is essential that the syntax analyzer can respond sensibly to *all* inputs. The process normally used to handle errors is called error "recovery". That is, when an error is discovered the parser attempts to continue by making local adjustments to the input marker (e.g. skipping a number of symbols) and/or to the state of the parse (e.g. by proceeding to a point where a reserved word like **begin** is expected). The standard of error recovery in commercially distributed compilers is distinctly variable, as the reader is, no doubt, already aware. In order to try to remedy this situation this chapter aims to develop a coherent theory of the *repair* of syntax errors. The philosophy behind our approach is that the best way to design the error-analysis phase of a syntax analyzer is to try to model the way the programmer would correct his own syntax errors. We do not advocate that errors should be "corrected" by the syntax analyzer because it is impossible to guarantee that an automatic technique, however well formulated, will always find the "correct" repair of the input. What we are seeking to guarantee is that the syntax analyzer will always *suggest* to the user one way of editing his program, with a minimum of effort, into an acceptable form. The term "repair" is, therefore, used advisedly to mean "patch" or "restore to good (but not necessarily the intended) condition".

Sections 5.1, 5.2 and 5.3 consider in turn the repair of spelling errors, regular languages and context-free languages. The approach is to consider all possible ways of repairing an input string and to define in each case the concept of the "best" repair. In Secs. 5.1 and 5.2 the outlook is very optimistic; performing a complete global analysis of the input string to determine a so-called "least-cost repair" would appear to be feasible. But, in Sec. 5.3 the situation deteriorates; although the model of error repair developed in the first two sections generalizes nicely to context-free languages, we discover that a global analysis of syntax errors is quite impractical. Consequently, in Chap. 6 we are obliged to compromise the ideal of least-cost repair with the practical constraint on the time required for the analysis. This chapter and the next offer, in the author's opinion, a good illustration of the interaction between theory and practice.

5.1   STRING-TO-STRING REPAIR

5.1.1   Edit Operations

We shall begin our discussion of error repair by considering the most elementary form, namely string-to-string repair. The problem is this. Suppose we are given two strings, the first of which is a misspelling of the second. How should the first string be "repaired" or "edited" in order to make it identical to the second? For instance we might be given the two words "ASASIN" and "ASSASSIN" and be asked to suggest edit operations to transform the first to the second.

To formulate the problem precisely we need to specify all allowable edit operations and we need some measure of the "best" repair. The most common errors which occur through misuse of a keyboard are (a) character mistyped (b) character omitted (c) character incorrectly inserted and (d) two adjacent characters transposed. Inversely the most frequent edit operations which are used to repair pieces of text are as follows:

1. change one character to another;
2. insert a character;
3. delete a character;
4. transpose two adjacent characters.

In addition it will be convenient for us to regard leaving a character unchanged as an edit operation. Thus to our list we add

5. character OK. Leave unchanged.

These five edit operations have the important property of being primitive —that is all edit operations (such as deleting a whole word) can be decomposed into a sequence of operations from this list. Throughout this chapter we shall assume, therefore, that the operations (1)–(5) are the only operations which may be applied to transform one string to another.

Operation (4) requires further clarification. We make the assumption that:

Exactly one edit operation must be applied to each character of the (misspelt) string.

The implication of this assumption with regard to (4) is that a character may not be transposed and then transposed again (thus having the effect of moving it two characters along). Additionally a character may not be changed and changed again, or changed and then deleted, etc.

5.1.2 The "Best" Repair

We have yet to formulate a measure of the "best" repair. This we shall do using the two strings "ASASIN" and "ASSASSIN" as an example.

Let us suppose that we are given the word "ASSASSIN" and are told to expect the individual characters of a second word which will be input one at a time. We are told to find the "best" repair—expressed as a sequence of edit operations—which will transform the input word to "ASSASSIN". In Figs. 5.2 to 5.4 we have drawn a number of graphs which represent the various ways in which "ASASIN" may be edited to form "ASSASSIN". Each point in these graphs corresponds to a position in the word "ASSAS-SIN" and a position in the input string. For example if, at any stage, we reach node 4 in Fig. 5.2, it will mean that we have edited "ASASI" to form "ASSASS".

Consider Fig. 5.1. Here we suppose that we have read the first input character "A" but do not know any of the remaining characters. At this stage there are (at least) three possible actions we could have taken. Firstly the input character "A" matches with the first character of "ASSASSIN" so we could follow the arc from node 0 to node 1 of the graph. That is, at node 1 we have used the OK operation to repair "A" to "A". Alternatively, we could have chosen to simply delete the input character "A" on the assumption

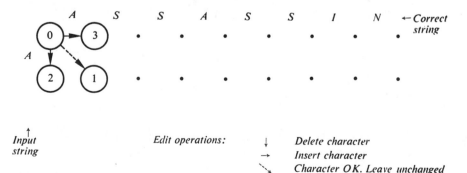

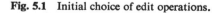

Fig. 5.1 Initial choice of edit operations.

that it had been incorrectly inserted. This is represented in Fig. 5.1 by the
arc from node 0 to node 2. Node 2 thus represents the situation where the
input character "A" has been edited to form the empty word. Finally, without
bothering to look at the input character, we may have decided that the first
character "A" of "ASSASSIN" had been omitted and so the first step in
repairing the input string should be to insert the character. This is represented
by the arc from node 0 to node 3 in Fig. 5.1. At node 3 we have repaired the
empty word to "A" by inserting the character "A".

The above analysis can be generalized. At any point in the editing process
some initial portion of "ASASIN" will have been edited into some initial
portion of "ASSASSIN". At each such point we can continue by inserting
the next character in the remaining portion of "ASSASSIN". This action is
represented by the horizontal arcs in Fig. 5.2. Alternatively we can always
continue by deleting the next character in the input string. This action is
represented by the vertical arcs in Fig. 5.2. These two edit operations already
give us one way of editing "ASASIN" to form "ASSASSIN". Indeed to
repair "ASASI" to "ASSASS" we can delete all the characters of "ASASI"
and then insert all the characters of "ASSASS". This is represented by the
path from 0 to 5 to 4 in Fig. 5.2.

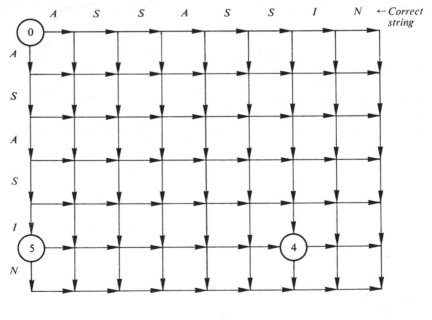

Fig. 5.2 Insert and delete operations.

Figure 5.3 represents the edit operations (1) and (5)—changing a character or leaving it unchanged. Whether a character is changed or left unchanged depends, of course, on whether it matches the character in the correct form. In Fig. 5.3 dotted arcs represent OK characters and solid arcs represent changing the character.

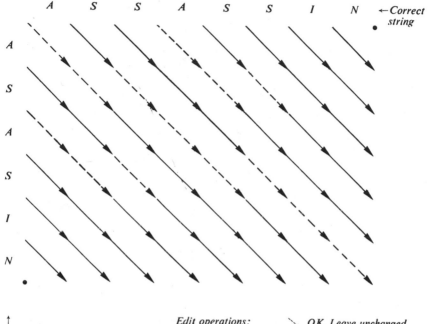

Fig. 5.3   Change and OK operations.

Finally, Fig. 5.4 shows those instances where a transposition of two characters is possible. For example if "A" has been edited into "ASS" then "ASA" can be edited into "ASSAS" by transposing the characters "S" and "A". This corresponds to the arc from node 6 to node 7 in Fig. 5.4.

Figure 5.5 is a combination of Figs. 5.2 to 5.4. Any path through this graph from node 0 to node 8 defines a sequence of edit operations which transforms "ASASIN" into "ASSASSIN". Suppose, however, that we give a cost to each edit operation. For simplicity, let the edit operations (1) to (4) have a cost of 1 and the edit operation (5) (leave unchanged) have a cost of 0.

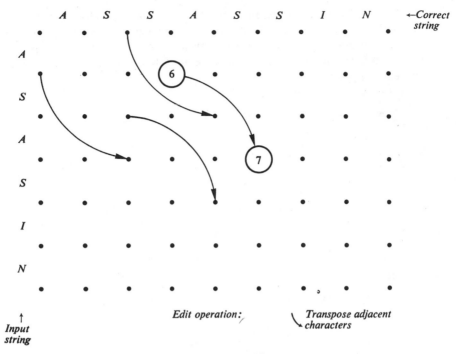

Fig. 5.4   Transpositions.

Correspondingly, each arc in Fig. 5.5 has an associated cost, the solid arcs having unit cost and the dotted arcs having zero cost. The cost of a path or, equivalently, a sequence of edit operations is the sum of the costs of the arcs forming the path. A "best" repair is then defined to be a path with least cost through the graph from node 0 to node 8. One such path has been marked in Fig. 5.5 and clearly corresponds to inserting "S" after "AS" and, again, after "ASAS".

The graph of Fig. 5.5 is the basis of a formal model of error repair which is presented in the next section. Note carefully how the construction of the graph embodies the earlier assumption that exactly one edit operation must be applied to each character—arcs in the graph proceed from left to right and/or vertically downwards but not upwards or from right to left. It is possible to relax this assumption but then the graphs constructed are necessarily larger and more complex. However, the assumption seems a reasonable one and so we shall adopt it throughout.

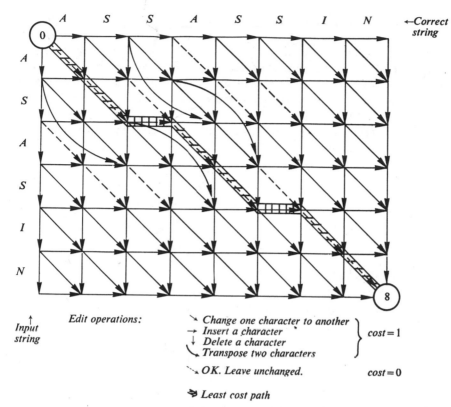

Fig. 5.5   Graph showing least-cost repair.

5.1.3   A Formal Model

This section summarizes the previous discussion by providing a formal model of string-to-string repair. Both this section and the next (Sec. 5.1.4) are fundamental to later sections (notably 5.3 and almost all of Chap. 6) but some readers may prefer to skim it or proceed directly to Sec. 5.2 on a first reading.

We begin by describing the construction of the repair graph for arbitrary strings u and v. Then, in Sec. 5.1.4, we express the problem of finding a least-cost repair as finding a solution to a set of simultaneous equations. This latter approach enables one to take advantage of a variety of algorithms for finding least-cost paths including, most importantly, the elimination techniques and Dijkstra's algorithm. These algorithms are discussed briefly in Sec. 5.4.

Definition (Repair graph)   Let $u = a_1a_2 \ldots a_m$ (the incorrect string) and $v = b_1b_2 \ldots b_n$ (the correct string) be arbitrary strings of length m and n, respectively, where $m \geq 0$ and $n \geq 0$. (If $m = 0$ or $n = 0$ the empty word is understood.) The repair graph $G(u, v) = (N, A)$ is constructed as follows. The set of nodes N of G consists of the set of ordered pairs $\langle i, j \rangle$ where $0 \leq i \leq m$ and $0 \leq j \leq n$. The set of labeled arcs A of G comprises a set of quadruples $\langle x, y, c, e \rangle$, where x and y are nodes, c is the cost (i.e. a non-negative integer) and e is the edit operation associated with the arc. The arcs are split into five sets corresponding to each type of edit operation:

1. For each $\langle i, j \rangle$, where $0 \leq i < m$, $0 \leq j < n$ and $a_{i+1} \neq b_{j+1}$, there is an arc
    $\langle\langle i,j \rangle, \langle i+1, j+1 \rangle, cost(a_{i+1} \rightarrow b_{j+1}), \text{change} \rangle$ in A.

2. For each $\langle i, j \rangle$, where $0 \leq i \leq m$ and $0 \leq j < n$, there is an arc
    $\langle\langle i,j \rangle, \langle i, j+1 \rangle, cost(\Lambda \rightarrow b_{j+1}), \text{insert} \rangle$ in A.

3. For each $\langle i, j \rangle$, where $0 \leq i < m$ and $0 \leq j \leq n$, there is an arc
    $\langle\langle i,j \rangle, \langle i+1, j \rangle, cost(a_{i+1} \rightarrow \Lambda), \text{delete} \rangle$ in A.

4   For each $\langle i, j \rangle$, where $0 \leq i < m-1$, $0 \leq j < n-1$, $a_{i+1} = b_{j+2}$ and $a_{i+2} = b_{j+1}$, there is an arc
    $\langle\langle i,j \rangle, \langle i+2, j+2 \rangle, cost(a_{i+1}a_{i+2} \rightarrow a_{i+2}a_{i+1}), \text{transpose} \rangle$ in A.

5. For each $\langle i, j \rangle$, where $0 \leq i < m$, $0 \leq j < n$ and $a_{i+1} = b_{j+1}$, there is an arc
    $\langle\langle i,j \rangle, \langle i+1, j+1 \rangle, cost(a_{i+1} \rightarrow a_{i+1}), \text{OK} \rangle$ in A.

Here the cost function is defined on pairs of strings and, as always, Λ denotes the empty word. Normally $cost(a_{i+1} \rightarrow a_{i+1})$ will be zero, but otherwise the costs are arbitrary non-negative integer values.

Definition   A *path* through the graph $G(u, v)$ from node x to node y is a sequence of arcs $\langle x_1, y_1, c_1, e_1 \rangle, \langle x_2, y_2, c_2, e_2 \rangle, \ldots, \langle x_r, y_r, c_r, e_r \rangle$ where $x_1 = x$, $y_r = y$ and $y_k = x_{k+1}$ for all k, $1 \leq k < r$. The *cost of the path* is

$$\sum_{k=1}^{r} c_k.$$

A *least-cost path* from x to y is a path whose cost equals the minimum cost of all paths from x to y.

Each path through $G(u, v)$ clearly defines a sequence of edit operations. If the sequence of arcs is

$$\langle x_1, y_1, c_1, e_1 \rangle, \ldots, \langle x_r, y_r, c_r, e_r \rangle,$$

then the type of the kth edit operation is e_k.

Definition   A *least-cost repair of u to v* is a sequence of edit operations defined by a least-cost path from $\langle 0, 0 \rangle$ to $\langle m, n \rangle$.

Note that there may well be more than one least-cost repair of u to v. In such cases we shall not be concerned with the choice that is made.

An example of a least-cost repair is that of "ASASIN" to "ASSASSIN":

$$A \rightarrow A$$
$$S \rightarrow S$$
$$\Lambda \rightarrow S$$
$$A \rightarrow A$$
$$S \rightarrow S$$
$$\Lambda \rightarrow S$$
$$I \rightarrow I$$
$$N \rightarrow N$$

Note that "$\Lambda \rightarrow S$" means "insert S" and "$A \rightarrow A$" means "A is OK". The notation "$X \rightarrow \Lambda$" will be used (and has already been used) to signify "delete X", "$Y \rightarrow Z$" will be used to signify "change Y to Z" and "$XY \rightarrow YX$" will be used to signify "transpose X and Y".

5.1.4   Equational Characterization

Let $cost^*(a_1 \ldots a_i \rightarrow b_1 \ldots b_j)$ be the cost of a least-cost edit sequence which transforms $a_1 \ldots a_i$ into $b_1 \ldots b_j$. The previous sections have shown that this is equal to the cost of a least-cost path from the node $\langle 0, 0 \rangle$ to the node $\langle i, j \rangle$ in the graph $G(u, v)$. We are, therefore, at liberty to identify these two costs and, accordingly, we will abbreviate $cost^*(a_1 \ldots a_i \rightarrow b_1 \ldots b_j)$ to $cost^*(i, j)$. We will use $cost^*(0, j)$ to denote both $cost^*(\Lambda \rightarrow b_1 \ldots b_j)$ and the cost of a least-cost path from $\langle 0, 0 \rangle$ to $\langle 0, j \rangle$. Similarly $cost^*(i, 0)$ will be used to denote $cost^*(a_1 \ldots a_i \rightarrow \Lambda)$ and the cost of a least-cost path from $\langle 0, 0 \rangle$ to $\langle i, 0 \rangle$. Note once again the use of *. Here it indicates that the cost of a repair is the sum of the costs of an indefinite number of edit operations.

The values of $cost^*(i, j)$ can be expressed by a set of simultaneous equations. When $2 \leq i \leq m$ and $2 \leq j \leq n$, there are three or four methods of reaching node $\langle i, j \rangle$. Firstly, $\langle i, j \rangle$ can be reached from $\langle i-1, j \rangle$ by performing a delete operation; secondly, it may be reached from $\langle i, j-1 \rangle$ by an insert operation; thirdly, it may be reached from $\langle i-1, j-1 \rangle$ by either a change operation or an OK operation and finally, if $a_{i-1}a_i = b_j b_{j-1}$, $\langle i, j \rangle$ can be reached from $\langle i-2, j-2 \rangle$ by a transposition. Thus

$$
\begin{aligned}
cost^*(i,j) = min\{ &cost^*(i-1,j)+cost(a_i{\rightarrow}\Lambda), \\
&cost^*(i,j-1)+cost(\Lambda{\rightarrow}b_j), \\
&cost^*(i-1,j-1)+cost(a_i{\rightarrow}b_j), \\
&\textbf{if } a_{i-1}=b_j \textbf{ and } a_i=b_{j-1} \\
&\textbf{then } cost^*(i-2,j-2)+cost(a_{i-1}a_i{\rightarrow}a_ia_{i-1}) \\
&\textbf{else} \infty \}
\end{aligned}
$$

The boundary nodes—nodes $\langle i,j\rangle$, where $i=0$ or $j=0$—must be treated separately since there are fewer arcs to these nodes. The complete set of equations is given by (5.1).

$$
\left.
\begin{aligned}
&cost^*(0,0) = 0 \\
&cost^*(0,j) = cost^*(0,j-1)+cost(\Lambda{\rightarrow}b_j) \qquad 1\le j\le n \\
&cost^*(i,0) = cost^*(i-1,0)+cost(a_i{\rightarrow}\Lambda) \qquad 1\le i\le m \\
&\text{For each } \langle i,j\rangle \text{ where } i=1 \text{ or } j=1 \text{ or} \\
&\quad (i\ge 2 \text{ and } j\ge 2 \text{ and } (a_{i-1}\ne b_j \text{ or } a_i\ne b_{j-1})) \\
&\quad cost^*(i,j) = min\{cost^*(i-1,j)+cost(a_i{\rightarrow}\Lambda), \\
&\qquad\qquad\qquad\quad cost^*(i,j-1)+cost(\Lambda{\rightarrow}b_j), \\
&\qquad\qquad\qquad\quad cost^*(i-1,j-1)+cost(a_i{\rightarrow}b_j)\} \\
&\text{For each } \langle i,j\rangle, \text{ where } 2\le i\le m,\ 2\le j\le n \\
&\quad \text{and } a_{i-1}=b_j \text{ and } a_i=b_{j-1}, \\
&\quad cost^*(i,j) = min\{cost^*(i-1,j)+cost(a_i{\rightarrow}\Lambda), \\
&\qquad\qquad\qquad\quad cost^*(i,j-1)+cost(\Lambda{\rightarrow}b_j), \\
&\qquad\qquad\qquad\quad cost^*(i-1,j-1)+cost(a_i{\rightarrow}b_j), \\
&\qquad\qquad\qquad\quad cost^*(i-2,j-2)+cost(a_{i-1}a_i{\rightarrow}a_ia_{i-1})\}.
\end{aligned}
\right\} (5.1)
$$

It is not difficult to devise an algorithm to solve equations (5.1). The important feature of the graph $G(u,v)$ is that it is acyclic (i.e., there is no path from any node x to itself). Thus the values of $cost^*(i,j)$ can be found by a forward-substitution process which calculates them in the order

$$
\langle 0,0\rangle, \langle 0,1\rangle, \ldots, \langle 0,n\rangle, \langle 1,0\rangle, \langle 1,1\rangle, \ldots,
$$
$$
\langle 1,n\rangle, \ldots, \langle m,0\rangle, \ldots, \langle m,n\rangle.
$$

A least-cost path from $\langle 0,0\rangle$ to $\langle m,n\rangle$ can be found at the same time by storing with each node $\langle i,j\rangle$ the edit operation used to reach $\langle i,j\rangle$. If the reader is in doubt about this process he is invited to construct the system of equations corresponding to the graph in Fig. 5.5 and to begin to solve them. By doing so it should become evident that there is a natural order in which the equations can be solved. (*Note*: there is more than one such order. The only requirement is that whenever there is an arc from $\langle i',j'\rangle$ to $\langle i,j\rangle$, say, in the graph then $cost^*(i',j')$ is evaluated before $cost^*(i,j)$. Any ordering of the nodes which meets this requirement is called a *topological* ordering.)

Although natural and obvious, the above technique is not necessarily the most efficient. An alternative is to use Dijkstra's algorithm. Both algorithms will be discussed in more detail for the more general cases of regular and context-free language repair in Sec. 5.4.

5.2 REPAIR OF REGULAR LANGUAGES

5.2.1 An Example

The informal approach to the development of a model for string-to-string repair can be applied equally well to the repair of regular languages. Here we suppose that we are given a string u and a regular language R. A best repair of u to R is defined to be a sequence of edit operations which transforms u to a word $v \in R$ such that the cost of the sequence is less than or equal to the cost of any other sequence which transforms u to a word in R. Let us suppose that R is specified by a deterministic finite-state machine. (When we consider the repair of context-free languages we shall see that this supposition is inessential.) As an example we shall use the finite-state machine shown in Fig. 5.6. This machine recognizes declarations in ALGOL 60.

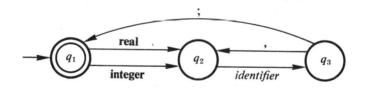

Fig. 5.6 Deterministic machine.

We shall take as sample input the string

real *identifier* ; ,

The repair graph for this string is shown in Fig. 5.7. In Fig. 5.7 each node has been labeled by a pair $\langle i, q \rangle$, where i is a position in the input string and q is a state of the finite-state machine. The method used to construct the graph is depicted in Figs. 5.8 to 5.11. Firstly, at any input position i, a transition can be made from state q_k to state q_j simply by inserting any symbol a which takes q_k into q_j in the finite-state machine (Fig. 5.8). For example, at input position 0 and in state q_1, it is possible to make the transition to state q_2, remaining at input position 0, by inserting either the symbol **real** or the symbol **integer**. A second possibility is that, in any state q_j, it is possible to move from input position $i-1$ to input position i by deleting the ith input symbol (Fig. 5.9). Thirdly the OK or change operations can be used to make both a state transition and an advance in the input position (Fig. 5.10). For instance, suppose the ith input symbol is ",". Then a transition can be made from $\langle i-1,q_1\rangle$ to $\langle i,q_2\rangle$ by changing "," to **"real"**. Similarly an OK transition can be made from $\langle i-1,q_3\rangle$ to $\langle i,q_2\rangle$ (dotted arc in Fig. 5.10). In the repair graph of Fig. 5.7 no transpositions are possible. However, Fig. 5.11 shows an instance where a transposition would be possible. If the $(i-1)$th and ith input symbols are "," and "*identifier*" respectively then, by transposing these symbols, one can go from $\langle i-2,q_2\rangle$ to $\langle i,q_2\rangle$. (The state transition is from q_2 to q_2 because under input "*identifier*" q_2 goes to q_3; then under input "," q_3 returns to q_2.)

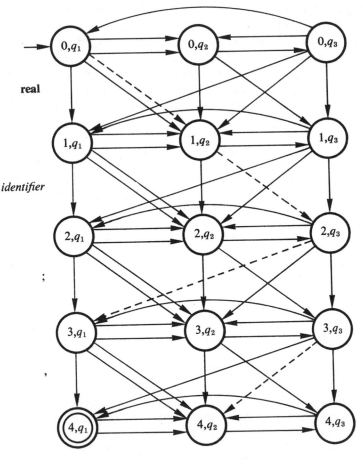

Fig. 5.7 The repair graph.

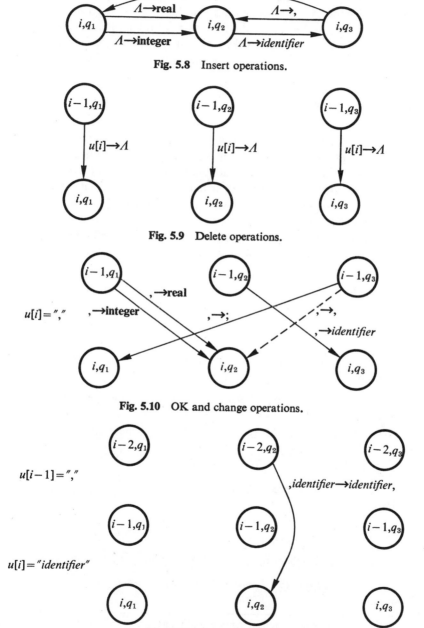

Fig. 5.8   Insert operations.

Fig. 5.9   Delete operations.

Fig. 5.10   OK and change operations.

Fig. 5.11   A transposition.

The start node in the repair graph is the node labeled $\langle 0, q_1 \rangle$. This node corresponds to the input position 0 and the start state of the finite-state machine. The final node in the repair graph—node $\langle 4, q_1 \rangle$—corresponds to the end of the input (position 4) and the final state of the finite-state machine. A best repair of u to R can be obtained by finding a least-cost path from $\langle 0, q_1 \rangle$ to $\langle 4, q_1 \rangle$. This procedure will now be given a formal treatment.

5.2.2   The Formal Model

Let $u = a_1 \ldots a_m$ be an arbitrary string, and let R be a regular language. In this section we shall assume that R is specified by a deterministic† finite-state machine $M = (Q, T, \delta, S, F)$. An error state of Q is a state q such that $\delta^*(q, v) \notin F$ for all $v \in T^*$. Q' will be used to denote the non-error states of Q.

The repair graph $G(u, R)$ is constructed as follows. The set of nodes N of G consists of the set of ordered pairs $\langle i, q \rangle$, where $0 \leq i \leq m$ and $q \in Q'$. The set of labeled arcs A of G comprises a set of quadruples $\langle x, y, c, e \rangle$, where x and y are nodes, c is the cost and e is the edit operation associated with the arc. The arcs are split into five sets corresponding to each type of edit operation:

1.   For each $\langle i, q \rangle$, where $0 \leq i < m$ and $q \in Q'$, and for each $t \in T$, where $t \neq a_{i+1}$ and $\delta(q, t) \in Q'$ there is an arc

$$\langle \langle i,q \rangle, \langle i+1, \delta(q,t) \rangle, cost(a_{i+1} \rightarrow t), \text{change} \rangle$$

   in A.
2.   For each $\langle i, q \rangle$, where $0 \leq i \leq m$ and $q \in Q'$, and for each $t \in T$, where $\delta(q, t) \in Q'$, there is an arc

$$\langle \langle i,q \rangle, \langle i, \delta(q,t) \rangle, cost(\Lambda \rightarrow t), \text{insert} \rangle$$

   in A.
3.   For each $\langle i, q \rangle$, where $0 \leq i < m$ and $q \in Q'$, there is an arc

$$\langle \langle i,q \rangle, \langle i+1, q \rangle, cost(a_{i+1} \rightarrow \Lambda), \text{delete} \rangle$$

   in A.
4.   For each $\langle i, q \rangle$, where $0 \leq i < m-1$ and $q' = \delta(\delta(q, a_{i+2}), a_{i+1}) \in Q'$, there is an arc

$$\langle \langle i,q \rangle, \langle i+2, q' \rangle, cost(a_{i+1}a_{i+2} \rightarrow a_{i+2}a_{i+1}), \text{transpose} \rangle$$

   in A.
5.   For each $\langle i, q \rangle$, where $0 \leq i < m$ and $\delta(q, a_{i+1}) \in Q'$, there is an arc

$$\langle \langle i,q \rangle, \langle i+1, \delta(q,a_{i+1}) \rangle, cost(a_{i+1} \rightarrow a_{i+1}), \text{OK} \rangle$$

   in A.

---

†The assumption of determinism is not essential, as will be evident when we consider the repair of context-free languages.

Note that a special case of the above construction is when $R = \{v\}$ is a language consisting of a single string. If the states of a finite-state machine to recognize $\{v\}$ are identified with the positions $0, 1, 2, \ldots$ in v, then $G(u, \{v\})$ constructed as above is identical to the graph constructed in Sec. 5.1.3.

It is worthwhile digressing at this stage to note the size and structure of the graph. Let α be the number of pairs $\langle q, t \rangle$ where $q \in Q'$, $t \in T$ and $\delta(q, t) \in Q'$. (α is the number of arcs in the finite-state machine, not counting those which enter error states.) Let s be the number of non-error states in the machine. Then the number of arcs in the repair graph due to OK or change operations is $m\alpha$. The number of arcs due to deletions is ms and to transpositions at most $(m-1)s$. Finally the number of arcs due to insert operations is $(m+1)\alpha$. The total number of arcs is therefore at most $2m\alpha + 2ms + \alpha - s$. Moreover *the graph has a distinctive acyclicity*—i.e. there is no path from a node $\langle i, q \rangle$ to a node $\langle j, q' \rangle$, where $i > j$. Together, these facts indicate that it should not be too difficult to design an algorithm which finds a least-cost repair in time proportional to the length of the input string, m. This is quite startling and, perhaps, counter-intuitive. But it is certainly encouraging and gives us hope for the more practical problem of context-free language repair.

We have complicated the above description slightly by always referring to Q' (the non-error states) rather than Q. Indeed it is equally valid to replace Q' by Q everywhere in the construction. However, nodes $\langle i, q \rangle$, where q is an error state, can never enter into a repair of u and so can always be ignored. Moreover substantial improvements ensue in the running time of the repair algorithm by omitting error states (since the running time depends on the number of arcs in the graph).

5.2.3 Equational Characterization

As in Sec. 5.1.4 we can again express the problem of finding a least-cost repair in terms of solving a system of simultaneous equations. We shall not give a general treatment of the construction of the equations—this is left as an exercise for the reader—but we shall present some of the equations which would be constructed for the example shown in Fig. 5.7.

Let Q_i be the set of all words which take the start state q_1 of Fig. 5.6 into the state q_i ($i = 1, 2, 3$). Let $cost^*(u \rightarrow Q_i)$ be the cost of a least-cost edit sequence which transforms the string u into a word $v \in Q_i$. Referring to Fig. 5.7 we can write down the following equations.

$$cost^*(\Lambda \rightarrow Q_1) \qquad\qquad = min\{0,\ cost^*(\Lambda \rightarrow Q_3) + cost(\Lambda \rightarrow;)\}$$

$$cost^*(\Lambda \to Q_2) \qquad = min\{cost^*(\Lambda \to Q_1) + cost(\Lambda \to \textbf{real}),$$
$$cost^*(\Lambda \to Q_1) + cost(\Lambda \to \textbf{integer}),$$
$$cost^*(\Lambda \to Q_3) + cost(\Lambda \to ,)\}$$

$$cost^*(\Lambda \to Q_3) \qquad = cost^*(\Lambda \to Q_2) + cost(\Lambda \to identifier)$$

$$cost^*(\textbf{real} \to Q_1) \qquad = min\{cost^*(\Lambda \to Q_1) + cost(\textbf{real} \to \Lambda),$$
$$cost^*(\Lambda \to Q_3) + cost(\textbf{real} \to ;),$$
$$cost^*(\textbf{real} \to Q_3) + cost(\Lambda \to ;)\}$$

$$cost^*(\textbf{real} \to Q_2) \qquad = min\{cost^*(\Lambda \to Q_1) + cost(\textbf{real} \to \textbf{real}),$$
$$cost^*(\Lambda \to Q_1) + cost(\textbf{real} \to \textbf{integer}),$$
$$cost^*(\Lambda \to Q_3) + cost(\textbf{real} \to ,),$$
$$cost^*(\Lambda \to Q_2) + cost(\textbf{real} \to \Lambda),$$
$$cost^*(\textbf{real} \to Q_1) + cost(\Lambda \to \textbf{real}),$$
$$cost^*(\textbf{real} \to Q_1) + cost(\Lambda \to \textbf{integer}),$$
$$cost^*(\textbf{real} \to Q_3) + cost(\Lambda \to ,)\}$$

$$cost^*(\textbf{real} \to Q_3) \qquad = min\{cost^*(\Lambda \to Q_2) + cost(\textbf{real} \to identifier),$$
$$cost^*(\Lambda \to Q_3) + cost(\textbf{real} \to \Lambda),$$
$$cost^*(\textbf{real} \to Q_2) + cost(\Lambda \to identifier)\}$$

$$cost^*(\textbf{real } identifier \to Q_1) = min\{cost^*(\textbf{real} \to Q_1) + cost(identifier \to \Lambda),$$
$$cost^*(\textbf{real} \to Q_3) + cost(identifier \to ;),$$
$$cost^*(\textbf{real } identifier \to Q_3) + cost(\Lambda \to ;)\}$$

etc.

It is important to note the relationship between this set of equations and the graph of Fig. 5.7. If y is a node in the graph then the general form of the equation for $cost^*(y)$ is

$$cost^*(y) = \min_{arcs\ from\ x\ to\ y} \{cost^*(x) + cost\ of\ arc(x, y)\}.$$

Additionally the equation for the start node—the node corresponding to $\Lambda \to Q_1$—is

$$cost^*(y) = min\{0, \min_{arcs\ from\ x\ to\ y} \{cost^*(x) + cost\ of\ arc(x, y)\}\}.$$

5.3 REPAIR OF CONTEXT-FREE LANGUAGES

Our diagrammatic approach to error repair breaks down when one considers context-free languages. Figure 5.12 gives a rough idea of what the repair graph looks like for a very simple context-free language. The important feature of this graph is that it is infinite because a context-free language has an "infinite-state" recognizer. The construction of such a diagram follows the same principles as those used earlier for regular languages, but it is extremely difficult to give a clear picture of the graph for all but the very simplest context-free languages. Nevertheless, the equational characterization of least-cost repairs can be generalized to context-free languages and so it is this approach which we shall now consider.

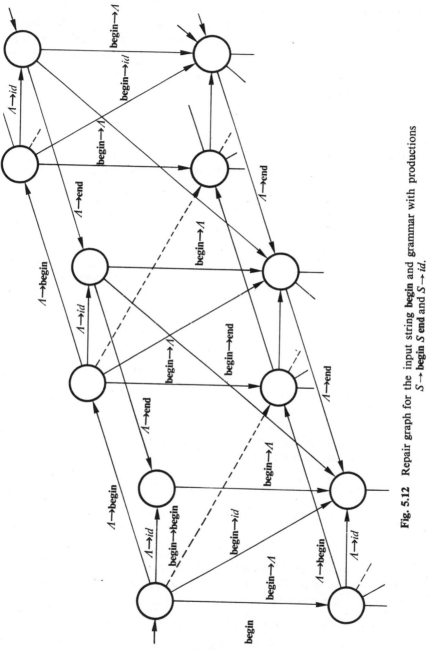

Fig. 5.12 Repair graph for the input string **begin** and grammar with productions $S \rightarrow$ **begin** S **end** and $S \rightarrow id$.

Regrettably, the effect of transpositions is difficult to incorporate into the equations and we shall not consider them any further. (We could argue that syntax errors caused by transpositions occur so rarely that they may be neglected. However, it would be dishonest to claim that this is the reason for neglecting them.) From now on by an "edit operation" we shall, therefore, mean an OK, change, insert or delete operation.

Consider a context-free grammar $G = (N, T, P, S)$ and let $X \in N \cup T$. A best repair of u to X is defined to be a sequence of edit operations which transforms the string u to a string $v \in L(X)$ such that the cost of the sequence is less than or equal to the cost of any other sequence which transforms u to a string in $L(X)$. Let us denote the cost of the best repair of u to X by $cost^*(u \rightarrow X)$. Then the above definition can be restated as

$$cost^*(u \rightarrow X) = \min_{v \in L(X)} \{cost^*(u \rightarrow v)\}.$$

Given a string u we are required to find the best repair of u to S. We can do this by constructing a set of simultaneous equations enabling us to determine $cost^*(u \rightarrow X)$ for each $X \in N \cup T$ and, in particular, $cost^*(u \rightarrow S)$. When constructing the equations we shall find it necessary to extend the definition of $cost^*$. This we shall do at the appropriate point in the development.

Consider, firstly, the case when $X \in T$. Transforming u to X is then an application of string-to-string repair. We have already shown how to construct the equations determining $cost^*(u \rightarrow X)$ but we shall repeat them here for greater clarity and because we shall adopt a slightly different notation.

There are three ways of transforming $u = a_1 \ldots a_m$ to X.

1. Delete a_1 and then transform $a_2 \ldots a_m$ to X.
2. Change a_1 to X and then transform $a_2 \ldots a_m$ to Λ.
3. Insert X and then transform u to Λ.

Thus the equation for $cost^*(u \rightarrow X)$ is

$$cost^*(a_1 \ldots a_m \rightarrow X) = min\{cost^*(a_1 \rightarrow \Lambda) + cost^*(a_2 \ldots a_m \rightarrow X),$$
$$cost^*(a_1 \rightarrow X) + cost^*(a_2 \ldots a_m \rightarrow \Lambda), \quad (5.2)$$
$$cost^*(\Lambda \rightarrow X) + cost^*(a_1 \ldots a_m \rightarrow \Lambda)\}.$$

Similarly one can construct the equation for $cost^*(a_i \ldots a_m \rightarrow X)$ for each i, $2 \leq i \leq m$ (noting that $i = m$ is a special case). These equations together with the equation

$$cost^*(\Lambda \rightarrow \Lambda) = 0 \quad (5.3)$$

can then be solved as described in Sec. 5.1.

Now consider the case when $X \in N$. Let $v \in L(X)$. Two steps in the generation of v from X can be identified. The first step is to pick a production $X \to Y_1 \ldots Y_n$, say, with lhs X. The second step is to generate strings w_1, $w_2, \ldots, w_n$ from $Y_1, \ldots, Y_n$ respectively where $v = w_1 w_2 \ldots w_n$. The first step can be expressed equationally as follows:

$$cost^*(u \to X) = \min_{\text{productions } X \to Y_1 \ldots Y_n} \{cost^*(u \to Y_1 \ldots Y_n)\}. \qquad (5.4)$$

Here we have extended the functionality of $cost^*$ in an obvious way. Specifically, we define $cost^*(u \to \alpha)$, where $u \in T^*$ and $\alpha \in (N \cup T)^*$, to be the cost of a sequence of edit operations which transforms the string u to a string $v \in L(\alpha)$ such that the cost of this sequence is less than or equal to the cost of any other sequence which transforms u to a string in $L(\alpha)$.

The equations (5.4) need to be constructed for each $X \in N$ and combined with the equations (5.2) and (5.3). To obtain a complete set of equations we now need to construct the equations for $cost^*(u \to Y_1 \ldots Y_n)$ where $n \geq 2$. Consider then the problem of transforming $u = a_1 \ldots a_m$ into a string $v \in L(Y_1 \ldots Y_n)$ where $n \geq 2$. This can be achieved in one of three ways.

1. Delete a_1 and transform $a_2 \ldots a_m$ to a word in $L(Y_1 \ldots Y_n)$.
2. If $Y_1 \in T$ change a_1 to Y_1 and then transform $a_2 \ldots a_m$ to a word in $L(Y_2 \ldots Y_n)$. If $Y_1 \in N$ pick an integer k, $1 \leq k \leq m$, transform $a_1 \ldots a_k$ into a word in $L(Y_1)$ and then transform $a_{k+1} \ldots a_m$ into a word in $L(Y_2 \ldots Y_n)$.
3. Insert a word in $L(Y_1)$ and then transform $a_1 \ldots a_m$ to a word in $L(Y_2 \ldots Y_n)$.

Equationally these three possibilities can be expressed as

$$cost^*(a_1 \ldots a_m \to Y_1 \ldots Y_n)$$
$$= \min\{cost(a_1 \to \Lambda) + cost^*(a_2 \ldots a_m \to Y_1 \ldots Y_n),$$
$$\quad cost(a_1 \to Y_1) + cost^*(a_2 \ldots a_m \to Y_2 \ldots Y_n),$$
$$\quad cost(\Lambda \to Y_1) + cost^*(a_1 \ldots a_m \to Y_2 \ldots Y_n)\} \qquad (5.5)$$
$$\qquad \text{if } Y_1 \in T$$
$$= \min\{cost(a_1 \to \Lambda) + cost^*(a_2 \ldots a_m \to Y_1 \ldots Y_n),$$
$$\quad \min_{0 \leq k \leq m} \{cost^*(a_1 \ldots a_k \to Y_1) + cost^*(a_{k+1} \ldots a_m \to Y_2 \ldots Y_n)\}\}$$
$$\qquad \text{if } Y_1 \in N.$$

In these equations we have adopted the convention that $a_i \ldots a_j$ shall denote Λ when $j < i$. Note that there are always three terms on the right-hand side of equation (5.5) when $Y_1 \in T$, but when $Y_1 \in N$ there are $m+2$ terms on the right-hand side. The reduction in the number of terms when $Y_1 \in T$ is important for reasons of efficiency.

The equations (5.2) to (5.5) still do not form a complete set but the general form of the equations is now apparent. We shall need to write an equation for $cost^*(a_i \ldots a_j \rightarrow \alpha)$ for each substring $a_i \ldots a_j$ of u (including Λ) and for each string $\alpha \in (N \cup T)^*$ such that there is a production $A \rightarrow \beta\alpha$ in G, for some $\beta \in (N \cup T)^*$. Below we present a schema for constructing a complete set of equations for $cost^*(u \rightarrow S)$ for any string $u \in T^*$. In these equations we have used the following notation: i and j denote integers where $1 \le i \le j \le m$ and m is the length of u, $A \in N$, $t \in T$, $X \in N \cup T$, $\alpha \in (N \cup T)^*$ and $\beta \in (N \cup T)^+$.

$$
\left.
\begin{aligned}
cost^*(\Lambda \rightarrow \Lambda) &= 0 \\
cost^*(\Lambda \rightarrow X\beta) &= cost^*(\Lambda \rightarrow X) + cost^*(\Lambda \rightarrow \beta) \\
cost^*(\Lambda \rightarrow t) &= cost(\Lambda \rightarrow t) \\
cost^*(\Lambda \rightarrow A) &= \min_{\text{productions } A \rightarrow \alpha} \{cost^*(\Lambda \rightarrow \alpha)\}
\end{aligned}
\right\} \quad (5.6)
$$

$$
cost^*(a_i \ldots a_j \rightarrow \Lambda) = cost(a_i \rightarrow \Lambda) + cost^*(a_{i+1} \ldots a_j \rightarrow \Lambda) \quad (5.7)
$$

$$
\left.
\begin{aligned}
cost^*(a_i \ldots a_j \rightarrow t) = \min\{&cost(a_i \rightarrow \Lambda) + cost^*(a_{i+1} \ldots a_j \rightarrow t), \\
&cost(a_i \rightarrow t) + cost^*(a_{i+1} \ldots a_j \rightarrow \Lambda), \\
&cost(\Lambda \rightarrow t) + cost^*(a_i \ldots a_j \rightarrow \Lambda)\}
\end{aligned}
\right\} \quad (5.8)
$$

$$
cost^*(a_i \ldots a_j \rightarrow A) = \min_{\text{productions } A \rightarrow \alpha} \{cost^*(a_i \ldots a_j \rightarrow \alpha)\} \quad (5.9)
$$

$$
\left.
\begin{aligned}
cost^*(a_i \ldots a_j \rightarrow t\beta) = \min\{&cost(a_i \rightarrow \Lambda) + cost^*(a_{i+1} \ldots a_j \rightarrow t\beta), \\
&cost(a_i \rightarrow t) + cost^*(a_{i+1} \ldots a_j \rightarrow \beta), \\
&cost(\Lambda \rightarrow t) + cost^*(a_i \ldots a_j \rightarrow \beta)\}
\end{aligned}
\right\} \quad (5.10)
$$

$$
\left.
\begin{aligned}
cost^*(&a_i \ldots a_j \rightarrow A\beta) \\
&= \min\{cost(a_i \rightarrow \Lambda) + cost^*(a_{i+1} \ldots a_j \rightarrow A\beta), \\
&\qquad \min_{i-1 \le k \le j} \{cost^*(a_i \ldots a_k \rightarrow A) + cost^*(a_{k+1} \ldots a_j \rightarrow \beta)\}\}
\end{aligned}
\right\} \quad (5.11)
$$

Example 1   Let $G = (\{S\}, \{a, b\}, P, S)$ where P consists of the two productions

$$S \rightarrow aSb \qquad S \rightarrow b$$

Below we present the complete system of equations when the string to be repaired is ab. Each of the equations is preceded by a reference to the equation schema used in its construction.

$$
\left.
\begin{aligned}
((5.9)) \quad cost^*(ab \rightarrow S) &= \min\{cost^*(ab \rightarrow aSb), cost^*(ab \rightarrow b)\} \\
((5.10)) \quad cost^*(ab \rightarrow aSb) &= \min\{cost(a \rightarrow \Lambda) + cost^*(b \rightarrow aSb), \\
&\qquad cost(a \rightarrow a) + cost^*(b \rightarrow Sb), \\
&\qquad cost(\Lambda \rightarrow a) + cost^*(ab \rightarrow Sb)\}
\end{aligned}
\right\}
$$

$$((5.11)) \quad cost^*(ab \to Sb) = min\{cost(a \to \Lambda) + cost^*(b \to Sb),$$
$$cost^*(\Lambda \to S) + cost^*(ab \to b),$$
$$cost^*(a \to S) + cost^*(b \to b),$$
$$cost^*(ab \to S) + cost^*(\Lambda \to b)\}$$
$$((5.8)) \quad cost^*(ab \to b) = min\{cost(a \to \Lambda) + cost^*(b \to b),$$
$$cost(a \to b) + cost^*(b \to \Lambda),$$
$$cost(\Lambda \to b) + cost^*(ab \to \Lambda)\}$$
$$((5.7)) \quad cost^*(ab \to \Lambda) = cost(a \to \Lambda) + cost^*(b \to \Lambda)$$

(5.12)

$$((5.9)) \quad cost^*(a \to S) = min\{cost^*(a \to aSb), cost^*(a \to b)\}$$
$$((5.10)) \quad cost^*(a \to aSb) = min\{cost(a \to \Lambda) + cost^*(\Lambda \to aSb),$$
$$cost(a \to a) + cost^*(\Lambda \to Sb),$$
$$cost(\Lambda \to a) + cost^*(a \to Sb)\}$$
$$((5.11)) \quad cost^*(a \to Sb) = min\{cost(a \to \Lambda) + cost^*(\Lambda \to Sb),$$
$$cost^*(\Lambda \to S) + cost^*(a \to b),$$
$$cost^*(a \to S) + cost^*(\Lambda \to b)\}$$
$$((5.8)) \quad cost^*(a \to b) = min\{cost(a \to \Lambda) + cost^*(\Lambda \to b),$$
$$cost(a \to b) + cost^*(\Lambda \to \Lambda),$$
$$cost(\Lambda \to b) + cost^*(a \to \Lambda)\}$$
$$((5.7)) \quad cost^*(a \to \Lambda) = cost(a \to \Lambda) + cost^*(\Lambda \to \Lambda)$$

(5.13)

$$((5.9)) \quad cost^*(b \to S) = min\{cost^*(b \to aSb), cost^*(b \to b)\}$$
$$((5.10)) \quad cost^*(b \to aSb) = min\{cost(b \to \Lambda) + cost^*(\Lambda \to aSb),$$
$$cost(b \to a) + cost^*(\Lambda \to Sb),$$
$$cost(\Lambda \to a) + cost^*(b \to Sb)\}$$
$$((5.11)) \quad cost^*(b \to Sb) = min\{cost(b \to \Lambda) + cost^*(\Lambda \to Sb),$$
$$cost^*(\Lambda \to S) + cost^*(b \to b),$$
$$cost^*(b \to S) + cost^*(\Lambda \to b)\}$$
$$((5.8)) \quad cost^*(b \to b) = min\{cost(b \to \Lambda) + cost^*(\Lambda \to b),$$
$$cost(b \to b) + cost^*(\Lambda \to \Lambda),$$
$$cost(\Lambda \to b) + cost^*(b \to \Lambda)\}$$
$$((5.7)) \quad cost^*(b \to \Lambda) = cost(b \to \Lambda) + cost^*(\Lambda \to \Lambda)$$

(5.14)

$$cost^*(\Lambda \to S) = min\{cost^*(\Lambda \to aSb), cost^*(\Lambda \to b)\}$$
$$cost^*(\Lambda \to aSb) = cost^*(\Lambda \to a) + cost^*(\Lambda \to Sb)$$
$$((5.6)) \quad cost^*(\Lambda \to Sb) = cost^*(\Lambda \to S) + cost^*(\Lambda \to b)$$
$$cost^*(\Lambda \to a) = cost(\Lambda \to a)$$
$$cost^*(\Lambda \to b) = cost(\Lambda \to b)$$
$$cost^*(\Lambda \to \Lambda) = 0$$

(5.15)

It is painfully evident from the last example that least-cost repair of context-free languages is impossibly inefficient (unless, of course, a better model is invented). The number of equations that have to be solved is alarmingly large, even for short strings and small grammars. It is not difficult to get a rough estimate of the number of equations. Given a string u of length m one must construct a set of equations in $cost^*(a_i \ldots a_j \rightarrow \alpha)$ for each value of i, where $1 \leq i \leq m$, and for each value of j, where $i \leq j \leq m$. Thus there are $O(m^2)$ equations, where the constant of proportionality is generally more than the total length of right-hand sides of productions in the grammar. More importantly, the total number of terms on the right-hand sides of the equations is $O(m^3)$, as is evident from (5.11). This is very disappointing, particularly in view of our optimism after analyzing the size of the repair graph for a regular language.

Although least-cost repair is an impractical proposition, the concept is of fundamental importance, as are the techniques we have described for characterizing a problem as finding the solution to a system of simultaneous equations. Indeed, in Chap. 6 we shall present a method of incorporating error recovery into a recursive-descent syntax analyzer which essentially involves applying a least-cost repair of a string into a context-free language for the particular case when the string has length one.

5.4 ALGORITHMS FOR FINDING LEAST-COST REPAIRS

In spite of the impracticality of the problem it is an interesting challenge to computer scientists to devise efficient algorithms for finding least-cost repairs—that is, algorithms which solve the equations in time roughly proportional to the number of terms they contain. Many of our readers would therefore (we hope) be disappointed if we did not at least present a brief overview of such algorithms. This we shall now do. We shall relate our discussion to the repair of regular languages since here we have, literally, a much clearer picture of the problem.

Least-cost repair of regular languages amounts to finding a least-cost path through the repair graph. Algorithms for finding least-cost paths are well-known, but they are normally referred to as "shortest-path" algorithms. (Finding shortest paths is algebraically identical to finding least-cost paths.) The algorithms all fall into one of two types—the elimination techniques or the iterative techniques. We shall briefly overview an example of each.

The graph of Fig. 5.13 will be used to illustrate the algorithms. In Fig. 5.13 the arc labels are the costs of edit operations. Node 1 is the start node and we wish to find a least-cost path to node 4. The costs attached to the arcs have been chosen specifically to indicate where identities occur. For example, all the delete arcs—arcs from 1 to 4, from 2 to 5 and from 3 to 6—have been given the same cost, namely 6.

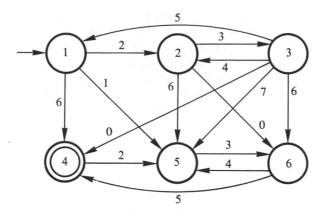

Fig. 5.13　A repair graph.

For brevity, we shall use y_i to denote the cost of a least-cost path from node 1 to node i. The equations for the y_i are then as follows:

$$
\begin{aligned}
y_1 &= min\{y_3+5, & 0\,\} \\
y_2 &= min\{y_1+2, y_3+4, & \infty\} \\
y_3 &= min\{y_2+3, & \infty\} \\
y_4 &= min\{y_1+6, y_3+0, y_6+5, & \infty\} \\
y_5 &= min\{y_1+1, y_2+6, y_3+7, y_4+2, y_6+4, \infty\} \\
y_6 &= min\{y_2+0, y_3+6, y_5+3, & \infty\}
\end{aligned}
\qquad (5.16)
$$

Let us note first how one can construct a least-cost repair knowing the solution to such a system of equations. By inspection of Fig. 5.13 one may verify that $y_1 = 0$, $y_2 = 2$, $y_3 = 5$, $y_4 = 5$, $y_5 = 1$ and $y_6 = 2$. Knowing these values we can *retrace* a least-cost path from node 1 to node 4. Specifically, we begin by asking which terms on the rhs of the equation for y_4 are equal to y_4. In fact

$$y_4 = 5 = y_3+0,$$

whilst $y_4 \neq y_1+6$ and $y_4 \neq y_6+5$. We infer that the predecessor of node 4 on a least-cost path from node 1 is node 3. Now, examining y_3 we have

$$y_3 = 5 = y_2+3.$$

That is, the predecessor of node 3 is node 2. Finally,

$$y_2 = 2 = y_1+2.$$

Therefore the predecessor of node 2 is node 1. Summarizing, the least-cost path from node 1 to 4 goes from 1 to 2 to 3 to 4. It is now straightforward to deduce the least-cost repair.

This technique, of comparing the known solution to the lhs of an equation with each term on the rhs, and thus retracing the repair, can be applied equally well to a system of equations whose underlying language is context-free. It may happen that the lhs equals more than one term on the rhs, indicating that there is more than one least-cost repair. In such circumstances an arbitrary choice of a term equaling the lhs can be made.

Let us now discuss how to solve (5.16).

5.4.1 Dijkstra's Algorithm

An iterative technique solves equations such as (5.16) by finding an approximation to each y_i and then repeatedly substituting the approximations into the right-hand sides in order to obtain new approximations. This process is repeated until the right-hand and left-hand sides become equal.

Let us use the notation y_i^a for an approximation to y_i. Then, a first approximation to equations (5.16) is

$$y_1^a = 0, \qquad y_2^a = y_3^a = y_4^a = y_5^a = y_6^a = \infty.$$

Substituting these values into the right-hand sides we obtain the new approximations:

$$
\begin{aligned}
y_1^a &= min\{\infty + 5, & 0\} = 0 \\
y_2^a &= min\{0 + 2, \infty + 4, & \infty\} = 2 \\
y_3^a &= min\{\infty + 3, & \infty\} = \infty \\
y_4^a &= min\{0 + 6, \infty + 0, \infty + 5, & \infty\} = 6 \\
y_5^a &= min\{0 + 1, \infty + 6, \infty + 7, \infty + 2, \infty + 4, \infty\} = 1 \\
y_6^a &= min\{\infty + 0, \infty + 6, \infty + 3, & \infty\} = \infty
\end{aligned}
$$

Various strategies can now be adopted for deciding when or when not to substitute a new approximation into the right-hand side of the equations. One strategy (the Jacobi method) is to substitute *all* the new approximations into the right-hand sides. This method, though very simple, is too inefficient to recommend in this application. A second strategy is to choose *one* value and substitute that value into all the right-hand sides in which it appears. Adopting this strategy we might now choose to substitute y_5^a into the equation for y_6. This would give a new value for y_6^a, namely $y_6^a = min\{\infty + 0, \infty + 6, 1 + 3, \infty\}$ $= 4$.

On what basis should this choice be made? Well, clearly, the fewest number of substitutions will be made if we can always choose i such that i has not already been chosen and $y_i^a = y_i$. (If $y_i^a \neq y_i$ when i is chosen, then i must be rechosen at some later stage to guarantee correctness.) Now, it is clear that $y_1^a = y_1$. We can also establish that $y_5^a = y_5$, thus justifying our choice of y_5^a. This is because the label of the arc from node 1 to node 5 is less than the labels of all other arcs from node 1. Since any path from node 1 to node 5 must begin with an arc from node 1, and all costs are non-negative, the direct path is of least cost. The nodes 1 and 5 are therefore said to be *permanently* labeled, whilst nodes 2, 3, 4 and 6 are said to be *temporarily* labeled. Our problem is: which, if any, of nodes 2, 3, 4 and 6 can be reclassified as permanent? A reasonable conjecture, which turns out to be correct when all costs are non-negative, is that any node i with the property that y_i^a is the least value among the temporary values can be chosen and declared permanent. In our example this implies that the next choice is node 2, since $y_2^a = 2 < y_6^a = 4 < y_4^a = 6 < y_3^a = \infty$.

This is the essence of the well-known shortest-path algorithm due to E. W. Dijkstra. Dijkstra's algorithm consists of repeatedly choosing the temporary value y_i^a of least cost among the temporary values, relabeling it as permanent and substituting it into the equations in which y_i appears. The process is terminated when a final node is labeled as permanent. The correctness of Dijkstra's algorithm relies on the assumption that all costs are non-negative, but this assumption is valid for repair graphs.

In designing a repair algorithm a reasonable consideration is to expect the efficiency of the algorithm to be comparable with that of a non-repair algorithm when both are presented with correct strings. The commending feature of Dijkstra's algorithm is that this requirement can be incorporated into the algorithm with only a relatively small overhead on the running time. Whenever a node is declared permanent and there is an arc of zero cost from the node to a temporary node, then this temporary node can immediately be declared permanent. Thus the processing of arcs of zero cost can be factored out of Dijkstra's algorithm and accomplished using a non-repair procedure. In this way, the best-case running time of Dijkstra's algorithm (which occurs when the input string has no errors) can be made to depend primarily upon the efficiency of the non-repair algorithm.

There is no reason why Dijkstra's algorithm cannot also be applied to the repair of context-free languages, but, so far as the author is aware, no-one has worked out the details. Should any reader wish to tackle this problem we would suggest that he begin by generalizing Dijkstra's algorithm to the following problem. Given a context-free grammar $G = (N, T, P, S)$, find $cost^*(A{\rightarrow}A)$ for each $A \in N$. The latter problem is a generalization of the terminating-productions problem discussed in Chap. 1, and the techniques used there in developing an efficient program are equally applicable. It is also a special case of the problem one is really concerned with (finding $cost^*(u{\rightarrow}A)$ for any string u), and so a thorough understanding of its solution should help considerably.

5.4.2 Gaussian Elimination

Presented with a system of equations like (5.16) it is more than likely that the reader would use an *elimination technique* to solve them. Thus to solve (5.16) one might begin by eliminating y_1 by *forward-substituting* its equation into the equation for y_2:

$$y_2 = min\{min\{y_3+5,0\}+2, y_3+4, \qquad\qquad \infty\} \qquad (5.17)$$

$$= min\{y_3+4, \qquad\qquad min\{0+2, \infty\}\}. \qquad (5.18)$$

Now y_2 is *forward-substituted* into the equation for y_3:

$$y_3 = min\{y_3+4+3, \qquad\qquad min\{0+2, \infty\}+3, \infty\}. \qquad (5.19)$$

Equation (5.19) can be simplified to

$$y_3 = min\{ \qquad\qquad min\{0+2, \infty\}+3, \infty\}. \qquad (5.20)$$

Summarizing the steps so far, we have

$$\begin{aligned}
y_1 &= min\{y_3+5, &&0\} \\
y_2 &= min\{y_3+4, &&min\{0+2, \infty\}\} \qquad (5.21) \\
y_3 &= min\{ &&min\{0+2, \infty\}+3, \infty\}.
\end{aligned}$$

Clearly $y_3 = 5$ and so its value can be *back-substituted* into the equations for y_1 and y_2, giving

$$y_2 = min\{5+4,2\} \quad \text{and} \quad y_1 = min\{5+5,0\}. \qquad (5.22)$$

That is, $y_1 = 0$ and $y_2 = 2$.

Now that we know the values of y_1, y_2 and y_3 we can *forward-substitute* them into the equations for y_4, y_5 and y_6. Thus, we obtain

$$\begin{aligned}
y_4 &= min\{y_6+5, &&5\} \\
y_5 &= min\{y_4+2, y_6+4, &&1\} \qquad (5.23) \\
y_6 &= min\{y_5+3, &&2\}.
\end{aligned}$$

And so it goes on . . . .

Elimination techniques are particularly well-suited to finding paths through graphs having distinctive structural qualities, and repair graphs have those qualities to a marked degree. The particular features of repair graphs which suggest the use of Gaussian elimination are

(a) the OK, change, delete and transpose operations define an *acyclic* subgraph of the repair graph, and
(b) the subgraph defined by the insertions repeats itself at all positions in the input string.

These properties are strikingly evident in Fig. 5.7. They also show themselves in equations (5.16) in that

(a) y_1, y_2 and y_3 are interdependent but do not depend on y_4, y_5 and y_6;

(b) there is a commonality between the equations for y_1, y_2 and y_3 and those for y_4, y_5 and y_6. This commonality is highlighted by comparing equations (5.23) with those defining y_1, y_2 and y_3 in (5.16).

Property (a) is exploited by evaluating the costs at each position in the input string, starting at position 0 and proceeding in order to position m. Property (b) is less easy to exploit, but we have tried to indicate how this is done by the way equations (5.17) to (5.23) have been structured. Effectively, Gaussian elimination avoids repeated computations by performing *offline* the simplifications used to go from (5.17) to (5.18) and from (5.19) to (5.20). The simplifications which have not been made in equations (5.21) and (5.22) are those not common to each position in the input string. Thus to calculate y_4, y_5 and y_6 one solves the equations:

$$y_4 = min\{y_6+5, \qquad\qquad\qquad\qquad 5\}$$
$$y_5 = min\{y_6+4, \qquad\qquad min\{5+2, 1\}\} \qquad (5.24)$$
$$y_6 = min\{ \qquad\qquad min\{5+2, 1\}+3, 2\}.$$

In fact, Gaussian elimination makes use of a so-called *product form* to solve (5.24) (numerical analysts may recognize this term), but it is beyond our scope to go into details.

It is quite straightforward to adapt Gaussian elimination to the problem of repairing context-free languages. One's experience with the regular language problem suggests examining the equation schema (5.6) to (5.11) for an acyclic structure and for a commonality in the terms involving insertions. The acyclicity is readily apparent; the values of $cost^*(w\rightarrow\alpha)$ (where $w \in T^*$ and $\alpha \in (N \cup T)^*$) depend on $cost^*(w'\rightarrow\beta)$ ($w' \in T^*$ and $\beta \in (N \cup T)^*$), where w' is a *substring* of w. Thus the equations should be solved beginning with the shortest substring, $w = \Lambda$, and successively increasing the length of w until $w = u$.

It is not so easy to identify the commonality due to insertions, but it is there. To illustrate it we have reproduced equations (5.12) and (5.14) below, but terms not involving insertions have been omitted.

$$\left.\begin{array}{l} cost^*(ab\rightarrow aSb) = min\{cost(\Lambda\rightarrow a)+cost^*(ab\rightarrow Sb), \dots\} \\ cost^*(ab\rightarrow Sb) \ = min\{cost^*(\Lambda\rightarrow S)+cost^*(ab\rightarrow b), \\ \qquad\qquad\qquad cost^*(\Lambda\rightarrow b)+cost^*(ab\rightarrow S), \dots\} \\ cost^*(ab\rightarrow b) \ \ = min\{cost(\Lambda\rightarrow b)+cost^*(ab\rightarrow\Lambda), \dots\} \end{array}\right\} \quad (5.25)$$

$$cost^*(b{\rightarrow}aSb) = min\{cost(\varLambda{\rightarrow}a)+cost^*(b{\rightarrow}Sb), \dots \}$$
$$cost^*(b{\rightarrow}Sb) = min\{cost^*(\varLambda{\rightarrow}S)+cost^*(b{\rightarrow}b),$$
$$cost^*(\varLambda{\rightarrow}b)+cost^*(b{\rightarrow}S), \dots \}$$
$$cost^*(b{\rightarrow}b) = min\{cost(\varLambda{\rightarrow}b)+cost^*(b{\rightarrow}\varLambda), \dots \}. \qquad (5.26)$$

Insertions, which are the only cause of cycles in the equations, can thus be handled by computing a "product form" in exactly the same way as for regular languages.

EXERCISES

5.1 Find least-cost repairs of all printing errors in this text. Please let the author know when you have completed this exercise!

5.2 Construct the repair graph for the following pairs of strings.

PREPARE   REPAIR
NESSERY   NECESSARY
MISIPI   MISSISSIPPI

In each case, find least-cost repairs assuming unit edit costs.

5.3 Construct the repair graph for the string

real ; *identifier*

using Fig. 5.6 as the basic recognizer.

5.4 Formalize the process of constructing the system of simultaneous equations defining the cost of repairing the string u to the regular language R. Assume that R is specified by a right-linear grammar.

5.5 Construct the system of equations defining the cost of repairing ba to S, where the grammar

$$G = (\{S,A\},\{a,b\},\{S \rightarrow baA, A \rightarrow Sb, A \rightarrow b\},S).$$

5.6 A problem related to least-cost repair is the *longest common subsequence problem*. A *subsequence* of a string $u = u_1u_2 \cdots u_m$ is any string $w = u_{i_1}u_{i_2} \cdots u_{i_k}$, where

$$1 \leq i_1 < i_2 < \cdots < i_k \leq m.$$

A *common subsequence* of a pair of strings u and v is a string w which is a subsequence of both u and v. For example, *aba* is a common subsequence of *abcbacca* and *adbcacb*. The longest common subsequence is *abcac*.

Express the problem of finding the longest common subsequence as finding the longest path through a suitably constructed graph. Describe how to construct the graph from a given pair of strings. Also, characterize the problem in terms of finding a solution to a suitably constructed system of equations.

BIBLIOGRAPHIC NOTES

The model of error repair developed in Secs. 5.1–3 is based on the work of Wagner and Fischer [5.18], Wagner [5.17] and Aho and Peterson [5.2]. Wagner and Fischer [5.18] consider only insertions, deletions and changes but do not assume that only one change operation may be applied to any symbol. If transpositions are included and a symbol may be transposed any number of times, finding least-cost repairs becomes intractable—see [5.12] for a discussion. The model of regular language repair discussed by Wagner [5.17] leads to rather less efficient algorithms than those presented here. When the edit operations have unit cost the least-cost repair is called the "minimum-distance correction"—hence the title of [5.2]. (We prefer the term "repair" to "correction" since the former is more apt and less emotive.) An alternative description of essentially the same algorithm for minimum-distance repair of context-free languages is given by Lyon [5.13]. (Note: [5.13] is singularly mistitled— the algorithm is far from "practical".)

The basic principle behind the construction of the model is the principle of "dynamic programming". Dynamic programming is a technique pioneered by Bellman [5.5] and used in operations research to evaluate policies in multi-stage processes. Some applications of dynamic programming to computer science have been noted in [5.1] but, in the author's view, it is a technique which has not yet realized its full potential.

The correction of spelling errors has many applications—computer-aided instruction and airline-reservation systems are particular examples—and a number of algorithms have been developed to cope with the problem [5.3, 5.6, 5.10, 5.14]. Alberga [5.3] gives a good review. Usually, specialized algorithms are more efficient and just as effective as least-cost repair and the latter is not recommended.

Backhouse and Carré [5.4] and Carré [5.7] show how Gaussian elimination can be applied in a variety of path-finding problems. The treatment is theoretical and may be hard going for some readers; Carré [5.8] gives a more leisurely account as well as providing yet more applications of Gaussian elimination. Carré [5.8] also discusses the Jacobi method alluded to in Sec. 5.4, as well as the related and better Gauss–Seidel and double-sweep methods. The latter method is due to J. Y. Yen [5.19].

Dijkstra's algorithm [5.9] is an excellent paradigm for the choice of data structures. Discussions of appropriate data structures are included in [5.1, 5.11, 5.15, 5.16]. Johnson's paper [5.11] is particularly lucid. For the repair of regular languages, Wagner's implementation of Dijkstra's algorithm can be recommended [5.16].

5.1 Aho, A. V., J. E. Hopcroft and J. D. Ullman, *The Design and Analysis of Computer Algorithms*, Addison-Wesley, Reading, Mass. (1974).

5.2 Aho, A. V. and T. G. Peterson, "A minimum-distance error-correcting parser for context-free languages", *SIAM J. Comput.*, **1**, 305–12 (1972).

5.3 Alberga, C. N., "String similarity and misspellings", *Comm. ACM*, **10**, 302–13 (1967).

5.4 Backhouse, R. C. and B. A. Carré, "Regular algebra applied to path-finding problems", *J. Inst. Maths. Applics.*, **15**, 161–86 (1975).

5.5 Bellman, R., *Dynamic Programming*, Princeton University Press, Princeton, New Jersey (1957).

5.6 Blair, C. R., "A program for correcting spelling errors", *Info. and Control*, **3,** 60–7 (1960).

5.7 Carré, B. A., "An algebra for network routing problems", *J. Inst. Maths. Applics*, **7,** 273–94 (1971).

5.8 Carré, B. A., *Graphs and Networks*, Oxford University Press, Oxford (1979).

5.9 Dijkstra, E. W., "A note on two problems in connexion with graphs", *Numerische Mathematik*, **1,** 269–71 (1959).

5.10 Damerau, F., "A technique for computer detection and correction of spelling errors", *Comm. ACM*, **7,** 171–6 (1964).

5.11 Johnson, D. B., "Efficient algorithms for shortest paths in sparse networks", *J. ACM*, **24,** 1–13 (1977).

5.12 Lowrance, R. and R. A. Wagner, "An extension of the string-to-string correction problem", *J. ACM*, **22,** 177–83 (1975).

5.13 Lyon, G., "Syntax-directed least-errors analysis for context-free languages: a practical approach", *Comm. ACM*, **17,** 3–14 (1974).

5.14 Morgan, H. L., "Spelling correction in systems programs", *Comm. ACM*, **13,** 90–4 (1970).

5.15 Vuillemin, J., "A data structure for manipulating priority queues", *Comm. ACM*, **21,** 309–15 (1978).

5.16 Wagner, R. A., "A shortest path algorithm for edge-sparse graphs", *J. ACM*, **23,** 50–7 (1976).

5.17 Wagner, R. A., "Order-*n* correction for regular languages", *Comm. ACM*, **17,** 269–71 (1974).

5.18 Wagner, R. A. and M. J. Fischer, "The string-to-string correction problem", *J. ACM*, **21,** 168–73 (1974).

5.19 Yen, J. Y., "An algorithm for finding shortest routes from all source nodes to a given destination in general networks", *Quart. Appl. Maths.*, **27,** 526–30 (1970).

6   ERROR RECOVERY

The development of least-cost repair in Chap. 5 has reached a crisis point; although the model is aesthetically pleasing and mathematically tractable, it is damned by the apparent impossibility of designing algorithms which accomplish it in an acceptable running time. In this chapter we shall make a rather crude simplification of our notation of least-cost repair, with the sole objective of guaranteeing that the repair algorithm does not significantly influence the running time of an LL parser. The resulting process is described as *error recovery*.

It has been traditional to regard error recovery and error repair as two quite distinct processes: error recovery is the process of determining how to continue analyzing a program when an error is found; error repair involves specifying how the incorrect program can be edited to form a syntactically correct program. We do not accept that there is a distinction. Instead, our argument is that the best way of determining how to continue analyzing a program is to evaluate the repairs that can be made *locally* at the point where the error is detected. More specifically, we consider error recovery as a special case of error repair in which no "back-tracking" is allowed when constructing the repair.

To clarify the notion, consider again the repair graph of Fig. 5.7. Using Dijkstra's algorithm one would perform the OK transitions from the node $\langle 0, q_1 \rangle$ to the node $\langle 3, q_1 \rangle$ before detecting an error in the input string. To find the least-cost repair one must allow the possibility that any of the OK transitions is incorrect. Accordingly, Dijkstra's algorithm may "back-track" and choose another node at position 0, 1 or 2 in the input string. In contrast, by an *error recovery algorithm* we shall mean any algorithm which finds a repair of the input string *without* retracing any earlier steps.

This constraint on the algorithm is the crude simplification to which we referred in the opening paragraph. It is an obvious technique to try to ensure that the error analysis is fast, but its limitations are easily exposed. The following statement illustrates a common syntactic error in the use of ALGOL-like languages:

$$\textbf{if } a = 0 \textbf{ then } b := 1; \textbf{ else } c := 2$$

The error in the statement (the spurious ";") is only detected when "**else**" is encountered. According to our definition an error *recovery* algorithm would declare the semicolon to be OK and would repair the error by editing the string "**else** $c := 2$"—probably by deleting "**else**".

In spite of its drawbacks, error recovery is the technique which is pre- dominantly used in error analysis and it will, no doubt, continue to be used when speed is an important factor. The mitigating feature of programming languages which makes its use feasible is that the "costs" of editing different symbols are widely disparate. For instance, if the symbol **while** is erroneously encountered in a PASCAL program and it is possible to continue the parse by inserting a semicolon, then it is very likely that this is the appropriate repair. In other words the "cost" of inserting a semicolon is low relative to the "cost" of other repairs, e.g. deleting the symbol **while**. (Deleting **while** is one way of continuing the parse but it is very easy to forget this possibility because it is so unlikely!)

The objective of this chapter is to present a recovery technique based upon a notion of "locally optimal" repairs. Our view of error *recovery* as a special case of error *repair* is relatively novel and, perhaps, not readily accept- able to some readers. The main aim of Secs. 6.1 and 6.2 is, therefore, to con- vince the reader that this is so. In Sec. 6.1 we describe a recovery technique essentially identical to one advocated by Wirth and successfully used in a number of compilers. The method is reasonably effective and sufficiently uncomplicated that it can be programmed by hand. Although it was not conceived as a repair technique we shall argue that the best way to evaluate its effectiveness is to evaluate the actions taken by the recovery process in terms of the repairs they simulate. Having made this point, the remaining sections are all concerned with choosing recovery actions which simulate a "locally optimal" repair.

Section 6.3 defines precisely the meaning of a "locally optimal repair" and shows how such a repair can be factored into one or more actions like calling a procedure or jumping from one position to another in a procedure. A scheme for incorporating a locally optimal repair strategy in a recursive- descent syntax analyzer is then described. Section 6.2 is interposed between Secs. 6.1 and 6.3 to give the reader an overview of the main points in the subsequent theoretical development. It contains a description of a recursive-descent syntax analyzer to which error recovery has been added using the locally optimal repair technique.

Some aspects of the development in Sec. 6.3 are conceptually quite difficult and open to doubt. This is particularly true of the idea of factoring repairs into sequences of recovery actions. Section 6.4 has therefore been included to allay the reader's fears about the correctness of the method. Finally, Sec. 6.5 presents a complete syntax analyzer for a simple programming language PL/0. A sample output from the syntax analyzer demonstrates the effectiveness of using a repair strategy to design the error-recovery procedure.

6.1 A SIMPLE RECOVERY SCHEME

The scheme we are about to describe exploits the rich structure of recursive-descent syntax analyzers. We shall assume that one has already been constructed for the given grammar as described in Chap. 3. To illustrate the method and, subsequently, our own method, we shall apply both to the construction of a syntax analyzer for the grammar in Table 6.1. This grammar defines a statement list (mnemonic: SL) to be a sequence of statements (mnemonic: ST) each of which is terminated by a semicolon. Statements are either **if** . . . **then** . . . **fi** statements or unconditional statements (mnemonic: U). To simplify matters the syntax of U is trivial: U generates the terminal symbol id (think of U as a procedure call). Also, for the purposes of illustration, the construct immediately following **if** in a conditional statement is assumed to be U.

Table 6.1   Grammar underlying Programs 6.1 and 6.2.

$$G = (\ \{S,SL,ST,E,U\},\ \{id,\text{if},\text{then},\text{else},\text{fi},;,.\},P,S)\ \text{where } P \text{ consists of:}$$

$$
\begin{array}{ll}
S\ \to SL\,. & \\
SL \to ST\,;\,SL & SL \to \Lambda \\
ST \to \text{if } U \text{ then } SL\ E \text{ fi} & ST \to U \\
ST \to \Lambda & \\
E\ \to \text{else } SL & E\ \to \Lambda \\
U\ \to id &
\end{array}
$$

Table 6.1 is, of course, much too simple to allow specific comparisons to be made between the technique described here and that to follow based on locally optimal repairs. Indeed, we do not intend to provide such a comparison. Rather, our aim is to use the insight accrued in Chap. 5, together with the experience of engineering a simple recovery scheme, to expose the fundamental issues and hence develop a mathematical model which encompasses both.

The main idea underlying the scheme is that, when an error is detected, part of the input text is skipped until a symbol is recognized which can legally follow the current state of the parse. Control of the parser is then allowed to proceed to the point at which the symbol is expected and the parsing resumes.

The realization of this simple strategy involves a number of elements. Firstly, the set of symbols which are "admissible" following each procedure call must be known. Secondly, a procedure to skip symbols must be included in the program and invoked at suitable intervals. Finally, the logic of the program must permit control to proceed to and from instances of the latter procedure whenever an error is detected.

The set of "admissible" symbols following each procedure call is defined by the structure of the syntax analyzer. Specifically, let us suppose that each non-terminal procedure has been assigned a parameter *folset*, say, of type **set of** *symbol*. The initial value of *folset* passed to *pS* (where S is the sentence symbol of the grammar) is the empty set—denoted by [ ] in PASCAL. Subsequently, when the procedure *pB*, say, is called from within *pA*, say, (i.e. there is a production $A \rightarrow \ldots B \ldots$) then the value of *folset* passed to *pB* is the union of the value passed to *pA* and the set of terminal symbols which are tested following the call to *pB* within *pA*.

Program 6.1

program $Z1(input, output)$;

. . .

type $symbol = (qif, qthen, qelse, qfi, qid, qsemicolon, qdot, qx)$;
  $symset = $ **set of** $symbol$;
  $errorno = 0 \ldots 10$;

var . . .
  $nextsymbol$: $symbol$;
  $noerrors$: $integer$;
  $chposn$: $1 \ldots 81$; {*position of last input character read*}

procedure $error(k: errorno)$;
begin $write(' ***', '   ' : chposn, '×')$; $noerrors := noerrors + 1$;
case k **of**
  0: $writeln('SYMBOL DELETED')$;
  1: $writeln('END OF FILE—ANALYSIS TERMINATED')$;
  2: $writeln('MISSING SEMICOLON—INSERTED')$;
  3: $writeln('THEN EXPECTED—INSERTED')$;
  4: $writeln('FI EXPECTED—INSERTED')$;
  5: $writeln('ID EXPECTED—INSERTED')$;
  6: $write('INVALID BEGINNING TO STATEMENT LIST')$;

Program 6.1   (Continued)

```
7: write('ID EXPECTED');
8: write('INVALID TERMINATION OF U');
9: write('INVALID TERMINATION OF STATEMENT');
10: writeln('DOT EXPECTED—INSERTED AND ANALYSIS ',
    'TERMINATED');
 end;
end; {error}
. . .
procedure  test(s1,s2: symset;  n: integer);
begin
if not (nextsymbol in s1) then
    begin error(n);  s1 := s1 + s2;
    if not (nextsymbol in s1) then
        begin writeln('—SYMBOL DELETED'); getsymbol;
        end
    else writeln;
    while not (nextsymbol in s1) do
        begin error(0);  getsymbol;
        end;
    end;
end; {test}


procedure pSL(folset: symset);
    procedure pST(folset: symset);
        procedure pU(folset: symset);
        begin test([qid], folset + [qsemicolon,qif], 7);
        if nextsymbol = qid then getsymbol
                            else error(5);
        test(folset, [qsemicolon, qif, qid], 8);
        end; {pU}


        procedure pE(folset: symset);
        begin getsymbol;  pSL(folset);
        end; {pE}

    begin {pST}
    if nextsymbol = qid then pU(folset)
    else if nextsymbol = qif
    then begin getsymbol;
        pU(folset + [qthen, qelse, qfi]);
```

Program 6.1   (Continued)

```
        if nextsymbol = qthen then getsymbol
                                else error(3);
        pSL(folset + [qelse, qfi]);
        if nextsymbol = qelse then pE(folset + [qfi]);
        if nextsymbol = qfi then getsymbol
                                else error(4);
        test(folset, [qid, qif], 9);
        end;
    end; {pST}


begin {pSL}
test(folset + [qid, qif, qsemicolon], [ ], 6);
while nextsymbol in [qid, qif, qsemicolon] do
    begin pST(folset + [qsemicolon]);
    if nextsymbol = qsemicolon then getsymbol
                                else error(2);
    test(folset + [qid, qif, qsemicolon], [ ], 6);
    end;
end; {pSL}

begin {main program}
. . .
getsymbol; {initialize nextsymbol}
pSL([qdot]);
if nextsymbol ≠ qdot then error(10);

. . .
end.
```

Program 6.1 shows how this works for the grammar in Table 6.1. Consider, for instance, the call to *pSL* within *pST*. Following this call there are tests for equality of *nextsymbol* with *qelse* and *qfi*. Thus the call to *pSL* is parameterized by *folset* + [*qelse*,*qfi*]. Similarly, again within *pST*, there are two calls to *pU*, one of which is parameterized by *folset* (since no test on *nextsymbol* occurs after the call) and one which is parameterized by *folset* + [*qthen*, *qelse*,*qfi*].

The second element in the scheme is the implementation of the procedure *test* shown in Program 6.1. This procedure has three parameters, the last of which is simply the code of an error diagnostic. The first parameter is a set *s*1 which includes all the symbols which can legally occur as the next symbol in the input stream. The second parameter is a set *s*2 of "stopping" symbols. Typically, *s*2 will contain symbols like **while** or **procedure** which are not in *s*1 but begin constructs which should not be overlooked by the parser.

In Program 6.1 the stopping symbols are *id*, **if** and semicolon. *test* ascertains whether the next symbol is in *s*1 and, if not, skips symbols until one in *s*1 or *s*2 is encountered.

In practice, the distinction between the admissible symbols and the stopping symbols is often blurred. As we have described it, the admissible symbols are those symbols which would be parsed successfully without involving a procedure call; the stopping symbols do require a procedure call before they can be parsed, but usually they signal the start of an important construct. The important requirement whenever *test* is called is that all symbols in *s*1 or *s*2 can follow the current state of the parse, and *s*1 should contain the set of symbols which are expected to follow immediately.

test is called at the beginning and end of each non-terminal procedure, except where the logic of the program makes the call unnecessary. Thus *test* is called on first entering *pA*, say, if *pA* is called unconditionally and does not itself immediately call another procedure *pB*, say. In Program 6.1 such a call occurs on entering *pU* and *pSL*, but not on entering *pST* or *pE*, since *nextsymbol* is checked before either of the latter two procedures is called. In such calls *s*1 is set to the set of symbols which can occur next, whilst *s*2 is set to the union of *folset* with the set of stopping symbols, excepting those symbols already in *s*1. (Cf. the calls of *test* on entering *pU* and *pSL* in Program 6.1.)

Before leaving the procedure *pA*, say, *test* is called unless the last action in *pA* was to call a procedure *pB*, say. This is exemplified by *pST* in Program 6.1. If *id* is encountered on entering *pST*, then *pU* is called. On its return *no* call to *test* occurs because such a call has already occurred in *pU*. On the other hand, if *pST* recognizes a conditional statement, a call to *test* occurs immediately after the test for **fi**.

The final element in the scheme is to allow control to "fall through" the procedure body when an error is detected. By this we simply mean that all comparisons on *nextsymbol* take the form

$$\textbf{if } \textit{nextsymbol} = qt \textbf{ then } \textit{getsymbol} \textbf{ else } \textit{error}(n);$$

That is, should the comparison fail, the parser prints an error diagnostic and then proceeds to the next production position. Note that this is equivalent to *inserting* the symbol *t*. Alternative techniques are to use the construct

$$\textbf{if } \textit{nextsymbol} \neq qt \textbf{ then } \textit{error}(n); \textit{getsymbol};$$

which is equivalent to *changing* the next symbol to *t*, or

$$\begin{aligned}
&\textbf{while } \textit{nextsymbol} \neq qt \textbf{ do}\\
&\qquad\textbf{begin } \textit{error}(n); \textit{getsymbol}\\
&\qquad\textbf{end};\\
&\quad\textit{getsymbol};
\end{aligned}$$

The latter is equivalent to deleting symbols until *t* is encountered, but its use would negate the purpose of *test*.

To conclude this section Table 6.2 shows a typical output from Program 6.1.

Table 6.2 Output from Program 6.1.

```
    IF ID THEN ID ;
         ELSE ID;
    FI;
    ID;
    IF ID THEN IF ID THEN ID;
               FI;
    FI;
    ID
    IF ID THEN ID ELSE ID FI
***  × INVALID TERMINATION OF U
***  × MISSING SEMICOLON—INSERTED
***               × MISSING SEMICOLON—INSERTED
***                    × MISSING SEMICOLON—INSERTED
    ID
***   × INVALID TERMINATION OF STATEMENT
***   × MISSING SEMICOLON—INSERTED
    IF ID ID; FI;
***   × INVALID TERMINATION OF U
***   × MISSING SEMICOLON—INSERTED
***       × INVALID TERMINATION OF U
***       × THEN EXPECTED—INSERTED
    IF ID THEN ID; ID;
    X;
***   × INVALID BEGINNING TO STATEMENT LIST—SYMBOL DELETED
    IF X ID THEN ID; FI;
***      × ID EXPECTED—SYMBOL DELETED
    IF FI;
***      × ID EXPECTED
***      × ID EXPECTED—INSERTED
***      × THEN EXPECTED—INSERTED
    IF ID . THEN FI;
***      × THEN EXPECTED—INSERTED
***      × FI EXPECTED—INSERTED
***      × MISSING SEMICOLON—INSERTED
***      × FI EXPECTED—INSERTED
***      × MISSING SEMICOLON—INSERTED
  20  SYNTAX ERRORS
```

6.2 OUR OBJECTIVE

As Table 6.2 hopefully suggests, the method we have just described is reasonably effective. Its main drawback is that it is *ad hoc*. It is composed of an assortment of tricks which fit together nicely, but it is not clear why.

To understand Program 6.1 properly it is necessary to relate the actions taken by it to repairing the input string. To this end, most of the error messages generated by Program 6.1 are qualified by either "— INSERTED" or by "— SYMBOL DELETED". In this way, the messages indicate how the parser thinks the input string ought to be corrected. Another way of looking at it is that the actions taken by the parser are exactly those actions which it would have taken had the input string been modified as indicated by the error messages.

It may be a surprise to the reader that this recovery scheme embodies a repair algorithm. After all, it was not conceived as such. Nevertheless, it is indeed true that *every* recovery scheme simulates a process of repairing the input string. For, whatever action is taken before parsing is resumed, we can always ask the question: "What input would have caused the parser to enter the state it is currently in?" Sometimes there are many such strings, but a knowledge of any one of them tells us how to repair the input string to a syntactically correct form.

Having accepted this fact the inevitable question is: "Why not choose recovery actions according to the repairs they simulate?" It is our objective to show just how this can be done.

In anticipation of its development, Program 6.2 shows how a syntax analyzer might look after the addition of a locally optimal repair strategy. This program was generated with the assistance of a software tool. The input to the tool was the grammar in Table 6.1, together with a list of edit costs, viz. the cost of deleting and inserting each terminal symbol (Table 6.3) and the cost of changing one symbol to another (Table 6.4). The symbol x in these tables represents a spurious symbol.

Table 6.3 Insert and delete costs.

Terminal symbol	Insert cost	Delete cost
if	3	1000
then	3	2
fi	1	5
else	3	2
;	1	1000
id	1	1000
.	1	2
x	1	2

Table 6.4 Change costs— $cost$ $(t_1 \rightarrow t_2)$.

t_1 \ t_2	if	then	fi	else	;	id	.	x
if	0							
then		0						
fi			0			∞		
else		∞		0				
;					0			
id	1	1	1	1	∞	0		
.	∞	∞	∞	∞	∞	∞	0	
x	∞	∞	∞	∞	∞	∞	∞	0

Program 6.2

```
program Z2(input, output);
 . . .
type  symbol = (qif, qthen, qelse, qfi, qid, qsemicolon, qdot, qx);
      symset = set of symbol;
      errorno = 0 .. 15;
var   . . .
      nextsymbol: symbol;
      chposn: 1 .. 81;  {position of last character read}
      noerrors: integer;

procedure error(k: errorno);
begin  write(' ***' , ' ' : chposn,  ' × ');  noerrors := noerrors + 1;
case k of
      0: writeln('SYMBOL DELETED');
      1: writeln('END OF FILE—ANALYSIS TERMINATED');
      2: writeln('MISSING SEMICOLON—INSERTED');
      3: writeln('THEN EXPECTED—INSERTED');
      4: writeln('FI EXPECTED—INSERTED');
      5: writeln('ID EXPECTED—INSERTED');
      6: writeln('INVALID BEGINNING TO STATEMENT LIST ',
         '—SYMBOL DELETED');
      7: writeln('ID EXPECTED—SYMBOL DELETED');
      8: writeln('U THEN EXPECTED—INSERTED');
      9: writeln('. EXPECTED—SYMBOL DELETED');
     10: writeln('THEN EXPECTED—SYMBOL DELETED');
     11: writeln('THEN EXPECTED—SYMBOL CHANGED');
     12: writeln('ELSE OR FI EXPECTED—SYMBOL ',
         'DELETED');
     13: writeln('SEMICOLON EXPECTED—SYMBOL ',
         'DELETED');
```

Program 6.2   (Continued)

```
14: writeln('FI EXPECTED—SYMBOL DELETED');
15: writeln('FI EXPECTED—SYMBOL CHANGED');
    end;
end; {error}
```

. . .

```
procedure delete(s: symset; n: errorno);
begin while nextsymbol in s do begin error(n);  n := 0;
                               getsymbol;
                               end;
end; {delete}

procedure pSL(sfi, selse, sdot: integer);
var d: symset; {symbols to be deleted}

    procedure pST;
    label 3, 4, 5, 6, 7;

        procedure pU;
        begin getsymbol;
        end; {pU}

        procedure pE;
        begin getsymbol;
        delete([qdot, qthen, qelse, qx], 14);
        pSL(0, 2, 2);
        end; {pE}

    begin {pST}
    if nextsymbol = qid then pU
    else if nextsymbol = qif then
        begin getsymbol;                                 {if}
        delete([qdot, qelse, qx], 7);
        case nextsymbol of                               {U}
            qid: pU;
            qif, qsemicolon: begin error(8); goto 4 end;
            qthen: begin error(5); goto 3 end;
            qfi: begin error(8); goto 6 end;
            end;
        delete([qdot, qx], 10);
3:      case nextsymbol of                               {then}
            qthen: getsymbol;
            qif, qsemicolon: begin error(3); goto 4 end;
            qelse: begin error(3); goto 5 end;
```

Program 6.2   (Continued)

```
              qid: begin error(11); getsymbol end;
              qfi: begin error(3); goto 6 end;
              end;
          delete([qdot,qthen,qx],6);
4:        case nextsymbol of                                          {SL}
              qif,qsemicolon,qid:  pSL(0,0,2);
              qfi:  goto 6;
              qelse: goto 5;
              end;
          delete([qdot,qthen,qx], 12);
5:        case nextsymbol of                                          {E}
              qelse: pE;
              qfi:;  {OK}
              qid:;  {not OK but do nothing}
              qif,qsemicolon: begin error(4);  goto 7 end;
              end;
          delete([qdot,qthen,qelse,qx],14);
6:        case  nextsymbol of                                         {fi}
              qfi: getsymbol;
              qid: begin error(15); getsymbol; end;
              qif, qsemicolon: error(4);
              end;
7:        end;
      end; {pST}

begin {pSL}
d := [qthen,qx]; {symbols to be deleted}
if sdot ≥ 1 then d := d+[qdot];
if sfi ≥ 4 then d := d+[qfi];
if selse ≥ 1 then d := d+[qelse];
while nextsymbol in [qif,qsemicolon,qid] do
      begin pST;
      delete(d,13);
      if nextsymbol = qsemicolon then getsymbol else error(2);
      delete(d,6);
      end;
end; {pSL}

begin {main program}
. . .
getsymbol; {initialize nextsymbol}
delete([qthen,qfi,qelse,qx],6);
```

Program 6.2   (Continued)

$pSL(5, 2, 0)$;
$delete([qif, qthen, qfi, qelse, qsemicolon, qid, qx], 9)$;
$\{nextsymbol = qdot\}$
if not eof($input$)
then $delete([qif, qthen, qfi, qelse, qsemicolon, qid, qx, qdot], 0)$;
. . .
end.

Programs 6.1 and 6.2 are quite different in structure but their effect, viewed as repair algorithms, is roughly the same—as can be seen by comparing the output from Program 6.2 (Table 6.5) with that from Program 6.1 (Table 6.2). This similarity is not accidental—the costs used to generate Program 6.2 were manipulated with that effect in mind. Specifically, the stopping symbols (*id*, **if** and semicolon) in Program 6.1 were each given a very high delete cost. Also, those symbols which Program 6.1 readily inserts (e.g. semicolon) were given insert costs of 1, the remaining symbols (e.g. **else**) being given insert costs of 3. The delete costs not already set were then set to 2, except for **fi**. The delete cost of **fi** had to be set to 5 to ensure that the analysis of an **if** statement was aborted whenever **fi** was erroneously encountered.

A minor difference between Programs 6.1 and 6.2 is the action taken when **then** is expected, but *id* encountered. In Program 6.1 **then** is inserted; in Program 6.2 *id* is changed to **then**. This difference was included solely to illustrate how a change can be simulated.

A more major respect in which Programs 6.1 and 6.2 do differ is in their actions when the symbol "." is encountered. Program 6.1 always aborts the analysis by inserting sufficient symbols to terminate incomplete statements (see the last seven lines of Table 6.2). The action taken by Program 6.2 depends on whether or not the statement being parsed is an **if** statement. If so the dot is deleted and parsing of any following symbols continues. If not the analysis is aborted as in Program 6.1. This tendency of the simple recovery scheme to "fall out" of procedure calls is its major disadvantage. It shows itself readily in the error diagnostics. For instance, on the PASCAL implementation used by the author, messages like "END EXPECTED" and "UNTIL EXPECTED" occur frequently. These indicate, respectively, that an error has caused the parser to give up parsing a compound statement or a **repeat** statement. A particularly unfortunate occurrence of this sort of message is within **record** declarations, where "giving up" the parse causes a cascade of "UNDECLARED IDENTIFIER" later on in the program.

Careful study of Program 6.2 both now and later will help the reader's understanding of the theoretical development which follows. Let us begin by overviewing the main features of Sec. 6.3 using Program 6.2 as a concrete example.

Table 6.5 Output from Program 6.2.

```
        IF ID THEN ID ;
             ELSE ID;
        FI;
        ID;
        IF ID THEN IF ID THEN ID;
                     FI;
        FI;
        ID
        IF ID THEN ID ELSE ID FI
***     × MISSING SEMICOLON—INSERTED
***                        × MISSING SEMICOLON—INSERTED
                              × MISSING SEMICOLON—INSERTED
***     ID
***     × MISSING SEMICOLON—INSERTED
        IF ID ID; FI;
***     × MISSING SEMICOLON—INSERTED
***          × THEN EXPECTED—SYMBOL CHANGED
        IF ID THEN ID; ID;
        X;
***     × INVALID BEGINNING TO STATEMENT LIST—SYMBOL DELETED
        IF X ID THEN ID; FI;
***          × ID EXPECTED—SYMBOL DELETED
        IF FI;
***          × U THEN EXPECTED—INSERTED
        IF ID . THEN FI;
***          × THEN EXPECTED—SYMBOL DELETED
        .
***     × INVALID BEGINNING TO STATEMENT LIST—SYMBOL DELETED
***                        × END OF FILE—ANALYSIS
                                         TERMINATED
```

12 SYNTAX ERRORS

The main idea behind locally optimal repair is that, in any state of the parse, the next symbol in the input string is repaired, at least cost, to a string which will allow the parse to continue normally. (If the next symbol is OK, then it is "repaired" to itself.) The next symbol is not, however, physically repaired. Instead, the repair is factored into a sequence of one or more recovery "actions" which together *simulate* repairing the next symbol. This step is conceptually a difficult one to make but it is fundamental to the whole process. The recovery actions depend on

(a) the next symbol in the input string,
(b) the position reached in the parse, and
(c) (sometimes) the history of the parse.

To illustrate this let us return to Program 6.2. The labels in *pST* correspond
to positions in the production

$$ST \rightarrow \textbf{if } U \textbf{ then } SL \; E \textbf{ fi.}$$

Thus label 3 is the point at which **then** is expected. At each of these positions
a choice of action has been taken depending on the value of *nextsymbol*.
Either

1. the next symbol is deleted,
2. a jump to another position occurs,
3. a procedure is called, or
4. effects occur equivalent to
   (a) changing the next symbol to the next expected symbol, or
   (b) inserting the next expected symbol.

In *pST* the "history" of the parse is not needed to determine the recovery
action. However, in *pSL* it is used to determine whether **fi, else** and *"."*
should be deleted. More precisely, the "history" of the parse is reflected by
the parameters passed to *pSL*. The parameter-passing mechanism is more
complicated than in Program 6.1, but its function is similar. The parameters
correspond to individual terminal symbols (thus *sfi* corresponds to **fi**) and
determine the cost of the repair if the chosen action were to return from the
current procedure call. Thus, in *pSL* the parameters are used to choose between deleting **fi, else** and *"."* or (implicitly, from the program structure)
returning from the call.

Program 6.2 is notably longer and more complex than Program 6.1.
Generally, the implementation of locally optimal repairs is a task too complex
to undertake without the assistance of a software tool—there are just too
many decisions to be taken—and the resulting programs are longer. However,
they need not be as long as Program 6.2 would suggest. Program 6.2 could
have been shortened and many of the **goto**s omitted, but this would have
obscured the main principles of the method. At the end of this chapter we
present a PL/0 parser written in a more realistic style.

6.3 LOCALLY OPTIMAL REPAIRS

This section presents a theoretical account of the choice of recovery policies
using locally optimal repairs. We begin by defining the term "locally optimal
repair". The important feature of this definition is that it is quite independent
of any parsing algorithm. This is an indicator that the definition is a natural
one and that we are not simply trying to "patch" our favourite parsing
technique. It does, however, leave us with the problem of relating repairs to

the actions taken by a parser. Here we shall restrict our attention to LL(1) parsers implemented by recursive descent. First we need to define precisely the position at which the recovery action is to be taken. This is done in Sec. 6.3.2. Essentially, we identify the earliest point in the parse at which an error can be detected and there is a choice of action available. Having done this we then tabulate in Sec. 6.3.3 the initial recovery action corresponding to each type of repair. (This is the most questionable step in the development and so Sec. 6.4 is devoted to reassuring the reader of its correctness.) The final step is to observe that much of the effort involved in finding a locally optimal repair can be done once and for all by preprocessing the grammar. Specifically, the recovery actions are divided into two sets. The first set contains the single action of returning from the procedure call; the second set contains the remaining actions. Preprocessing the grammar then involves two things: (a) finding the best non-return action at each "production position" and (b) determining how procedure calls should be parameterized. At any point in the parse a choice can then be made between the best non-return action and returning from the procedure by determining whether the appropriate parameter exceeds a given boundary cost.

Some simplifying assumptions have been made, the principal one being that the edit costs must be finite. This assumption can be relaxed (and for practical purposes it is important to do so) but it is beyond the scope of this text to present the more complex proofs required.

6.3.1   The Definition

In the definitions below we shall make precise our notion of a locally optimal repair. Before doing so a brief overview might be helpful. Figure 6.1 is a diagrammatic representation of a possible state of the parse when an error is detected. That portion of the input string which has currently been read is $u't$; some editing may have already been performed to transform u' to u, and t is the next symbol. A partial derivation tree has been constructed and, currently, position i in the production $A \rightarrow X_1 \ldots X_m$ has been reached. Also, after parsing A, a string in $L(\gamma)$ is anticipated.

To continue the parse we consider all possible strings w' which can follow u in a sentence of the grammar. Of these we pick that one, w say, to which t can be transformed at least cost. (If no error is detected in ut, then t is transformed to t.) The recovery actions are chosen which *simulate* the transformation of t to w. In other words we shall identify a sequence of recovery actions which have the effect of (a) advancing the input marker beyond t and (b) modifying the derivation tree to the form it would take had the input string been $uw \ldots$.

Let $G = (N, T, P, Z)$ be a context-free grammar with no useless productions. We assume that G has been augmented in the now familiar way by a
production $Z \rightarrow S\mathbf{eof}$. The input is a string $v\mathbf{eof}$ where none of the symbols of
v is $\mathbf{eof}$. The symbol $\mathbf{eof}$ cannot be changed, inserted or deleted and the recovery action whenever $\mathbf{eof}$ is erroneously encountered is always to abort the
analysis. Therefore, the symbol $\mathbf{eof}$ is *not* included in the alphabet T. We
assume that each terminal symbol has been assigned (strictly positive and non-
infinite) insert and delete costs, and each ordered pair of distinct terminal
symbols has been assigned a (non-negative, but possibly infinite) change
cost.

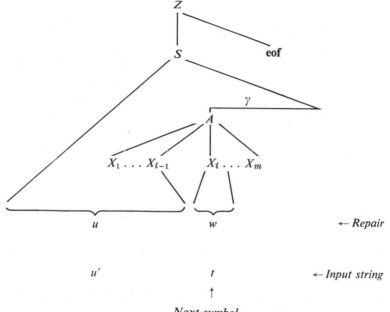

Fig. 6.1 An error situation.

Definition Let $\alpha \in (N \cup T)^*$. The set of prefixes of α, denoted $pr(\alpha)$, is
defined by

$$pr(\alpha) = \{v \mid v \in T^* \text{ and } vw \in L(\alpha) \text{ for some } w \in T^*\}.$$

Definition The string u is said to be a *valid prefix* (of S) if and only if $u \in pr(S)$.
Let u be a valid prefix. The set of (*valid*) *continuations of* u, denoted $C(u)$, is
defined by

$$C(u) = \{v \mid v \in T^* \text{ and } uv \text{ is also a valid prefix}\}.$$

Example 1 Let $G = (\{R, S, A, Z\}, \{a, b, c\}, P, Z)$ where P consists of

$$Z \rightarrow Seof$$
$$S \rightarrow bAbR \qquad S \rightarrow cAcR$$
$$A \rightarrow aa$$
$$R \rightarrow \Lambda \qquad R \rightarrow b$$

The strings Λ, a, ab and abb are all valid continuations of ba. Similarly, the strings Λ, a, ac and acb are all valid continuations of ca. (See Figs. 6.2(a) and (b).)

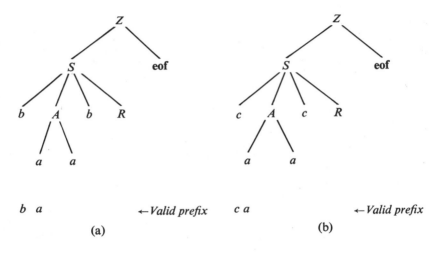

(a)   ←Valid prefix   (b)

Fig. 6.2 Valid continuations.

Definition Let u be a valid prefix and $t \in T$. A *locally optimal repair of t following u* is defined to be $t \rightarrow w$, where $w \in T^*$ is such that

$$w \in C(u) \qquad \text{and} \qquad cost^*(t \rightarrow w) \leq cost^*(t \rightarrow w')$$

for all $w' \in C(u)$.

(Equivalently:

$$cost^*(t \rightarrow w) = cost^*(t \rightarrow C(u)).)$$

Example 2 Consider again the grammar of Example 1. Suppose that the cost of inserting any symbol is two, the cost of deleting any symbol is three and the cost of changing any symbol to any other symbol is four. Suppose the valid prefix is ba and the next symbol is b. As there are only a finite number of continuations of ba we can enumerate the cost of repairing b to each of them. These costs are as follows:

$$cost^*(b{\to}\Lambda) \quad = 3 \ (= \text{cost of deleting } b)$$
$$cost^*(b{\to}a) \quad = 4 \ (= \text{cost of changing } b \text{ to } a)$$
$$cost^*(b{\to}ab) \quad = 2 \ (= \text{cost of inserting } a)$$
$$cost^*(b{\to}abb) = 4 \ (= \text{cost of inserting } ab)$$

Thus the locally optimal repair of b following ba is $b{\to}ab$. That is, the symbol a should be inserted before b. Similarly, if the valid prefix is ba and the next symbol is c one can determine that the locally optimal repair is $c{\to}\Lambda$, i.e. c should be deleted (see Fig. 6.2(a)).

Compare these actions with the actions to be taken when the valid prefix is ca (Fig. 6.2(b)). If the next symbol is b the locally optimal repair is $b{\to}\Lambda$, i.e. b should be deleted, and if the next symbol is c the symbol a should be inserted. This is an example of a situation in which a procedure call needs to be parameterized—in this case to distinguish between the two rhs occurrences of A.

"The" locally optimal repair may not be unique. In such cases we will allow an arbitrary choice to be made. We will also be careful to refer to a locally optimal repair rather than *the* locally optimal repair.

6.3.2 Production Positions

The definition of a locally optimal repair in Sec. 6.3.1 is a very general one and is quite independent of any parsing algorithm. Our problem now is how to implement it in a recursive-descent parser. The feature of LL(1) grammars which facilitates our task is that the valid prefix u defines a unique "state of the parse" represented diagrammatically by Fig. 6.1. Moreover, in such a state of the parse the valid continuations of u can be easily determined. Referring to Fig. 6.1 we have

$$C(u) = pr(X_i \ldots X_m \gamma).$$

Finding locally optimal repairs is thus a special case of context-free language repair where the string to be repaired has length one.

Our claim that u defines a unique state of the parse when G is LL(1) can be justified as follows. Consider any string $\xi \in (N \cup T)^*$ such that $Z \Rightarrow_l^* u\xi$. Let a leftmost derivation of $u\xi$ be

$$Z = \alpha_0 \Rightarrow_l \cdots \Rightarrow_l \alpha_k = u\xi.$$

Suppose $\alpha_i = x_i A_i \psi_i$, where $x_i \in T^*$, $A_i \in N$ and $\psi_i \in (N \cup T)^*$. If $u = \Lambda$, then we shall define the state of the parse to be, simply, Z. Suppose $u \neq \Lambda$

and let us consider the points in the derivation sequence at which the individual symbols of u are introduced. In particular, let us note the step at which the last symbol of u is introduced. That is, let the index m be defined to be the maximum index i such that x_{i-1} is a proper prefix of u. Thus

$$\alpha_{m-1} = x_{m-1}A_{m-1}\psi_{m-1}$$

where $u = x_{m-1}y$ for some $y \in T^+$, $x_m = uz$ for some $z \in T^*$ and $\alpha_m = x_m A_m \psi_m$. Clearly the condition that G is LL(1) *uniquely* defines the derivation sequence

$$Z = \alpha_0 \Rightarrow_l \alpha_1 \cdots \Rightarrow_l \alpha_{m-1} \Rightarrow_l \alpha_m.$$

The derivation tree defined by this sequence is what we mean by the unique "state of the parse" defined by u. For later reference we shall summarize the above argument in the form of a lemma.

Lemma 6.1   Let $G = (N, T, P, Z)$ be an LL(1) grammar and let u be a valid prefix of S. Then there is a *unique* leftmost derivation sequence

$$Z = \alpha_0 \Rightarrow_l \alpha_1 \Rightarrow_l \cdots \Rightarrow_l \alpha_m = u\gamma$$

(where $\gamma \in (N \cup T)^*$) having the properties:

(a)   if $u = \Lambda$, then $m = 0$ and $\gamma = Z$;
(b)   if $u \neq \Lambda$, then $m > 0$, $\alpha_{m-1} = vB\beta$ and $\alpha_m = vw\mu\beta$, where $w \neq \Lambda$, $vw = u$ and $B \rightarrow w\mu \in P$.

Example 3   Let

$$G = (\{Z, S, R\}, \{a, b, c\}, \{Z \rightarrow \mathbf{Seof}, S \rightarrow aRS, S \rightarrow b, R \rightarrow bR, R \rightarrow c\}, Z).$$

The unique leftmost derivation sequence defined by aca is

$$Z \Rightarrow \mathbf{Seof} \Rightarrow aR\mathbf{Seof} \Rightarrow ac\mathbf{Seof} \Rightarrow acaR\mathbf{Seof}.$$

The unique leftmost derivation sequence defined by abc is

$$Z \Rightarrow \mathbf{Seof} \Rightarrow aR\mathbf{Seof} \Rightarrow abR\mathbf{Seof} \Rightarrow abc\mathbf{Seof}.$$

The next step is to identify the production position at which the recovery action must be chosen. Figures 6.3(a) and (b) show the derivation trees corresponding to the two derivation sequences in Example 3. In Fig. 6.3(a) the relevant production position is clearly the second position on the rhs of $S \rightarrow aRS$. Figure 6.3(b) is a little more complicated. Here, if an error is detected in the next symbol, the appropriate recovery action should be initiated at the third position in $S \rightarrow aRS$. This is not the last production used in the derivation sequence but the position is the first where a choice of action is available.

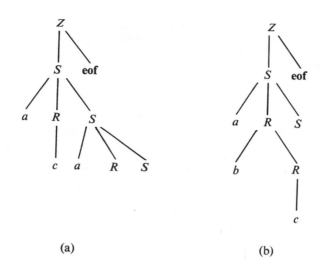

(a)   (b)

Fig. 6.3   State of the parse defined by (a) *aca*, and (b) *abc*.

Definition   A *production position* is a pair $\langle A \rightarrow X_1 \ldots X_m, i \rangle$ where $1 \leq i \leq m$ and $A \rightarrow X_1 \ldots X_m \in P$.

Lemma 6.2   Let $G = (N, T, P, Z)$ be an LL(1) grammar and let u be a valid prefix of S. Then there is a unique production position $\langle A \rightarrow X_1 \ldots X_m, i \rangle$ defined by u and having the properties:

(a)   if $u = \Lambda$, the position is $\langle Z \rightarrow S\text{eof}, 1 \rangle$;
(b)   if $u \neq \Lambda$, then

$$Z \Rightarrow_l^* vA\gamma \Rightarrow_l vX_1 \ldots X_m\gamma \Rightarrow_l^* vwX_i \ldots X_m\gamma,$$

where $1 < i \leq m$, $w \neq \Lambda$ and $vw = u$. (*Note: i is greater than 1.*)

6.3.3   Repairs and Actions

We are now able to relate repairs to recovery actions. Table 6.6 shows the recovery action which should be taken for a given locally optimal repair. The production position referred to is the unique position defined by the valid prefix u. The actions are uniquely defined when the grammar is LL(1).

Table 6.6 Correspondence between recovery actions and repairs.

Recovery action at position $\langle A \to X_1 \dots X_m, i \rangle$	Locally optimal repair
1. Delete t	$t \to \Lambda$
2. Change t to X_i ($X_i \in T$) (includes OK action)	$t \to X_i$
3. Call pX_i ($X_i \in N$)	$t \to w$ where $X_i \Rightarrow^* wv$ for some $v \in T^*$
4. Jump to position j	$t \to w$ where $j > i$ is the largest index such that $X_i \dots X_{j-1} \Rightarrow^* v$ and $w = vx$ for some $x \ne \Lambda$.

It is important to observe that actions 3 and 4 simply *initiate* the repair; they do not complete it. For example, the action of jumping to position j simulates the insertion of some string v. At position j a further recovery action is necessary. This may be an OK or change action, or it may be to call pX_j. (The action at position j will always be arranged not to be another jump or a deletion.)

When the action is to call a procedure pB, say, the next step must be to choose a production with left-hand side B. How this choice is made has not been shown in Table 6.6. The rule for choosing a production is as follows:

Let t be the next symbol in the input string when pB is called.
The production chosen is $B \to Y_1 \dots Y_n$ if for some $u \in T^*$ and
$\alpha \in (N \cup T)^*$, $Z \Rightarrow^* uB\alpha$ and the chosen locally optimal repair of t
following u is $t \to w$, where $w \in pr(Y_1 \dots Y_n)$.   (6.1)

At this point the reader may, quite rightly, have doubts about the correctness of the recovery process. Instead of specifying the repair for each combination of production position and next symbol, we have factored it into a sequence of actions like: skip positions $i \dots j-1$ of $A \to X_1 \dots X_m$, call pB, skip positions $1 \dots k$ of $B \to Y_1 \dots Y_n$, call pC, skip positions $1 \dots l$ of $C \to Z_1 \dots Z_p$, etc. How can we be sure that this sequence of actions will always terminate? Also, if the action at position i of $A \to X_1 \dots X_m$ is to jump to position j, will the action at j be appropriate to complete the repair commenced at i? Position j might be reached by some other means, e.g. a successful parsing action at position $j-1$. It is not immediately obvious that the recovery action at a given position does not depend on how that position was reached. Finally, does the choice of a production after calling a procedure depend on the point of call? (That is, is the rule (6.1) well defined?) These questions will be answered in Sec. 6.4, but, for the moment, the reader must bear with us while we add the final link between recovery actions and repairs— the parameterization of procedures.

6.3.4 Program 6.2 Again

Before presenting the final step in the development, let us show the reader how some of the recovery policies in Program 6.2 might have been calculated. Reference should be made to Tables 6.3 and 6.4 for the edit costs. Consider *pST* and, in particular, consider the actions to be taken when the production being parsed is

$$ST \rightarrow \textbf{if}\ U\ \textbf{then}\ SL\ E\ \textbf{fi}$$

and the next symbol at each position is **if**. We shall evaluate the recovery policies from right to left because, as it turns out, this is the easiest way.

At position 6 the symbol **fi** is expected. If, however, the symbol **if** is input the possible actions are

1. Delete **if**. This has been given the cost 1000.

2. Return from the procedure call. In order to perform this action we must, in effect, insert the symbol **fi** incurring a cost of 1. However, following *ST* one always expects a semicolon and then a new *ST* can begin. Thus the cost of the complete recovery is the cost of inserting **fi** and inserting a semicolon i.e. 2.

Of these two actions the second is the cheaper. Thus the locally optimal repair is **if→fi;if** and the appropriate action is to return from the procedure call. Note that the repair is completed when, in *pSL*, error message 2 is printed.

At position 5 an optional **else** part (i.e. *E*) is expected. Both the possibilities (1) and (2) are open to us and, because *E* is nullable, it costs nothing to skip the call of *pE*. Thus the costs of options (1) and (2) are the same as at position 6. We must add one more possibility to our list, namely:

3. Call *pE*. If this action is taken we must choose a production with lhs *E* and decide on the recovery action at the first position on the rhs of that production. Now, we never allow the possibility of choosing an empty-word production since this is included in the option of skipping the call. Thus, if *pE* is called the way to recover is by repairing **if** to **else if**, i.e. by inserting **else**. Thus calling *pE* has cost 3. (Strictly we can also recover by repairing **if** to **else** or **else** *id* etc. but it is obvious that these are more costly.)

Option (2) has the least cost and so the action is to return from the procedure. This is implemented by the statement **goto 7**.

At position 4 an *SL* is expected. Now **if** can begin *ST* which can begin *SL*. The occurrence of **if** in this position is, therefore, not erroneous and clearly *pSL* should be called. This fits into the general schema because the locally optimal repair is **if**→**if** and has cost 0.

The remaining positions in the production can be dealt with in the same way. It would appear that, as one proceeds from right to left, the number of possibilities to be considered increases dramatically. This is not so. At position 3, for instance, the only possibilities that need to be considered are deleting **if** or jumping to position 4. We do not need to consider the possibility of jumping to positions 5, 6 or 7 because it is known that these possibilities have been overruled at position 4.

A possibility which did not occur in the above analysis was changing the next symbol. Only *id* has been given finite change costs (Table 6.4) and the only instance where a change is the locally optimal policy is at label 3 in *pST*. This is the point at which **then** is expected. Here, if the next symbol is *id* the options available are

1. Insert **then** (i.e. jump to position 4) and then call *pSL*. This has cost 3.
2. Change *id* to **then**. That is, advance the input marker and jump to position 4. This has cost 1 and hence is the chosen option.

(Again, there are many other options but they are all clearly of higher cost and need not be considered.)

6.3.5 Passing Parameters

It would be very fortunate if, for a given value of *t*, there were a one-to-one correspondence between locally optimal repairs and production positions. Occasionally, however, the locally optimal repair depends not only on the production position but also on how the lhs symbol was introduced into the parse. The solution to this problem is to parameterize procedure calls. The function of such parameterization is to indicate, roughly, which strings are expected once the current procedure call has been completed. This is illustrated by the procedure *pSL* in Program 6.2, where it is necessary to use parameters to decide which symbols ought to be deleted. The explanation for the parameters is simple: Consider, for example, the case when the next symbol is **fi** and a semicolon is expected. One possibility is that *SL* is part of an **if** statement and the semicolon is missing. Clearly, therefore, a return from *pSL* should be executed. Alternatively, it may be that no **if** statement has previously been encountered and so **fi** is entirely unexpected. In this case the only reasonable recourse is to delete it and continue to the next symbol.

Although Program 6.2 is typical of the level of parameterization which is usually necessary, it is not a good example of the full complexity of the parameter-passing mechanism which is required. The following example illustrates what is involved.

Example 4   Let $G = (\{E, L\}, \{a, (,), ;\}, P, L)$ where P consists of

$$L \to E ; L \qquad L \to \Lambda$$
$$E \to a \qquad E \to (E)$$

The language defined by this grammar consists of sequences of expressions terminated by semicolons. Expressions may be parenthesized to any depth. Let us focus our attention on the recovery action to be taken when a semicolon is erroneously encountered in the middle of an expression. Suppose the cost of deleting a semicolon is 2 and the cost of inserting a closing parenthesis is 1. Figures 6.4(a) and (b) illustrate two instances where reading a semicolon flags an error. In Fig. 6.4(a) recovery from the error can be achieved, at a cost of 1, by inserting a closing parenthesis—or, equivalently, returning from pE. In contrast, in Fig. 6.4(b), inserting matching parentheses would incur a cost of 3, whilst deleting the semicolon has cost 2. Therefore the latter is preferred. Choosing between the actions of deleting the semicolon or returning from the procedure is achieved by passing a parameter to pE which, effectively, counts the number of opening parentheses up to a threshold of 2. (6.2) shows how this is achieved.

```
procedure pL;
     procedure pE(esemicolon: integer);
     var d: symset;
     begin
     case nextsymbol of
         . . .
         qleftparenthesis:  begin getsymbol;
                            pE(min(esemicolon + 1, 2));
                            d := . . . ;                        (6.2)
                            if esemicolon ≥ 2 then
                                d := d + [qsemicolon];
                            delete(d, 1);
                            if nextsymbol = qrightparenthesis
                                then getsymbol else error(2);
                            end;

         . . .
         end;
     end; {pE}
begin {pL}
     . . .
```

> **while** *nextsymbol* **in** [*qa, qleftparenthesis*] **do**
>   **begin** $pE(0)$;
>   · · ·
>   **end**;
>   **end**; {*pL*}

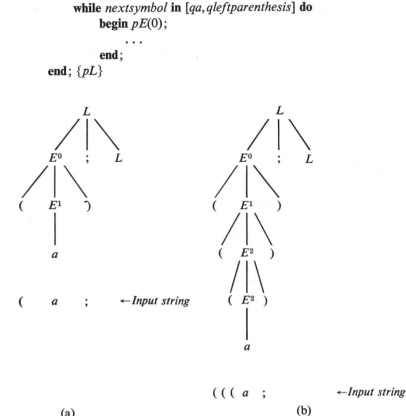

Fig. 6.4   Parameterization of nested procedures.

Note the two calls of *pE*. When called from *pL* the parameter *esemicolon* is set to 0. This indicates that a semicolon would be OK immediately after returning from the call. Within *pE* the call to *pE* sets *esemicolon* to *min{esemicolon* + 1, 2}. The new value of *esemicolon* is the cost of repairing a semicolon after returning from *pE*.

Let us now present a more rigorous development of the parameter-passing mechanism. Consider once again the state of the parse shown in Fig. 6.1. That is, suppose the production position defined by the valid prefix u is $\langle A \rightarrow X_1 \ldots X_m, i \rangle$ and suppose $Z \Rightarrow^{*}_{l} vA\gamma \Rightarrow^{*}_{l} uX_i \ldots X_m\gamma$. In such a state we can split the valid continuations, $C(u)$, into two sets, namely:

$$C(u) = L(X_i \ldots X_m) \cdot pr(\gamma) \cup pr(X_i \ldots X_m). \tag{6.3}$$

Whence

$$cost^*(t{\rightarrow}C(u)) = min\{cost^*(t{\rightarrow}pr(\gamma)) + cost^*(\Lambda{\rightarrow}X_i \ldots X_m),$$
$$cost^*(t{\rightarrow}pr(X_i \ldots X_m))\}. \tag{6.4}$$

Now, of the terms on the right-hand side of (6.4), $cost^*(\Lambda{\rightarrow}X_i \ldots X_m)$ and $cost^*(t{\rightarrow}pr(X_i \ldots X_m))$ are independent of u. Therefore, they can (and should) be calculated and tabulated *once and for all* before the parser is constructed. (This is one of the functions of the software tool we mentioned.) The value of $cost^*(t{\rightarrow}pr(\gamma))$ does depend on u and reflects the "history" of the parse. This then is the value passed to pA.

Equation (6.4) is very important; an understanding of its implications is crucial to the efficient implementation of locally optimal repairs. Consider first the term $cost^*(t{\rightarrow}pr(X_i \ldots X_m)) = c$, say. Suppose that $c = cost^*(t{\rightarrow}w)$, where $w \in pr(X_i \ldots X_m)$. As mentioned above, c and its associated repair, $t{\rightarrow}w$, can be evaluated offline. The corresponding recovery action does not involve returning from pA and so is called the *non-return policy* associated with t at the position $\langle A \rightarrow X_1 \ldots X_m, i \rangle$. To determine whether it should be chosen we need to compare c with

$$cost^*(t{\rightarrow}pr(\gamma)) + cost^*(\Lambda{\rightarrow}X_i \ldots X_m) = c',$$

say. Specifically, suppose $c' = cost^*(t{\rightarrow}w')$, where $w' \in pr(X_i \ldots X_m\gamma)$. Now, if $c \leq c'$ the non-return policy should be chosen. Otherwise, the repair $t{\rightarrow}w'$ should be chosen; the corresponding action is then to return from the procedure call.

The details of whether to choose the non-return policy are actually a little different to the method described above. Each procedure, pA, in the syntax analyzer is assigned a parameter At, say, for each $t \in T$. The value of At is calculated such that

$$At = cost^*(t{\rightarrow}pr(\gamma)), \tag{6.5}$$

and the non-return policy is chosen when

$$At \geq cost^*(t{\rightarrow}pr(X_i \ldots X_m)) - cost^*(\Lambda{\rightarrow}X_i \ldots X_m). \tag{6.6}$$

The right-hand side of (6.6) is called the *boundary cost* associated with t at the position $\langle A \rightarrow X_i \ldots X_m, i \rangle$. As observed earlier, it is independent of u.

It is surprisingly straightforward to arrange that (6.5) holds at all times during the parse. The trick is to observe that $cost^*(t{\rightarrow}pr(\gamma))$ is the cost of repairing t immediately after a return from pA is executed. Thus when pS is initially called the parameter St passed to it is

$$St = cost(t{\rightarrow}\Lambda), \tag{6.7}$$

since on returning from pS the only option is to delete any remaining symbols. Subsequently, suppose u has been successfully parsed and the position $\langle A \to X_1 \ldots X_m, i \rangle$ reached. Let $X_i = B$ and suppose the action is to call pB. Then the value Bt passed to pB is

$$Bt = min\{cost^*(t \to pr(X_{i+1} \ldots X_m)), At + cost^*(A \to X_{i+1} \ldots X_m)\}. \qquad (6.8)$$

The justification for (6.8) is inductive. We have already argued the correctness of (6.7). Now, assuming inductively that $At = cost^*(t \to pr(\gamma))$, we have

$$\begin{aligned} Bt &= min\{cost^*(t \to pr(X_{i+1} \ldots X_m)), \; cost^*(t \to pr(\gamma)) \\ &\quad + cost^*(A \to X_{i+1} \ldots X_m)\} \\ &= cost^*(t \to pr(X_{i+1} \ldots X_m \gamma)). \end{aligned} \qquad (6.9)$$

This is, indeed, the required value.

Lemma 6.3 summarizes the parameter-passing mechanism and its required property.

Lemma 6.3   Let $G = (N, T, P, Z)$ be an LL(1) grammar. Suppose that each procedure, except pZ, in a recursive-descent parser of G has a parameter defined for each terminal symbol. During a parse the parameters are passed according to the following rules:

Let $B (\neq Z) \in N$ and $t \in T$. The parameter Bt, passed to pB, is given by:

1. If $B = S$ and the calling procedure is pZ, then $Bt = cost(t \to A)$.

2. Otherwise, if the calling procedure is pC and the corresponding rhs occurrence of B is $C \to \alpha B \beta$, then $Bt = min\{Ct + cost^*(A \to \beta), cost^*(t \to pr(\beta))\}$.

Now, suppose u is a valid prefix of Z defining the production position $\langle A \to X_1 \ldots X_m, i \rangle$. Let

$$Z \Rightarrow^*_l vA\gamma \Rightarrow^*_l uX_i \ldots X_m\gamma.$$

Then, on calling pA, $At = cost^*(t \to pr(\gamma))$. $\square$

If every procedure had to be parameterized for every terminal symbol, as suggested by Lemma 6.3, then the method would be unacceptably inefficient. Luckily, as evidenced by Program 6.2, parameters turn out to be the exception rather than the rule. Thus in most cases it can be argued that the parameter is unnecessary because one of the two possibilities—returning or executing the non-return policy—will never be chosen. Minimizing the amount of parameterization is quite a complex process, but it is a topic which is outside our scope.

6.3.6 A Summary

Let us quickly review the development in Secs. 6.3.1 to 6.3.5.

We began (Sec. 6.3.1) by defining the notion of a locally optimal repair. Specifically, if u has been successfully parsed (i.e. is a valid prefix) we consider all strings v such that uv is also a valid prefix. We then choose to repair the next symbol t, at least cost, to one such string. Now, to simulate the repair it is factored into a sequence of recovery actions. In order to do this we need to identify the earliest position in the parse at which a choice of action is available (Sec. 6.3.2). Table 6.6 (Sec. 6.3.3) then enables us to convert the chosen repair into the *initial* recovery action. The final step, passing and using parameters (Sec. 6.3.5) eliminates the dependency on the valid prefix u. The parameters encode all the information one needs to know about the history of the parse and are used within the parser to determine whether a non-return policy (computed offline) is to be executed in preference to returning from the procedure call.

6.4 DOES IT WORK?

In Sec. 6.3.3 we deliberately cast doubts in the reader's mind about the validity of the whole recovery process. The questions we need to resolve are:

1. Will the recovery actions always terminate?
2. Do the actions initiated at a production position truly simulate a locally optimal repair?

Theorem 6.10 answers both these questions in the affirmative, but, before we can prove it, we need six preliminary results. The difficulty is caused by jump actions. Jumping from one position to another in a production is equivalent to inserting some string. Thus the repair may be factored into a number of insertions followed by an OK, change or delete operation. We must, therefore, prove that such a factorization is safe. We must also prove that the mechanism we have built up for evaluating policies, namely parameter passing, does not break down under this process. That is, we must prove that the recovery action following the valid prefix u is, indeed, characterized by the production position, $\langle A \rightarrow X_1 \dots X_m, i \rangle$, defined by u and the parameters passed to pA.

We begin with a simple but very important lemma which effectively states that, if a locally optimal repair involves any insertions, then these will always precede any change, OK or delete operation. Lemma 6.5 then asserts that a locally optimal repair can be safely factored into two repairs, the first of which is an insertion.

Lemma 6.4 If a locally optimal repair of t following u is $t{\rightarrow}w$ and $w = xy$, where $y \neq \Lambda$, then

$$cost^*(t{\rightarrow}w) = cost^*(\Lambda{\rightarrow}x) + cost^*(t{\rightarrow}y).$$

Proof Figure 6.5 is a diagrammatic representation of the repair graph of the pair of strings $\langle t, xy \rangle$. Now, either a least-cost path from $\langle \Lambda, \Lambda \rangle$ to $\langle t, xy \rangle$ passes through the node $\langle \Lambda, x \rangle$ or none does. In the former case

$$cost^*(t{\rightarrow}w) = cost^*(\Lambda{\rightarrow}x) + cost^*(t{\rightarrow}y)$$

and the lemma holds. In the latter case, the path must pass through $\langle t, x \rangle$ and so

$$cost^*(t{\rightarrow}x) = cost^*(t{\rightarrow}w) - cost^*(\Lambda{\rightarrow}y) < cost^*(t{\rightarrow}w).$$

But x is also a valid continuation of u. This contradicts the choice of the repair $t{\rightarrow}w$ and so cannot occur. $\square$

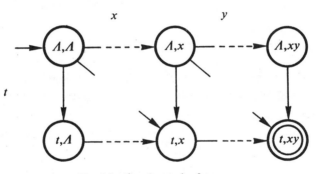

Fig. 6.5   Repair graph of $t{\rightarrow}xy$.

Lemma 6.5 Suppose a locally optimal repair of t following u is $t{\rightarrow}w$ and $w = xy$ where $y \neq \Lambda$. Suppose, also, that $t{\rightarrow}z$ is a locally optimal repair following ux. Then $t{\rightarrow}y$ and $t{\rightarrow}xz$ are locally optimal repairs following ux and u, respectively.

Proof y is certainly a valid continuation of ux and xz is a valid continuation of u. So $t{\rightarrow}y$ and $t{\rightarrow}xz$ are possible repairs following ux and u, respectively. Suppose

$$cost^*(t{\rightarrow}z) < cost^*(t{\rightarrow}y).$$

Then

$$
\begin{aligned}
cost^*(t{\rightarrow}xz) &\leq cost^*(\Lambda{\rightarrow}x) + cost^*(t{\rightarrow}z)\\
&< cost^*(\Lambda{\rightarrow}x) + cost^*(t{\rightarrow}y)\\
&= cost^*(t{\rightarrow}xy) \qquad \text{(by Lemma 6.4)}.
\end{aligned}
$$

But this contradicts the choice of the repair $t{\to}xy$ following u. Therefore, $cost^*(t{\to}z) \geq cost^*(t{\to}y)$. But, by the choice of z, $cost^*(t{\to}z) \not> cost^*(t{\to}y)$. We conclude that $cost^*(t{\to}z) = cost^*(t{\to}y)$ and, so, $cost^*(t{\to}xz) \leq cost^*(t{\to}xy)$. Thus $t{\to}y$ is a locally optimal repair following ux as is $t{\to}xz$ following u. $\square$

Let us now justify the parameter-passing mechanism. What we have to prove is that the parameters passed to each procedure and the production position do, indeed, characterize locally optimal repairs. The first step is to show that, if u_1 and u_2 both define the position $\langle A \to X_1 \ldots X_m, i \rangle$, and, after parsing u_1 and u_2, the parameter At passed to pA is the same, then the same *initial* recovery action is applicable on encountering t. There are two complications in the lemmas. The first is that locally optimal repairs are not necessarily unique and so we can only claim that the initial recovery action for u_1 is equally as good as the initial recovery action for u_2. The second complication is that, if the recovery action is to return from pA, the subsequent actions for u_1 and u_2 may differ—hence our emphasis of "initial". It then remains for us to use an inductive argument to establish that the sequence of recovery actions initiated by $\langle u, t \rangle$ is finite and simulates a locally optimal repair of t following u.

Lemma 6.7 considers the case when the action following u_1 is not to return from pA, Lemma 6.9 considers the opposite case. Lemma 6.6 is a preliminary to both these lemmas. In all the lemmas the assumption that G is LL(1) is implicit.

Lemma 6.6 Suppose u is a valid prefix defining the production position $\langle A \to X_1 \ldots X_m, i \rangle$ and suppose $Z \Rightarrow^*_l vA\gamma \Rightarrow^*_l uX_i \ldots X_m\gamma$. If a locally optimal repair of t following u is $t{\to}xy$, where $x \in L(X_i \ldots X_m)$ and $y \neq \Lambda$, then $cost^*(t{\to}y) = cost^*(t{\to}pr(\gamma))$.

Proof By Lemma 6.4, $cost^*(t{\to}xy) = cost^*(\Lambda{\to}x) + cost^*(t{\to}y)$. Suppose $cost^*(t{\to}pr(\gamma)) < cost^*(t{\to}y)$. Then $\exists\ z \in pr(\gamma)$ such that $cost^*(t{\to}z) < cost^*(t{\to}y)$. But xz is a valid continuation of u and

$$cost^*(t{\to}xz) \leq cost^*(\Lambda{\to}x) + cost^*(t{\to}z) < cost^*(t{\to}xy).$$

This contradicts the choice of the repair xy. $\square$

Lemma 6.7 Suppose u_1 and u_2 are valid prefixes which both define the production position $\langle A \to X_1 \ldots X_m, i \rangle$. Suppose

1. $Z \Rightarrow^*_l v_1A\gamma_1 \Rightarrow^*_l u_1X_i \ldots X_m\gamma_1$ and
2. $Z \Rightarrow^*_l v_2A\gamma_2 \Rightarrow^*_l u_2X_i \ldots X_m\gamma_2$, where
3. $cost^*(t{\to}pr(\gamma_1)) = cost^*(t{\to}pr(\gamma_2))$.

Then, if $w_1 \in pr(X_i \ldots X_m)$ and $t{\to}w_1$ is a locally optimal repair of t following u_1, it is also a locally optimal repair of t following u_2.

Proof Let $t{\to}w_2$ be a locally optimal repair following u_2. There are two cases to consider: (i) $w_2 \in pr(X_i \ldots X_m)$ and (ii) $w_2 = xy_2$ where $x \in L(X_i \ldots X_m)$, $y_2 \neq \Lambda$ and $y_2 \in pr(\gamma_2)$. Let us consider these cases in turn.

Case (i) Here, w_1 and w_2 are valid continuations of both u_1 and u_2. Hence, by the choice of w_1,

$$cost^*(t{\to}w_1) \leq cost^*(t{\to}w_2).$$

Also, by the choice of w_2,

$$cost^*(t{\to}w_2) \leq cost^*(t{\to}w_1).$$

Hence $cost^*(t{\to}w_1) = cost^*(t{\to}w_2)$ and w_1 is a locally optimal repair following u_2.

Case (ii) Again, w_1 is a valid continuation of u_2 and so we must prove that

$$cost^*(t{\to}w_1) \leq cost^*(t{\to}xy_2).$$

Now, by the choice of w_1,

$$cost^*(t{\to}w_1) \leq cost^*(t{\to}\{x\} \cdot pr(\gamma_1))$$
$$\leq cost^*(\Lambda{\to}x) + cost^*(t{\to}pr(\gamma_1)).$$

Hence

$$cost^*(t{\to}w_1) \leq cost^*(\Lambda{\to}x) + cost^*(t{\to}pr(\gamma_2)) \qquad \text{(by assumption (3))}$$
$$= cost^*(t{\to}xy_2) \qquad \text{(by Lemmas 6.4 and 6.6).}$$

That is,

$$cost^*(t{\to}w_1) \leq cost^*(t{\to}w_2).$$

Thus $t{\to}w_1$ is also a locally optimal repair following u_2. $\square$

Corollary 6.8 The rule (6.1), for choosing productions when a procedure is first called, is well-defined.

Proof Let us rewrite (6.1) in the notation of Lemma 6.7. The production $B \to Y_1 \ldots Y_n$ is chosen following u_1 if $B = X_i$ and a locally optimal repair of t is $t{\to}w_1$, where $w_1 \in pr(Y_1 \ldots Y_n)$. Now

$$pr(Y_1 \ldots Y_n) \subseteq pr(X_i) \subseteq pr(X_i \ldots X_m).$$

Hence, by Lemma 6.7, $t{\to}w_1$ is also a locally optimal repair following u_2 and $B \to Y_1 \ldots Y_n$ is an appropriate choice of production. $\square$

Lemma 6.9 Suppose, again, that the properties (1), (2) and (3) of Lemma 6.7 are true of the valid prefixes u_1 and u_2. Then, if $w_1 = x_1y_1$, where $x_1 \in$

$L(X_i \ldots X_m)$, $y_1 \neq \Lambda$ and $t \rightarrow w_1$ is a locally optimal repair following u_1, there is a locally optimal repair $t \rightarrow x_1 y_2$ of t following u_2, for some $y_2 \in T^*$.

Proof   Let $t \rightarrow w_2$ be a locally optimal repair following u_2. Again we have two cases to consider: (i) $w_2 \in pr(X_i \ldots X_m)$ and (ii) $w_2 = x_2 y_2$, where $x_2 \in L(X_i \ldots X_m)$, $y_2 \neq \Lambda$ and $y_2 \in pr(\gamma_2)$.

Case (i)   Choose $y_2 \in pr(\gamma_2)$ such that $cost^*(t \rightarrow pr(\gamma_2)) = cost^*(t \rightarrow y_2)$. Then $x_1 y_2$ is a valid continuation of u_2 and

$$
\begin{aligned}
cost^*(t \rightarrow x_1 y_2) &\leq cost^*(\Lambda \rightarrow x_1) + cost^*(t \rightarrow y_2) \\
&= cost^*(\Lambda \rightarrow x_1) + cost^*(t \rightarrow pr(\gamma_1)) \\
&\qquad \text{(by the choice of } y_2 \text{ and assumption (3))} \\
&= cost^*(t \rightarrow w_1) \qquad \text{(by Lemmas 6.6 and 6.4).}
\end{aligned}
$$

But w_2 is a valid continuation of u_1. Hence

$$cost^*(t \rightarrow w_1) \leq cost^*(t \rightarrow w_2) \qquad \text{(by the choice of } w_1)$$

and

$$cost^*(t \rightarrow x_1 y_2) \leq cost^*(t \rightarrow w_2).$$

That is, $t \rightarrow x_1 y_2$ is also a locally optimal repair following u_2.

Case (ii)   In this case $x_1 y_2$ is a valid continuation of u_2 and $x_2 y_1$ is a valid continuation of u_1. We must prove that $cost^*(t \rightarrow x_1 y_2) \leq cost^*(t \rightarrow x_2 y_2)$. Now, by Lemma 6.6 and assumption (3),

$$cost^*(t \rightarrow y_1) = cost^*(t \rightarrow y_2).$$

Hence

$$
\begin{aligned}
cost^*(t \rightarrow x_1 y_2) &\leq cost^*(\Lambda \rightarrow x_1) + cost^*(t \rightarrow y_2) \\
&= cost^*(\Lambda \rightarrow x_1) + cost^*(t \rightarrow y_1) \\
&= cost^*(t \rightarrow x_1 y_1) \qquad \text{(by Lemma 6.4)} \\
&\leq cost^*(t \rightarrow x_2 y_1) \qquad \text{(by the choice of } x_1 y_1) \\
&\leq cost^*(\Lambda \rightarrow x_2) + cost^*(t \rightarrow y_1) \\
&= cost^*(\Lambda \rightarrow x_2) + cost^*(t \rightarrow y_2) \\
&= cost^*(t \rightarrow x_2 y_2) \qquad \text{(by Lemma 6.4).}
\end{aligned}
$$

Thus $t \rightarrow x_1 y_2$ is also a locally optimal repair of t following u_2. $\square$

Theorem 6.10   Consider an LL(1) parser for the grammar $G = (N, T, P, Z)$ in which each non-terminal procedure has an integer parameter corresponding to each terminal symbol. Parameters are passed to procedures according to the rules given in Lemma 6.3, and, on calling a procedure, productions are chosen according to the rule (6.1). Also, at the production position $\langle A \rightarrow X_1 \ldots X_m, i \rangle$, the recovery action on encountering the symbol t is chosen according to the following rules:

Let $w \in pr(X_i \ldots X_m)$ be such that

$$cost^*(t \rightarrow pr(X_i \ldots X_m)) = cost^*(t \rightarrow w).$$

Let At be the parameter passed to pA corresponding to t. (At is undefined if $A = Z$ or $t = \textbf{eof}$.)

1. If $t = \textbf{eof}$ and the position is $\langle Z \rightarrow Seof, 2 \rangle$ a return from pZ is executed. If $t = \textbf{eof}$ and the position is not $\langle Z \rightarrow Seof, 2 \rangle$, the analysis is terminated. (*Note:* encountering **eof** at a position other than $\langle Z \rightarrow Seof, 2 \rangle$ may or may not signal an error.)
2. If the position is $\langle Z \rightarrow Seof, 1 \rangle$, then pS is called if $w \neq \Lambda$, otherwise t is deleted.
3. If the position is $\langle A \rightarrow X_1 \ldots X_m, i \rangle$ and $A \neq Z$, then
   (a) if $At + cost^*(A \rightarrow X_i \ldots X_m) < cost^*(t \rightarrow w)$ a return from pA is executed.
   (b) if $At + cost^*(A \rightarrow X_i \ldots X_m) \geq cost^*(t \rightarrow w)$, then w is used to choose the recovery policy as follows:
      (i) if $w = \Lambda$, then t is deleted.
      (ii) if $w = X_i \, (\in T)$, then t is changed to w.
      (iii) if $w \in pr(X_i)$ and $X_i \in N$, then pX_i is called.
      (iv) otherwise, let $j > i$ be the maximum index such that w can be expressed as xy where $x \in L(X_i \ldots X_{j-1})$ and $y \neq \Lambda$. The recovery policy is then to jump to position j.

Suppose that the input utv is supplied to the parser, where u is a valid prefix of S. Then, on encountering t, the parser will perform a finite sequence of actions equivalent in their final effect to having parsed uw', where $t \rightarrow w'$ is a locally optimal repair of t following u.

Proof If $t = \textbf{eof}$, we have nothing to prove. Suppose that $t \neq \textbf{eof}$. Let the sequence of actions initiated when t is encountered be $a_1, a_2, \ldots$, where each a_i is either OK, change, delete, call or $\langle jump, j_i \rangle$, where j_i is an index to a rhs position. We argue, by induction on i, that immediately before a_i is executed the parser will be in a state equivalent to having parsed ux_{i-1}, where $t \rightarrow x_{i-1}y_{i-1}$ is a locally optimal repair following u, for some x_{i-1}, $y_{i-1} \in T^*$.

The basis $i = 1$ is obvious. Let $x_0 = \Lambda$ and $y_0 = w$ where $t \rightarrow w$ is a locally optimal repair following u.

Now suppose the induction hypothesis is true immediately before a_i is executed. At this point the parser is in a state equivalent to having parsed ux_{i-1} and, by Lemma 6.5, if $t \rightarrow z_{i-1}$ is a locally optimal repair following ux_{i-1}, then $t \rightarrow x_{i-1}z_{i-1}$ is a locally optimal repair following u. Suppose the position before executing a_i is $\langle B \to Y_1 \ldots Y_n, j\rangle$. If $j = 1$ (i.e. pB has just been entered and a production chosen) then Corollary 6.8 assures us that the recovery action is appropriate to a locally optimal repair of t following ux_{i-1}. If $j > 1$, Lemmas 6.7 and 6.9 assure us of its appropriateness (Lemma 6.7 when the action does not involve returning, Lemma 6.9 when the action is to return). It remains for us to identify the strings x_i and y_i.

Let us consider the various possibilities for a_i. These are as follows:

1. OK, change or delete. In this case there is no $(i+1)$th action and we have nothing more to prove.
2. Call. In this case let $x_i = x_{i-1}$ and $y_i = y_{i-1}$. Trivially, the induction hypothesis is true before the $(i+1)$th action.
3. $\langle \text{jump}, j_i\rangle$. Suppose the position before executing a_i is $\langle B \to Y_1 \ldots Y_n, j_{i-1}\rangle$. By the choice of action, there is some string $w_i \in L(Y_{j_{i-1}} \ldots Y_{j_i-1})$ such that $t \to w_i y_i$ is a locally optimal repair following ux_{i-1}, for some y_i. Let $x_i = x_{i-1}w_i$. Then after the jump the parser will be in a state equivalent to having parsed ux_i. Moreover, by Lemma 6.5, $t \to x_i y_i$ is a locally optimal repair following u.

In all three cases we have re-established the induction hypothesis and so, by induction, it is valid for all i.

The final step, proving that the sequence of actions is finite, is straightforward. Suppose, on the contrary, that the sequence does not terminate. We argue that this implies that G is left-recursive, contradicting the assumption that it is LL(1).

After i actions the parser is in a state equivalent to having parsed ux_i. Hence $Z \Rightarrow_l^* ux_i v_i$ for some $v_i \in T^*$. Also, by Lemma 6.4,

$$cost^*(\Lambda \to x_i) = cost^*(t \to x_i y_i) - cost^*(t \to y_i).$$

Thus $cost^*(\Lambda \to x_i) \leq cost^*(t \to x_i y_i)$. (All costs are zero or positive.) Now $cost^*(t \to x_i y_i)$ is finite (an upper bound is $cost(t \to \Lambda)$ which is assumed to be finite) and all insertion costs are strictly positive. Therefore, we deduce from the latter inequality that the length of the strings, $x_1, x_2, \ldots$ cannot be strictly increasing. That is, for some k, $x_k = x_{k+1} = x_{k+2} = \cdots$.

Suppose $i \geq k$ and suppose the position before the ith action is $\langle B_i \to Y_{i_1} \ldots Y_{n_i}, j_i\rangle$. Because $x_i = x_{i+1}$ the ith action is a call or a jump. Moreover, if the action is a jump we must have $Y_{j_i} \ldots Y_{j_{i+1}-1} \Rightarrow^* \Lambda$. In either case we therefore have

$$Y_{j_i} \in N \ (i \geq k) \qquad \text{and} \qquad Y_{j_k}\alpha_k \Rightarrow_l^+ Y_{j_{k+1}}\alpha_{k+1} \Rightarrow_l^+ Y_{j_{k+2}}\alpha_{k+2} \Rightarrow_l^+ \cdots \quad (6.10)$$

for some strings $\alpha_k, \alpha_{k+1}, \alpha_{k+2}, \cdots$. Now, the only way the derivation sequence (6.10) can continue indefinitely is if G is left-recursive. (Exercise 6.9

asks the reader to prove the latter claim.) But G is not left-recursive since it is LL(1). We conclude, therefore, that the sequence of actions will always terminate. □

Corollary If an LL(1) parser is constructed as detailed in Theorem 6.10 then, given any input *ueof*, the parser will always terminate.

Proof Straightforward induction on the length of the input string. □

6.5 ERROR RECOVERY IN A PL/0 PARSER

To conclude this chapter, Program 6.3 is a recursive-descent syntax analyzer of the language PL/0. This language has a syntax very similar to PASCAL but much fewer features are included. The basis for the construction of Program 6.3 was the PL/0 parser with no recovery facilities written by N. Wirth.† Some minor modifications had to be made to Wirth's program because of restrictions on the PASCAL implementation used by the author. After making these modifications, a software tool was used to tabulate the non-return policies, procedure parameterization and boundary costs at each production position. These were then incorporated by hand into the syntax analyzer.

To construct the table of recovery policies the terminal symbols were divided into a number of classes. For example, all reserved words which can begin a statement—**if**, **while**, **begin** and **call**—form the class *begcl*, and the symbols "," and ";" form the class *delimcl*. The elements in each class are evident from the initializations in the main program. A grammar for PL/0 was then constructed from its BNF description by replacing each terminal symbol by its class. Effectively this is equivalent to allowing symbols in a class to be interchanged at zero cost. Each class was assigned an insert and a delete cost. These values were set at either 1, 2 or 3 except for the delete cost of the classes *begcl*, *delimcl* and *deccl* which were all set to 10. (The class *deccl* contains symbols like **const** which introduce a sequence of declarations.) Setting the costs is, at present, very much an empirical process but, essentially, the costs were adjusted to give an impressive performance on the one sample output which we present in Table 6.7. (A calculus for setting the costs, based on the analysis of common errors and the appropriate repairs, is not out of the question but has not yet been formulated.)

---

†In Wirth [6.10], Program 5.4, pp. 314–20. By permission of Prentice-Hall, Inc., Englewood Cliffs, New Jersey, U.S.A.

Having generated the table of recovery policies it was then a painless exercise to code Program 6.3. For greater ease a procedure *leave* was written in addition to *delete*. Given a set *l*, *leave* deletes all the symbols not in *l*. Error messages are prefixed by a letter to indicate whether the recovery action involves an insertion ("I"), a deletion ("D") or a change ("C"). Table 6.8 lists all the error messages.

Table 6.7   Output from PL/0 parser.

```
 1   VAR X,Y,Z,Q,R;
 2   CONST M = 7, N = 85
***          × M1
 3   PROCEDURE MULTIPLY;
***             × I1
 4     VAR A,B
 5     BEGIN A := U; B := Y; Z := Q
***          × I1     × C1
 6     WHILE B > 0 DO
***          × I1
 7       BEGIN IF ODD B DO Z := Z+A;
***                       × C3
 8       A := 2A; B := B/2;
***            × I16
 9       END
10     END;
11   PROCEDURE DIVIDE
12     CONST TWO = 2, THREE = 3;
***          × I1
13     VAR W;
14     BEGIN R = X; Q := 0; W := Y;
***             × C7
15     WHILE W < R DO W := TWO*W;
16     WHILE W > Y
17       BEGIN Q := (2*Q; W := W/2);
***            × I4           × I5        × D16
18       IF W < R THEN BEGIN R := R−W Q := Q+1;
***                                      × I16
***                                        × D16
***                                          × I1
***                                            × I11
19                       END
20     END
21     END;
22   PROCEDURE GCD;
23     VAR F,G;
24     BEGIN F := X; G := Y
25     WHILE F ≠ G DO
***          × I1
```

Table 6.7   (Continued)

26	BEGIN IF F < G THEN G := G − F;
27	IF G < F THEN F := F − G;
28	Z := F;
29	END;
30	END;
31	BEGIN X := M; Y := N; CALL MULTIPLY;
32	X := 25; Y := 3; CALL DIVIDE;
33	X := 84; Y := 36; CALL GCD;
34	CALL X; X := GCD; GCD = X
***	× C2 × C4 × I2
***	× D16
***	× I1
35	END.
***	× I11
***	× I15
24	SYNTAX ERRORS DETECTED

Two *ad hoc* additions were thought necessary. Firstly, if an identifier is encountered on first entering *statement*, its type—procedure, variable or undeclared—is checked. If the identifier has not been declared it is assumed to be a variable and, hence, to begin an assignment. If the identifier is a procedure identifier it is assumed that **call** is missing and the appropriate action is taken. The second addition was caused by misplaced declarations. As in PASCAL, PL/0 requires that declarations appear in the specific order **const** section, **var** section, **procedure** section. Misplacing sections is a problem we have not attempted to model and, consequently, it causes insuperable problems to a locally optimal recovery scheme (and to the simple recovery scheme described in Sec. 6.1!). The solution adopted in Program 6.3 is to allow declarations in any order but to output the message "M1" when the ordering is violated. ("M" signifies "miscellaneous".)

Strictly, the procedures *expression*, *term* and *factor* should have parameters corresponding to the classes *begcl* and *delimcl*. However, roughly speaking, the parameters indicate that symbols in these classes should be deleted when the level of parenthesization of expressions exceeds 10. Consequently it is highly unlikely that they would ever be deleted and the parameters were ignored.

For the most part the error messages in Table 6.7 require no explanation. Lines 8 and 18 deserve some comment though. When constructing the costs an attempt was made to anticipate both the possibility of a missing operator (as in line 8) or a missing semicolon (as in line 18). The insert costs of an operator and a semicolon were, therefore, both set to 1. In retrospect, this was foolish because it is impossible to cater for both possibilities. In a situation such as occurs in lines 8 and 18, both of the repairs *identifier* → *operator identifier* and *identifier* → ; *identifier* are locally optimal. The policy chosen arbitrarily when generating the table of recovery policies was to insert *operator*—probably the least likely to be the appropriate repair.

Table 6.8   Error messages

D	—	Action is to delete symbol	I	— Action is to insert one or more
D1		Invalid beginning to program		symbols
D2		Program must be terminated	I1	Semicolon missing
		by "."	I2	"call" missing
D3		Identifier expected	I3	"then" missing
D4		"=" expected	I4	"do" missing
D5		Number expected	I5	")" missing
D6		Semicolon or comma expected	I6	Comma or semicolon missing
D7		Invalid beginning to **var**		—semicolon assumed
		section	I7	Missing identifier
D8		Semicolon expected	I8	"=" missing
D9		Invalid beginning to **procedure**	I9	Missing number
		section	I10	Faulty procedure heading
D10		Invalid beginning to statement	I11	":=" missing
D11		":=" expected	I12	"begin" missing
D12		Invalid beginning of expression	I13	"while" missing
D13		Invalid beginning of condition	I14	Relational operator missing
D14		"then" expected	I15	Faulty expression
D15		")" expected	I16	Missing operator
D16		Semicolon or "end" expected	I17	"end" missing
D17		Invalid beginning of block	I18	Missing condition
D18		Relational operator expected	I19	Missing declaration
D19		Invalid expression		
C	—	Action is to change symbol	M	— Miscellaneous
C1		Identifier not declared—	M1	Declarations should be in the
		variable assumed		order **const** section, **var**
C2		Identifier not declared—		section, **procedure** section.
		procedure identifier assumed		
C3		"then" expected		
C4		Invalid use of identifier—		
		variable assumed		
C5		"=" expected		
C6		Semicolon expected		
C7		":=" expected		
C8		"do" expected		
C9		"end" expected		
C10		"odd" expected		

One point worthy of note is the printing of error messages when *delete* is called. Deplorably, many compilers recover from syntax errors by skipping symbols but no indication is given of the number of symbols skipped. For instance, in PASCAL compilers it is common that an extra **end** in a **record** declaration will cause the syntax analyzer to skip all symbols until **begin** or **procedure** is encountered. Because only one message is printed the user is deceived into believing that subsequent declarations have been processed normally. The inevitable cascade of undeclared identifiers can be very perplexing to the novice. The simple, honest alternative is to do as in *delete* i.e. print a message on first detecting an error and then print " × " under every deleted symbol.

Our final comment on the theory developed in this chapter is to emphasize its use as a tool to *assist* in the preparation of a syntax analyzer with good recovery facilities. Locally optimal repairs are not sacrosanct, and the good designer will not slavishly adopt the policies they dictate. Used in this way there is no reason why one should be unable to ensure excellent error recovery with a minimum of effort.

Program 6.3

```
program  PL0Parser(input, output);
label 99;
const norw = 11;     {no. of reserved words}
      txmax = 100;  {length of identifier table}
      al = 7;        {length of identifiers}
      {alfa is predeclared as packed array[1 .. 7] of char}

type  symbol = (nul, ident, number, plus, minus, times, slash, oddsym, equal,
               nequal, lt, gt, lparen, rparen, comma, semicolon, period, becomes,
               beginsym, endsym, ifsym, thensym, whilesym, dosym, callsym,
               constsym, varsym, procsym);
      object = (constant, variable, proc);
      symkind = (begcl, deccl, docl, endcl, relopcl, idcl, eqcl, delimcl, opcl,
               lparcl, rparcl, numcl, dotcl, nulcl);
      symkindset = set of symkind;

var   ch: char;       {last character read}
      sym: symbol;    {last symbol read}
      id: alfa;        {last identifier read}
      cc: integer;    {character count}
      ce: integer;    {character count—errors}
      ll: integer;     {line length}
      lineno: integer; nosyntaxerrors: integer;
```

Program 6.3 (Continued)

```
    kk: integer;
    line: array[1 .. 81] of char;
    a: array[1 .. al] of char;
    word: array[1 .. norw] of alfa;
    wsym: array[1 .. norw] of symbol;
    ssym: array[char] of symbol;
    table: array[0 .. txmax] of record name: alfa; kind: object
                                end;
    tx: integer;
    class: array[symbol] of symkind;
    symclass: symkind; {class of last symbol read}


function min(i,j: integer): integer;
begin if i < j then min := i else min := j end;

procedure error(ch: char; n: integer);
var   nodigits: integer;
begin if ce = 0 then write(' ***        ')
        else if ce > cc − 2 then begin writeln; write(' ***         '); ce := 0
                        end;
    if cc = ce + 2 then write(' × ') else write('    ': cc − ce − 2, ' × ');
    if n = 0 then ce := cc − 1
    else begin if n ≥ 10 then nodigits := 2 else nodigits := 1;
        write(ch,n: nodigits); ce := cc + nodigits;
        end;
    nosyntaxerrors := nosyntaxerrors + 1;
end; {error}

procedure getsym;
var i,j,k: integer;
    function letter(c: char): Boolean; {N.B. machine dependent}
    begin letter := ((ord(c) ≥ ord('A')) and (ord(c) ≤ ord('I')))
                or ((ord(c) ≥ ord('J')) and (ord(c) ≤ ord('R')))
                or ((ord(c) ≥ ord('S')) and (ord(c) ≤ ord('Z')))
    end; {letter}

    procedure getch;
    begin if cc = ll then
            begin if eof(input) then
                        begin write('PROGRAM INCOMPLETE'); goto 99;
                        end;
```

Program 6.3 (Continued)

```
        if ce >0 then writeln; ce : = 0;
        ll := 0; cc := 0; lineno :=lineno+1;
        write('  ', lineno: 3, '        ');
        while not eoln(input) do
                begin ll := ll+1; read(ch); write(ch); line[ll] := ch;
                end;
        writeln; ll := ll+1; read(line[ll]);
        end;
    cc := cc+1; ch := line[cc];
    end; {getch}

begin {getsym}
while ch= '   ' do getch;
if letter(ch) then
    begin {identifier or reserved word} k := 0;
    repeat if k < al then
                begin k := k+1; a[k] := ch;
                end;
            getch;
    until  not letter (ch) and not (ch in ['0' .. '9']);
    if k ≥ kk then kk :=k
    else repeat a[kk] := '   '; kk := kk−1;
        until kk = k;
    pack(a, 1, id); i : = 1; j := norw;
    {binary search of reserved word table}
    repeat k := (i+j) div 2;
        if id ≤ word[k] then j := k−1;
        if id ≥ word[k] then i := k+1;
    until i > j;
    if i−1 >j then sym := wsym[k] else sym := ident
    end

else if ch in ['0' .. '9'] then
    begin {number} sym := number;
    repeat getch;
    until not (ch in ['0' .. '9']);
    end

else if ch = ' : ' then
    begin getch;
    if ch = '=' then begin sym := becomes; getch;
```

Program 6.3   (Continued)

```
                      end
                  else sym := nul;
      end
 else begin sym := ssym[ch]; getch;
       end;
 symclass := class[sym];
 end; {getsym}

 procedure add(var s: symkindset; x: symkindset; c1, c2: integer);
 {adds x to s if c1 > c2}
 begin if c1 > c2 then s := s+x;
 end; {add}

 procedure leave(l: symkindset; n: integer);
 begin while not (symclass in l) do
            begin error('D', n); getsym; n := 0 end;
 end; {leave}

 procedure delete(d: symkindset; n: integer);
 begin while symclass in d do
            begin error('D', n); getsym; n := 0 end;
 end; {delete}

 procedure block(bend, bdelim, bdot: integer);
 label 4;
 var firstentry: integer; l, d: symkindset;
     procedure enter(k: object);
     begin {enter object into table}
         tx := tx+1;
         with table[tx] do begin name := id; kind := k;
                           end;
     end; {enter}

     function position(id: alfa): integer;
     var i: integer;
     begin {find identifier id in table}
         table[0] .name := id; i := tx;
         while table[i].name ≠ id do i := i-1;
         position := i;
     end; {position}

     procedure constdeclaration;
     label 4;
```

Program 6.3 (Continued)

begin if *sym* = *ident* **then** *getsym* **else** *error*('*I*', 7);
leave([*begcl*, *deccl*, *eqcl*, *delimcl*, *numcl*], 4);
if *symclass* **in** [*begcl*, *deccl*, *delimcl*] **then goto** 4;
if *symclass* = *eqcl* **then begin if** *sym* ≠ *equal* **then** *error*('*C*', 5);
                       getsym;
                      end
                else *error*('*I*', 8);
leave([*begcl*, *deccl*, *delimcl*, *numcl*], 5);
if *sym* = *number* **then begin** *enter*(*constant*); *getsym*;
                      end
                else *error*('*I*', 9);
4:    **end**; {*const declaration*}

procedure *vardeclaration*;
begin *enter*(*variable*); *getsym*;
end; {*var declaration*}

procedure *statement*(*send*,*sdelim*, *sdot*: *integer*);
label 2;

var *i*: *integer*; *leaveset*, *deleteset*: *symkindset*;

    procedure *expression*(*edo*, *eend*, *erelop*,*eeq*, *erpar*, *edot*: *integer*);
    var *d*: *symkindset*;

       procedure *term*(*tdo*, *tend*, *trelop*, *teq*, *trpar*, *tdot*: *integer*);
       var *d*: *symkindset*;

          procedure *factor*(*fdo*,*fend*,*frelop*,*feq*,*frpar*,*fdot*: *integer*);
          var *i*: *integer*; *d*: *symkindset*;
          begin
          if *sym* = *ident* **then**
             begin *i* := *position*(*id*);
             if *i* = 0 **then** *error*('*C*', 1) **else**
             if *table*[*i*].*kind* = *proc* **then** *error*('*C*', 4);
             getsym;
             end
          else if *sym* = *number* **then** *getsym*
          else if *sym* = *lparen* **then**
             begin *getsym*;
             d := [*relopcl*, *eqcl*, *dotcl*, *nulcl*];
             add(*d*, [*docl*],*fdo*, 1); *add*(*d*, [*endcl*],*fend*, 1);
             delete(*d*, 19);

Program 6.3   (Continued)

```
        if symclass in [idcl, opcl, lparcl, numcl]
        then expression(min(fdo + 1, 3), min(fend + 1, 3),
                           min(frelop + 1, 2), min(feq + 1, 2), 0,
                           min(fdot + 1, 2))
        else error('I', 15);
        d := [idcl, lparcl, numcl, nulcl];
        add(d, [docl], fdo, 2); add(d, [endcl], fend, 2);
        add(d, [relopcl], frelop, 1); add(d, [eqcl], feq, 1);
        add(d, [dotcl], fdot, 1);
        delete(d, 15);
        if sym = rparen then getsym else error('I', 5);
        end;
    end;  {factor}


begin  {term}
{determine symbols to be deleted}
d := [nulcl]; add(d, [docl], tdo, 2); add(d, [endcl], tend, 2);
add(d, [relopcl], trelop, 1); add(d, [eqcl], teq, 1);
add(d, [rparcl], trpar, 2); add(d, [dotcl], tdot, 1);
factor(tdo, tend, trelop, teq, trpar, tdot);
while sym in [times, slash, ident, lparen, number] do
    begin if sym in [times, slash] then getsym else error('I', 16);
    delete(d, 19);
    if symclass in [idcl, lparcl, numcl]
    then factor(tdo, tend, trelop, teq, trpar, tdot)
    else error ('I', 15);
    end;
end;  {term}


begin {expression}
{determine symbols to be deleted}
d := [nulcl]; add(d, [docl], edo, 2); add(d, [endcl], eend, 2);
add(d, [relopcl], erelop, 1); add(d, [eqcl], eeq, 1);
add(d, [rparcl], erpar, 2); add(d, [dotcl], edot, 1);
if sym in [plus, minus] then getsym;
delete(d, 19);
if symclass in [idcl, lparcl, numcl]
then term(edo, eend, erelop, eeq, erpar, edot)
else error('I', 15);
```

Program 6.3 (Continued)

```
while sym in [plus, minus, ident, lparen, number] do
    begin if sym in [plus, minus] then getsym else error('I', 16);
    delete(d, 19);
    if symclass in [idcl, lparcl, numcl]
    then term(edo, eend, erelop, eeq, erpar, edot)
    else error('I', 15);
    end;
end; {expression}

procedure condition(cend, cdot: integer);
begin
if symclass in [relopcl, eqcl] then
        begin if sym ≠ oddsym then error('C', 10); getsym;
        delete([relopcl, eqcl, rparcl, dotcl, nulcl], 17);
        if symclass in [idcl, opcl, lparcl, numcl]
        then expression(0, cend, 2, 2, 3, cdot)
        else error('I', 15);
        end
else begin expression(2, 3, 0, 0, 3, 2);
        delete([endcl, rparcl, dotcl, nulcl], 18);
        if (symclass = relopcl) or (sym = equal) then getsym
        else if sym = becomes then begin error('C', 5); getsym end
                              else error('I', 14);
        delete([relopcl, eqcl, rparcl, dotcl, nulcl], 12);
        if symclass in [idcl, opcl, lparcl, numcl]
        then expression(0, cend, 2, 2, 3, cdot)
        else error('I', 15);
        end;
    end;  {condition}

begin {statement}
if symclass in [eqcl, idcl] then
        begin {assignment}
        if sym ≠ ident then error('I', 7)
        else begin i := position(id);
            if i = 0 then error('C', 1)
            else if table[i].kind = proc then
                        begin error('I', 2); goto 2;
                        end
            else if table[i].kind = constant then error('C', 4);
            getsym;
            end;
```

Program 6.3 (Continued)

leaveset := [*begcl, deccl, idcl, eqcl, opcl, lparcl, numcl*];
if *send* ≤ 1 **then** *leaveset* := *leaveset* + [*endcl*];
if *sdelim* ≤ 8 **then** *leaveset* := *leaveset* + [*delimcl*];
leave(*leaveset*, 11);
if *sym* = *becomes* **then** *getsym*
else if *sym* = *equal* **then begin** *error*('C', 7); *getsym* **end**
        else *error*('I', 11);
leaveset := [*begcl, deccl, idcl, opcl, lparcl, numcl*];
if send ≤ 2 **then** *leaveset* := *leaveset* + [*endcl*];
if *sdelim* ≤ 9 **then** *leaveset* := *leaveset* + [*delimcl*];
if *sdot* ≤ 1 **then** *leaveset* := *leaveset* + [*dotcl*];
leave(*leaveset*, 12);
if not (*symclass* **in** [*endcl, dotcl*])
then *expression*(3, *send*, 2, 2, 3, *sdot*) **else** *error*('I', 15);
end

else if *sym* = *callsym* **then**
    begin {*procedure call*} *getsym*;
    leaveset := [*begcl, deccl, idcl*];
    if *send* ≤ 2 **then** *leaveset* := *leaveset* + [*endcl*];
    if *sdelim* ≤ 9 **then** *leaveset* := *leaveset* + [*delimcl*];
    if *sdot* ≤ 1 **then** *leaveset* := *leaveset* + [*dotcl*];
    leave(*leaveset*, 3);
2: **if** *sym* = *ident* **then begin** *i* := *position*(*id*);
                          if *i* = 0 **then** *error*('C', 2) **else**
                          if *table*[*i*].*kind* ≠ *proc* **then** *error*('C', 2);
                          getsym;
                          end
                  else *error*('I', 7);
    end

else if (*sym* = *beginsym*) **or** (*symclass* **in** [*delimcl, endcl*]) **then**
    begin {*compound statement*}
    if *sym* ≠ *beginsym* **then** *error*('I', 12) **else** *getsym*;
    deleteset := [*docl, rparcl, nulcl*];
    add(*deleteset*, [*dotcl*], *sdot*, 1); *delete*(*deleteset*, 10);
    if *symclass* **in** [*begcl, relopcl, idcl, eqcl, opcl, lparcl, numcl*]
    then *statement*(0, 0, *min*(*sdot* + 1, 2));
    leaveset := [*begcl, deccl, endcl, idcl, delimcl*];
    if *sdot* ≤ 1 **then** *leaveset* := *leaveset* + [*dotcl*];
    leave(*leaveset*, 16);

Program 6.3   (Continued)

```
while not (symclass in [endcl, dotcl, deccl]) do
    begin if sym = semicolon then getsym
        else if sym = comma then begin error('C', 6); getsym end
                            else error('I', 1);
        delete(deleteset, 10);
        if symclass in [begcl, relopcl, idcl, eqcl, opcl, lparcl, numcl]
        then statement(0, 0, min(sdot + 1, 2));
        leave(leaveset, 16);
        end;
    if sym ≠ endsym then error('I', 17) else getsym;
    end

else if (sym = whilesym) or (symclass in [relopcl, opcl, lparcl, numcl])
    then begin {while statement}
    if sym = whilesym then getsym else error('I', 13);
    deleteset := [endcl, dotcl, nulcl];
    add(deleteset, [delimcl], sdelim, 1); delete(deleteset, 13);
    if symclass in [relopcl, idcl, eqcl, opcl, lparcl, numcl]
    then condition(min(send + 1, 2), min(sdot + 1, 2))
    else error('I', 18);
    leaveset := [begcl, deccl, docl, idcl];
    if send ≤ 1 then leaveset := leaveset + [endcl];
    if sdelim ≤ 1 then leaveset := leaveset + [delimcl];
    if sdot ≤ 1 then leaveset := leaveset + [dotcl];
    leave(leaveset, 10);
    if sym = dosym then getsym
    else if sym = thensym then begin error('C', 8); getsym end
    else error('I', 4);
    delete([docl, rparcl, nulcl], 10);
    if (symclass in [begcl, relopcl, idcl, eqcl, opcl, lparcl, numcl])
        or ((symclass = endcl) and (send > 1))
        or ((symclass = delimcl) and (sdelim > 1))
    then statement(send, sdelim, sdot);
    end

else if sym = ifsym then
    begin {if statement} getsym;
    deleteset := [endcl, dotcl, nulcl];
    add(deleteset, [delimcl], sdelim, 1); delete(deleteset, 13);
    if symclass in [relopcl, idcl, eqcl, opcl, lparcl, numcl]
```

Program 6.3 (Continued)

```
then condition(min(send + 1, 2), min(sdot + 1, 2))
else error('I', 18);
leaveset := [begcl, deccl, docl, idcl];
if send ≤ 1 then leaveset := leaveset + [endcl];
if sdelim ≤ 1 then leaveset := leaveset + [delimcl];
if sdot ≤ 1 then leaveset := leaveset + [dotcl];
leave(leaveset, 10);
if sym = thensym then getsym
else if sym = dosym then begin error('C', 3); getsym end
else error('I', 3);
delete([docl, rparcl, nulcl], 10);
if (symclass in [begcl, relopcl, idcl, eqcl, opcl, lparcl, numcl])
    or ((symclass = endcl) and (send > 1))
    or ((symclass = delimcl) and (sdelim > 1))
then statement(send, sdelim, sdot);
end;
    end; {statement}


begin {block}
firstentry := tx;
l := [begcl, deccl, endcl, idcl, delimcl];
if bdot ≤ 1 then l := l + [dotcl];
d := [docl, rparcl, nulcl]; if bdelim > 1 then d := d + [delimcl];
while symclass = deccl do
    begin if sym = constsym then
        begin getsym;
        leave([begcl, deccl, idcl, eqcl, delimcl], 3);
        if symclass in [idcl, eqcl] then constdeclaration else error('I', 19);
        leave(l, 6);
        while sym in [comma, ident] do
            begin if sym = comma then getsym else error('I', 6);
            leave([begcl, deccl, idcl, eqcl, delimcl], 3);
            if symclass in [idcl, eqcl] then constdeclaration else error('I', 19);
            leave(l, 6);
            end;
        if sym = semicolon then getsym else error('I', 1);
        end;
    delete(d, 7);
    if sym = varsym then
        begin getsym;
```

Program 6.3   (Continued)

```
            leave([begcl, deccl, idcl, delimcl], 7);
            if sym = ident then vardeclaration else error('I', 7);
            leave(l, 6);
            while sym in [comma, ident] do
                    begin if sym = comma then getsym else error('I', 6);
                    leave([begcl, deccl, idcl, delimcl], 7);
                    if sym = ident then vardeclaration else error('I', 7);
                    leave(l, 6);
                    end;
            if sym = semicolon then getsym else error('I', 1);
            end;
        delete(d, 9);
        while sym = procsym do
                begin getsym;
                leave([begcl, deccl, idcl, delimcl], 3);
                if sym = ident then begin enter(proc); getsym end
                else begin error('I', 10);
                        if symclass in [begcl, deccl] then goto 4;
                        end;
                leave([begcl, deccl, endcl, idcl, delimcl], 8);
                if symclass ≠ delimcl then error('I', 1)
                else begin if sym ≠ semicolon then error('C', 6); getsym
                        end;
                delete(d, 1);
                block(2, 0, min(bdot + 1, 2));
                leave(l, 8);
                if symclass ≠ delimcl then error('I', 1)
                else begin if sym ≠ semicolon then error('C', 6); getsym
                        end;
                delete([docl, rparcl, nulcl], 9);
                end;
            if symclass = deccl then error('M', 1);
            end;
    if (symclass ≠ dotcl) and ((symclass ≠ delimcl) or (bdelim > 1))
    then statement (bend, bdelim, bdot);
4:  tx := firstentry;
    end;  {block}

begin  {main program}
for  ch := '0' to '''' do ssym[ch] := nul;
```

Program 6.3   (Continued)

```
word[1]   := 'BEGIN    ';  word[2]  := 'CALL     ';
word[3]   := 'CONST    ';  word[4]  := 'DO       ';
word[5]   := 'END      ';  word[6]  := 'IF       ';
word[7]   := 'ODD      ';  word[8]  := 'PROCEDU' ';
word[9]   := 'THEN     ';  word[10] := 'VAR      ';
word[11]  := 'WHILE    ';
wsym[1]   := beginsym;  wsym[2]  := callsym;
wsym[3]   := constsym;  wsym[4]  := dosym;
wsym[5]   := endsym;    wsym[6]  := ifsym;
wsym[7]   := oddsym;    wsym[8]  := procsym;
wsym[9]   := thensym;   wsym[10] := varsym;
wsym[11]  := whilesym;
ssym['+'] := plus;      ssym['-'] := minus;
ssym['*'] := times;     ssym['/'] := slash;
ssym['('] := lparen;    ssym[')'] := rparen;
ssym['='] := equal;     ssym[','] := comma;
ssym['.'] := period;    ssym['≠'] := nequal;
ssym['<'] := lt;        ssym['>'] := gt;
ssym[';'] := semicolon;
class[nul]        := nulcl;    class[ident]      := idcl;
class[number]     := numcl;    class[plus]       := opcl;
class[minus]      := opcl;     class[times]      := opcl;
class[slash]      := opcl;     class[oddsym]     := relopcl;
class[equal]      := eqcl;     class[nequal]     := relopcl;
class[lt]         := relopcl;  class[gt]         := relopcl;
class[lparen]     := lparcl;   class[rparen]     := rparcl;
class[comma]      := delimcl;  class[semicolon]  := delimcl;
class[period]     := dotcl;    class[becomes]    := eqcl;
class[beginsym]   := begcl;    class[endsym]     := endcl;
class[ifsym]      := begcl;    class[whilesym]   := begcl;
class[dosym]      := docl;     class[callsym]    := begcl;
class[constsym]   := deccl;    class[varsym]     := deccl;
class[procsym]    := deccl;    class[thensym]    := docl;
nosyntaxerrors := 0; ce := 0; cc := 0; ll := 0;
ch := ' '; lineno := 0; kk := al; tx := 0;
page(output); getsym;
delete([docl, rparcl, nulcl], 1);
if sym ≠ period then block(3, 10, 0);
leave([dotcl], 2);
99: writeln; writeln; writeln;
```

Program 6.3 (Continued)

if *nosyntaxerrors* $= 0$ **then** *writeln*(' *NO SYNTAX ERRORS'*)
else *writeln*(' ', *nosyntaxerrors*: 4, ' *SYNTAX ERRORS DETECTED'*);
end.

EXERCISES

6.1 (Programming project) Use the scheme described in Sec. 6.1 to add error recovery to your syntax analyzer for the simple programming language defined by Table 3.1 on p.93.

6.2 Consider the recovery scheme described in Sec. 6.1. Assuming that the set of stopping symbols is empty, prove that a syntax analyzer so constructed will always terminate. Should any conditions be imposed on the set of stopping symbols in order to ensure that the recovery scheme will always terminate?

6.3 Consider the grammar $G = (\{S,R\}, \{a,b,c\}, P, S)$, where P consists of

$$S \to RS \qquad S \to cR \qquad S \to \Lambda$$
$$R \to aRb \qquad R \to baaS$$

Suppose that the cost of inserting any symbol is 1 and the cost of deleting any symbol is 3. No changes are allowed. Compute a locally optimal repair for the following combinations of the valid prefix, *u*, and next symbol, *t*. In which cases is the repair non-unique?

Valid prefix, *u*	Λ	*a*	*ab*	*aaa*	*abaabc*
Next symbol, *t*	*a*	*c*	*b*	*c*	*c*

6.4 Consider again the grammar of Exercise 6.3. Using a locally optimal repair strategy, how might the following strings be repaired? In which cases does the repair differ from the least-cost repair as defined in Chap. 5?

$$ccc \qquad acb \qquad abc$$

6.5 In the following grammars the set of terminal symbols is $T = \{a,b,c\}$. The symbol *x* is used to denote a spurious symbol. The insert, delete and change costs for each symbol are specified by Tables 6.9 and 6.10.

Table 6.9   Insert and delete costs.

Symbol	Insert cost	Delete cost
a	1	5
b	3	3
c	7	10
x	∞	2

Table 6.10   Change costs—$cost(t_1 \to t_2)$

t_1 \ t_2	*a*	*b*	*c*	*x*
a	0	3	4	∞
b	4	0	∞	∞
c	∞	∞	0	∞
x	∞	∞	1	0

(a) $Z \to Seof$ $S \to ABCA$
     $A \to a$ $B \to b$ $C \to c$

Construct the non-return policy at each position in the production $S{\to}ABCA$ for each possible value of the next symbol.

(b) $Z \to Seof$ $S \to AaB$
     $A \to cB$ $B \to b$
     $A \to \Lambda$ $A \to Bb$

In a recursive-descent parser of this grammar, which procedures would you expect to be parameterized, and for which terminal symbols?

6.6 Design an algorithm for evaluating $cost^*(t{\to}pr(\gamma))$. The input is a context-free grammar $G = (N,T,P,S)$, the value of $t \in T$ and $\gamma \in (N \cup T)^*$, and a set of edit costs.

6.7 Prove Lemmas 6.1, 6.2 and 6.3.

6.8 Suppose that the recovery action corresponding to a locally optimal repair of t at the position $\langle A \to X_1 \ldots X_m, i \rangle$ is to jump to position j, where $j > i$. Prove that, at each position k, where $i \leq k < j$, there is a locally optimal repair of t for which the corresponding recovery action is also to jump to position j. (For simplicity, assume that the parameter $At > cost^*(A \to X_i \ldots X_m)$.)

6.9 Let $G = (N,T,P,S)$ be a context-free grammar and suppose that for all $k > 1$, there is a leftmost derivation sequence

$$Y_1\alpha_1 \Rightarrow_l Y_2\alpha_2 \Rightarrow_l \cdots \Rightarrow_l Y_k\alpha_k$$

where $Y_i \in N$ and $\alpha_i \in (N \cup T)^*$ ($1 \leq i \leq k$). Prove that G is left-recursive. (This result is used in the proof of Theorem 6.10).

BIBLIOGRAPHIC NOTES

Error recovery is of great practical importance and various techniques have been developed for particular parsing algorithms [6.1–5, 6.7–10]. Gries [6.6] gives a good survey of the topic. The simple scheme presented in Sec. 6.1 is essentially that described by Wirth [6.10]. The notion of a locally optimal repair was developed from ideas of Fischer *et al.* [6.4]. Both techniques are effective when errors are simple clerical errors. Errors involving systematic misuse of a language (e.g. declarations in ALGOL 60 style within PASCAL programs or incorrect ordering of the **var, const** and **type** declarations) cause problems. Aho and Johnson [6.1] describe a technique which involves adding extra "error productions" to the grammar and is better able to cope with this type of error.

6.1 Aho, A. V. and S. C. Johnson, "LR parsing", *Computing Surveys*, **6**, 99–124 (1974).

6.2 Conway, R. W. and T. R. Wilcox, "Design and implementation of a diagnostic compiler for PL/1", *Comm. ACM*, **16**, 169–79 (1973).

6.3 Feyock, S. and P. Lazarus, "Syntax-directed correction of syntax errors", *Software—Practice and Experience*, **6**, 207–19 (1976).

6.4 Fischer, C. N., D. R. Milton and S. B. Quiring, "An efficient insertion-only error-corrector for LL(1) parsers", *4th ACM Symposium on Principles of Programming Languages* (1977), 97–102.

6.5 Graham, S. L. and S. P. Rhodes, "Practical syntactic error recovery", *Comm. ACM*, **18**, 639–50 (1975).

6.6 Gries, D., "Error recovery and correction—an introduction to the literature", in F. L. Bauer and J. Eickel (eds.) *Compiler Construction: An Advanced Course* (2nd edn), Springer-Verlag Lecture Notes in Computer Science (1976).

6.7 James, E. B. and D. Partridge, "Adaptive correction of program statements", *Comm. ACM*, **16**, 27–37 (1973).

6.8 Levy, J. P., "Automatic correction of syntax errors in programming languages", *Acta Informatica*, **4**, 271–92 (1975).

6.9 Mickunas, M. D. and J. A. Modry, "Automatic error recovery for LR parsers", *Comm. ACM*, **21**, 459–65 (1978).

6.10 Wirth, N., *Algorithms + Data Structures = Programs*, Prentice-Hall, Englewood Cliffs, N.J. (1976).

7 LIMITATIONS

In Chap. 1 we suggested four criteria against which the definition of a programming language can be evaluated. The previous chapters are a tribute to the success of the "Revised Report on ALGOL 60" in satisfying these criteria, particularly the final criterion—"the method should facilitate the systematic construction of a compiler". This success is due, in no small measure, to the basis which the Report provided for a sound *theory* of syntax analysis. But every theory has its limitations, and the theory developed in this text is no exception to this rule. The aim of this concluding chapter is to state, precisely, what the limitations are and to direct the reader towards a further study of the problems involved in defining programming languages.

The main limitation of context-free grammars is that they fail to satisfy our fourth criterion. That is, the grammar used in the Report to describe ALGOL 60 does not completely define its syntax. Moreover, as we shall see in Sec. 7.1, it is quite impossible to modify the definition to overcome the deficiency.

Before proceeding, let us emphasize that the recognition of the limits of a theory does not mean that the theory should be abandoned altogether—Newton's laws of motion are still used, although strictly they have been superseded by Einstein's special theory of relativity. Context-free grammars fall a long way short of specifying the whole of the syntax of typical programming languages; nevertheless, they are here to stay.

7.1 THE *uvwxy* THEOREM

The syntactic features of programming languages which cannot be described by a context-free grammar are those involving the declaration and use of identifiers. Such features are called "context-sensitive" (because they are not "context-free") and are exemplified by the restriction in ALGOL 60 that all identifiers of a program must be declared (Sec. 5 of the "Revised Report"), but may be of any length (Sec. 2.4.1, "Revised Report"). All ALGOL programmers would recognize the following as syntactically incorrect because the identifier b has not been declared:

$$\textbf{begin integer } a; \quad b := 0 \textbf{ end}$$

Yet the context-free definition of ALGOL 60 does recognize it as a valid ⟨*program*⟩. An outline of the derivation tree is shown in Fig. 7.1.

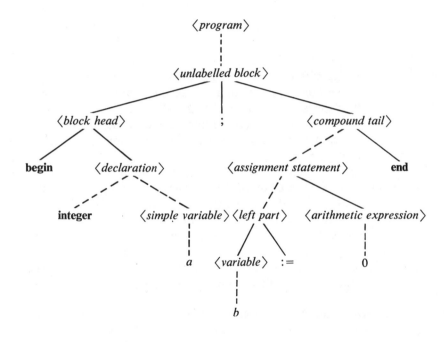

Fig. 7.1 Derivation of a syntactically incorrect ALGOL 60 program.

Theorem 7.2 exploits this restriction to highlight the limitations of context-free grammars using a fundamental result of language theory—the *uvwxy* theorem (or, as it is sometimes called, the *pumping lemma*). The *uvwxy* theorem describes the mechanism by which a *finite* grammar can define an *infinite* set. More precisely, it characterizes the mechanism for iteration which is inherent in a context-free grammar. Here is its statement and proof.

Theorem 7.1 (*uvwxy* theorem)   Let G be a context-free grammar defining the language $L = L(G)$. Then there exists a constant k such that if $z \in L$ has length greater than k, we can write

$$z = uvwxy$$

where

1. $length(vx) \geq 1$
2. $length(vwx) \leq k$, and
3. for all $i \geq 0$, uv^iwx^iy is in L.

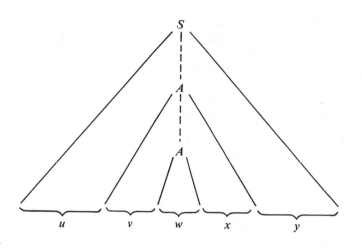

Fig. 7.2   Essence of Theorem 7.1.

Proof   The essential idea behind the proof of this theorem is that, if a word $z \in L(G)$ is long enough, then in any derivation tree for z some non-terminal symbol must be repeated (see Fig. 7.2). Thus we have $S \Rightarrow^* uAy$; also, $A \Rightarrow^* vAx$ and $A \Rightarrow^* w$.

Hence

$$S \Rightarrow^* uAy \Rightarrow^* uvAxy \Rightarrow^* \cdots \Rightarrow^* uv^iAx^iy \Rightarrow^* uv^iwx^iy \qquad \text{for all } i.$$

The formal proof now follows.

Let G be a context-free grammar defining the language $L = L(G)$. Let the number of non-terminal symbols in G be m, and let l be the length of the longest right-hand side of productions in G. Let $k = l^{m+1}$.

To make the argument clear we introduce some terminology regarding trees. A *path* through a *tree* is any traversal of the branches which starts at the root node S and proceeds downwards to a leaf. The *length* of the path is the number of nodes on the path excluding the final leaf. The *height of the tree* is the length of the longest path through the tree.

Consider any word $z \in L$ such that $length(z) > k$, and consider all derivations of z. Among these, pick a shortest derivation sequence and let T be the derivation tree corresponding to the sequence.

Now, in any derivation of a word w, the replacement of a non-terminal A by a string α (corresponding to applying the production $A \rightarrow \alpha$) can only introduce $length(\alpha) \leq l$ symbols into the string. We observe, therefore, that:

1. If the height of the derivation tree for w is 1, then $length(w) \leq l$.
2. If the height of the derivation tree for w is 2, then $length(w) \leq l^2$.
3. If the height of the derivation tree for w is h, then $length(w) \leq l^h$.

Conversely $length(z) > k = l^{m+1}$ implies that the derivation tree T for z has height greater than $m+1$.

There is, therefore, at least one path p through T of height greater than $m+1$. But by assumption there are only m non-terminals in G, so on this path at least one non-terminal labeling the nodes must be repeated.

Suppose we traverse the path p upwards from the leaf, searching for repeated non-terminal symbols. Let A be the first encountered in this way. The tree must then have the form shown in Fig. 7.3.

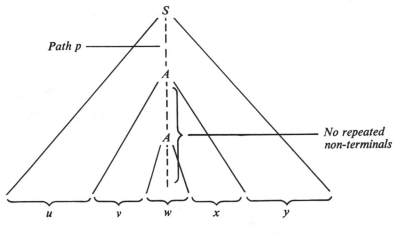

Fig. 7.3   Identifying u,v,w,x and y.

That is, there are strings u, v, w, x and y such that $z = uvwxy$, $S \Rightarrow^* uAy$, $A \Rightarrow^* vAx$ and $A \Rightarrow^* w$. (More precisely, w is the terminal string generated by the subtree whose root is the lower occurrence of A and vwx is the terminal string generated by the tree whose root is the upper occurrence of A.) Clearly, therefore, we have $S \Rightarrow^* uv^iwx^iy$ for all $i \geq 0$. By the choice of A, there are no repeated non-terminals on the path p below the upper occurrence of A and so the height of the tree whose root is the upper occurrence of A is $\leq m+1$. Thus, by our earlier observation $length(vwx) \leq l^{m+1} = k$. Finally, by the choice of a shortest derivation sequence for z, we cannot have

$$S \Rightarrow^* uAy \Rightarrow^+ uAy \Rightarrow^* uwy = uvwxy.$$

That is, $length(vx) \geq 1$. We have thus shown that the strings v, w and x satisfy all the conditions of the theorem and so the theorem is proved.   □

Theorem 7.2   There is no context-free grammar which completely defines the syntax of ALGOL 60.

Proof   Let us assume that there is indeed a context-free grammar defining the syntax of ALGOL 60, including the two rules (1) identifiers may have arbitrary length, and (2) all identifiers must be declared. The *uvwxy* theorem applies to this grammar, so let k be the constant mentioned in the theorem.

Let P_1 be the syntactically correct ALGOL program:

begin real a^nb^m; $a^nb^m := 0$ **end**

where a^r denotes a sequence of r a's, and n and m are any integers greater than k.

P_1 certainly has length greater than k, and so it must be possible to write $P_1 = uvwxy$, where the program P_i, defined by $P_i = uv^iwx^iy$, is also a syntactically correct ALGOL 60 program, for all $i \geq 0$.

We now perform a case analysis on the characters forming the substrings v, w and x and show that in all cases we obtain a contradiction.

Note firstly that, since $length(vwx) \leq k$, $n > k$ and $m > k$ we have

1. vwx is a substring of **begin real** a^nb^m, or

2. vwx is a substring of $a^nb^m := 0$ **end**, or

3. vwx is a substring of b^m; a^n.

In case (1) the symbols **begin** and **real** cannot appear in v or x, since it is clear that P_0 would not then be a syntactically correct ALGOL program. Therefore, v and x must be substrings of a^nb^m. However, since $length(vx) \geq 1$, the program P_0 would then involve an assignment in which the identifier was not declared. Thus case (1) cannot hold.

In case (2) a similar argument applies. The symbols $:=$, 0 and **end** cannot appear in v or x since otherwise P_2 would be syntactically incorrect. However, if v and x are substrings of $a^n b^m$, the program P_0 would again involve an assignment in which the identifier was not declared. Thus case (2) cannot hold.

Case (3) is the simplest of all. The semicolon cannot be a symbol of v or x, since P_0 would not be syntactically correct. Thus either vwx is a substring of b^m or a substring of a^n, or v is a substring of b^m, w is a substring of $b^m; a^n$ and x is a substring of a^n. Again, since $length(vx) \geq 1$, the program P_0 would involve an undeclared identifier and so case (3) cannot hold.

In all cases we have established a contradiction, so our initial assumption that the syntax of ALGOL 60 is context-free must be invalid. $\square$

It is evident from Theorems 7.1 and 7.2 that context-free grammars are capable of defining "matching" symbols, where the process of "matching" is no more complicated than that used in, for example, parenthesized expressions. Any restriction based on a correspondence between the declaration of an identifier and the subsequent use of that identifier cannot, therefore, be defined using a context-free grammar.

Two further examples of matching processes which cannot be so defined are parameters in procedures and the Hollerith count in FORTRAN FORMAT statements—whenever a procedure is called, the number of parameters must be the same as in the procedure heading, and in a FORMAT of the form

$$nH\langle\text{string of characters}\rangle$$

the number of characters must be equal to the value of the decimal number n.

A number of methods have been proposed for enhancing context-free grammars, but none has gained widespread acceptance. Context-sensitive grammars, mentioned in Chap. 1, are capable of defining all the above restrictions, but their use is not recommended because they do not reflect the way in which the restrictions are normally checked. A variety of criticisms can be leveled at other proposals. In some cases, the proposed metalanguage models certain aspects of programming language syntax, but has to be artificially extended to model other aspects. This is true, for instance, of W-grammars—the metalanguage used to define ALGOL 68. Using such grammars one can provide lucid descriptions of the restrictions on identifiers, but processes involving counting (e.g. in FORMAT statements) can only be expressed in a very primitive and unnatural way. A second criticism of the novel methods is that for none has an adequate amount of effort been expended on producing software tools to help the compiler writer.

7.2 SEMANTIC AMBIGUITIES IN ALGOL 60

One might argue that there is no need to look beyond context-free grammars. After all, the scope rules in ALGOL 60 are not difficult to understand and their description, in English, in the "Revised Report" is quite unambiguous. To counteract this argument, we discuss in this section ambiguities which are apparent in the "Revised Report on ALGOL 60", and, in Sec. 7.3, ambiguities in the definition of PASCAL. Our comments on ALGOL 60 are based solely on Knuth [7.9], to which the reader is referred for a more complete account.

The ambiguities of ALGOL 60 have long since been clarified and this section may seem highly pedantic. Indeed, as Knuth comments "The . . . list (of ambiguities) is actually more remarkable for its shortness than its length. A complete critique which goes to the same level of detail would be almost out of the question for other languages comparable to ALGOL 60, since the list would probably be a full order of magnitude longer". Our intention is, therefore, not to deplore the definition, but to learn from its mistakes and, by so doing, hope to achieve higher standards in the future.

7.2.1 Side Effects

The main ambiguities in the "Revised Report on ALGOL 60" arise from the use of "side effects". The function *sneaky* in (7.1) has the side effect of changing the value of x. Thus one cannot presume that the value of $x + sneaky$ is the same as the value of $sneaky + x$.

$$
\begin{aligned}
&\textbf{integer procedure } sneaky;\\
&\textbf{begin} \quad \textbf{comment } x \textit{ is a global variable};\\
&\qquad x := x + 1;\\
&\qquad sneaky := 0;\\
&\textbf{end } sneaky;
\end{aligned}
$$

(7.1)

The "Revised Report" does not state whether side-effects are allowed or not, and if so how arithmetic expressions should be evaluated in their presence. For example, how should $x + sneaky$ be evaluated? Is x to be evaluated before or after *sneaky*? In Sec. 3.3.5 the "Revised Report" says "The sequence of *operations* within one expression is generally from left to right" (my italics), but nowhere does it refer to the order in which the *operands* are evaluated.

Side effects also introduce ambiguities in the evaluation of value parameters. Consider the procedure f in (7.2):

$$
\begin{aligned}
&\textbf{integer procedure } f(a, b);\\
&\textbf{value } b, a; \quad \textbf{integer } a, b;\\
&f := a + b;
\end{aligned}
$$

(7.2)

Note that the order of a and b in the value list is different to that in the parameter list. The definition of value parameters in Sec. 4.7.3.1 states that they
are to be evaluated just after entry to a procedure and before execution of the
procedure body. The order in which they are to be evaluated is unspecified.
Yet, if $f(sneaky, x)$ is called, the final value depends critically on this order
of evaluation. One interpretation is that code equivalent to

$$a := sneaky;$$
$$b := x;$$
$$f := a+b;$$

is executed; alternatively, the call can be interpreted as

$$b := x;$$
$$a := sneaky;$$
$$f := a+b;$$

It is easily seen that the value of f differs by one in the two cases.

Another source of ambiguity, caused by side effects, is the evaluation
of array subscripts. Here the "Revised Report" explicitly states in Sec. 4.2.3.1:
"Any subscript expressions occurring in the left part variables are evaluated
in sequence from left to right", but even this is not clear. Does it mean, for
example, in the assignment

$$a[sneaky + b[x]] := 0$$

that $sneaky + b[x]$ is evaluated first, and then x is re-evaluated? Is x to the
right of $sneaky + b[x]$?

7.2.2   for Statements

for statements would appear to be quite innocuous, yet their interpretation
in certain circumstances has caused a great deal of debate. Section 4.6.4.2
of the "Revised Report" defines the construction:

$$\textbf{for } V := A \textbf{ step } B \textbf{ until } C \textbf{ do } S \qquad (7.3)$$

in terms of additional ALGOL statements. Expanding the definition slightly,
we can regard (7.3) as equivalent to a call of the procedure *for* in (7.4).

$$\textbf{procedure } for(V, A, B, C, S);$$
$$\langle specifications\ of\ V,\ A,\ B,\ C\ and\ S\rangle;$$
$$\textbf{begin } V := A;$$
$$\quad L1: \textbf{ if } (V-C) \times sign(B) > 0$$
$$\qquad\qquad \textbf{then goto } element\ exhausted; \qquad (7.4)$$

$$S;$$
$$V := V + B;$$
goto $L1$;
element exhausted:
end *for*;

The point at issue is the specifications of V, A, B, C and S. The four variables can be called either by name or by value—which method should be used? If statement S is executed n times and they are all called by name, A is evaluated once, B is evaluated $2n+1$ times and C is evaluated $n+1$ times. On the other hand, if all of V, A, B and C are called by value then each is evaluated once only. A simple example of the difference this can make is the statement:

$$\textbf{for } i := 1 \textbf{ step } i \textbf{ until } 16 \textbf{ do } S$$

If B ($= i$) is called by value, S is executed 16 times; if B is called by name, S is executed 5 times.

The specification of S causes further problems. Within (7.4) S is regarded as a procedure. But if S contains statements which access V, A, B or C, then the parameter-passing mechanism needs to be defined once again. A complex illustration of the problems is provided by (7.5).

```
begin integer array v, b, c[1:2]; integer i,k;
k := 0; i := 1; v[2] := 0;
b[1] := 1; b[2] := −1; c[1] := 1; c[2] := −1;          (7.5)
for v[i] := 1 step b[i] until c[i] do
    begin k := k + v[i];
    i := i+1; if i > 2 then i := 1;
    end;
write(k);
end
```

If all of V, A, B and C are called by value then the execution of the **for** statement will be equivalent to executing (7.6).

```
V := 1;
for V := 1 step 1 until 1 do
    begin k := k + V;                                 (7.6)
    i := i+1;  if i > 2 then i := 1;
    end;
```

That is, the value 1 will be output. If, however, all of V, A, B and C are called by name, code equivalent to (7.7) will be executed.

$$k := 0; \; i := 1; \; v[2] := 0;$$
$$b[1] := 1; \; b[2] := -1; \; c[1] := 1; \; c[2] := -1;$$
$$v[i] := 1;$$

L1: **if** $(v[i] - c[i]) \times sign(b[i]) > 0$ (7.7)
         then goto *element exhausted*;
     begin $k := k + v[i]$;
     $i := i+1$; **if** $i > 2$ **then** $i := 1$;
     end;
     $v[i] := v[i] + b[i]$;
     goto L1;
element exhausted:

In this case, i will take the values 1, 2 and then 1 before the program terminates. The value of k output is 0.

Various remarks in the "Revised Report" conflict on the interpretation of V. On the one hand, if the **for** loop is terminated by a **goto** in S the value of V is well-defined (Sec. 4.6.5), thus suggesting that V is called by name. However, if the loop is terminated via the label *element exhausted* then the value of V is undefined (Sec. 4.6.5, again), thus suggesting that V is called by value. One can argue about each of V, B or C and so there are potentially 8 possible interpretations of any **for** loop. In practice, most programs use only the simple type of the form

               for $i := 1$ **step** 1 **until** n **do** . . .

or

               for $i := n$ **step** -1 **until** 1 **do** . . .

and none of the problems arise. Consequently, PASCAL restricts **for** statements to the form

               for $i := j$ **to** k **do** . . .

or

               for $i := j$ **downto** k **do** . . .

The step size is always 1 or -1 and i, j and k are effectively defined to be value parameters of the corresponding procedure.

7.3 SYNTACTIC AMBIGUITIES IN PASCAL

Unlike those in ALGOL 60, the ambiguities in the definition of PASCAL are still a subject of contention. The main ones are, also, syntactic and not semantic ambiguities.

In the following discussion, we shall refer to the PASCAL *Report* which is the second part of *PASCAL: User Manual and Report*, by Kathleen Jensen and Niklaus Wirth.† Our comments are drawn from the work of Welsh *et al.* [7.16] together with the experiences of the author in developing the programs for this text.

7.3.1 Types

A profound innovation in PASCAL was the notion of **type** and the facility this allowed for structuring the declarations in a program. The implications of typing are far reaching—it helps to document a program and facilitates compile-time checks on the movement of data. Yet the rules governing typing are, sadly, poorly defined in the PASCAL report. In an assignment statement the two sides must be of "identical" type (Sec. 9.1.1 of the PASCAL report) but nowhere is the meaning of "identical" defined. To illustrate the problems that this introduces, let us consider the program segment shown in (7.8).

type *hashindex* = 0 . . *primenomin*1 ;
    terminal = *hashindex*; *terminallink* = ↑*terminalitem*;
    terminalitem = **record** *t*: *terminal*; *next*: *terminallink*;
                end;
    nonterminal = *hashindex*; *nonterminallink* = ↑*nonterminalitem*;   (7.8)
    nonterminalitem = **record** *next*: *nonterminallink*; *A*: *nonterminal*;
                end;
var *h*1: 0 . . *primenomin*1 ; *h*2: 0 . . *primenomin*1 ;
    *t*1, *t*2: *terminal*; *A*: *nonterminal*;
    pt: *terminallink*; *pA*: *nonterminallink*;
    right: **array**[*nonterminal*] **of** *nonterminallink*;

There are essentially two ways of defining the notion of identical types, namely *name equivalence* and *structural equivalence*. Name equivalence is very strict and easily checked: two variables have identical types only if they are declared together or their type is defined by the same type identifier. Under this definition *t*1 and *t*2 have identical types but *h*1 and *h*2 do not. Also, *right*[*A*] and *pA* have identical types. Structural equivalence offers the other extreme—it is very loose and is difficult to check: two types are *identical* if and only if they have the same name or their components have *identical* types and are structured in equivalent ways. This definition is recursive, as we have tried to indicate by the use of italics. It is also incomplete because we haven't defined "structured in equivalent ways". However, under any

---

†"PASCAL: User Manual and Report", Corrected Reprint of 2nd Edition, Jensen, K. and N. Wirth, Springer-Verlag: New York (1976).

interpretation $h1$, $h2$, $t1$, $t2$ and A all have the same type. Also under the least restrictive interpretation of equivalent structures *nonterminallink* and *terminallink* are identical. On the other hand, if the order of the fields in a record is considered important they do not have identical types.

The intention of the declarations in (7.8) should be evident. Firstly, the introduction of the types *terminal* and *nonterminal* was meant to improve the documentation of the program and to avoid the necessity for comments. (A good maxim is that a well-written program is one which doesn't need comments.) Secondly, the separation of *terminallink* from *nonterminallink* was intended to provide a degree of security when constructing lists of terminal and non-terminal symbols—the use of pointers is hazardous at the best of times and any safeguards are welcome. Yet neither name equivalence nor structural equivalence achieves the objective. Name equivalence is too strict and structural equivalence is too loose. The dilemma is caused by the fact that PASCAL confuses the mathematical notion of *type* with the internal representation of that type and restrictions on the use of variables of that type. Consequently, there is no easy solution to the dilemma and, in practice, a compromise dictated by implementation considerations is made between name and structural equivalence. Thus, on the implementation used by the author $h1$, $h2$, $t1$, $t2$ and A have identical types, but pt and pA do not (and would not even if the components *next* and A in *nonterminalitem* were interchanged).

7.3.2 Scope Rules

The scope rules in PASCAL are ambiguous because their definition in the Report is virtually non-existent! Identifiers declared in the main program are said to be "global" (Sec. 2) but neither the meaning of "global" nor the scope of such identifiers is ever defined. Indeed, after introducing the term "global" it is never used again. One is, therefore, led into believing that the scope rules of ALGOL 60 apply in PASCAL, in particular, that an identifier may not be used before the *textual* appearance of its declaration. However, this cannot be so, as (7.9) illustrates. Unless the scope rules of ALGOL 60 are relaxed, it would be impossible to define a simple construct, like a list of characters, using pointer variables, because of the recursive nature of the type declaration.

$$\textbf{type } charlist = \textbf{record } c: char; \quad next: \uparrow charlist; \qquad (7.9)$$
$$\textbf{end};$$

A careful reading of the PASCAL report reveals that, within procedures (and by implication within the main program), there is no requirement for an identifier to be declared before it is used. In Sec. 10 it is stated that "All identifiers in the formal parameter part, the variable, procedure or function declaration parts are *local* to the procedure declaration which is called the *scope* of these identifiers. They are not known outside their scope", As a definition this seems perfectly reasonable, but it causes problems to implementors of one-pass compilers. Indeed, it seems that *no* PASCAL compiler has been written which sticks to the definition in the Report (even the one implemented by the language designers). Instead, the requirement of declaration before use is imposed except for pointer types. Thus (7.9) is syntactically incorrect; a new type *charlink* = ↑*charlist* must be defined before *charlist* and used in place of ↑*charlist*. A second example of an intrinsically recursive data structure is (7.10). Note that *production* has a pointer to *rhsitem* which has a pointer to *production*. To conform to the generally accepted rule, pointer types *rhslink* and *productionlink* preface the declarations.

type   *rhslink* = ↑*rhsitem*;
      productionlink = ↑*production*;
      production = **record** *lhs*: *nonterminal*; *length*: *integer*;
                    firstrhsposn: *rhslink*;
         end;
      rhssymbol = **record** *h*: *symbol*;   (7.10)
                    nextoccurrence: *rhslink*;
         end;
      rhsitem = **record** *x*: *rhssymbol*; *next*: *rhslink*;
                p: *productionlink*;
        end;

Now, this new rule *seems* reasonable but it contains a subtle trap into which a number of implementors have fallen. The trap is illustrated by (7.11). Within the procedure X the assignment statement should be OK, but a syntax error is flagged by some compilers! Note that r is declared twice, once globally to X and once within X following the declaration of p. When the declaration of p is processed the global declaration of r should *not* be assumed; instead, p should be associated with the following declaration of r.

        type   *r* = *integer*;
        procedure X;
            type *p* = ↑*r*;
                r = **record** *c*: *char*; *pc*: *p*   (7.11)
                end;
            var *q*: *p*;
            begin *q*↑.*c* := '*A*' **end**; {X}

This is a very serious ambiguity because it means that it is impossible to test the reliability of a procedure independently of any calling procedures— any change in the declarations in, for example, the main program could precipitate syntax errors (if one is lucky) or runtime errors (if one is unlucky) in a well-tested procedure. Moreover, this is not an improbable occurrence. Program 7.1 abstracts the main features of a very weird phenomenon which occurred when the author was developing a program using Gaussian elimination to perform error repair (see Sec. 5.4). The procedure *constructproductform* was written, tested and declared satisfactory. Then it was placed, quite unchanged, within the program *Gaussrepair*. As a result the declarations of *charlist* were duplicated (see Program 7.1), but being identical no problems were anticipated. Unfortunately, as Program 7.1 demonstrates, problems did occur. The point to note is that the assignment $pc\uparrow := cl$ is equivalent to the two assignments

$$pc\uparrow.c := cl.c \quad \text{and} \quad pc\uparrow.next := cl.next$$

One would expect, therefore, that all three are syntactically correct but, in fact, the first is declared illegal. We shall leave the reader to puzzle out the reason why—the example combines both the ambiguity in this section and that in Sec. 7.3.1.

```
program Gaussrepair(input, output);
type . . .
     charlink = ↑charlist;
     charlist = record c: char; next: charlink;
                 end;
     procedure constructproductform;
     type charlink = ↑charlist;
          charlist = record c: char; next: charlink;
                      end;
     var pc: charlink; cl: charlist;
     begin . . .
          pc↑ := cl;
               × 17
          pc↑.c := cl.c; pc↑.next := cl.next;
     end; {construct product form}
begin . . .
end.
 1 SYNTAX ERROR DETECTED
17 EXPRESSION IS OF WRONG TYPE.
```

Program 7.1

7.4 CONCLUSION

In this text we have argued the case for a sound theory of programming language syntax in the best way we know how—by demonstrating the practical application of the theory in its present form. Increasingly now, programming languages are being designed which emphasize the use of syntactic restrictions in designing reliable programs, and the limitations of context-free grammars are strikingly apparent. Yet it is not enough to supplement the context-free description of a language with an English description of the additional constraints. Errors of omission or inconsistencies are bound to ensue, causing frustration and inconvenience to users of the language many years after it is published. The need for a more powerful metalanguage is indisputable.

In many ways, the features of a good metalanguage should coincide with those of a good programming language. The metalanguage should enable and, indeed, encourage the construction of a well-structured grammar. It should be possible to separate the grammar into modules, each describing some individual aspect of the syntax (or semantics) of the object language, and each sufficiently succinct to allow easy comprehension. Finally, the steps used to refine the grammar should be apparent from its structure, allowing some (for example, users of the object language) to examine broad aspects and others (for example, the compiler writer) to study minute details. These requirements have not yet been achieved by programming languages, where the need is more urgent, and so it is not surprising that neither have they been achieved by metalanguages.

EXERCISES

7.1 Consider the grammar $G = (\{S,A,B\}, \{a,b\},P,S)$, where P consists of

$$S \to a \qquad S \to A$$
$$A \to aAB \qquad A \to aba$$
$$B \to b$$

For the sentence $z = aaababb$, find all possible ways of splitting z into strings u,v,w,x and y such that $z = uvwxy$ and $S \Rightarrow^* uv^iwx^iy$ for all $i \geq 0$.

7.2 Repeat Exercise 7.1 for the grammar $G = (\{S,A,B\},\{a,b\},P,S)$ and the sentence $z = baabaab$, where P consists of

$$S \to AB$$
$$A \to Aa \qquad A \to bB$$
$$B \to a \qquad B \to Sb$$

7.3 Use the $uvwxy$ theorem to prove that the following languages are not context-free:

(a) $\{a^nb^nc^n \mid n \geq 1\}$
(b) $\{a^nb^ma^nb^m \mid n,m \geq 1\}$

(c) $\{a^nba^nba^n \mid n \geq 1\}$

(d) $\{nHa^n \mid n$ is an integer expressed in decimal notation$\}$

(*Hint:* Consider the string $z = \underbrace{11\ldots1}_{k} Ha \underbrace{{}^{11\cdots1}}_{k}$.)

7.4 Consider the *uvwxy* theorem when G is a *right-linear* grammar. What can you say about x and y? Use your observation to prove the following:

uvw Theorem. Let G be a regular grammar. Then $\exists$ a constant k such that if $z \in L(G)$ has length greater than k, we can write $z = uvw$, where

(a) $length(v) \geq 1$

(b) $length(vw) \leq k$, and for all $i \geq 0$

(c) $uv^iw \in L(G)$.

Use the *uvw* theorem to prove that $\{a^nb^n \mid n \geq 1\}$ is not regular.
What features of ALGOL 60 are not regular? Name three.

7.5 Use the *uvw* theorem to prove that postfix expressions cannot be generated by a regular grammar. (A postfix expression is an arithmetic expression in which the operators follow the operands. For example, $ab+$ and $ab+c\times$ are postfix expressions which, conventionally, would be written $a+b$ and $(a+b)\times c$ respectively.)

7.6 Consider (7.5) again. What value will be output if B is called by name, but all of V, A and C are called by value?

BIBLIOGRAPHIC NOTES

The *uvwxy* theorem was first proved by Bar Hillel *et al.* [7.1]; its application to ALGOL 60 was observed by Floyd [7.4].

As mentioned in the text, our comments on the ambiguities in ALGOL 60 and PASCAL are based on the work of Knuth [7.9] and Welsh *et al.* [7.16], respectively. Consult these references for a discussion of further ambiguities in the definitions of the languages. Habermann [7.5] and Wirth [7.18] offer further (contrasting) views on PASCAL. Sale [7.12] collates a number of variations in existing PASCAL compilers, the variations arising from loopholes or omissions in the PASCAL report.

Two noteworthy techniques for defining context-sensitive restrictions on the syntax of a programming language are "W-grammars" and "attribute grammars". Both are reviewed by Marcotty *et al.* [7.10]. W-grammars were developed by van-Wijngaarden and used to describe ALGOL 68. The ALGOL 68 report has been revised several times; [7.17] is the most up-to-date version. Cleaveland and Uzgalis [7.2] provide an excellent introduction to W-grammars.

There is an abundance of published literature on the definition of the semantics of programming languages, but a dearth of introductory material. Three techniques are prominent—"axiomatic", "denotational" and "operational" semantics. An axiomatic definition is essential to a completely rigorous, formal verification of assertions in a program. The seminal paper on axiomatic definitions is Hoare's [7.6]. An axiomatic definition of a major part of PASCAL can be found in [7.8].

Specifying the operational semantics of a language boils down to describing an interpreter of the language on an abstract machine. PL/1 has been defined in this way [7.15]. Ollongren's book [7.11] provides a detailed study of this method.

Denotational semantics involves associating a function with each construct in the language. The most complex and most rewarding part of the definition is describing the type (i.e. domain and range) of the functions—the remainder of the definition is usually self-evident. Stoy [7.13] and Tennent [7.14] provide introductory accounts.

There is a growing feeling that more than one definition of a language is necessary. At one extreme, the implementor of a language requires a very detailed definition; at the other extreme, the first-time user wishes to know only the basic properties of the facilities provided by the language. This idea, initiated by Hoare and Lauer [7.7], has led to the development of complementary definitions which are then checked for mutual consistency. In his thesis, Donahue [7.3] applies the idea to a (small) subset of PASCAL.

7.1 Bar-Hillel, Y., M. Perles and E. Shamir, "On formal properties of simple phrase structure grammars" *Z. Phonetik, Sprachwiss. Kommunikationsforsch*, **14**, 143–72 (1961).

7.2 Cleaveland, J. C. and R. C. Uzgalis, *Grammars for Programming Languages*, Elsevier North-Holland, New York (1977).

7.3 Donahue, J. E., "Complementary Definitions of Programming Language Semantics", *Springer-Verlag Lecture Notes in Computer Science*, **42**, Berlin (1976).

7.4 Floyd, R. W., "On the non-existence of a phrase-structure grammar for ALGOL 60", *Comm. ACM*, **5**, 483–4 (1962).

7.5 Habermann, A. N., "Critical comments on the programming language PASCAL", *Acta Informatica*, **3**, 47–57 (1973).

7.6 Hoare, C. A. R., "An axiomatic basis for computer programming", *Comm. ACM*, **12**, 576–80 and 583 (1969).

7.7 Hoare, C. A. R. and P. E. Lauer, "Consistent and complementary formal theories of the semantics of programming languages", *Acta Informatica*, **3**, 135–53 (1974).

7.8 Hoare, C. A. R. and N. Wirth, "An axiomatic definition of the programming language PASCAL", *Acta Informatica*, **2**, 335–55 (1973).

7.9 Knuth, D. E., "The remaining trouble spots in ALGOL 60", *Comm. ACM*, **10**, 611–18 (1967).

7.10 Marcotty, M., H. F. Ledgard and G. V. Bochmann, "A sampler of formal definitions", *ACM Computing Surveys*, **8**, 191–276 (1976).

7.11 Ollongren, A., *Definition of Programming Languages by Interpreting Automata*, Academic Press, London (1974).

7.12 Sale, A., *PASCAL Compatibility Report*, Department of Information Science, University of Tasmania, Report No R77–5 (1977).

7.13 Stoy, J. E., *Denotational Semantics: The Scott–Strachey Approach to Programming Language Theory*, The MIT Press, Cambridge, Mass. (1977).

7.14 Tennent, R., "The denotational semantics of programming languages", *Comm. ACM*, **19,** 437–56 (1976).

7.15 Wegner, P., "The Vienna definition language", *ACM Computing Surveys*, **4,** 5–63, (1972).

7.16 Welsh, J., W. J. Sneeringer and C. A. R. Hoare, "Ambiguities and insecurities in PASCAL", *Software—Practice and Experience*, **7,** 685–96 (1977).

7.17 van Wijngaarden, A., *et al.* (eds.) "Revised report on the algorithmic language ALGOL 68", *ACM Sigplan Notices* **12** (5), 1–70 (May 1977).

7.18 Wirth, N., "An assessment of the programming language PASCAL", *IEEE Trans. Software Engineering*, **SE–1,** 192–8 (1975).

INDEX